They Planted Well

They Planted Well
New England Planters in Maritime Canada

**Edited by
Margaret Conrad**

Acadiensis Press
Fredericton, New Brunswick

1988

Canadian Cataloguing in Publication Data

They Planted Well

Includes bibliographical references.
Proceedings of the Planter Studies Conference sponsored by the Planters Studies Committee, and held in Wolfville, N.S., October 1987.
ISBN 0-919107-20-6

1. Maritime Provinces — Emigration and immigration — History.
2. New England — Emigration and immigration — History.
3. Land Settlement — Maritime Provinces.
4. Farmers — Maritime Provinces.
5. Maritime Provinces — History — to 1867.*
I. Conrad, Margaret.
II. Planters Study Conference (1987: Acadia University).
III. Acadia University. Planter Studies Committee.

FC2032.T53 1988   971.500413   C88-098642-5

Acadiensis Press gratefully acknowledges the financial support of the Publishers Assistance Programme of the New Brunswick Department of Tourism, Recreation and Heritage and of Acadia University.

COVER: William Morrison, engraved by J. Clark for *Letters from Nova Scotia,* published by Colburn & Bentley, London, 1830.

THEY PLANTED WELL
NEW ENGLAND PLANTERS IN MARITIME CANADA
Edited by Margaret Conrad

TABLE OF CONTENTS

ACKNOWLEDGEMENTS... 7

INTRODUCTION.. 9

IMMIGRATION AND SETTLEMENT

R.S. Longley, The Coming of the New England Planters
to the Annapolis Valley 14
D. Murray Young, Planter Settlements in the
St. John Valley 29
Esther Clark Wright, Cumberland Township: A Focal Point
of Early Settlement on the Bay of Fundy............................. 36
Ernest A. Clarke, Cumberland Planters and the Aftermath
of the Attack on Fort Cumberland 42

HISTORIOGRAPHICAL CONTEXT

Jack Greene, Recent Developments in the Historiography
of Colonial New England... 61
George Rawlyk, J.B. Brebner and Some Recent Trends in
Eighteenth-Century Maritime Historiography 97
Barry Cahill, New England Planters at the Public Archives
of Nova Scotia.. 120
Terrence Punch, Genealogy, Migration and the
Study of the Past 132

CULTURE AND SOCIETY

Graeme Wynn, The Geography of the Maritime Provinces
in 1800: Patterns and Questions... 138
Debra McNabb, The Role of the Land in Settling Horton
Township, Nova Scotia, 1766-1830 151
Elizabeth Mancke, Corporate Structure and Private Interest:
The Mid-Eighteenth Century Expansion
of New England 161
Allen Robertson, Methodism Among Nova Scotia's
Yankee Planters.. 178

Daniel Goodwin, From Disunity to Integration:
Evangelical Religion and Society in
Yarmouth, Nova Scotia, 1761-1830 190
Thomas Vincent, Henry Alline: Problems of Approach
and Reading the Hymns as Poetry.. 201
Gwendolyn Davies, Persona in Planter Journals 211

MATERIAL CULTURE

Allen Penney, A Planter House: The Simeon Perkins House,
Liverpool, Nova Scotia.. 218
Daniel Norris, An Examination of the Stephen Loomer House,
Habitant, Kings County, Nova Scotia 236
Heather Davidson, Private Lives from Public Artifacts:
The Architectural Heritage of Kings County Planters........... 249
M.A. MacDonald (with **Robert Elliot**), New Brunswick's
'Early Comers': Lifestyles Through Authenticated
Artifacts, a Research Project 262
Deborah Trask, 'Remember Me As You Pass By':
Material Evidence of the Planters
in the Graveyards of Nova Scotia 298

FUTURE DIRECTIONS

Phillip Buckner 307
Brian Cuthbertson.. 310
Marie Elwood 313
James Morrison 315
William Naftel.. 318
Esther Clark Wright 320

ACKNOWLEDGEMENTS

Turning conference proceedings into a bound volume is more difficult than most people realize. I am particularly indebted to Hazel Ward and Sherri Davis who entered the manuscript on disks for nothing more than the experience of doing it. Deborah Eaton had the thankless task of keeping paper moving, badgering delinquent authors and copy-editing their work. Without her constant presence (funded by a SEED grant) and efficient ways (surely a manifestation of her Planter roots) the manuscript may never have been completed. Acadia University Archivist Patricia Townsend was her usual helpful self during this project and Edith Haliburton cheerfully tolerated our many demands for "rare" books at a time when the Library was officially closed. The History Department at Acadia University, particularly its head Sam Nesdoly and his assistant Carolyn Bowlby, were supportive in ways too numerous to mention. The other members of the Planter Studies Committee — Douglas Baldwin, Gwendolyn Davies, Richard Davies, Alan MacIntosh, Barry Moody, James Snowdon and Patricia Townsend — gave me a free hand to do as I wished and spared me the trouble of endless editorial meetings.

Since books like these rarely pay for themselves, I am also grateful to those who dug even deeper into their purses to provide publication subsidies; in particular, Lois Vallely-Fischer, Dean of Arts, Marshall Conley, acting Director of Graduate Studies, and President James Perkin of Acadia University. The remainder of an Occasional Conference Grant provided by the Social Sciences and Humanities Research Council for the Planter Conference was essential in putting us "over the top" and I am grateful to the Council for its support. Finally, I would like to thank the contributors, most of whom scrupulously met my unrealistic deadlines and graciously accepted my editorial nit-picking. It is to them, both longtime and recent Planter scholars, that the book is dedicated.

Margaret Conrad
Acadia University

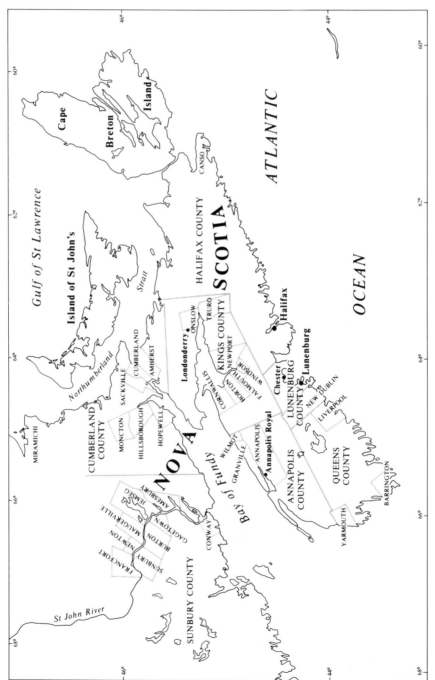

Planter Nova Scotia, 1767

Introduction

Between 1759 and 1768 some 8000 New Englanders emigrated to what are now the provinces of Nova Scotia and New Brunswick. Known as "planters," the old English term for colonist, they were among the first anglophone immigrants to the area of present-day Canada. In October 1987 nearly 150 people converged on Acadia University in Wolfville, Nova Scotia, to attend a conference billed as "New England Planters in Maritime Canada." It was the first time that the Planters had ever been made the exclusive focus of an academic conference, and the unexpectedly large turn-out suggested that the time was long overdue for such an event.

The obscurity into which the New England Planters have fallen is a curious phenomenon of Canadian historical scholarship. In numbers, the Planters included almost as many people as migrated to Quebec during the whole period of the French regime, and they equal or surpass the Icelandic, Doukhobor and Mennonite migrations to the Prairies in the nineteenth century. Yet, as George Rawlyk points out in his article in this volume, authors of Canadian history texts give short shrift to the Planters, if they mention them at all.

Part of the explanation for the "missing" Planters must surely lie in their motives for coming to Nova Scotia. Because the Acadian deportation and Loyalist migration were far more dramatic events than the peaceful migration of a mass of land-hungry Yankees, the Planters have received less scholarly attention than their numbers and impact warrant. But this explanation alone is not enough. Other migrant groups endowed with a healthy strain of possessive individualism have not been expunged from our textbooks. Nor can it be said that little is known about the Planters. J.B. Brebner, whose book, *The Neutral Yankees of Nova Scotia,* was first published in 1937, explored, at great length, the period during which the Planters dominated the population base of Nova Scotia. Why have Brebner's mighty labours, and those who have followed in his footsteps, not guaranteed the Planters their place in the Canadian mosaic?

It would be easy to blame the Toronto-dominated Canadian history profession for deliberately down-playing the Planter heritage in the Maritimes. However, this explanation, appealing though it may be, will not do. And it would be equally remiss to blame the Americans for refusing to acknowledge that people have actually left the United States for opportunity elsewhere. Indeed, it is the Planters themselves who must share much of the blame for the neglected state of Planter Studies. As Ernest A. Clarke reveals in his discussion of Cumberland Township during the American Revolution, Planter identity was a fragile concept, at best, during the first generation of settlement. It more or less easily gave way to

Loyalist rhetoric once it became clear that Nova Scotia would remain a British possession. Even the term "Planter" atrophied from disuse. Although the New Englanders called themselves "planters," a generic term for colonist, they did not see themselves collectively as an exclusive group called "Planters." Nor did ninteenth-century historians find the term particularly useful. A.W.H. Eaton in his *History of Kings County*, published in 1910, described his ancestors as "Planters" but Brebner referred to them only as "New Englanders" or "Yankees." By the 1960s "Planter" was again in vogue, an attempt on the part of historians to avoid the obviously ahistorical use of the term "pre-Loyalist" to lump together all anglophone immigrants to Nova Scotia prior to the American Revolution. Nevertheless, as the articles in this collection indicate, Planter is still not a widely accepted term. In New Brunswick, a colony established in 1784 as a response to Loyalist pressure, "early comer" still vies with "pre-Loyalist" as a way of establishing the Loyalist migration as the benchmark against which all other immigrants are measured.

It is instructive to consider how the Planter identity would have evolved had Nova Scotia joined the newly formed United States of America in 1776. Surely New England origins would have served the Planters well in establishing their claim to citizenship in the great republic. Such roots were considerably less useful, however, in making one's argument for position and privilege before Loyalist claims commissions and British-appointed governors. In fact, American citizenship has rarely been an asset in Canada — officially at least. As a result, the Planters have had to remain content with the more mundane boast, still often heard in the Maritimes, that their ancestors are among the oldest European settlers in Canada.

While the Planter heritage withered in the official canon of Canadian identity, locally it grew and flourished. Thomas Chandler Haliburton, himself of Planter origins, described the circumstances surrounding the arrival of his ancestors in his *History of Nova Scotia*, published by Joseph Howe in 1829. Most nineteenth-century provincial and county historians dutifully acknowledged the New England heritage in Nova Scotia and New Brunswick. In the twentieth century two Planter descendants, both graduates of, and at various times professors at Acadia University, endeavoured to keep the Planters in the scholarly limelight to which Brebner had raised them. Esther Clark Wright's article, "Cumberland Township: A Focal Point of Early Settlement on the Bay of Fundy," appeared in the *Canadian Historical Review* in 1946. Her book *The Loyalists of New Brunswick*, published in 1955, revealed important insights about the Planter experience. On the occasion of the Planter bicentennial, R. S. Longley, a member of Acadia's history department (1929-64) and Vice President from 1957 to 1964, delivered a paper entitled, "The Coming of the New England Planters to the Annapolis Valley" to the

Nova Scotia Historical Society. It appeared in the society's collections published in 1961. Unfortunately, administrative duties and poor health made it difficult for Longley to pursue his interest in the Planters.

In the 1970s and 1980s an increased enthusiasm for heritage, and the annual request from the University of Maine for presentations to their Canadian Studies students brought pressure upon the history department at Acadia University to formally embrace the Planters. Esther Clark Wright's publication of *Planters and Pioneers* in 1978, and her insistence that the younger generation of historians at Acadia do justice to the Planters, was also a spur to action. Finally, in 1983 the Canadianists in the history department created a Planter Studies Committee to co-ordinate research on the people who had figured so prominently in the founding of Acadia University in 1838. It was the committee's aim to produce a bibliography of primary and secondary sources relating to the Planters, to host a Planter Conference and ultimately to create a Planter Studies Centre at Acadia University. *A Checklist of Secondary Sources for Planter Studies* compiled by Daniel Goodwin appeared in 1987, in time for the conference, the proceedings of which form the basis for this publication. Plans are underway for a *Checklist of Primary Sources for Planters Studies*, scheduled to appear in 1990. As part of the celebrations marking Acadia's 150th anniversary, the university launched a fund-raising drive to establish a Planter Studies Centre.

The members of the Planters Studies Committee made a conscious decision to use the term "Planter" to describe the people who migrated from New England to take up land in the old province of Nova Scotia between 1759 and 1768. While we recognized that it would be opposed in some quarters and produce as many problems as it solved, "Planter" seemed a better term than "pre-Loyalist," "Yankee" or any of the other suggestions put forward. Our committee tends to take an inclusive approach in deciding who was a Planter but there will, no doubt, be some debate as to whether New England merchants and officials in Halifax — especially those who took advantage of the free grants of land in the Planter townships — should be included under the term. We, of course, use the term only as a means of making distinctions for scholarly purposes and not as a label bestowing some imaginary status on people who can trace their origins to the Planters.

Having never staked a claim to be included among the founding people of Canada, the Planters nevertheless left an idelible mark on their Maritime homeland and further afield. Descendants of the Planters include major educators, theologians, inventors, industrialists, social reformers, politicians and at least two Canadian prime ministers. Planter descendants have spread across Canada and, during the great exodus from the Maritime Provinces in the late nineteenth and early twentieth centuries, they found their way back to New England. Like their ancestors, they were quickly absorbed into the larger Anglo-American identity and left few visible traces of their Canadian sojourn.

A few words of explanation are in order concerning the content of this book. Readers will see that, in addition to the papers presented at the conference, the articles by Esther Clark Wright and R.S. Longley, mentioned above, are published in this volume. Both articles have much to offer and document the Acadia University connection to Planter scholarship. It therefore seemed appropriate to include them.

Readers might have expected the historiographical articles to appear first in the table of contents. Although this was the original intent, it became clear as the conference was being organized that, even among the academic community, the details of the Planter migration were not widely known. A 'preface' to the interpretative articles seemed in order. In the section entitled "Immigration and Settlement," R.S. Longley and D. Murray Young outline the contours of Planter migration to and settlement of Nova Scotia and what would become New Brunswick, while Esther Clark Wright and Ernest A. Clarke provide a glimpse of the complexity for the Planters of both the migration experience and the American Revolution by focusing specifically on Cumberland Township.

The "Historiographical Context" includes a comprehensive discussion by Jack Greene, Mellon Professor of the Humanities at Johns Hopkins University, of recent developments in the writing of the history of colonial New England. Since it is their New England roots that define the Planters as a group, such an overview is suggestive of future directions for Planter research. George Rawlyk, a friend of Planter Studies, describes developments in Canadian scholarship relating to eighteenth-century Maritime history since the appearance of Brebner's work over fifty years ago. Barry Cahill's discussion on the sources for Planter Studies at the Public Archives of Nova Scotia provides an excellent starting point for anyone interested in pursuing the Planters, while Terrence Punch issues a timely reminder that historical genealogy has much to offer the academic historian.

Graeme Wynn, one of Canada's foremost geographers, prefaces the section on "Culture and Society" with an overview of the Maritime Provinces in 1800. He is followed by four young scholars, Debra McNabb, Elizabeth Mancke, Allen Robertson and Daniel Goodwin, who studied the Planters as part of their graduate school experience. Their careful research into land holding patterns, religious beliefs, and comparative developments in British North America and the United States testify to the new questions now being asked about the Planters. Thomas Vincent and Gwendolyn Davies, both established scholars in the field of eighteenth-century British North American literature, explore aspects of the Planter written heritage.

Some of the most vital Planter scholarship currently underway is focused on material culture. Allen Penney, in his fine study of the Simeon Perkins House, cautions us against wearing rose-coloured glasses in our efforts to interpret the Planters. Daniel Norris and Heather Davidson demonstrate that the Planter material heritage is a changing and evolving reality, not one that can be fixed for all time. M.A. MacDonald and Robert Elliot describe Planter artifacts which have surfaced in their search for material culture from New Brunswick's "early comers." Finally, Deborah Trask explains what grave markers reveal about Planter society.

To conclude the conference, five people were asked to offer brief comments on future directions for Planter Studies. Phillip Buckner, Brian Cuthbertson, Marie Elwood, James Morrison and William Naftel are people who, both through their offices and their research, have had a significant impact on the history of Atlantic Canada in recent years. They offer wise counsel to scholars considering the Planters as a field of study. Esther Clark Wright's banquet address, which stirred a few comments among her listeners, is also published here. At the banquet, Dr. Wright was proclaimed the first Planter Scholar by the Planter Studies Committee. Dr. Wright's lifetime interest in the history of the Maritime Provinces in general, and the Planters in particular, made her an obvious choice for this distinction. From her address to the banqueters at Blomidon Inn, it is clear that she has lost none of her fighting spirit or her commitment to regional scholarship. Her comments and her injunction to "hang on" to our spelling provide a fitting ending to the volume.

A highlight of the conference was a presentation of selections from *Around Alline*, an opera/drama composed by Michael R. Miller of Mount Allison University. Professor Miller, pianist, and David Carle (Atlantic Baptist College), Baritone, performed in Acadia's Manning Memorial Chapel on a beautiful autumn day. The capacity audience was delighted with yet another interpretation of Planter evangelist Henry Alline, whose spirit seemed to hover over the conference deliberations. Unfortunately, it is impossible to publish the opera in this forum but readers will be happy to know that the performance was captured for posterity on video by Acadia's Audio Visual Department.

They Planted Well serves up a veritable Maritime "hodge-podge" of methodologies and queries relating to the Planters. Most of the research is tentative — "work in progress" — and little of it definitive. Much remains to be done. For that reason Planter Studies, and eighteenth-century Maritime history generally, is an exciting field and one which promises to make the New England Planters in Maritime Canada conference but the first of many on the Planter experience.

MARGARET CONRAD

The Coming of the New England Planters to the Annapolis Valley

R.S. LONGLEY
Department of History, Acadia University, 1929-64
(Read before the Nova Scotia Historical Society, April 1960)[1]

It is now more than a century since the well known humorist, Judge Thomas Chandler Haliburton, had his inimitable Yankee salesman, Sam Slick, exclaim: "Now if you want to know all about us and the Bluenoses — a pretty considerable share of Yankee blood in them too, I tell you — the old stock comes from New England and the breed is tolerable pure yet, near about one-half apple sarce and t'other half molasses, except to the easterd where there is a cross of the Scotch."[2] Today the ebullient Clockmaker's obvious attempt to assign certain personal characteristics to the people of western Nova Scotia has little meaning, but his racial and geographical descriptions still stand. Most of the settlers commonly known in the province as Planters, or Pre-Loyalists, came from Sam Slick's native Connecticut. Others were from Massachusetts and Rhode Island. They came by sea to the Basins of Minas and Annapolis to occupy the lands made vacant by the deportation of the Acadians five years before. As we observe the bi-centenary of their arrival, a number of questions suggest themselves: who where the Planters, why did they come to Nova Scotia, where did they settle, and what customs and institutions did they bring with them? To answer these questions in detail would require a large book, but a few bi-centennial observations may be made.

I

The original New England Planters were not those who came to Nova Scotia in 1760, but their ancestors, the hardy middle class folk, commonly known as Pilgrims and Puritans, who for religious, political, and economic motives left their homes in the midlands and south of England more than a century before, to *plant* a new England on the Atlantic coast of North America. Their numbers increased rapidly, both by immigration and by births. At the outbreak of the Revolution in 1775 New England had a population of 800,000.[3]

---

1   Reprinted from the Nova Scotia Historical Society, *Collections* (Halifax, 1961), 81-101. We would like to thank the officers of the Royal Nova Scotia Historical Society for permission to include this article in our collection.

2   T. C. Haliburton, *Sam Slick*, ed. Ray Palmer Baker (New York, 1923), 46.

3   H. L. Osgood, *American Colonies in the Seventeenth and Eighteenth Centuries,* 7 Vols. (New York, 1904-25) passim. Simeon Perkins, *Diary*, ed. H. Innis (Champlain Society, 1948), 88.

One of the distinguishing features of pioneer New England was the constant *migration* of people from the coast to the interior, to what has been called the *frontier*, the meeting place of civilization and wilderness, beyond which lay the unbroken forest, the home of Indians and wild animals. Here the fur trader had his hut, and here the adventurer found activity and excitement. Here also was abundant land, the desire of the Planter. Thus almost as soon as New England was founded, individuals, groups, and even whole congregations, were on the move "trekking" westward to find free land.

An early example of organized migration to the frontier was a congregation from Newtown, near Boston, who, led by their minister, Rev. Thomas Hooker, crossed one hundred miles of uncharted wilderness to settle in the Connecticut Valley. They lived in tents and wagons, carried their personal belongings, and drove their cattle before them. When asked why they withdrew from Massachusetts, for they were not compelled to do so, Hooker replied that the many communities on, or near, the coast were too close together to give them all sufficient land, that the Connecticut Valley was commodious and fruitful, and that "it was the strong bent of their spirits to remove thither."[4] In later years other motives, political and religious, also inspired migrations, but always the major consideration was land.

Since most of the Planters who settled in the Annapolis Valley came from south-western New England, a glance at this area will indicate some reasons for the emigration. In 1637 Connecticut had only 800 people. A century later the number had grown to 38,000. In the next ten years the population doubled, and in 1760 it was 141,000.[5] In our industrial age more than this number are found in many a North American city, but in the 18th century fully 90 per cent of the population tilled the soil, and as farming in New England was extensive rather than intensive, many a Planter with a limited acreage found it difficult to make a comfortable living for his "teeming" offspring. New England families were large, from five to fifteen children being quite common.[6] As the sons grew up, one generally remained with his parents, and the others set out for the nearest unoccupied area to carve homes and farms for themselves in the virgin forest. Girls married young and accompanied their husbands to the frontier. The pioneers had no tasteful surveyor or landscape artist to lay off

---

4 R.L. Morrow, *Connecticut Influences in Western Massachusetts and Vermont* (New Haven, 1936), 2.

5 *Ibid.*

6 Two examples of large families may be cited. On the tombstone of Mrs. Joseph Parker is written she "left two hundred or upward of children and grandchildren." She had fourteen children. *Tercentenary of Groton, Mass., 1655-1955* (Groton, 1955), 40. Joseph DoLittle of Connecticut had 13 children, 72 grandchildren, and 232 great-grandchildren. Morrow, 2.

their lots. They got land when and where they could, from the Indians, from Governments, and by squatters' rights. After 1727 the government of Connecticut began to sell land at public auction, which gave wealthy persons wanting estates, and business men desiring investments, an opportunity to purchase it. Thus with Planters constantly making farms, and speculators seeking profits, it was not long before the best land in the lower Connecticut Valley was occupied, and what remained was so full of swamps, hills, and rocks that it could be gained only "out of fire as it were, by hard blows and for small recompense."[7] Under these conditions, an area which had once been a Paradise for the land hungry farmer, began to send emigrants to other frontiers. At first they crossed to Long Island and the New Jersey Shore. Later they went to Upper New York, Pennsylvania, and even as far south as the Carolinas and Georgia. In the middle of the 18th century the stream turned northward, through western Massachusetts into the wooded valleys of New Hampshire and Vermont. Sometimes young men serving in the armed forces passed an unoccupied area of great beauty and fertility, and after the conclusion of hostilities returned alone or with others, to make it their home. Connecticut became like bees when the hive is full. The surplus population "swarmed" and went off to found new communities and townships. The method of migration was patterned on the New England Town Meeting. A group wishing to move met in some convenient place, elected a moderator and clerk, appointed a committee of management, and decided upon fees. The committee in turn employed agents to negotiate the necessary grants, and to arrange for the "trek." It was in the midst of all this activity that lands in Nova Scotia were opened for settlement. Here was a new frontier. It was further away than the vales of the Green and White mountains, but travel was by water rather than over rough country, and the land was cleared and fertile. It is not surprising, therefore, that for a few years New England had an eastern, as well as a western and northern, frontier. That it ceased so soon was not due to a lack of either people or land, but to the American Revolution which placed Nova Scotia and New England under separate flags. After the revolution, the frontier of the United States continued westward until there was no more free land.[8]

II

Although Nova Scotia became a British colony in 1713, it was thirty-six years before any serious attempt was made to settle it, and forty-five years before it was granted that birthright of Englishmen at home and abroad,

---

7   Morrow, 2.

8   For a discussion on the importance of the Frontier see F.J. Turner, "The Significance of the Frontier in American History," *Proceedings of the State Historical Society* (Wisconsin, 1893).

an elected assembly. At least six schemes intended to promote immigration were mooted. One of these came from the Waldos of Boston who, soon after the capture of Louisburg in 1745, proposed to bring 66,000 settlers from Europe, chiefly Great Britain, to Nova Scotia in return for a large grant of land, and an expected profit of two million dollars.[9] This offer was not accepted, but soon after the Board of Trade, looking forward to the end of the war, planned to settle 3000 disbanded soldiers in the province. Giving land to men discharged from the services was a common procedure, but was not always popular with civil administrations, on the ground that the ex-soldier was in general a poor farmer. The New England Planter, on the other hand, because of his love of the soil, sobriety, industry, and thrift, would be a most acceptable immigrant.

With this in mind, the dynamic Governor of Massachusetts, William Shirley, offered what is known as the *Great Plan*, which was to bring 6000 settlers to Nova Scotia in the next ten years. Two thousand of these were to be disbanded soldiers, 2000 were to be brought from Great Britain and Western Europe, and 2000 were to come from New England.[10] The first did not become of immediate concern as the wars with the French were not yet over, but the second part of the plan was realized by the founding of Halifax in 1749. It had, of course, political implications, such as the establishment of a capital on the Atlantic coast, but as an organized migration it followed a pattern. Advertisements in the *Royal Gazette*, handbills through the Customs Houses and Post Offices, and personal interviews were used to attract settlers. The volunteer emigrants were sent out on ships hired by the British Government, and Parliament voted money to pay the costs. Governor Edward Cornwallis brought more than 2000 people to settle in Nova Scotia.[11]

To tap the third source of Shirley's proposed immigrants, New England, two conditions were necessary: there must be certainty that Nova Scotia would not be reconquered by, or restored to, France; and the province must have an elected Assembly. The French danger was removed by the capture of Fort Beausejour and the deportation of the Acadians in 1755, and the surrender of Louisburg, the Dunkirk of America, in 1758. The Lords of Trade instructed Governor Lawrence to call an Assembly, and members of his Council, such as Jonathan Belcher, favored it. In spite of its obvious connection with the desired immigration, Lawrence delayed action for several years. Then came the great year, 1758. On October 2nd, a few weeks after the fall of Louisburg, the first Assembly met in Halifax. The way was thus opened for the New England Planters to come to Nova

---

9 Norman MacDonald, *Canada: Immigration and Settlement, 1763-1841*(Toronto, 1939), 40; Chester Martin, *Empire and Commonwealth* (Toronto, 1929), 59.

10 This was known as Shirley's *Great Plan*, Martin, 60.

11 A. Basye, *Lords Commissioners of Trade and Plantation* (New Haven, 1925), 40 ff.

Scotia.

On October 12, just ten days after the Assembly convened, Lawrence, with the advice of his Council, prepared a Proclamation which was published in the *Boston Gazette*. It informed the people of New England that since the enemy which had formerly disturbed and harassed the province was no longer able to do so, the time had come to people and cultivate, not only the lands made vacant by the removal of the Acadians, but other parts of "this valuable province" as well. The Proclamation concluded with the words "I shall be ready to receive any proposals that may be hereafter made to me for effectually settling the vacated, or any other lands within the said province."[12] Applications could be made directly to Halifax, or through two well known business and colonizing agencies, Thomas Hancock of Boston and Delancey and Watts in New York.

The Governor's Proclamation was widely read, and created immediate interest, especially in Southern Connecticut. It appealed to several classes of people, adventurers, speculators, and especially land hungry Planters. Although complete evidence is lacking, it seems that a considerable group from New London, Norwich, Lebanon, Lyme, Tolland, and other townships in south-eastern Connecticut, and some from neighboring Rhode Island, met in the Town Hall at Norwich and formed a grantee's organization. The Boston *News Letter* and *Gazette* in the years 1758 to 1763 contain many notices of similar meetings in Massachusetts, but as Connecticut did not then have a newspaper, records are not available.[13] There must have been a number of these organizations, for inquiries came in from individuals and groups, both to Lawrence in Halifax and to the agents in Boston and New York. To answer questions regarding the amount of land an individual could receive, and to describe conditions in Nova Scotia, Lawrence issued a second Proclamation dated January 11, 1759. Townships were being established to contain 100,000 acres. Land would be granted according the grantee's ability to enclose and cultivate it. Every head of a family was entitled to receive 100 acres of wild land for himself and an additional 50 acres for each member of his household. No quit rent would be charged for the first ten years; after that it would be one shilling for each fifty acres. The grantee would be required to plant, cultivate, and improve one-third of his holdings each decade until all was under cultivation. Land along the Bay of Fundy Shore would be so distributed as to give each grantee a share of upland, meadow and marsh. To prevent speculation, no person could receive more than 1000 acres. As to the government, the Province had an Assembly, and every township

---

12 Public Archives of Nova Scotia, Minutes of Council, 12 October 1758.
13 The meeting in Norwich is suggested in Frances Caulkins, *History of Norwich* (Norwich, 1874).

with at least fifty families had the privilege of electing two members to it. The courts were like those of New England. Religious freedom was enjoyed by all Protestants who were allowed to build their own Meeting Houses and choose their own ministers.[14]

These answers were reasonably satisfactory, although no specific mention was made of New England's most prized institution, the Town Meeting. The grantees held further meetings. At one of these it was voted to send five agents, Major Robert Denison, Joseph Otis, Jonathan Harris, Amos Fuller, and John Hicks, to look over the lands in Nova Scotia, and if, in their judgement, conditions were favorable, to make an agreement with the Provincial Government. The first four of the envoys were from Connecticut; Hicks was from Rhode Island. Dennison, Otis and Harris were the seniors of the group; Fuller and Hicks were younger.

In 1759 Robert Denison was sixty-two years of age. He was a landowner in the north-eastern section of New London, having inherited land purchased by his father from the Indians in 1710. He donated land to the Congregational Church in New London, in return for which he was permitted to build a pew in the church for himself and his heirs forever.[15] He took part in the French and Indian wars, and in 1745 commanded one of the eight companies of Walcott's Connecticut Brigade at the seige of Louisburg. He was not discharged from the army until 1761. He settled at Horton and was one of the first members of that township in the Assembly, 1761-1765. He represents the soldier and adventurer, as well as the Planter, in the migration. He was seeking land for himself and his family.[16]

Joseph Otis emigrated to New London from Massachusetts, where he had been a judge of the Court of Common Pleas and a member of the General Court, or Assembly. Like Denison, his family pew was in the front of the Church. He was by no means a land hungry Planter, for he owned considerable property in north-eastern Connecticut. His interest in Nova Scotia was largely that of an agent for others, or as a speculator. It was probable that when he saw the individual grants were limited, he lost interest. He did not settle in the province.

Jonathan Harris was a son-in-law of Otis, and no doubt shared his attitudes and interests. He too did not become a Nova Scotia Planter, but his brother, Lebbeus, and his son, James, were grantees of Horton. Like Denison, Lebbeus Harris was elected to the House of Assembly.

Fuller was a fellow townsman of Denison, Otis, and Harris, but he was much younger, being but thirty-eight years of age. Because of age, or

---

14 Minutes of Council, 11 Jan. 1759.

15 F. M. Caulkins, *History of New London* (Hartford, 1852), passim. A pew in the front of the church was a recognition of distinction.

16 Denison was twice married and had 15 children. The first family were all grown up and on their own in 1760. Many of the younger family had also reached maturity.

interests, or both, he became friendly with Hicks, and the two later worked together in their colonizing ventures.

Hicks was a Rhode Island Quaker. His ancestor, Robert Hicks, was one of the Pilgrims. He was definitely a Planter, and he and his eldest son, Benjamin, were grantees in the township of Falmouth. Later they sold their lots in Falmouth and moved to Annapolis County. Here the father was elected to the Assembly, and the son achieved a considerable degree of affluence.[17]

The five agents came to Halifax by ship, and on April 18, 1759, appeared before the Council. They were men of influence and position and were treated as such. The Governor and four Councilors, Jonathan Belcher, Benjamin Green, Charles Morris, and John Collier, were present. The first three were New Englanders, and understood the aspirations of the agents and their associates; Collier, like Lawrence, was of the British military tradition.[18]

Before admitting the agents, Lawrence raised the question as to whether negotiations should be undertaken without the knowledge and approval of the British Lords of Trade, but after due deliberation it was decided that since delay might dampen the enthusiasm of the agents, discussions should proceed. The Council was encouraged by the fact that the aspiring immigrants seemed willing, apart from transportation, to pay all cost of removal.[19]

On being admitted to the Council, the agents asked a number of questions which were duly answered. These were concerned with what happened to land if the grantee should die before the terms of the grant had been fully met, the possibility of remitting the quit rent of some settlers unable to pay it, and the condition of the Minas dykes. It was agreed that if settlement were made, the Planters should be given weapons to defend themselves, and that they would not be subject to impressment in the army or navy for ten years. The agents then asked to be taken at Government expense to look over the proposed place of settlement. The request was granted, with the understanding that if all was satisfactory, grants would be made as soon as the surveys were completed. Surveyor-General Charles Morris was to accompany them to aid in choosing sites for future townships.[20]

The agents set out on a Government ship with the Surveyor-General in command, and nine soldiers as guards. The vessel sailed around Yarmouth into the Bay of Fundy which enabled the visitors to view the lands along

---

17 W.A. Calnek, *History of Annapolis County* (Toronto, 1897), 332. Elizabeth Coward, *History of Bridgetown* (Kentville, 1955).

18 T.B. Akins, *Selections from the Public Documents of the Province of Nova Scotia* (Halifax, 1869), 255-56; 293, and 315 footnote.

19 Minutes of Council, 18 April 1759.

20 *Ibid.*

the Annapolis river before proceeding to Minas Basin. They landed on the shore of the Basin and spent many busy days studying the topography and soil of the large area between Cape Blomidon and Piziquid, now Windsor. They were delighted with all they saw. Seven rivers emptied their waters into the Basin, and on the banks of each was an abundance of fertile soil. The hills were covered with forests and the apple trees planted by the Acadians were almost ready to bud, the grass on the dykes was green, and the uplands seemed to be waiting for the plough.[21] When the inspection was over, the agents hurried back to the capital where they arrived on May 17. They at once resumed negotiations with the Council. The latter wanted settlers, and the agents were ready to supply them, so an agreement was concluded without delay. The now enthusiastic agents were quite ready to settle two townships, Horton and Cornwallis, each of 100,000 acres, with 200 and 150 families respectively. These were to be brought to Nova Scotia at Government expense, and each passenger might bring stock, tools, building materials, and household goods up to a weight of two tons.[22] To families of several members this concession was quite a boon. Most of the prospective settlers were quite able to pay all expenses save transportation, but fifty families were reported too poor to do so. For these the agents requested one bushel of grain a month for each individual for one year, or until the first harvest.[23] Lawrence hesitated to make this grant, feeling that free land and free transportation were sufficient. Also, thus far the Lords of Trade had been unable to express an opinion on the new immigration policy, and there was a real possibility that it might be rejected, especially if the costs were high. On the other hand, the Council did not wish to lose more than two hundred settlers for the sake of a few hundred bushels of corn, so the free grain was included in the agreement.[24]

Well pleased with what they had accomplished, the three senior agents, Denison, Otis, and Harris, hastened back to Connecticut to report what had been arranged and to seek additional grantees. Fuller and Hicks remained in Halifax to present a supplementary plan of settlement.

While scouting at Minas, Fuller and Hicks came upon a former Acadian settlement on the north bank of the Avon river, opposite Fort Piziquid. The marshes and uplands were fertile, and half-destroyed buildings still dotted the landscape. The two men requested a grant of 50,000 acres on which to settle one hundred families from Rhode Island, fifty in 1759 and fifty in 1760.[25] The Council agreed to the terms and promptly created the township of Falmouth. Fuller then returned home, but Hicks remained to

---

21 A.W.H. Eaton, *History of Kings County* (Salem, 1910), 63.

22 Minutes of Council, 18 May 1759.

23 *Ibid.*

24 *Ibid.*

25 *Ibid.*, 19 May 1759.

submit a list of potential grantees.[26]

With the return of the four Connecticut agents news of their successful negotiations in Nova Scotia spread rapidly, and led to the formation of other immigration societies, not only in Connecticut, but in Massachusetts and Rhode Island as well. Soon more agents arrived in Halifax. Most of them were representatives of actual organizations and grantees, but a few proved impostors.[27]

The first of the new applicants for land were James Read and John Grow of Massachusetts, and Paul Crocker of eastern New Hampshire, who represented a group from those colonies. They knew the country around Annapolis, and wished to have the protection of the old fort. They therefore requested a grant of a township of the usual 100,000 acres in the picturesque area between the Annapolis River and the Bay of Fundy. The Council approved the grant on June 27, 1759, and thus established the township of Granville. It was to be settled by 200 Planters, but at the moment the agents could list only 138. They were to find 40 more. The remaining 22 were to come later. The grant was to "Mr. Crocker, Mr. Grant, and others."[28]

Next to appear before the Council were four agents from Connecticut, Edward Mott, Benjamin Kimball, Bliss Willoughby, and Major Samuel Starr. Some of their prospective settlers had served with Colonel Robert Monckton at Beausejour in 1755, and so knew of the isthmus of Chignecto. Knowing the success of Denison and associates, they requested free transportation to the proposed site of settlement.[29] The Governor complied with their wishes. The details of their visit to Chignecto are beyond the scope of this paper, except for the activities of Samuel Starr. He and Willoughby decided not to return to Halifax by ship, and so travelled overland to Cobequid, and by whaleboat to Windsor. Here Willoughby rejoined Mott and Kimball in Halifax, but Starr turned west to Grand Pré. Later he crossed the Cornwallis river and explored the new township between the river and the Bay of Fundy. He was so pleased with what he saw that he abandoned the Chignecto project and became a Cornwallis Planter.[30] He settled at Starr's Point where he lived highly respected until his death in 1799. His descendants have been active in the political, industrial, military, and social life of Kings County.[31]

The fifth request for land in this momentous year came from Daniel Knowlton who made application on behalf of himself and fifty-two others

---

26 *Ibid.*, 16 July 1759.

27 *Ibid.*, 3 Oct. 1759.

28 *Ibid.*, 27 and 29 June, 67 and 71.

29 *Ibid.*, 19 July 1759, 77

30 From the papers in the possession of the Starr family, Eaton, 531-2.

31 Eaton, 824-6.

for land at Cobequid. The Council thereupon established the township of Onslow.[32]

The final grant for 1759 was to a well organized group from central Massachusetts whose managing committee was Ebenezer Felch, John Woodward, and Jason Glezen. Associated with them were Abner Morse, Samuel Bent, and Henry Evans. Like the Granville grantees, they wished to settle near the fort, and so applied for a grant on the south side of the river in the township of Annapolis.[33]

The success of his Proclamations of 1758-59 gave Lawrence great satisfaction. Hardly had Denison and his fellow agents withdrawn from their first meeting with the Council, when the Governor wrote the Lords of Trade that those who had arrived represented "some hundreds of associated families" and that they intended to "chuse lands for the immediate establishment of two or more townships."[34] Later he explained to an attentive House of Assembly that "very extensive tracts of the vacated lands on the Bay of Fundy" had been granted, "to industrious and substantial farmers," and that applications for more were coming in faster than he could prepare the grants. "And I make no doubt," he concluded "but that the well peopling of the whole " will keep pace with our warmest and most rapid wishes."[35]

Even before these optimistic and cheering words had been spoken, word reached Halifax that fishing vessels had been seized near Canso, several persons had been killed near Dartmouth, and prospective settlers had been fired upon near Cape Sable. Also bands of Indians, with a few Frenchman, had threatened the forts at Windsor, Lunenburg, and Sackville.[36] Lawrence gave this news to his Council, and consulted with John Hicks who was still in the province. All agreed that the immigration from New England should be postponed until more peaceful conditions prevailed.[37] It was then decided that all agreements made for 1759 would not become operative until the spring of 1760.

Although the anticipated activity for 1759 was thus delayed, the next few months were far from uneventful, either in New England or Nova Scotia. In Connecticut meetings of enthusiastic grantees continued, even in the face of official coldness and hostility. Some of the original promoters, such as Otis and Harris, withdrew from active participation and transferred their shares to others. Some lost their enthusiasm because

---

32 Minutes of Council, 24 July 1759, 78, and 26 Oct. 26 1759, 90.

33 *Ibid.*

34 J.B. Brebner, *The Neutral Yankees of Nova Scotia,* (New York, 1937), 31.

35 T.C. Haliburton, *An Historical and Statistical Account of Nova Scotia,* 2 Vols. (Halifax, 1829), I , 225.

36 Minutes of Council, 16 July 1759.

37 *Ibid.*

opportunities for speculation were lacking. Others were dropped when they did not pay the required fees, but their places were taken by new applicants. Thus while names might appear today and be gone tomorrow, which accounts for grantees who did not come to Nova Scotia, there were no fundamental changes in either plans or numbers.

Meanwhile Lawrence in Halifax made changes in the Council and Assembly in preparation for the incoming tide. The Council, because of withdrawals from the province, had been reduced to four members. It was strengthened by the addition of Richard Bulkeley, Thomas Saul, and Joseph Gerrish.[38] In the first Assembly there were many who served as "members at large." Under the revised order, five counties, Annapolis, Cumberland, Halifax, Horton, and Lunenburg, received two members each. Four townships, Annapolis, Cumberland, Horton, and Lunenburg, as agreed by the Proclamation of January 11, 1759, were given two members each, which, with four from Halifax, gave the province the original number, twenty-two seats.[39] An election was held on November 20. Thus a new Assembly greeted the Planters on their arrival the following spring and within a year they had representatives in it. In the same month of November an angry sea swept over the Minas dykes which, after five years of neglect, were in a state of disrepair. The Governor visited the area and found the damage severe, but not disastrous. Soldiers and Acadians later helped repair the dykes, and to make other improvements.

Meanwhile Lawrence received a dispatch from the Lords of Trade. As was anticipated, they viewed the Governor's immigration project with some doubt. The cost, it was feared, would be great, and the money should be used to place disbanded soldiers on the land. In a well reasoned reply the Governor pointed out that in an earlier dispatch their Lordship had admitted that Planters from the older colonies made excellent farmers. It was an equally well known fact that disbanded soldiers did not make good Planters. As proof of this, it could be shown that every soldier who had come to Nova Scotia since the founding of Halifax had either left the province or had become a dramseller. In addition, to place soldiers on the land the Government must find, not only transportation, but stock, utensils, and building materials. It would be much better, the Governor concluded, to place disbanded soldiers in the older colonies where, if they failed as farmers, they could find other employment.[40] These statements, supported as they were by facts, convinced the Lords of Trade that Lawrence's policy was sound. He was therefore given the authority to carry "the same into execution."[41] There was still room for the disbanded

---

38 *Ibid.*, 17 Aug. 1759, 80.

39 *Ibid.*, 22 Aug. 1759, 82.

40 Haliburton, *An Historical and Statistical Account of Nova Scotia*, I, 235 ff.

41 Lords of Trade to Lawrence, 16 Feb. 1760, Boston *Gazette*, 28 July 1760.

soldier to settle in the province, but the Governor's immediate concern was the Planter migration of 1760.

In New England the associations of grantees continued their preparations to emigrate. Those who were owners of property disposed of it, and purchased stock and materials which could be used in the new homes. Some received gifts from parents. Then came the journey to the place of embarkation. In Connecticut it was near at hand, in other colonies more distant. The chief problem was to know just when the ships would arrive. During the waiting, food had to be obtained for both man and beast. Finally spring came and the migration began.

It is from the pen of Chief Surveyor Morris, that we learn of the early arrivals. He left Halifax in May to visit the various centres of activity. Calling first at Liverpool, he found the newcomers busy and satisfied. He then sailed to the Annapolis Basin where he greeted forty-five settlers for the township of Annapolis, and a small group of lot layers who came in advance of the Granville grantees. Those in the township of Annapolis sailed on a ship, the *Charming Molly*, and landed a short distance up the river from the fort. According to Morris, the ship had been chartered from Hancock in Boston to make two voyages to Annapolis for Henry Evans and associates.[42]

From the Boston *News Letter* we know that the Annapolis grantees held an important meeting at the inn of William Bryant in Sudbury, Massachsuetts, on February 13, 1760. Here, with business-like precision, preparations were made for the removal to Nova Scotia. All who decided they did not want to emigrate, or had not paid their fees, were dropped. Henry Evans was employed to go to Halifax, to conclude negotiations with the Government so that the settlers might be at work in their new homes by the end of May.[43] Receipts for money paid Evans for his services are among the Caleb Davis papers in the New England Historical Society in Boston.

According to his *Journal*, Evans left Marblehead on April 4, 1760, and after a tedious voyage of nine days arrived at Halifax. Here he completed his business with the Governor and Council, and notified authorities at Annapolis to expect the settlers within a month. By May 1st he was back in Boston where on the 5th he visited Hancock's and engaged the *Charming Molly* for two voyages. He then attended a final meeting of the grantees at Framington. On the 15th those who were to form the advance group, or working party, were ready to sail. As was so often the case with sailing ships, a sequence of contrary winds and aggravating calms prevented a speedy crossing. Evans reports the arrival at Annapolis in June, but Morris found settlers there at the end of May.[44]

---

42 Morris to Governor Lawrence, 1 June 1760, Minutes of Council.

43 Boston *News Letter*, 31 Jan. 1760.

44 Evans, *Journal* in Calnek, 148-50. Morris to Lawrence, *op. cit.*

On her first voyage the *Charming Molly* carried thirty-one men, two women, and twelve children, as well as stock and equipment.[45] Most of the the men left their wives and families in Massachusetts until they had prepared living quarters for them. These and other families came later in the year.[46] The grantees met to appoint lot layers and other necessary officials, and so introduced the New England Town Meeting to Nova Scotia. The lot layers, of whom Evans was one, divided the land, after which individuals holdings were determined by lot. Each head of a family received the normal share of 500 acres, and some of the low land which had been cultivated by the Acadians. Defence was provided by the garrison at Annapolis and the organization of the male settlers as militia. The building of homes went forward rapidly. Within a few years the Annapolis township had a population of 500. The arrival of the Granville grantees late in 1760, and early in 1761, completed the initial migration, but settlers continued to arrive for the next two or three years. The Granville grants were also 500 acres each, and extended from the river to the Bay of Fundy. As in Annapolis, the location was determined by lot. Later a number of exchanges and sales were made in both townships to bring relatives and friends together.[47] The Town Meeting was used as a system of local government and administration, but the central village or town plot was not adopted as in the eastern end of the Valley. The chief occupation was farming, although some of the Planters became fishermen, millers and sawyers.

From Annapolis, Surveyor Morris sailed to Windsor where he arrived just in time to see six vessels under the command of a Captain Rogers come up the Avon river and dock a little distance from the fort. These contained the first contingent of between two and three hundred of the Connecticut Planters whose destination was the township of Horton. The ships had been hired by Lawrence and Council, as nearly as can be determined, at the cost of ten shillings per ton weight of the vessel per month. Thus a ship of eighty tons cost £40 a month.[48] In the case of the six ships, winds and high seas kept them hiding in coves and harbours, so that it took three weeks to make the crossing from New London to Windsor, and must have cost the Government nearly £200. The passengers arrived weary and half sick, and fodder for the stock had been exhausted. But once on land, the settlers regained their optimism, and they were soon off to their new homes, in true

---

45 For the names of the passengers, see Calnek, 151. Such names as Kent, Bent, Rice, Morse, and others are still to be found in the Valley.

46 Calnek, 151.

47 Calnek, Chapter XI; Coward, 10-14.

48 This was approximately the rate paid for the ships which took away the Acadians. Akins, 285-93.

pioneer fashion, driving their cattle before them.[49]

On June 4, 1760, the main flotilla, consisting of twenty-two ships hired by the Government of Nova Scotia to transport the Connecticut Planters to Horton and Cornwallis rounded Cape Blomidon and anchored in the estuary of the Avon and Gaspereau rivers. It was escorted by a brig of war under the command of Captain Pigot. Assuming that the vessels were the usual sloops and schooners of average size, they must have carried an average of fifty passengers each, plus stock and equipment.[50] The total cost of the Rogers and Pigot ships was about £1500.[51]

The Cornwallis settlers landed at what was Boudreau's Bank, now Starr's Point, and the Horton settlers at Horton Landing. At first they lived in tents and temporary shelter. Almost at once they held Town Meetings, or assemblies of grantees, at which the usual lot layers and other officials such as clerk, constable, and herdsmen were appointed. The lot layers divided the land which was drawn for in the usual way. Most heads of families received the regular share of 500 acres, but some were granted a share and a half, and a few a half-share. Each had a town lot and a portion of marshland, upland, and woodland. Soon all were busy building houses and tilling the soil.[52]

An outstanding characteristic of the Planter settlements in Horton and Cornwallis was the central community ot Town Plot. It was an inheritance from both old and new England, and was used here also for purposes of defense, trade, and social life. At Annapolis there was a fort near the settlements, but in Horton and Cornwallis it was necessary to construct a palisaded area, and it was desirable to have the families as near to it as possible. As danger from the Indians ceased, the Planters found it more convenient to live on the land they tilled. Thus the present community system replaced the town plot. To consolidate their holdings, the owners began a series of sales and exchanges in the process of which the shrewd often obtained the best lands.[53] Farming continued for some time extensive rather than intensive, with younger sons still seeking land. This resulted in the divisions of the original grants, and the occupation of ungranted areas west of the settlements. In the 19th and early 20th centuries many sons and daughters of Planters found their way back to

49 Morris to Lawrence, *op. cit.* Morris suggested that the six ships made a second voyage to bring many who were waiting at New London.

50 The estimate of 1100 people in the flotilla fits with a census taken in 1763-64 when there were 122 families or 689 people in Horton, and 125 families or 656 people in Cornwallis.

51 See I. G. MacKinnon, *Settlements and Churches in Nova Scotia* (Montreal 1930).

52 Eaton, *op. cit.* Grants to those who settled in the two townships were issued in 1761. The Horton committee was William Welch, Lebbeus Harris, and Samuel Read. For Cornwallis the committee was Eliakim Tupper, Stephen West and Jonathan Newcomb.

53 Harriet B. Weld, *The History and Genealogy of the Borden Family* (1899), 122.

New England. Here their descendants still reside.

The Rhode Island Planters came to Falmouth in four ships of which two were the *Sally* commanded by Captain Jonathan Lovett, and the *Lydia* commanded by Captain Samuel Toby.[54] The former carried 35 passengers and the latter 23. The cost to each passenger was 25 shillings.[55] Among the leaders of this group were John Hicks, Henry Denny Denson, and Shubal Dimock.[56] There were 73 families in all. Almost at once those who settled on the east side of the river wished to have their own township, and so Newport was established. In Falmouth, more than in any of the other settlements, the town meeting was used as the means of dividing the land and of regulating almost every activity of the community, even to the distribution of the Acadian ruins, the cutting of firewood, the earmarks for the cattle, and the use of the commons for grazing.

By the end of the year 1760, Annapolis County had a new Massachusetts, Kings County a new Connecticut, and the present Hants County a new Rhode Island. The whole Valley was a new New England, with a population of nearly 2000 people.[57]

Governor Lawrence was so well pleased with his new settlers that he wrote Thomas Hancock he was prepared to receive further applications for land.[58] He visited the Minas settlements during the summer and found contentment and activity everywhere. His death on October 19th left the work well advanced, but incomplete. It was continued by acting Governor Jonathan Belcher. Today after two hundred years many Planter descendants are still in the area, some residing on the original grants. Other descendants have made places for themselves in politics, business, the professions, and in the church. Their contributions to Nova Scotia, Canada, and the United States justify the policy that brought the New England Planters to the beautiful Vale of Annapolis.[59]

---

54 Lovett was the captain of one of the ships that carried the Acadians into exile.

55 R.G. Huling, "The Rhode Island Emigration to Nova Scotia," *Narragansett Historical Register*, VII, 1899, 92 ff.

56 Hick's associations with Falmouth have been given. Denson was active in the early life of the settlement. In 1775 he was distributor of arms and ammunition in Kings County. Eaton, 431. Dimock was a dissenting preacher who emigrated to escape persecution.

57 A.W.H. Eaton, *Americana* (March 1915).

58 Boston *Gazette*, 28 July 1760.

59 See *Canada and Its Provinces*, XIII, 110.

Planter Settlements in the St. John Valley

D. Murray Young
Department of History
University of New Brunswick

The new settlements founded or projected in the St. John Valley in the 1760s were of three distinct types: first there was one "do-it-yourself" settlement[1] ; second, there was one mercantile settlement; and third, there were a number of townships and estates projected either on managerial-proprietorial or on landlord-tenant principles.

The one "do-it-yourself" settlement was the township of Maugerville. It became a "dominating influence up and down the St. John River" and, in Dr. Esther Clark Wright's estimation, "one of the most successful [townships] in the old province of Nova Scotia." This settlement was Massachusetts in origin and inspiration and in its incarnate self-help principles. Its founding father figure was Captain Francis Peabody, who had served as a sergeant in a Massachusetts company at Annapolis in 1755 and had later distinguished himself as the commander of a company in the western campaign.[2] The most active promoter of Maugerville was Israel Perley,[3] another former officer. He visited the St. John River Valley at the head of a scouting expedition that came overland from Machias in 1761 to look at lands recently abandoned by the French, and came again by way of Saint John in 1762 when the site was chosen. A trained surveyor, Perley was one of five petitioners who in 1763 made a request to the Board of Trade and Plantations for a grant of the lands on which Peabody, Perley and a number of fellow colonists had already settled. Both were natives of Boxford in Essex County. Most of the other "do-it-yourself" pioneers were from there or from neighboring areas.

The land on which they had settled was a low-lying plain on the east bank of the St. John River about seventy miles inland. Three years later Beamsley Glasier described it as:

> flat, not a stone or pebble....It runs level...such land as I cannot describe. The New England people have never plowed but harrowed in their grain, such Grain of all kinds, such Hemp, Flax, etc. as was never seen.[4]

1 The phrase is from E.C. Wright *Planters and Pioneers, Nova Scotia, 1749-1775* (Hantsport, 1982), 12.

2 W.O. Raymond, *The River St. John* (Saint John, 1950), 141; New England Historical Society, "New England Enlistments in Gov. Shirley's Regiments 1755."

3 S.E. Patterson, "Perley (Pearley), Israel," *Dictionary of Canadian Biography*, V, 665-7.

4 Raymond, *The River St. John*, 178-9.

The quality of the grass on the intervales met with similar enthusiastic approval: "I never in my life," he says, "saw fatter beef...." The grant was laid out in 101 freehold lots extending for twelve and a half miles along the river bank.[5] They were equal in size, each, that is, of 500 acres. Two large islands in the river were divided into sections and assigned to individual lots. At the rear of the grant an area about the same size as the surveyed section was left undivided. The land at the upriver end was less desirable than the lower part of the township and most of the grantees at the extreme upper end abandoned their properties; these later passed into the hands of incoming Loyalists. In the fertile lower section, where the height of land between the St. John River and a parallel waterway inland is today the Trans-Canada Highway, the lots had the advantage of having two fronts on navigable water — one on the St. John River, the other on French Lake or the Portobello Stream. The lakes had the potential for a useful fishery and the township's only sites for water-powered mills were on small streams flowing into this inland waterway.

After giving initial support to the successful effort of the settlers to gain title to the grant,[6] Halifax exerted very little influence in Maugerville, except to give at least nominal approval to the distribution of land. Internal affairs were managed largely through the traditional New England institutions of the congregational church and the town meeting,[7] with the Halifax-appointed justices of peace being local men who, for the most part, found it convenient to fit into the "do-it-yourself" system. Although from 1765, when the St. John Valley and Passamaquoddy were erected into the county of Sunbury, members were chosen for the assembly at Halifax, they seldom took their seats.

Maugerville and the commercial enterprise at the mouth of the St. John River were interdependent, the first merchant there, James Simonds,[8] being a Maugerville grantee who later "married into the settlement," choosing one of Captain Peabody's daughters as his life partner. Little ships employed by Simonds shuttled between the St. John River and Newburyport, carrying people, goods and information, and keeping the people of Maugerville in close contact with their relatives and their roots in and near Essex County. The St. John River was closer to Boston by sea than it was to Halifax.

While most of the settlers seem to have been attracted to the valley by the opportunity to continue, or to return to, the rural pattern of their

5 W.D. Moore, "Sunbury County 1760-1830," M.A. thesis, University of New Brunswick, 1977, 8.

6 Moore, "Sunbury County 1760-1830," 6-7.

7 Moore, "Sunbury County 1760-1830," 13-4, 17-9.

8 T.W. Acheson, "Simonds, James," *Dictionary of Canadian Biography*, VI, 717-20.

ancestors, what attracted James Simonds was the opportunity to participate in the North Atlantic trading system. Other notable examples of
commercial settlements in this corner of the world at the end of the Seven
Years' War include those of George Cartwright in Labrador, Charles
Robin on the Gaspé and, much nearer at hand, that of William Davidson
on the Miramichi.[9] Simonds began scouting for business opportunities in
the province of Nova Scotia in 1759, before the smell of gunpowder had
cleared from the harrying of the French in the St. John Valley. Three years
later, in 1762, he accompanied the vanguard of the Maugerville settlers and
established himself at Portland Point in Saint John harbour where, early
in 1764, he obtained a reserve of valuable marshland and a license "for
carrying on a fishery and for burning limestone." He also conducted an
illicit fur trade with the Indians until he was able to obtain a license for that
trade.

Armed with these assets he and his younger brother, Richard Simonds,
were able to enter into a partnership with their cousin William Hazen in
Newburyport and with a Boston merchant who provided capital and
access to a trading network. The partnership,[10] which changed somewhat
in its composition over the years, is the one popularly known as Simonds,
Hazen and White. Richard Simonds was killed by Indians in 1765 and
James White, another cousin, joined James Simonds as a resident partner
at Portland Point.

The firm's many activities — which included serving the garrison at Fort
Frederick; trading with the Indians for furs, feathers and castor; limeburn-
ing; a fishery; barrel-making; sawmilling; shipping and ship building —
provided employment for many hands in the years 1764 to 1774. In these
operations Simonds, Hazen and White employed workers from New
England, most of whom came to the St. John River on a seasonal basis,
though some became permanent settlers. Simonds and White also
employed local Acadians to drain part of the great marsh to provide hay
and pasture land, and also, probably, in preparing the way for a
tidal-powered sawmill.[11]

In the meantime, the several individuals and groups who form my third
category of sponsors of settlements had acquired blocks of land. Their
goals were either to found settlements or to establish agricultural estates

9   G.M. Story, "Cartwright, George," *Dictionary of Canadian Biography*, V, 165-7; David
    Lee, "Robin, Charles," *Dictionary of Canadian Biography*, VI, 652-4; W.A. Spray,
    "Davidson, William (John Godsman)," *Dictionary of Canadian Biography*, IV, 195-7.

10 R.C. Campbell, "Simonds, Hazen and White: A Study of a New Brunswick Firm in the
    Commercial World of the Eighteenth Century," M.A. thesis, University of New
    Brunswick, 1970.

11 Raymond, *The River St. John*, 193-4. For a reference to the mill irons, which were
    originally intended for another mill, see Massachusetts Historical Society, St. John's
    Society Collection, Simonds to Col. Glazier, 20 August 1765.

on the landlord-tenant principle, then so ably defended by Arthur Young and other British agricultural theorists. Most of these enterprises were idle speculations of men of influence, such as General Gage and Governor Wilmot, but one group did for a time actively promote development. This was the Canada Company, formed by officers in the Montreal garrison in 1764 to take advantage of the opportunities in Nova Scotia. Their headquarters later was in New York. They recruited to their numbers prominent persons such as Governor Thomas Hutchinson, Sir William Johnson and Frederick Haldimand, and also enlisted local men whose talents and resources were likely to be helpful, such as Charles Morris, the surveyor general, and James Simonds and William Hazen, who provided both a New England agency and local contacts.[12]

Their plans were ambitious and far-reaching, embracing the idea of an extensive fishery, a major lumbering and sawmilling enterprise, agricultural estates and a village community. The site they preferred for their colony was the Cape Sable area, but when that was denied them, their choice narrowed to either Prince Edward Island (Ile St.-Jean) or the lower St. John Valley. Their agent was another Essex county man, Beamsley Perkins Glasier,[13] who had served as a captain in the capture of Louisbourg in 1745. Glasier rejected Prince Edward Island without actually visiting it, assuring a director of the company who had favoured the island that "There is scarce any good land upon it...and all sumer (sic) covered with fogg....All that can be said for it is fish...."[14]

The Nova Scotia government reserved five townships in the valley, amounting in all to around 400,000 acres, and also an island in Passamaquoddy Bay, for the company, which renamed itself the St. John River Society. Four of these townships were on the west bank of the river and corresponded to the areas around West Saint John, Gagetown, Oromocto and Fredericton South. The fifth township was a grant centered on the waterfall, later called the Great Rapids, in the Nashwaak River at Marysville. There in 1766 Glasier expended a considerable part of the company's resources on the construction of a dam and what was planned as a large sawmill.[15] His preferred site for a village was St. Ann's Point at Fredericton, but it being unavailable, he chose Gagetown instead.

There is as yet no analytical study of the St. John River Society. In some respects its projects are reminiscent of the activities of the company

12 Raymond, *The River St. John*, 177, 179-80; W. Inglis Morse, ed., *The Canadian Collection at Harvard University: Harvard Library Bulletin VI* (1948-9), 54-7, 95.

13 D.M. Young, "Glasier (Glasior, Glazier), Beamsley (Bensley) Perkins," *Dictionary of Canadian Biography*, IV, 299-301.

14 Massachusetts Historical Society, St. John's Society Collection, Glasier to John Fenton, 1 March 1765.

15 Raymond, *The River St. John*, 182-4.

incorporated in Britain in 1832 for the development and sale of lands in central New Brunswick.[16] But there were great differences, for the nineteenth-century enterprise was a modern joint stock company, whereas the St. John River Society was essentially an extended partnership intended to be an instrument of both corporate and individual enterprise. In fact, it impresses me as being a creature designed by a committee — with very mixed objectives. In part it was grandiosely capitalist and business minded; in part it was a romantic dream of landed estates and deferential tenants. Above all, it gave institutional expression to the desire of mostly impecunious and temporarily rootless men to explore any opportunity that might yield a financial, social or political advantage. In 1767 the company suspended activities due to the failure of the proprietors to subscribe sufficient capital. In 1768 the land was alloted to the sixty-eight individual proprietors. Only the sawmill property and Perkin's Island in Passamaquoddy Bay were to continue to be held in common.[17]

Few permanent settlers had arrived in the Society's townships by 1768. Even the company store was in Maugerville, where the storekeeper, Sergeant Barlow, became a permanent resident. After 1768, the introduction of settlers depended upon the energy and enterprise of individual proprietors, and on the willingness of potential settlers to accept their terms. A few proprietors did make serious efforts, but only two of the townships contained significant numbers of settlers in 1783: Gagetown with at least 172 people and 34 houses, and Burton with 218 people and 32 houses.[18]

Burton and part of Gagetown lie directly across the river from Maugerville and in the 1770s became extensions of that community. Most of the settlers recruited by the proprietors were New Englanders, though some were sent from Ireland by proprietors from that country. Several of the most energetic of the townships' inhabitants, or at least those who left the greatest mark in the records, were "self-help" families from Maugerville who moved across the river to avoid the annual floods or to obtain better land.[19] Even Israel Perley established an outpost of his Maugerville property on the Burton side of the river. He occupied the high grassy knoll that later became the site of the Sunbury County courthouse (at the end of the Burton bridge).[20] It was a convenient refuge for his livestock during the

---

16 Raymond, *The River St. John*, 182-3; for the nineteenth-century company see Ivan Saunders, "The New Brunswick and Nova Scotia Land Company," M.A. thesis, University of New Brunswick, 1969.

17 Morse, *The Canadian Collection at Harvard University*, 62-70.

18 Raymond, *The River St. John*, 187; Wright, *Planters and Pioneers*, 25; Wright, *The Loyalists of New Brunswick* (Saint John, 1972), 116.

19 Raymond, *The River St. John*, 174.

20 Moore, "Sunbury County 1760-1830," 57-8.

spring freshets. Land records of the Loyalist era tell the stories of families who squatted in the Society's townships or made arrangements with the agents of the proprietors.[21]

Of the remaining townships, two, Sunbury and Newtown, remained little more than fur trading outposts on the frontier of the French settlements and of Indian territory. The third, Conway, was looked upon primarily as a base for the fishery. There, across the river from their Portland Point estate, Simonds and White placed a dozen useful Maugerville families in an effort to ensure title to lands alloted to them as proprietors.[22]

Within a decade of its founding Maugerville itself was showing signs of prosperity and stability, so much so that in 1774 it was able to attract a resident clergyman and two years later to provide a parsonage and a commodious framed meeting house.[23] How does one account for its early stability? Many reasons have been suggested by historians:[24] the benefits derived by the settlers from their corporate heritage and self-help institutions; the presence of a strong mercantile establishment near at hand; the advantages of having adequate capital and possessions at the time of arrival, of being first on the ground, of having the way prepared for them by earlier French settlers, of receiving outright grants of large lots of fertile land under a system of freehold tenure, of being beyond the administrative reach of Halifax, and of being able in the early years to maintain continuous contact with their roots in Massachusetts. In our era of genealogical enthusiasm and prosopographical history, it is probably safe to add to this list the advantage of the presence of a number of kinship groups as well as a mix of generations among the settlers. When eight Burpee children were orphaned by the deaths of their father in 1767 and their mother in 1771,[25] they were able to retain their identity as a nuclear family under the guardianship of their aged grandparents, Jonathan and Mehetable Burpee. Jonathan's other sons had not moved from Massachusetts, but the children had other relatives in Maugerville, including their mother's brother and sister, whose households were open to them.

Life in the settlements was disrupted by the break between Britain and Massachusetts in 1774. Two years later privateers, military adventurers and discontented Indians invaded the valley. Commercial enterprises collapsed. By 1778 both James Simonds from Portland Point and William

---

21 Moore, "Sunbury County 1760-1830," Chapter III.

22 Raymond, *The River St. John*, 187.

23 J.M. Bumsted, "Noble, Seth," *Dictionary of Canadian Biography*, V, 627-8.

24 W.S. MacNutt, *New Brunswick: A History, 1784-1867* (Toronto, 1963), 4-5; Wright, *The Loyalists*, 116; Moore, "Sunbury County 1760-1830," 14-21; Raymond, *The River St. John*, 166,174.

25 D.M. Young, "Burpee, David," *Dictionary of Canadian Biography*, VII (forthcoming).

Davidson from the Miramichi were living inland, in Maugerville.[26] The establishment of British garrisons at Saint John and at the mouth of the Oromocto in the winter and spring of 1777-8 brought a return to stability. The Indians gradually became less threatening, so that by late 1779 William Davidson was able to put a crew to work cutting masts for the navy.[27] William Hazen and Benjamin Glasier, who in person or on behalf of relatives had claims to large estates, moved to the valley during the time of troubles, bringing to an end the Planter migration from New England.[28] By 1781, Hazen and White, this time without Simonds, were back in the export business, with masting added to their list of trades.[29] By 1783, when a census of the old inhabitants was taken, there were signs that pioneers of the second generation were already moving into areas that had previously been left to the Indians. Later, the appearance of Planter family names in Loyalist settlements indicates that descendants of the Planters continued to play a remarkable role in the peopling of the frontiers.

Planter families also continued to thrive after 1783 in the heartland of the original settlements at Portland Point and Maugerville. The Hazen and Simonds extended families, with wealth derived from the property and skills acquired in the Planter era, occupied a central position in New Brunswick politics throughout the first half of the nineteenth century, with political influence resting initially in the Hazen connection and passing later to the Simonds connection. Other St. John Valley Planter clans — Burpees, Esteys, Hartts, Perleys, Pickards, Estabrooks, Coys and Glasiers — filled important niches in nineteenth-century lumbering, merchandising, manufacturing, education, religion and politics.[30]

26 Raymond, *The River St. John*, 222, 237.

27 Raymond, *The River St. John*, 237.

28 Raymond, *The River St. John*, 243, 278.

29 Raymond, *The River St. John*, 238.

30 Biographies of many descendants of Planter families appear in the *Dictionary of Canadian Biography*. For the Estabrooks family and its connections, see the publications of Florence C. Estabrooks and her papers in the New Brunswick Museum. The bibliographies attached to the individual biographies in the *Dictionary of Canadian Biography* serve as an invaluable guide to the extensive manuscript material available on the St. John River settlements, as well as to later writing on their history.

Cumberland Township: A Focal Point of Early Settlement on the Bay of Fundy[1]

Esther Clark Wright
Wolfville, Nova Scotia

It is the destiny of certain places to be ingathering and distributing centres for a time, and then, because of changes in means of transportation or because of the opening of new regions, to lose their local importance. During the eighteenth century, Philadelphia was the principal receiving and distributing centre of population for the Atlantic seaboard, and it was only slowly, and with much difficulty, that New York forged ahead to supremacy in the nineteenth century. For the Bay of Fundy region, Cumberland Township on Chignecto Isthmus was such a centre from 1750 to 1783 — the dates can be assigned quite definitely — and the story of how it became such a centre, of its functioning during the period of its supremacy, and of the way in which it lost its focal importance, is here set forth.

Port Royal-Annapolis had been the first Bay of Fundy centre. It was from Port Royal that the various French settlements around the Bay of Fundy and its inlets were established, including the one at the head of the middle passage which the French called Beaubassin, and the English Cumberland Basin. This settlement was begun by Jacques Bourgois shortly after 1671,[2] and granted as the Seigneury of Chignitou or Beaubassin to Michel le Neuf, Ecuyer, Sieur de la Vallière, on October 24, 1676.[3] Thanks to Vallière's energy and the fertility of the marshlands, this was the most successful seigneury in Acadie, and from 1738 to 1748 showed an annual increase of eleven per hundred inhabitants.[4]

The richness of the area was, however, only one factor in accounting for the stubbornness of the English attempt to capture the district, and of the French to retain it. The isthmus was a long used route of travel from the Gulf of St. Lawrence to the Bay of Fundy, familiar both to the Indians and the French. Furthermore, the area had a strategic value as offering the shortest possible front line for the opposing forces. In 1750, both sides moved to the isthmus — La Corne with the French forces, early in the year, to the hill of Beausejour, west of the Misseguash and Major Charles Lawrence, in September, to the ridge on the east — and both began

---

1 Reprinted with the permission of the University of Toronto Press from the *Canadian Historical Review*, 27 (1946), 27-32.

2 Rameau de Saint-Père, *Une Colonie féodale* (2 Vols., Paris, 1889), I, 168.

3 W.F. Ganong, "Historic Sites in New Brunswick," *Transactions* of the Royal Society of Canada, 1899, Section II, 315.

4 Rameau, *Une Colonie féodale*, II, 77.

fortifications. With the capture of Fort Beausejour by the English in 1755, control of the region passed to the English, and when Louisbourg was taken in 1758, their possession was confirmed.

The captured fort was renamed Fort Cumberland; the other forts on the isthmus, the English Fort Lawrence and the fort on Baie Verte, called Gaspereau by the French and Monckton by the English after its surrender, were destroyed by order of the Council at Halifax.[5] A considerable force was maintained at Fort Cumberland until 1768, when the soldiers were withdrawn from this and other forts in Nova Scotia to Halifax, and a small garrison thereafter.[6] The existence of a large garrison at the fort from 1755 to 1768 meant that there were vessels plying to and from the region with troops destined for the garrison, with troops being relieved of duty, and with supplies. It meant also the existence of a commissariat for provisioning the garrison, and the appearance of the traditional camp followers, a sort of irregular commissariat, who supplied the soldiers with services and goods, not always of a desirable kind. The danger of raids by the French and Indians held back for three or four years any attempt at building or farming, except in the immediate vicinity of the fort. It may have been this danger, but it was probably the unaccustomedness and the menace of the tides which led to there being no desire on the part of the New Englanders who took part in the capture and the early garrisoning of the fort to take up land in the region.

The first manifestation of desire to settle is found in the grant of the Township of Cumberland, in 1759, to ninety-one individuals, with a supplementary grant the next year, in which nine other names were included. Two groups had joined in the application, one of persons connected with the fort but mostly with the commissariat, and a committee from Connecticut who came up to Nova Scotia in July, 1759.[7] The two groups added the names, if not of their sisters, their cousins, and their aunts, at least of their brothers, their uncles, and their brothers-in-law. In addition, there were several names from Halifax, notably those of John Burbidge and William Best. (The Connecticut settlers were deflected to Cornwallis, for the most part, apparently by the deliberate purpose of the administration at Halifax to have settlers in a more accessible region.)[8]

Only about twenty percent of the one hundred persons named in the 1759-60 grants were at Cumberland long enough to have their names included in the second pair of grants, made in 1763 and 1764 — a few of the Connecticut settlers and a larger number of officers in the regular army or

5   J.C. Webster, *The Forts of Chignecto* (Saint John, 1930), 71.

6   *Ibid.*, 76.

7   A.W.H. Eaton, *The History of Kings County* (Salem, Mass., 1910), 64-5.

8   J.B. Brebner, *The Neutral Yankees of Nova Scotia* (New York, 1937), 60.

persons connected with supplying the garrison.[9] There were nearly as many names on the 1763-4 lists as on the previous grants, for the original grantees added the names of members of their families;[10] there were a few more members of the garrison,[11] new settlers from Massachusetts,[12] further arrivals resulting from the visit of the Connecticut committee,[13] and a few immigrants from the British Isles.[14]

It was the policy of the Nova Scotia Council at that time to make grants of 100,000 acres as townships. Cumberland township included the Fort Cumberland and Fort Lawrence ridges, with the Misseguash River between, and extended to the River Aulac, west of Fort Cumberland, to the river La Planche eastward, and north-east to Baie Verte. Since its bounds by no means included all the land dyked by Vallière's industrious settlers, two other townships were laid out and granted in 1763, Sackville, west of the Aulac, to include the great marsh of the Tantramar, and Amherst, east of the La Planche. The settlers for these districts were probably landed at Cumberland and distributed from there, and they were joined in their new homes by former Cumberland settlers. By 1770, when returns of the state of the townships were made, there were nine or ten

---

9 The Connecticut settler, chiefly Norwich names, were Ayer, Burnham, Fales, Fitch, Fillmore, Hunt, and Merrill. The garrison and commissariat group included William and John Allan, Halifax merchants of Scottish origin, William Bearsto, probably of Boston, head carpenter, Captain Benoni Danks, Jotham and Samuel Gay, traders, John Huston and his protégé, Brook Watson, Richard Jones of the 47th Regiment (Westmorland County Memorial no. 171, Crown Land Office, Fredericton), Captain Sennacherib Martyn, Henry McDonald, Abiel Richardson (formerly Innholder of Cambridge, who was drowned in 1765 on the way to his fish curing establishment on P.E.I., *Boston Evening Post*, March 24, 1766), Engineer Winckworth Tonge, and Josuha Winslow, Chief Commissariat Officer.

10 Abiel Richardson, for instance, added the names of his two sons, Abiel Jr., and Godfrey, although they were only eleven and seven years old, and the name of his bother-in-law, Jesse Converse, who remained fifty years in the region.

11 Lieutenant Thomas Dixson or Dickson, William How, whose father had been slain by the Indians in 1750 (Webster, *Forts of Chignecto*, 32), Daniel Goodwin or Gooden (said to be a native of Plymouth, England, who had been in Captain Adam's company from Newburyport) and his brother Enoch, Alexander Mills, who had been taken prisoner with Dickson, Martin Beck ("Marin Peck, der King's Paker, tam you." He is supposed to have said, according to the Steeves family tradition), and Samuel Wethered of Boston, who was connected with the commissariat.

12 Moses Barnes of Swansea, John and Jesse Bent of Milton, the Eddys from Sharon, the Gardners from Salem, Joseph Morse from Dedham, Zebulon Roe, perhaps from Newburyport, Gamaliel Smethurst and Ebenezer Storer, Boston merchants, Nehemiah Ward of Attleborough.

13 Chappels of Lebanon, Simeon Chester of Groton, Amos Fuller of Lebanon, Nathaniel Sheldon?, Josiah and Thomas Throop of Lebanon.

14 Anthony Burke, Windsor Eager, of Dumfries, William Maxwell, William Milburn, Robert Whatley.

Cumberland families at Sackville, and four at Amherst.[15]

Nor was it only to the adjacent townships that Cumberland distributed population: after the setting up in 1765 of the townships of Hopewell, Hillsborough, and Monckton on Shepody Bay and the Petitcodiac River, Cumberland passed along settlers to all three, in some cases its own, in some cases Horton and Cornwallis settlers who paused briefly at Cumberland and then moved on.[16]

The censuses of 1767 and 1770 show a decline in the population of Cumberland from 334 to 322, but the 1770 returns are admittedly incomplete and may have still other omissions. The shifts to Sackville and Amherst probably occured before 1767, when enthusiasm for the new grants was high. The lists for 1770 show that nearly half of the 1763-4 grantees were still at Cumberland, and that members of their households had set up households of their own. There were not many newcomers; two Rhode Island families, an army officer, four or five old country men who may have been soldiers, and three or four families who may have been among the dissatisfied tenants who disappeared from Hopewell and Monckton.[17]

Unfortunately, there are no later returns similar to those of 1770, with names of the householders and the numbers in the household. For the next phase in the history of Cumberland Township — the coming of the Yorkshire immigrants in the years before the war, 1772 to 1774 — it has been necessary to piece together the evidence from family histories,[18] from deeds, and from *Memorials* in the Crown Land Office, Fredericton. At least fourteen families came to the area, some directly, some after a brief sojourn elsewhere, those of the name of Atkinson, Carter, Chapman, Dobson, Harper, Keillor, Lowerison, Scurr, Siddall, Trenholm, Trueman, Wells, Wood. At the same time, the Copps and perhaps other families moved over from Horton. With these additions, Cumberland Township must have seemed well on the way to success, with an assured future; but already the storm was gathering which was, in the end, to wreck Cumberland's chances of remaining the principal port of the Bay of Fundy.

---

15 *1934 Report*, Public Archives of Nova Scotia (Halifax, 1935), 27, 33, 34, 47, 48.

16 The Copps, for instance. See Samuel Copp Worthen's articles in *New York Genealogical and Biographical Report*, LXII, 350, and LXVIII, 34. For other instances, see E. C. Wright, *The Peticodiac* (Sackville, N.B., 1945), passim.

17 The R.I. families were Hicks and Brownell, the officer, Edward Barron. John Ackley or Eckley, reported to be from Pennsylvania (*Maine Historical Magazine*, IX, 1894-5, 64-5), William Resty and wife listed as "Germans and other foreigners," John Leckhart, may have come from either Hopewell or Monckton.

18 Howard Truman, *The Isthmus of Chignecto* (Toronto, 1902), is particulary helpful, although the statements need checking occasionally.

The first events in the Revolutionary War, the so-called Eddy Rebellion, which culminated in the attack on Fort Cumberland, and the harrying of the settlements by American privateers, seemed to accentuate the importance of Cumberland. The Royal Fencible Americans were sent to hold the fort and to man outposts, and settlers from the outlying districts[19] moved to Cumberland within the protection of the fort. To balance this gain, however, there was a loss of population with the removal of some fourteen or fifteen Cumberland residents who found it expedient to withdraw after the unsuccessful attempt on Fort Cumberland.[20]

This outward movement, which probably would have occurred over a term of years but was hastened by the rebellion, was not the death blow to Cumberland Township: that came with the founding of Saint John and the division of Nova Scotia into two provinces. Had a larger body of Loyalists been sent to Cumberland, that district might have remained as the principal distributing centre on the Bay of Fundy, and might eventually have been selected as the capital of a single province, since its accessability by water from the peninsular portion (the present Nova Scotia), the mainland portion (the present New Brunswick), and the island portions (Prince Edward Island and Cape Breton) would have been an irresistible argument in favour of such a choice, sufficient even to overcome the jealousy with which Halifax guarded its prerogatives. As it was, only one body of Loyalists, the Westchester Loyalists,[21] was sent to Cumberland for distribution; the main body went to the mouth of the St. John River, where they found a hinterland, up the St. John River and its tributaries, of

---

19 The Lowerisons, Deslesderniers, and perhaps others moved from Hillsborough at this time. See Wright, *The Petitcodiac*, 50.

20 Jonathan Eddy listed the refugees (*Maine Historical Magazine*, IX, 1894-5, 64-5), who included the following from Cumberland, John Allan, Elijah Ayer, Obadiah Ayer, Anthony Burke, Simeon Chester, Parker Clarke, (Edward Cole?), Daniel Earl, John Eckley, Jonathan Eddy (Atwood Fales, who had moved to Amherst), Ebenezer Gardner, William How, William Maxwell, Nathaniel Reynolds, Zebulon Roe, Josiah Throop. These were given grants in Maine, and also in Ohio. See C.M. Layton, "Canadian Refugee Lands in Ohio," *Canadian Historical Review*, XXIV, December, 1943, 380. (Why *Canadian* Refugee Lands? The names given are nearly all traceable to Nova Scotia townships, to which the term Canada did not apply in the eighteenth century. Did any of them settle on the Ohio lands? Most of hem can be traced in Maine, but a few returned to Nova Scotia and New Brunswick.)

21 The Westchester Loyalists were a more or less organized group who operated in the area between the British and American armies and were largely concerned with getting supplies for the army in New York. They were called "cattle rustlers" by the Americans, who had a similar body. It was the proud boast of the Westchester Loyalists that they always took enough prisoners to be able to redeem their own men and to have some left over for bargaining purposes. They received grants at Ramsheg (Wallace) and Cobequid, but a few remained at Cumberland — Edgett, Hewson, Knapp, Palmer, Pugsley, Purdy, Teed — and spread westward rather than eastward as designated.

unexpected value and accessability. The St. John River Loyalists insisted on the division of the province, which not only split Cumberland Township in two, but also cut in half the Bay of Fundy empire. Cumberland might have prevailed against Halifax only; against the two way pull, of Halifax and Saint John, it was helpless. After 1783, the area which had been the township (the larger half, west of Misseguash, went to New Brunswick, the smaller went to Nova Scotia) received rather less incoming population than most areas in the two provinces, and distributed only the usual quota which went out from all such regions in the era of large families.

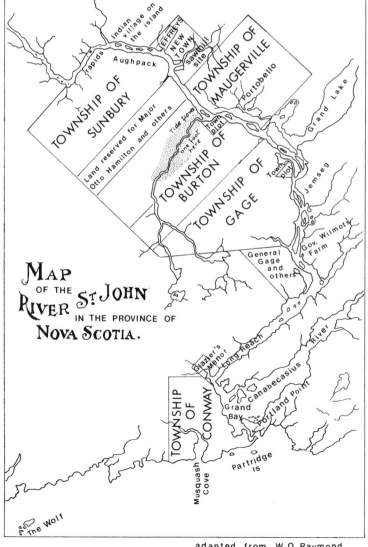

adapted from W. O. Raymond

Cumberland Planters and the Aftermath of the Attack on Fort Cumberland

Ernest A. Clarke
Halifax, Nova Scotia

"There are many timorous and weak persons among us, who aw'd by fear, are drove to do what they would avoid, if they durst." John Eagleson, Anglican missionary and acting chaplain of Fort Cumberland, describing Cumberland Planters during the rebellion.[1]

* * * * *

"O most mighty God," prayed the Society for the Propagation of the Gospel missionary at Windsor. "Ruler of Heaven and Earth," prayed the Rev. William Ellis as H.M.S. *Vulture* sailed out Minas Basin to relieve Fort Cumberland in November 1776. "Re-unite the Divided interests and Distracted minds of our Countrymen. Defend us from Seditious rage at home and from the Designs of all our...enemies, wheresoever they may be!"[2] A good many of the distracted wheresoevers were, even as Ellis prayed, surrounding Fort Cumberland where sedition had raged through the Planter community, for the past year and where the fort had been under attack for a month by a band of 180 guerrillas led by the self styled Colonel Jonathan Eddy.[3]

Inside the fort were about the same number of defenders: a garrison of provincial troops, the Royal Fencible Americans, and two dozen or more

---

1 Eagleson to John Butler, 27 January 1776, Public Archives of Canada (PAC), MG 11, Vol. 95, 112-7.

2 Prayer, Discourses and Sermons of the Rev. William Ellis, Dalhousie University Archives. Ellis also was a chaplain at Fort Edward.

3 The Planter community of Cumberland was an amalgam of halfpay officers, farmers, tradesmen and artisans heavily dependent on the fort for their livlihood. Cumberland Planters were not pioneers in the usual sense, having received land already rendered productive by the Acadians — not only extensive dykeland but cleared upland and abundant orchards. In addition, the local economy was strongly underpinned by the Fort Cumberland garrison of which the economic spinoff alone was sufficient to support no less than twenty-three non-agricultural occupations (from linen draper to tavern keeper) in the county before 1768.
   Despite economic infusion and ready-made farmland, community development was slow in part because Cumberland Planters, especially the ex-soldiers, were poor farmers. Visitors and settlers alike observed that New England farmers were a "lazy, indolent people," rising late in the morning and then only "to get a glass of rum" before breakfast and before going out to work. Abrupt withdrawal of the garrison in 1768 followed by severe economic recession damaged the Cumberland community fundamentally and prepared the groundwork for future political dissent.

loyal inhabitants, designated "the virtuous few" by the fort's commander, Colonel Joseph Goreham.[4] Numerous women and children were also in the garrison where supplies were running low and where many of the buildings had been burned down around them. Ill-trained and ill-equipped, the troops were without uniforms and half of them without a shoe to their feet. Because of their ragged appearance, the regiment was a joke to the Royal Marines on board the relief ship *Vulture*, blessed as they were, not only by the Rev. Ellis, but also with real uniforms. "The Fencibles not being all Cloth'd look so much like Yankees," howled one marine officer, "that [the prospect] of doing [service] with them gives me [the] Horrors!"[5]

The Rev. Ellis also blessed the captain of the ship, and he was well-advised to do so, for Captain James Feattus of H.M.S. *Vulture* was a hard drinker who had even been accused of "being in liquor" while guiding His Majesty's warship into Halifax Harbour.[6] Despite Ellis' blessing, the normally short, one day voyage from Windsor to Cumberland took Feattus a full six days and during the voyage *Vulture* strayed within three leagues of Annapolis Gut, farther away from Windsor than Cumberland was in the opposite direction.[7] But *Vulture* eventually reached Fort Cumberland and the Royal Marines (in their uniforms) condescended to join with the Nova Scotia Fencibles (in their rags) to defeat the Patriots at Camphill, lifting the month-long siege and ending the rebellion.[8] The

---

4   Attestation of service, December 1776, signed by Joseph Goreham and eighteen other officers. Claim of Christopher Harper, PAC, A.O. 13, Bundle 92.

5   William Feilding to Lord Denbigh, 23 May 1776, in Marion Balderston and David Syrett, eds., *The Lost War: Letters from British Officers during the American Revolution* (New York, 1975), 82.

6   Feattus Papers, Public Record Office (PRO), Admiralty (ADM) 1, 1790. When the navy removed Feattus from his command of the *Vulture* for drunkenness, nepotism and neglect of duty, the entire Executive Council of Nova Scotia expressed its displeasure and highly commended Feattus' service, but to no avail, and when *Vulture* assisted Benedict Arnold in his defection to the British in 1780, she had a new captain.

7   Journal of H.M.S. *Vulture*, National Maritime Museum (NMM), L/V/126, and Log, PRO ADM 51/1044. *Vulture* "unmoored" in the mouth of the Avon River, 21 November, and landed troops at Fort Cumberland, 27 November. Quite apart from the captain's personal problems. *Vulture* was delayed by bad weather and the schooner she convoyed. The voyage was bedeviled first by gale force winds, then by thick fog on a dead calm. The *Levinia* schooner carrying two companies of Royal Highland Emigrants, encountered a series of problems that slowed *Vulture*'s progress before contact was lost in the fog and a leaky *Levinia* returned to Windsor thereby reducing the relief force by more than half.

8   For a description of the siege from within the fort, see Goreham's Journals in *PAC Report*, 1894, 355-66; for Camphill, see Eddy's account in Frederic Kidder, *Military Operations in Eastern Maine and Nova Scotia During the [American] Revolution* (Albany, 1867), 67-72; and for a description of its climax, the Camphill Rout, see Thomas Batt's account in *Remembrancer*, Part III, 1776 (London, 1777), 297-8.

effects of the civil dispute lingered a very long time in Cumberland County, growing into a uniquely troublesome period which may be referred to as the aftermath of the siege. It is this unusual period which is here considered.

The foremath of the siege lasted a year, the siege itself exactly one month, but the aftermath persisted vigorously for twelve long years, from the day of the Camphill Rout to at least 1788 when the last legal case was settled and the embers of the last deliberately-set house fire had cooled to ashes. The effects of the aftermath, which spread far beyond the borders of Cumberland County, derived from the bitter nature of the civil strife and also from the peculiar propensity of Cumberland Planters for sustained acrimony.

The depth of bitterness can be judged by the number of homes destroyed. So far, I have been able to document forty-nine houses burned during and after the siege, with the arson evenly perpetrated between Patriots and Loyalists. Indications are that many more were destroyed and, of course, these were not your usual home fires. They were conflagrations malicious! A great serial arson rendered homeless at least 300 people, all neighbours, and out of the ashes there arose an industry of criminal and civil litigation that fueled the aftermath and skewed the legal system at all levels from justices-of-the-peace to Supreme Court judges.[9]

5 December 1776: six days after the end of the siege
Many prisoners have been taken. Over a hundred residents have availed themselves of Goreham's promise of amnesty by surrendering and taking the oath of allegiance. The senior Patriot leadership, including Colonel Eddy and most of his Committee-of-Safety, have fled with perhaps sixty refugees to Massachusetts. But five of the prisoners — Joseph Goreham calls them the "principal prisoners" — are being led down to Cumberland Creek to be put aboard H.M.S. *Vulture* and shipped to Halifax.[10]

It is a squally Thursday with fresh gales. Among the principal prisoners is Thomas Faulkner commander of the Cobequid contingent of Eddy's guerrilla army and James Avery the commissariat officer.[11] And there is Dr. Parker Clarke member of the unique collection agency sent out during

---

9 Jotham Gay, a Cumberland Planter, explained the destruction to Levi Ames, an absentee property owner in London: "I am very sorry for the Great Loss you sustained, as well as many Others in This Place, By This Garrison Being Invested in the fall of 1776. Your House and Barn was Burnt (Not by the Enemy) But by the Kings Troops when they Attacked and Drove the Enemy out of the Country, the Consequence of which was that the Country was Put into Great Confusion, Fences Destroyed and Lands layed Common for Several Years." Levi Ames Papers, PAC, MG 40, M 36.

10 Journal of H.M.S. *Vulture*, NMM L/V/126.

11 Avery was a brother-in-law of George Haliburton. See Jean Stephenson, "The Connecticut Settlement of Nova Scotia Prior to the Revolution," in *National Genealogical Quarterly* (American), XLII, 2 (June 1954), 59.

the siege by the Committee-of-Safety to collect old debts and extort money from loyal Cumberlanders. It was odd to see a doctor making house calls, as one who saw him said, with "a bayonet tied to his gun."[12] And there is Benoni Danks who, despite his sixty years, was in the Patriot front lines where he was wounded in the Camphill Rout, having "receiv'd a Spent Ball in his thigh."[13] But he has concealed the wound from his captors and now six days later infection is setting in. The fifth and last prisoner is Richard Uniacke, one of Eddy's out-guards, but who also must have performed more important service to be classified among the principal prisoners. Perhaps he looks back up the hill to catch a fleeting glimpse of his tearful teen-age wife who celebrated her fourteenth birthday three days ago.[14]

* * * * *

A feature of the aftermath was the growth of the provincial militia, whose members after the siege, were suddenly eager to serve even outside home districts. The Kings County militia had been active locally during the siege,[15] having made the initial discovery of the siege when it recaptured the Partridge Island ferry.[16] It has been assumed that another Planter, Thomas Dixson, brought first news of the siege to Windsor and Halifax and indeed it is difficult to correct an error bronzed, as it were, on a plaque at the Beausejour Museum, but Dixson did not escape the fort and reach Windsor until six days after the militia patrol made its discovery, by which time a relief force was already being organized at Windsor and H.M.S. *Vulture* was already en route from Halifax to pick up that force and go to Cumberland.[17] Militia improvement underscored Nova Scotia's growing

12 Deposition of Thomas Robinson in "Trials For Treason 1776-7," J.T. Bulmer, *Collections of the Nova Scotia Historical Society* (NSHS), I (Halifax, 1879), 111.

13 Massey to Germain, 4 January 1777, PANS, RG 1, Vol. 365, 3.

14 PANS BIO, Delesdernier. Also, family memorial plaque in St. Paul's Anglican Church, Halifax.

15 In addition to the Kings County militia, that of Annapolis Royal and Halifax were demonstrably active in their own districts during the siege. See "Expenses incurred for Militia employed on Sundry Services between 10 November 1776 and 30 July 1777," PAC, MG 11, Vol. 97, 299-300.

16 Michael Francklin to Joseph Pernette, 9 December 1776, PANS, MG 100, Vol. 143, 22. The five townships of Windsor, Newport, Falmouth, Horton and Cornwallis exhibited the strongest early loyalty of any district outside Halifax, especially during the critical winter of 1775, and early 1776 (see for example the correspondence of the Rev. William Ellis), hence the active response of Kings County to the perceived threat of Eddy's attack.

17 Thomas Dixson probably escaped through Patriot lines 11 November; certainly, he was unable to depart Cumberland sooner, Goreham's first journal, *PAC Report*, 1894. He reached Windsor 15 November, Francklin to Arbuthnot, 15 November 1776, and Francklin and Batt to "the Commanders of any of his Majesty's Ships at Annapolis," 15

determination in the aftermath of the siege to aggressively defend even its remote frontiers. When John Allan returned the next year to occupy the St. John River Valley with an invasion force larger and better organized than Jonathan Eddy's, Halifax reacted quickly and was able to use the militia directly. From Halifax, Windsor and Cumberland militiamen joined in the Hawker expedition to drive John Allan from the valley.[18] Sounding pleasantly surprised by this development, Marriott Arbuthnot, the lieutenant-governor, explained to Lord Sandwich how "the militia turned out volunteers with the greatest cheerfulness, many of them quitting their professions where they earned 15 to 20 shillings a day, to serve upon this painful business for one. So much, my Lord, is the complexion of the times altered in this province!"[19] In addition to their one shilling the militiamen were also eligible for prize money. Livestock, goods and chattels of leading Patriots on the river were seized and shipped over to Annapolis Royal where they were auctioned off with the proceeds going to the militia "as encouragement for another Party," explained the Nova Scotia army commander, Eyre Massey.[20]

So eager were militiamen to serve on the Hawker expedition, that there resulted a singular incident — the only scalpings I know to have occurred in Nova Scotia during the Revolutionary War. In the early hours of 1 July, in clear moonlight on the Manawogonish Trail, now in West Saint John, the bloodthirsty Planter militia caught up with several Patriots just

---

November 1776, PAC, MG 11, Vol. 96, 376-81. The Partridge Island ferry was re-captured 9 November and news of the siege was relayed directly to Halifax whence it spread quickly through the town and down the south coast to Liverpool where it was a topic of lunchtime conversation 15 November, Harold A. Innis, ed., *The Diary of Simeon Perkins, 1766-1780* (Toronto, 1948), 137. Via Liverpool, John Allan at Boston learned of the news as early as 13 November. Allan journal, PANS, RG 1, Vol. 364, 96. By the time Thomas Dixson arrived at Windsor (six days after the ferry's recapture) specific measures had been taken there by Michael Francklin to organize a relief force. In addition, Commodore Collier at Halifax had ordered Captain James Dawson of H.M.S. *Hope* 14 November (one day prior to Dixson's arrival at Windsor) to find the ships *Albany* and *Diligent*, then cruising near the mouth of the Bay of Fundy, and "proceed immediately to Fort Cumberland and destroy if possible the rebel Armament now employed against that Place." A week later the Commodore confirmed that he had given Dawson the order "upon the certainty that a Body of Rebels (reported about 500) had actually invested Fort Cumberland," Collier to Dawson, 14 November 1776, PAC, MG 11, Vol. 96, 332-4.

18 The task force raised to dispel the second Massachusetts attack comprised six ships led by H.M.S. *Mermaid* (Captain James Hawker). In charge of the regular provincial troops of the force was Gilfred Studholme while Michael Francklin and John George Pyke commanded the militia.

19 Arbuthnot to Lord Sandwich, 13 September 1777, G.R. Barnes and J.H. Owen, eds., *The Private Papers of John, Earl of Sandwich, First Lord of the Admiralty 1771-1782*, Vol. 1 (Navy Records Society, 1932), 296-8.

20 Massey to Germain, 10 June 1777, PAC, MG 11, Vol. 97, 170-3.

wounded in a skirmish and killed and scalped them (not necessarily in that order). The incident was mentioned by John Allan, described in lurid detail by Stephen Smith of Machias,[21] and I have recently verified the name of one of the victims.

Neutral? The Nova Scotia Planter militia certainly was not! Confused? Yes, but only (and unfortunately) in discerning the limits of their duty! Such alacrity appears the more startling when one considers that the militia commander on the Hawker expedition, John George Pyke, was the brother-in-law of John Allan, leader of the Patriot invasion.[22] In fact, most families (especially Planter families) had members on both sides of the dispute. An example is the Wethereds, called by Eyre Massey "the family of the worst Rebels in this Province."[23] Samuel Wethered kept a tavern near Fort Cumberland and during the siege entertained Eddy's guerrillas nightly. On one such occasion, while in his tavern, Wethered was severely wounded by a cannonball fired from the fort. This story has been discounted by some historians, but in an unpublished letter written only a week after the siege, we read that "Wethered has had about half his buttocks taken off by a cannon shot from the Fort, when he was in his own house, there being many rebels in it."[24] While the half-buttocked Wethered was so painfully laid up in his tavern, his two Loyalist sisters (Catherine Wethered, wife of Thomas Dixson of whom we have heard and Sarah Wethered, wife of James Law, barrack-master of the fort) were inside the fort with their husbands celebrating the defeat of Jonathan Eddy.[25]

---

21 Allan's journal in Kidder, *Military Operations*, 111. Stephen Smith to Mass. Council, 31 July 1777, PANS, MG 1, Vol. 364, 56.

22 Allan genealogy in Kidder, *Military Operations*, 25. For Pyke's service on the St. John River see indictments of Crath, Fulton and Crawford, 27 January 1778, and the deposition of John George Pyke, 3 February 1778, PANS, RG 1, Vol. 342; also, Fulton to Allan, 1 April 1778, Massachusetts Archives (MA) Vol. 218, 55-6.

23 Massey to Germain, 17 January 1777, PAC, MG 11, Vol. 96, 96-9. "Nothing but open Rebellion," wrote John Eagleson in January 1776, "will satisfy them, being stimulated and led on principally by Allen and Wethered, persons of Desperate Fortune."

24 Michael Francklin to Joseph Pernette, 9 December 1776, PANS MG 100, Vol. 143, 22. The Wethered incident appeared first in Knapp's folktales over-dressed in the embellishment of much re-telling. It was repeated by Bird before being denounced by Kerr who said it "need not be taken seriously," which advice has generally been followed by later historians. Kerr's comment and Webster's branding of another of Knapp's folktales as "ridiculous" have discredited the Knapp collection of stories about the siege, but while these stories must be approached warily, they are ignored at one's peril. All contain elements of verifiable fact and the Wethered incident — almost too bizarre to be false — is confirmed by the Francklin letter. Charles Knapp's "Folk Lore About Old Fort Beau-se-jeur," *Acadiensis* (October 1908), 300; W.R. Bird, *Century At Chignecto* (Toronto, 1928), 227-8; W.B. Kerr, "The American Invasion of Nova Scotia," *Canadian Defence Quarterly* (October 1936), 444.

25 Louise Walsh Throop, "Early Settlers of Cumberland Township, Nova Scotia," in

A curiosity of the aftermath was the collapse of military discipline in Fort Cumberland during the spring and summer of 1777. Any number of reasons might be given: post-siege doldrums, renewed heavy drinking of Joseph Goreham, spill-over from the general turmoil of Cumberland County, and certainly the neglect of Halifax authorities. "There is great dissensions among the Officers of the Garrison," gloated John Allan.[26] Chief among the dissensions was the row between Commander Joseph Goreham and Major Thomas Batt, hero of the Camphill Rout, which resulted in each of them being court-martialled.[27] But the strongest evidence of the breakdown of discipline was the series of duels fought between officers of the garrison. On 29 May for example, Lieutenant Constance Connor shot dead Lieutenant Lewis De Beaudoin. These two officers had actually led troops into battle together in the Camphill Rout only a few months earlier. With a successful duel in his curriculum vitae, Planter Constance Connor went on to lead a naval detachment on the Nova Scotia vessel *Buckram*, and became commander of Fort Hughes on the Oromocto River.[28]

Dueling was in fashion during this period of the aftermath and was not confined to junior officers of the garrison. Eyre Massey, in charge of the army in Nova Scotia, and George Collier, in charge of the navy, had developed their hatred of each other during the siege. They came within seconds of fighting a duel with pistols behind Citadel Hill and were only dissuaded at the last moment by Marriott Arbuthnot. "The impropriety," admitted Collier, "of the two chief officers of the Army and Navy going out to fight at a time when we were surrounded by the Enemies of our Country" could hardly be ignored.[29] One might ask if indigenous rebellion

---

National Genealogical Quarterly, 67, 3 and 4(September and December 1979), 189, 270. Both Eyre Massey and Joseph Goreham cited James Law for his failure to supply the fort with adequate fuel in the fall of 1776, as he had been contracted to do, and for which he had been paid. However, there is no doubt that Law was loyal — incompetent but loyal.

26 Allan to Mass. Council, 24 June 1777, in Kidder, *Military Operations*, 196.

27 Goreham was tried in 1777 and Batt in 1780. See the British Headquarters Papers (BHQ): the complaint against Goreham, 10 July 1777, and that against Batt, 18 June 1780.

28 Allan to Mass. Council, 24 June 1777, in Kidder, *Military Operations*, 196-7. Muster rolls of the Royal Fencible Americans, PAC, RG 8, Vol. 1893. Letter of William Handfield, 18 April 1782, PANS, RG 1, Vol. 369, 16-18. Lorenzo Sabine, *The American Loyalists* (Boston, 1847), 225. E.C. Wright, *The Loyalists of New Brunswick* (Yarmouth, 1955), 120. "Letterbook of Captain McDonald," *Collections of the New York Historical Society 1882* (New York, 1883), 348-9.

29 The near duel between the two heads of the army and navy in Nova Scotia is described in "A detail of some particular services performed in America during the years 1776-79 by Sir George Collier," NMM BGR/28. While this incident has not been corroborated, several other incidents between Collier, Massey and Arbuthnot, which are described in the same document, are supported by other evidence.

could have wished for a more divided military command than that provided by General Massey and Commodore Collier, or for that matter, a more inept lieutenant-governor than that forgetful senior citizen, Marriott Arbuthnot whose faculties, it was said, "(which were never brilliant)" were so impaired in 1776 that he lost important military instructions in the pocket of his own trousers![30] Arbuthnot's chief concern in November 1776 was not the outcome of the siege but the Christmas present he would get his patron, Lord Sandwich. Not just anything would do for the Lord! It had to be unusual. Finally, he found a live wildcat and shipped it off to England.[31] He must have surprised the Lord with that gift — hard to top it really! But throughout 1777, while discipline collapsed at his garrison outpost of Cumberland, the real issue for this affable old servant of the crown was what to get Lord Sandwich to match that wildcat!

A thorny political problem arising from the aftermath was the disposition of spouses and children left behind by absconding Patriots. An analysis of those who fled with Jonathan Eddy (who was careful to remove his own family before the siege) indicates that their families numbered above 200 persons, many of whom were destitute and a burden on the resources of the fort. Their continued presence was a source of conflict in Cumberland and exacerbated the mood of vengeance. The common term for Patriot women during the aftermath, according to John Allan, was "Damn'd Rebel Bitches and Whores, Excuse the rough Expression, and [they are] often kicked when met in the street. My unhappy Wife has often been accosted in this manner," added Allan whose wife, Mary, was one of those stranded in Cumberland after the siege."[32]

---

30 When Admiral Shuldham sailed away from Halifax with the North American fleet and army in June, he left behind with Arbuthnot secret written instructions regarding various matters including the New York destination. These papers, intended for the reinforcements soon to arrive from England were consigned to Arbuthnot's pocket where he promptly forgot about them and when Lord Howe's fleet arrived in July and Admiral Hotham's in August, he was unable to tell these gentlemen even where Shuldham had gone, leaving them to guess their intended destination. See "The War in America 1776. Original manuscript Journal by Admiral Sir George Collier," NMM JOD/9. This incredible incident is corroborated in a "Journal of occurrences from January 1776 to August 1787. Military Events etc. at Halifax, Nova Scotia kept by Lieut. Ferguson," PANS, RG 1, Vol. 365, 28 1/2.

31 Arbuthnot to Sandwich, 11 October 1777, Barnes and J.H. Owen, eds., *The Private Papers of John, Earl of Sandwich*, Vol. 1, 306. Arbuthnot's health worsened but did not prevent Lord Sandwich from promoting him to Admiral of the North American fleet. "I have been seized with very odd fits," complained Arbuthnot in his new position, "I faint, remain senseless and speechless sometimes four hours and sometimes longer, and when I recover am ignorant of the past." Incredibly, he was soon after leading a squadron of eight warships of the line into action against a similar French force off Chesapeake Bay. See Captain Donald MacIntyre, *Admiral Rodney* (London, 1962), 156.

32 Allan to Mass. Council, 24 June 1776, in Kidder, *Military Operations*, 196. When John Allan fled to Massachusetts before the siege, he abandoned Mary and the five Allan

Of course, families were not free to join Patriot husbands and fathers in Massachusetts with which Nova Scotia was at war, but early efforts to exchange them for Loyalist prisoners in New England looked promising. Joseph Goreham, with a view to alleviating the local situation, considered an application to permit the families to leave the province in the summer of 1777. A cartel ship filled with exchange prisoners was sent from Boston and actually docked at Windsor to receive the families. But Halifax intervened at the last minute to squelch the deal. Policy had hardened in the wake of John Allan's occupation of the St. John Valley and authorities refused permission for the women and children to leave the colony. The cartel ship was ordered to depart Windsor at once and the families to be removed to Halifax.[33] The implication of removing so many women and children from Cumberland to the capital was enormous. Nevertheless, some, if not all, were brought as far as Windsor before the absurdity of the order dawned on Halifax. As it was, at least five families of leading Patriots were taken on to the capital and held under house arrest through 1778.[34]

Not until the spring of 1779, when Nova Scotia felt much more secure militarily, and with the prospects of a general amnesty imminent, did the hardline policy soften towards the refugee families of Cumberland Patriots. An arrangement to exchange them for Loyalist prisoners in New

---

children to their fate. On the day of the Camphill Rout, the Nova Scotia troops advanced along the Baie Verte Road and burned the Allan home, barns and all the family belongings. Mary barely had time to flee with her five children into the woods where they were forced to spend the night. On that same night, a cold, wet, late November night, "severe with wind and rain," while Mary and the children huddled together, hungry and suffering from exposure, husband John was enjoying the warm reception and fine entertainment of Gray's tavern in Dedham, Massachusetts.

33 Executive Council Minutes, 16 September and 6 November 1777, PANS, RG 1, Vol. 212, and Bulkeley to Barron, 17 October 1777, PANS, RG 1, Vol. 136. Also, see petitions and letter of Robert Foster and other Patriots to Mass. Council, including a list of refugee families, and Mass. resolve, 22 September 1777, MA, Vol. 183, 171-76.

34 Bulkeley to Barron, 20 December 1777 and 25 February 1778, PANS, RG 1, Vol. 136. The five ladies were Mary Allan, Martha Throop, Mahitable Earle, Anne Burke and Mrs. Fales. John Allan is not to be believed when he complained publicly that his wife, Mary, was kept in gaol and severely treated while in Halifax. A Patriot agent explained to Allan that the women were provided with houses and given soldier rations. Mary Allan lived in the home of her sister-in-law, Elizabeth Pyke (whose husband, John George Pyke, commanded the militia that drove John Allan from the St. John River) while her children stayed with various other in-laws and the older ones attended school. Possibly, this young thirty-year-old mother of five young children enjoyed no quieter interlude in her married life than this period in Halifax. See John Fulton to John Allan, 1 April 1778, MA, Vol. 218, 55-6. Meanwhile, husband John Allan (as he confided to his journal) was throwing parties for the Malecite ladies of Aukpaque on the St. John River, dancing far into the night, delighting in the details of the fine jewellery these native ladies wore, and drinking wine, as he said, in their wigwams.

England was struck and those families still wishing to leave the province were permitted to board a cartel ship.[35]

* * * * *

15 December 1776: over two weeks after the siege was lifted and ten days after the five principal prisoners were put aboard 'Vulture'
It might reasonably be expected the prisoners would be in Halifax by now, but no, they were still in Cumberland Basin, shackled in a cold, damp ship's hold, crowded in with twenty-four other prisoners from Massachusetts, transferred from the captured American warship *Independence*. Captain Feattus had intended to sail away immediately but Joseph Goreham insisted that he stay longer at Cumberland. Anchorage was shifted daily as boat crews went ashore in search of Patriot stragglers. Temperatures dropped steadily as the weather fluctuated between squalls and gales, sleet and snow.

Crowded below decks are Commissary Avery, the "much terrified" Thomas Faulkner, the extra-billing Dr. Clarke, the future attorney-general of the province, Richard Uniacke, looking anything but prosecutorial in irons, and the badly wounded Planter Danks whose fever mounts as *Vulture* tosses about in the choppy waters of the basin. Today, their second Sunday on the *Vulture*, the prisoners are shifted across the harbour to the transport ship *Nancy* which is likewise crowded with Massachusetts prisoners.[36]

* * * * *

The legacy of the siege was the plethora of court proceedings that seriously derailed the legal system. The month of republican rule in Cumberland County, administered by the Committee-of-Safety, verged on anarchy.[37] It was the political equivalent of New Dispensationalism with William How's plundering party and Dr. Clarke's collection agency acting, as it were, "under the pretence of honouring free grace."[38] When Eddy's

---

35 Executive Council Minutes, 24 April 1779, PANS, RG 1, Vol. 212, and Bulkeley to Goreham, 26 April 1779 and 30 May 1779, PANS, RG 1, Vol. 136.

36 Journal of H.M.S. *Vulture*, NMM L/V/126. The brig *Independence* (Captain Simeon Sampson) was captured by H.M.S. *Hope* (Captain James Dawson) 25 November off the south coast of Nova Scotia while *Hope* with *Nancy* in convoy was en route to relieve Fort Cumberland.

37 "Anarchy" was the term used by John Allan to explain the Committee-of-Safety's rule in Cumberland. Allan to Mass. Council, 19 February 1777, PANS, RG 1, Vol. 365, 23.

38 Anti-nomianism, or radical anti-formalism, surfaced during the aftermath and extended well beyond it. Of the more than twenty accounts of anti-nomianism in Nova Scotia and

forces were driven out of the country a day of reckoning was predictable. Joseph Goreham's initial effort to deal leniently with Patriots who remained in Cumberland after the siege was soon eclipsed by a mood of vengeance. The loyal populace, encouraged by over-zealous authorities, indulged in a paroxysm of retribution that became the chief characteristic of the aftermath.

Less than a week after the Camphill Rout, even before the prisoners were put aboard *Vulture*, depositions were being collected for legal proceedings against them. These would lead to the so-called treason trials, more appropriately called the treason indictments since, while only two Patriots were ever tried, more than fifty were indicted for rebellious practices related to the siege.[39]

A dragnet, spread over Cumberland in the spring of 1777, caught many men who had been in arms. Their wives and children (amounting to hundreds of people) were thrown on the fort for charity. They were homeless, having come through a hard Nova Scotia winter (cold enough were such winters, it was said, to congeal the rum in an S.P.G. missionary's

New Brunswick between the 1780s and 1820s, it is of more than passing interest that the first account ("and the foulest," added William Black who witnessed the event in 1782) was in the Sackville area, also the centre of Nova Scotia rebellion. Moreover, the most common location of these accounts was the greater Cumberland region. The Sackville-Amherst axis was particularly subject to religious extravagance and in the 1790s entered into a phase of New Dispensationalism, the most virulent outburst of anti-nomianism. New Dispensationalism in Cumberland climaxed in the worst account of practical anti-nomianism, the Babcock tragedy of 1805, when Amos Babcock of nearby Shediac "ordered himself to be worshipped and thereafter divided his sister or cut her [in] twain." Not only was the venue of this sobering event in the greater Cumberland region, but one of the participants in the all-night religious exercises leading up to the ritual murder had been a soldier in Jonathan Eddy's Patriot army while a member of the jury also had been a member of the Committee-of-Safety. Not only did the Cumberland troubles continue into the nineteenth century, they spanned the political/social/religious gamut of this unique Planter community as political agitation, leading to open rebellion and military siege, was followed by an unruly and turbulent aftermath which itself was superceded by the religious anarchy of New Dispensationalism. New Dispensationalism and the Babcock tragedy are described in D.G. Bell, ed., *The Newlight Baptist Journals of James Manning and James Innis* (Saint John, 1984).

39 The two convicted of treason were Thomas Faulkner and Parker Clarke whose sentences were respited and eventually (after both had escaped gaol, although Faulkner was re-captured) their cases were overtaken by general proclamations of amnesty as were those of the many who in the meantime had been indicted for crimes related to the siege.

The indictments multiplied early in 1777, after the other two surviving principal prisoners, James Avery and Richard Uniacke, agreed to give King's evidence. By April, "more than 200 names" had been returned to the attorney-general out of which the dozens of indictments of Patriots from Cobequid to Passamaquoddy followed. Complaints had been collected in Cumberland by Joseph Goreham and local justices-of-the-peace, but even from the few surviving documents, it can be concluded that Avery and Uniacke also were of considerable assistance to the authorities. By the end of January Avery had

house)[40] and many were without food. One of those arrested was Planter Alpheus Morse who by April was languishing in Halifax gaol with ten of his comrades from Cumberland! His wife, Theodora, and their little ones showed up at the fort: "She had not one Mouthfull of Vitals to give her Children and she tould her child to take that Tray and ask me for a little flour!"[41] It was lucky for Theodora that out of all those soldiers she had picked Sergeant James Innis who would later become a minister of the gospel. "Glory be to his great name," he cried after helping her, "for that a man Sows of the Seam Shall he Reape!"[42]

Old inhabitant Loyalists like Christopher Harper, who suffered loss in the siege, demanded recompense through civil litigation. Such proceedings flourished after 1778 when the Rev. John Eagleson returned from captivity in New England to a glebe destroyed by the Patriots.[43] Those who had helped Jonathan Eddy (some through fear and compulsion), and who thought themselves protected by Joseph Goreham's promise of amnesty,

---

already given evidence against seven of his Cobequid comrades and the April trial of one of them, Charles Dixson, had to be postponed when Avery, the star witness, escaped gaol. At the same time, Uniacke had also given evidence against at least Faulkner and Clarke.

40 Joseph Bennett to the Society for the Propagation of the Gospel(S.P.G.), 21 February 1767, Reel 73, 106, 274.

41 Morse genealogy in W.C. Milner, *The Basin of Minas and its Early Settlers*, reprinted from the Wolfville Acadian, n.d., 121-2.

42 "The Journal of James Innis," Bell, *Newlight Baptist Journals of James Manning and James Innis*, 244-5. Sergeant Innis appears in the Royal Fencible Muster Roll, PAC, RG 8, Vol. 1893. Also appearing in the muster roll is a Private "James Maning," although there is no evidence that he was the Newlight Baptist minister who being born 1763-65, would have been no more than fourteen in 1777. However, he would not have been too young to be in the Fencibles, a regiment that commonly recruited boys. Thomas Dixson's son, who was "the Eldest volunteer in the Regiment" in 1778, was only "about 17 years of Age," and already had been in the regiment a year, maybe longer. Also in 1778, the soldier son of Captain George Burns, "a Sprightly fine Lad" of 15, was already a one year veteran of the Force. See Joseph Goreham to Robert MacKenzie, 3 January 1778, BHQ.

43 "He has returned to his place of abode to view with an aching heart the spot which once contained...the comforts of life, now without a bed for its owner. But what he laments is the entire loss of his library." S.P.G. Journals, letter of John Eagleson, 4 July 1778, Vol. 21, Reel 4, 330-2.

Eagleson's return from captivity was a milestone in his tempestuous, twenty-year Cumberland ministry, dividing it into two distinct phases of similar length: a vigorous and productive first phase (1766-1778) and a disastrous and tragic second phrase (1778-1790). His ministry began in 1766 as a Presbyterian missionary. After a year Eagleson left the Dissenting Church to join the Anglicans and went to London for ordination. When he returned to Cumberland in 1770, he found the local religious geography much altered. Baptists had divided into two separate and competing churches and a Dissenting Congregationalist Society had been established under the ministry of the Rev. Caleb Gannett of Boston. Contending vigorously in his new missionfield, Eagleson built up the Established Church and just as vigorously he contended in the courts for the township

found themselves besieged with lawsuits.[44] Several decisions, favorable to Loyalists were obtained and property was seized. Those Patriots whose properties were not seized were "under the Terror of the same prosecutions and the continual dread of being reduced to Wretched Indigence."[45]

Not surprisingly, "Wretched Indigence" was a condition to be avoided if possible, so after about 1780 it became difficult to levy judgments against Patriot farms. Lawsuits were commenced, on purpose it was said, between Patriots to protect their farms and effects from being used for making good the damages suffered by Loyalists. These suits were looked upon as collusive; they evoked strong emotions, being the cause, for example, of Christopher Harper "falling into a passion."[46] What followed was utter confusion. Justices-of-the-peace, now all Loyalists, exceeded their authority; judges issued confusing, even conflicting, instructions; sheriffs were faced with issuing several writs on the same land. Out-of-court settlements

ministerial grant which Gannett had already settled with the blessing of the Congregational society.

In a direct and emotional manner, the complex Cumberland glebe dispute challenged the residue of New England style local government in the Planter community, in this instance, the right of a committee of proprietors to allocate land. The dispute, which Eagleson won, broke Gannett's ministry and sent him back to New England. The Dissenting Church in Cumberland was decimated, but the dispute also provided a convenient reference point for later promoters of rebellion. The premature departure of Gannett, who at any rate was no advocate of the Patriot cause, and the collapse of his congregation meant that the Dissenting Church played no part in the Cumberland rebellion. The local revolutionary movement had its political leaders, the greatest concentration of republican zealots in the province, but it had no religious underpinning. Considering the importance of a strong Dissenting Church in the New England revolutionary movement, this was a fundamental flaw.

The desolate scene of his ruined home that was presented to Eagleson on his return from captivity was a foreboding omen of the tragic second phase of his ministry. Although he rebuilt, laboured on for a time in his mission, married and had a family, he developed a drinking problem and increasingly neglected his duties until in 1790 he was removed from his post by Bishop Inglis. Discouraged by property losses, broken by the ordeal of captivity, embittered by protracted legal battles, estranged from his family, and mentally deranged (his wife's brother-in-law, Charles Morris junior, referred to him at this time as "that unnatural monster"), the Rev. John Eagleson truly was a victim of the siege aftermath.

44 The onslaught of lawsuits prompted several of these people to petition Joseph Goreham to intervene on their behalf and stop the proceedings. Halifax was unequivocal in its reply to Goreham's subsequent enquiry: "The petitioners may be entitled by your Declaration and by several Proclamations to their Liberty and the re-possession of their property and to Pardon for the offenses they committed against the Crown, but not to an Exemption for the Injuries which they may have done to private people....The course of Law cannot be stopped," advised the provincial secretary, "and the injured have a right to seek remedy." Bulkeley to Goreham, 8 June 1779, PANS, RG 1, Vol. 136.

45 "Report of the Judges of the Supreme Court, relating to the Inhabitants of Cumberland," 8 September 1782, PANS, RG 1, Vol. 221, 61.

46 Deposition of William Black in Watson vs. Bent, PANS, RG 1, Vol. 36, 82.

were also pursued as more houses were burned in the night, and various Patriots were said to be "guilty of divers misdemeanors and atrocious behaviour."[47]

Certain delinquents of the county, according to the Rev. John Eagleson, "bid defiance to all law and last fall [1780] wrote several anonymous and seditious letters to the sheriff and other executive officers, threatening to burn their property, and maltreat their persons, should they presume to execute any writ of the courts against them."[48] Now John Eagleson was a baroque personality, much addicted to extravagant language (among other things), but I have found one of the letters to which he must have been referring, written in the fall of 1780 to deputy provost marshall, Thomas Watson, and deliciously seditious.

Sir,

I suppose you are not ignorant of the proceedings of some people of late days in which your hand is deeply engaged. You know that a number of Families have been ruined by the Diabolical proceedings of a perjured Wretch, you know who I mean....I warn you to desist from Executing any Instrument...against any persons...who have been under Arms against the Fort.

Your punishment, you may depend, will not delay as hitherto, for tho' Vengeance may nod, yet her Sleep is mostly very short.... Should you be obstinate and persist...I solemnly declare...that you will neither have House nor Barn many days after....Weigh these matters Seriously...for... there is Evil determined against you.

I am with Respect, according to your future demeanor, Sir, R. Revenge, Scrutiny River, 20 August 1780.[49]

It is not clear if Watson's home was put to the torch as threatened by Mr. Revenge, but court orders continued to be served through 1781. Abuses of the law and further instances of perjury followed. By the next year, matters had so deteriorated that a judicial enquiry was called for and was commenced by Supreme Court judges, Isaac Deschamps and James Brenton.

Christopher Harper was accused of having abused his office of justice-of-the-peace. He was guilty, found the judges, of violent and oppressive measures and they recommended his removal. They also recommended that a three-person committee be set up in Cumberland to account for the losses and apportion them among those "in any way

47 Executive Council Minutes, 16 April 1777, PANS, RG 1, Vol. 212.

48 Journals of the S.P.G., letter of Eagleson, 7 May 1781, Vol. 22, Reel 5, 257-60.

49 "Incendiary and anonymous letter," included in Bulkeley to Thomas Watson, 25 September 1780, PANS, RG 1, Vol. 170, 307-8. See also Executive Council Minutes, 22 September 1780, PANS, RG 1, Vol. 212.

concerned in supporting or aiding the Rebels during the Invasion at Fort Cumberland."[50] Although claiming to have support from both sides, this plan was not acted upon immediately and individual prosecutions continued, along with the burnings and threats of burnings.

At the same time (September 1780), court orders emanating not only from the Inferior Court at Cumberland but also from that of Horton and the Supreme Court of Halifax, concerning several cases relating to the siege, were judged to have been improperly levied to the probable injury of the many parties involved. At the urging of the General Assembly, the Supreme Court ordered the sheriff to cease further executions of the orders, further confounding the judicial process.[51]

The influx of American Loyalists the following year added a new confusion to the siege aftermath. Relations between new Loyalists and old inhabitants were strained, resulting in many disputes across the province, but in Cumberland County this pattern was more complex. Some disputes, supposed simply to have been between new Loyalists and old inhabitants, were more properly disputes between old inhabitants of varying degrees of Loyalty. And here I must lean on the Rev. William Ellis: "I apprehend," said he, "that there are degrees in this virtue of loyalty."[52]

An example is the dispute in July 1783 involving old inhabitant Moses Delesdernier and one Captain Kipp, a newly-arrived Loyalist who in a violent outrage, ejected Delesdernier from his own home.[53] It may at first seem strange that local justices-of-the-peace turned their backs on the incident and ignored Delesdernier's complaints. But it is not at all strange when one considers that the Delesdernier family had been labelled with the lowest degree of Loyalty as the result of its ambiguous role in the siege, while the justices-of-the-peace — in this instance, James Law, Christopher Harper and Charles Dixson — by virtue of their losses wore the badge of highest Loyalty. The lawsuits with neighbours of lesser loyalty, the abuses of power, the acrimony between the various factions of old inhabitants created just the atmosphere that would have tempted the likes of Captain Kipp to believe he could with impunity assault Moses Delesdernier.

A month later, the provincial secretary censured the three justices-of-the-peace for their mal-conduct in the Delesdernier affair,[54] but for one of

---

50 Report of the Judges, 8 September 1782, PANS, RG 1, Vol. 221, 61.

51 See Harper vs. Ayer *et al*, PANS, 39 'C', Box 25, 1782; also, Assembly Address to Executive Council, PANS, RG 1, Vol. 286, 147.

52 Prayer, Discourses and Sermons of the Rev. William Ellis, Dalhousie University Archives.

53 Diary (17-23 July 1783) and deposition (17 July 1783) of Moses Frederick Delesdernier, PANS, RG 1, Vol. 223, 7, 8.

54 Bulkeley to Law, Harper and Dixson, 2 August 1783, PANS, RG 1, Vol. 136.

them, Christopher Harper, the string had already run out. The Supreme Court Judges' Report had just been presented to Executive Council with its recommendation to remove Harper. With the Delesdernier incident fresh in their minds, the councillors acted immediately on the recommendation,[55] although it should be noted, that Christopher Harper later became a justice-of-the-peace in New Brunswick.

Undismayed by the setback and impatient with delays in court proceedings, Christopher Harper sailed to London in 1784 to plead his case before the special Board of Commissioners set up "to enquire into the Losses and Services of American Loyalists." I took "a decided and active part against the Rebels," claimed Harper, "and took up arms in consequence of which my House and property were destroyed by the Rebels." The commissioners, who had been appointed by King George for the sole purpose of judging who was a Loyalist, were sympathetic.

"It appears decidedly to us to have been a Loss sustained in Consequence of Loyalty" — "We therefore think ourselves justified in recommending a small allowance to Mr. Harper."[56] It mattered not that Harper was an old inhabitant of Nova Scotia, that his loyal service had been performed in Nova Scotia, or that his property loss had been sustained in Nova Scotia. And it was a good thing that Harper applied for certification when he did. The United Empire Loyalist Association of Canada has since proven that King George made a poor choice of a Board, that his Commissioners were incompetent in their job of certifying Loyalists (at least those who were old inhabitants of Nova Scotia) and that henceforth the job might be better carried out in Toronto (then known as York).

Neither the Loyalist diversion, the report of the Supreme Court Judges, the removal of Christopher Harper from public office, nor the passage of seven years, could diminish the fury of the aftermath. The General Assembly in 1784 recognized "the discontent and uneasiness which has long subsisted in the County of Cumberland," placed much of the blame on the justices-of-the-peace, and recommended more removals.[57] The Supreme Court judges were sent back for further investigation, but in the meantime, efforts were revived to find a more comprehensive solution.

Towards the end of the year, the three-person committee was finally set up to find a formula for the relief of old inhabitant Loyalists.[58] Some results were forthcoming over the next two years. Liability was appor-

---

55 Executive Council Minutes, 22 August 1783, PANS, RG 1, Vol. 212.

56 Claim of Christopher Harper, PAC, A.O. 12, Vol. 100 and A.O. 13, Bundle 92. See also E.A. Clarke, "Christopher Harper: Loyalist," *The Loyalist Gazette*, XXIV, 2(December 1986), 16.

57 Executive Council Minutes, PANS, RG 1, Vol. 212, 12 January 1784.

58 Executive Council Minutes, PANS, RG 1, Vol. 212, 8 December 1784. Committee members were Jotham Gay, Thomas Scurr and George Foster, all of Cumberland.

tioned and assets of absconded Patriots were assigned. But more significantly, these attempts at restitution and apportionment of blame rekindled the bitterness, triggered a new round of civil litigation, and caused the spectre of arson to rise again over Cumberland.

In January 1778, Christopher Harper, Loyalist, had just settled in a house awarded him in New Brunswick under the programme of restitution, and which had previously belonged to Elijah Ayer, member of the Committee-of-Safety. One cold evening, "either by accident or Intention, the latter is strongly suspected...the House was burned to the Foundation Stone."[59] It had been twelve years since the attack on Fort Cumberland and twelve years since the Harper's first home had been burned by the Patriots!

Not only had the civil litigation, not to mention the arson, spread to neighbouring New Brunswick, but the aftermath in Nova Scotia had by now infected the highest levels of the judicial system. The judges affair, which resulted in the impeachment of acting chief justice Isaac Deschamps and justice James Brenton, reviewed a number of court cases allegedly mis-handled by the judges. Two of these cases were related to the attack on Fort Cumberland. These cases were the successors to earlier cases about which, ironically, the judges had admitted in their report of 1782 that Patriots had been "harassed" by the courts. Their attempts to correct matters in the later two cases only compounded the problem and provided grist to their accusers. The judges affair was not simply a matter of untrained practitioners lapsing predictably into incompetence; rather it was a part of a larger context, and the judges were, at least in part, victims of the siege aftermath.[60]

* * * * *

17 December 1776: eighteen days after the end of the siege
Nancy transport ship docks at Windsor. Old judge Isaac Deschamps saw

---

59 Stephen Millidge to Ward Chipman, 23 January 1788, New Brunswick Museum, Hazen Collection, F 1, Pkt. 6.

60 The two cases were Thomas Watson vs. John Bent and Thomas Watson vs. Joseph Cozins. Watson was the deputy provost marshall who received the engaging letter from "R. Revenge." John Bent was a member of the Committee-of-Safety and brother-in-law of another member, Simeon Chester. His own brother, Jesse Bent, was a Patriot soldier and for "some months" after the siege Judith Clarke lived with John Bent while her Patriot husband, Parker Clarke, was on trial in Halifax. Joseph Cozins' house was burned by the Nova Scotia troops. For accusations against the judges and their defense see *The Reply of Mssrs. Sterns and Taylor, to the Answers Given by the Judges of His Majesty's Supreme Court of the Province of Nova Scotia*, Colonial Correspondence, 217/61/203b-232a, and a later report, *Collections of the Publications relating to the Impeachment of the Judges of His Majesty's Supreme Court of the Province of Nova Scotia*, copy in Acadia University Archives.

her anchor out in Minas Basin. After surviving ten terrible days on the *Vulture* only to be transferred to *Nancy*, the five principal prisoners have suffered the ordeal of a two-day winter voyage around to Windsor and are taken ashore. By this time Benoni Danks is in very bad shape, and according to an observer, was carried off the ship "half dead."[61] From his unattended wound "a mortification ensued of which he died."[62] Today — Tuesday — a day "squally with snow,"[63] a line of four shackled prisoners might be seen trudging towards Halifax — Avery, Clarke, Faulkner and Uniacke — facing gaol, trials for treason, very uncertain futures. But Planter Danks' trials are over. He has been left behind at Windsor where, it is said, he "had little better than the Burial of a Dog."[64]

* * * * *

The will of the province to defend itself was tested by a month-long siege driven as much by local issues as by external factors; most certainly, the long aftermath was nurtured strictly on local issues. The latent loyalty of Nova Scotians (some would say neutrality) was transformed to active loyalty by the successful defence of Fort Cumberland. Only one expression of that transformation was a dramatically improved militia by 1777,[65] a timely circumstance given the collapse of discipline in the provincial officer corps and deep divisions in the Nova Scotia command. The convoluted legal proceedings, which defied disentanglement for so long, reflected a volatility of opinion longstanding in Cumberland and paralleled that community's remarkable innovation in social, religious and political thinking. It is in this context of diversity and innovation that the Planter community of Cumberland became Nova Scotia's most unruly county during the American Revolution and supported the single instance of indigenous rebellion.[66]

---

61 A.G. Doughty, ed., *Captain John Knox: An Historical Journal of the Campaigns in North America for the Years 1757, 1758, 1759, and 1760*, Vol. 1, The Champlain Society (Toronto, 1914), 196-7.

62 Massey to Germain, 4 January 1777, PANS, RG 1, Vol. 365, 3.

63 Journal of H.M.S. *Vulture*, NMM L/V/126.

64 Doughty, *Knox Journal*, 196-7.

65 By 1782, even Cumberlanders who had been in arms against the fort, but who had "returned to their allegiance," were admitted to the county militia and armed. Bulkeley to Barron, 20 June 1782, PANS, RG 1, Vol. 136.

66 If Cumberland County was the region of rebellion in Nova Scotia, Sackville was its centre. It was to Sackville that Eddy went to recruit the Planters after his invasion and it was to Sackville that he retreated with the remnants of his guerrilla band after the Camphill Rout. Of the seven members of the General Assembly who also became soldiers in Eddy's army, three were from Sackville; more importantly, when several members lost their seats in July 1776 for rebellious activities after which constituencies re-elected loyal

In conclusion, some loose ends should be tied up.

You will be pleased to learn that Marriott Arbuthnot succeeded in finding a gift to send home to his mentor, Lord Sandwich, for Christmas 1777. From the exotic wilds of Nova Scotia he retrieved it, a live owl, "finest bird I ever saw," exulted the absent-minded Lieutenant-Governor![67]

In the event you have been holding your breath about what happened to Alpheus Morse whom we left languishing in Halifax gaol, charged with rebellious practices, wife Theodora thrown on the generosity of troops at Fort Cumberland, I can assure you that he and his colleagues were released and were never tried because of the general amnesty granted. Alpheus reformed himself with a swiftness matched only by Richard Uniacke, becoming justice-of-the-peace, and respected member of the community, appearing more loyal than the Loyalists. To illustrate this last point, it may be noted that a piece of china belonging to Alpheus Morse has survived and is included in the Weldon collection at Kings College: "Alpheus Morse, Loyalist,"[68] scribbled the unsuspecting Mrs. Weldon in her notebook. Alpheus' cracked sugar bowl may be seen at any time, sitting quietly in the display case among the crockery of the Botsfords, the Saunders and other notable Loyalists. Examine it closely! See its aura spreading slowly outwards, gradually infecting the good Loyalist teacups surrounding it! But I digress.

Finally, there is Planter Benoni Danks. A loose end? Was he not buried at Windsor and given the appropriate epitaph by one who knew him: "he liv'd under a general Dislike and died without [one] to regret his Death?"[69] Yes, but as it turned out General Eyre Massey was an old war buddy of Colonel Danks; they were together at the siege of Havana, Cuba, in 1761. So when Massey heard of Danks' death, he sent his surgeon to Windsor to investigate and dug him up, as he said, out of the grave.[70] This was the final indignity for poor old Danks, unable even to rest in peace, and so far as I know, he is the only Planter who was — re-planted!

---

members in by-elections, Sackville was unique in defiantly returning a Patriot, Robert Foster, a member of the Committee-of-Safety. In the aftermath of the siege, when the Sackville seat was again declared vacant, Richard Uniacke was elected by which time (1783), constituency reformation apparently matched that of its new member.

67 Arbuthnot to Sandwich, 11 October 1777, in Barnes and Owen, *The Private Papers of John, Earl of Sandwich*, Vol. I, 306.

68 While Mrs Weldon did not regard her collection as exclusively Loyalist, she apparently assumed the particular Morse piece to be Loyalist, and recorded in her notebook that Alpheus Morse was a Loyalist. See the Weldon Catalogue prepared by Marie Elwood and the original Weldon Notebook, both in Kings College Library.

69 Doughty, *Knox Journal*, 196-7.

70 Massey to Germain, 4 January 1777, PANS, RG I, Vol. 365, 3.

Recent Developments in the Historiography of Colonial New England

JACK GREENE
Mellon Professor of Humanities
John Hopkins University

The historiography of colonial New England, like that of colonial British America in general, has undergone a profound reorientation over the past two decades. The classic theme of the nature, implementation, and subsequent metamorphoses of Puritanism in Massachusetts Bay and Connecticut has continued to receive major attention from historians. Indeed, no other subject in the vast and variegated history of colonial British America has yet attracted more scholarly attention. Increasingly, however, religious history has had to share the stage with social history. How this development has changed our conceptions of colonial New England is the subject of this paper. For convenience, the subject has been broken down into three rough periods, the first stretching from the founding to 1660, the second from 1660 to about 1720, and the third from 1720 to about 1770. To the rather considerable extent that Nova Scotia was a socio-economic and cultural extension of New England during the third quarter of the eighteenth century, this analysis may help to illuminate important aspects of the immediate background of its early development.

Much of the work done on the first generation of English settlement in New England before 1660 speaks most directly to the question of the typicality of the New England experience in the process of establishing English colonies in the America. Early American historians have widely, if usually only implicitly, assumed that the New England experience can serve as model for the English American colonial experience in this regard. But recent research on New England and other areas of settlement have revealed the inapplicability of this assumption. With regard to almost every area of life, the New England experience, at least insofar as it was manifest in the histories of the two major colonies of Massachusetts Bay and Connecticut, deviated sharply from that of every other region of English colonial settlement — in Ireland, in North America, and in the Atlantic and Caribbean island colonies.

Demographically, for instance, the experience of New England was quite peculiar. Although a few hundred people had migrated to Plymouth and other small coastal settlements in the 1620s, New England, in contrast to most other areas, was initially peopled largely by a short, sudden, and carefully organized burst of immigration. Between 20,000 and 25,000 Englishmen poured into the colony and adjacent areas in just twelve short years between 1630 and 1642. As many as 70 per cent of these immigrants, moreover, came not, as was the case elsewhere, as unmarried, young, and unfree servants but as members of established families, independent farmers and artisans with some accumulated resources. Virtually from the beginning, therefore, the age structure and sex ratio in New England resembled those of established societies all over western Europe far more closely than was the case with any other new societies established by the English in America during the early modern era. Unlike the Chesapeake colonies which could never have sustained themselves without a constant flow of new arrivals from England, New England was the destination of relatively few new immigrants following the outbreak of the English Civil War in 1642. Nor does it appear that immigration from England to New England ever again became substantial during the colonial period.[1]

Nevertheless, New England population grew rapidly from the substantial base of initial immigrants. Largely free of serious epidemics, New England experienced much lower rates of mortality than either England or any of England's other colonies. Studies in the early 1970s by Philip Greven and Kenneth Lockridge suggested that infant mortality was low — of an average of 8.3 children born to a group of sample families in Andover, 7.2 survived to age 21 — and those who lived to 21 could anticipate long and healthy lives: 71.8 for men and 70.8 for women among the first generation of settlers, and 64.2 for men and 61.6 for women among the second. Combined with relatively young ages for first marriages for women (19.0 for the first generation and 22.3 for the second) and a correspondingly high number of births per marriage, this low rate of mortality sent population surging upwards. Within a generation, population had doubled. By 1660, New England as a whole contained between 55,000 and 60,000 inhabitants of European descent, more than twice the number in the Chesapeake colonies, which had been in existence for a full generation longer. In vivid contrast to the Chesapeake, moreover, most of these people were native born, New England becoming the first region of Anglo-American settlement to develop a predominantly creole population.[2]

---

1 Terry L. Anderson and Robert Paul Thomas, "White Population, Labor Force and Extensive Growth of the New England Economy in the Seventeenth Century," *Journal of Economic History*, XXXIII (1973), 639-41; T.H. Breen and Stephen Foster, "Moving to the New World: The Character of Early Massachusetts Immigration," *William and Mary Quarterly* [hereafter *WMQ*], XXX (1973), 189-222; Virginia Dejohn Anderson, "Migrants and Motives: Religion and the Settlement of New England, 1630-1640," *New England Quarterly*, LXVIII (1985), 340, 346-67; N.C.P. Tyack, "The Humbler Puritans of East Anglia and the New England Movement: Evidence from the Court Records of the 1630s," *New England Historical and Genealogical Register* [hereafter *N.E. Hist. & Gen. Reg.*] CXXXVIII (1984), 79-106.

2 Anderson and Thomas, "White Population", 639-42; Philip J. Greven, Jr., *Four Generations: Population, Land, and Family in Colonial Andover, Massachusetts* (Ithaca,

We have long known of course that the New England colonies had a much more deeply religious orientation than other English colonies; perhaps the most important finding of new scholarship is the considerable religious diversity among the early settlers. As William Stoever and Philip Gura have both stressed, participants in the great migration were far from being all of one mind with regard to theology, church government and other religious questions, and the congregational church polity preferred by most of them was conducive to the accommodation of a wide range of religious opinion. At the same time, this scholarship has continued to emphasize, with Perry Miller, the extent to which leaders of these colonies were moved by the vision of establishing a redemptive community of God's chosen people in the New World. They saw themselves as a special group joined in a binding covenant with God and sent by Him into the wilderness to establish the true Christian commonwealth that would thenceforth serve as a model for the rest of the Christian world. In the societies they created, the church and the clergy thus necessarily had unusually powerful roles, the relationship between clerical and secular leaders was both intimate and mutually supportive, and full civil rights, including the franchise, were in many communities limited to church members.[3]

1970), 21-40; Kenneth Lockridge, "The Population of Dedham, Massachusetts, 1636-1736," *Economic History Review*, 2d ser., XIX (1966), 318-44.

3 David D. Hall, "Understanding the Puritans," in Herbert Bass, ed., *The State of American History* (Chicago, 1970), 330-49; Michael McGiffert, "American Puritan Studies in the 1960's," *WMQ*, 3d ser. XXVII (1970), 36-67; and Anderson, "Migrants and Motives," 367-83. David D. Hall, "A World of Wonders: The Mentality of the Supernatural in Seventeenth-Century New England," in Hall and David Grayson Allen, eds., *Seventeenth-Century New England* (Boston, 1984), 239-74; William K.B. Stoever, *"A Faire and Easie Way to Heaven": Covenant Theology and Antinomianism in Early Massachusetts* (Middletown, Conn., 1978) and Philip F. Gura, *A Glimpse of Scion's Glory: Puritan Radicalism in Seventeenth-Century New England 1620-1660* (Middleton, Conn., 1984) stress the religious diversity among puritan settlers. See also Stephen Foster, "New England and the Challenge of Hersey, 1630 to 1660: The Puritan Crisis in Transatlantic Perspective," *WMQ*, XXXVIII (1981), 624-60; "The Godly in Transit: English Popular Protestantism and the Creation of a Puritan Establishment in America," in Hall and Allen, eds., *Seventeenth-Century New England*, 185-238; and "English Puritanism and the Progress of New England Institutions, 1630-1660," in David D. Hall, John M. Murrin, and Thad W. Tate, eds., *Saints & Revolutionaries: Essays on Early American History* (New York, 1984), 3-37; J.F. Maclear, "New England and the Fifth Monarchy: The Quest for the Millennium in Early American Puritanism," *WMQ*, 3d ser., XXXII (1975), 223-60; and Sacvan Bercovitch, *The American Jeremiad* (Madison, 1978), 3-61. Relations between church and state, ministry and magistracy in early New England are treated in David D. Hall, *The Faithful Shepherd: A History of the New England Ministry in the Seventeenth Century* (Chapel Hill, 1972); George Selement, *Keepers of the Vineyard: The Puritan Ministery and Collective Culture in Colonial New England* (Lanham, Md., 1984); and B. Katherine Brown, "The Controversy over the Franchise in Puritan Massachusetts, 1654 to 1674," *WMQ*, 3d ser., XXXIII (1976), p. 228. Other works on the complex issue of the franchise are T.H. Breen, "Who Governs: The Town

If most of these conclusions are generally compatible with the work of an earlier generation of historians, recent historians, especially Stephen Foster, have perhaps put more emphasis upon the social dimensions of the initial Puritan vision. Puritan colonists came to America not only because they were unable to realize their religious aspirations in Old England. They were also driven by a profound disquiet over the state of contemporary English society. In towns and rural areas alike, new social and economic forces seemed to be producing a disturbing and ever-widening gap between inherited prescriptions of social order and actual circumstances of life, while the Crown and its agents were more and more intruding into many aspects of local affairs — civil as well as religious. To an important degree, the great migration to New England was an "essentially defensive, conservative, even reactionary" response to these developments. Hence, its members were determined not only to achieve perfection in the church but also to create a society that, in contrast to the seemingly increasingly anarchic and beleaguered world they were leaving behind, would conform as closely as possible to traditional English conceptions of the ideal, well-ordered commonwealth.[4]

This determination accounted for the peculiar social organization of New England. In their grand design of building the ideal traditional ordered English world in the untamed American wilderness, the Puritan settlers tried to organize their new societies around a series of tightly constructed and relatively independent communities in which the inhabitants formally covenanted with each other to comprise unified social organisms. As David Grayson Allen and others have shown, there was considerable diversity in the form of these communities. Joseph Wood's recent research shows that only a few, like Andover, seem to have been classical nucleated villages in which the inhabitants lived around the meeting house and went forth each working morning to fields arranged

Franchise in Seventeenth-Century Massachusetts," *WMQ*, 3d ser., XXVII (1970), 460-74; Stephen Foster, "The Massachusetts Franchise in the Seventeenth Century," *ibid.*, XXIV (1967), 613-23; Arlin I. Ginsberg, "The Franchise in Seventeenth Century Massachusetts: Ipswich," *ibid.*, XXXIV (1977), 444-52; Robert E. Wall, "The Franchise in Seventeenth Century Massachusetts: Dedham and Cambridge," *ibid.*, 453-58, and "The Decline of the Massachusetts Franchise, 1647-1666," *Journal of American History*, LIX (1972), 303-10; and James A. Thorpe, "Colonial Suffrage in Massachusetts," *Essex Institute Historical Collections*, CVI (1970), 169-81.

4   T.H. Breen, "Transfer of Culture: Chance and Design in Shaping Massachusetts Bay, 1630-1660," *N.E. Hist. & Gen. Reg.*, CXXXII (1978), 3-17, and "Persistent Localism: English Social Change and the Shaping of New England Institutions," *WMQ*, 3d ser., XXXII (1975), 3-28; Andrew Delbanco, "The Puritan Errand Re-Viewed," *Journal of American Studies*, XVIII (1984), 342-60; Allen Cardin, "The Communal Ideal in Puritan New England, 1630-1700," *Fides et Histoiria*, XVII (1984), 25-38. The clearest and most perceptive discussion of puritan social goals in New England is Stephen Foster, *Their Solitary Way: The Puritan Social Ethic in the First Century of Settlement in New England* (New Haven, 1971).

according to the traditional open field system that still prevailed in some areas of England. Most communities like Sudbury, quickly broke up into dispersed rural settlements with the inhabitants living on individual farms. How any group of settlers organized themselves upon the land seems to have been determined to some significant degree by their own prior experience in England.[5] But everywhere, at least in the three "orthodox colonies" of Massachusetts Bay, Connecticut, and New Haven, the end of their settlements was the same. Although they were by no means disinterested in achieving sustenance and prosperity, they put enormous emphasis upon establishing well-ordered communities knit together by Christian love and composed only of like-minded people with a common religious ideology and a strong sense of communal responsibility. These tightly-constructed and communally-oriented villages were only one means of achieving order and harmony. Strong extended and highly patriarchal families, Greven's work on Andover suggests, also helped to preserve social control and guarantee a relatively high degree of peace throughout the first generation of settlement. So also did the quick establishment of an educational system that was both designed to promote religious and social cohesion and extraordinarily elaborate for a new colonial society.[6]

The Puritan colonial experiments in Massachusetts, Connecticut and New Haven were also unusual in the extent to which they were presided over by a numerous and highly visible group of established secular and clerical leaders. To a far greater extent than any other English colonists in America, the Puritans brought their leaders with them to New England. Political and religious authority and social status survived the Atlantic crossing and the process of reimplantation in the New World without serious disruption. Unlike the hothouse elites that sprang up among the winners in the race for profits in other early colonies, New England leaders at both the local and the provincial levels during the first decades were to a significant degree people who had brought all the traditional attributes of

5   Diversity among New England towns is admirably treated in David Grayson Allen, *In English Ways: The Movement of Societies and the Transferal of English Local Law and Custom to Massachusetts Bay in the Seventeenth Century* (Chapel Hill, 1981). See also Joseph S. Wood, "Village and Community in Early Colonial New England," *Journal of Historical Geography*, VIII (1982), 333-46; Sumner Chilton Powell, *Puritan Village: The Formation of a New England Town* (Middletown, Conn., 1964); Kenneth A. Lockridge, *A New England Town, The First Hundred Years: Dedham, Massachusetts, 1636-1736* (New York, 1970); Greven, *Four Generations*; John J. Waters, "Hingham, Massachusetts, 1631-1661: An East Anglian Oligarchy in the New World," *Journal of Social History*, I (1968), 351-70, and "The Traditional World of the New England Peasants: A View from Seventeenth-Century Barnstable," *N.E. Hist. and Gen. Reg.*, CXXX (1976), 3-21.

6   Foster, *Solitary Way*, 11-64, 99-152; Timothy H. Breen and Stephen Foster, "The Puritans' Greatest Achievement: A Study of Social Cohesion in Seventeenth-Century Massachusetts," *Journal of American History*, LX (1973), 5-22.

socio-political authority with them to the New World.

As Stephen Foster has pointed out, the political societies of the New England colonies were based not upon the "customary engines of social coercion of early modern Europe," not upon "a hereditary monarch, a titled nobility, a church hierarchy, and a landlord class," but upon "a radical voluntarism" derived out of the logic of the social covenants that served as the foundations for colonies and communities alike. Because all freemen, initially defined as church members who had assumed full civil rights, were theoretically parties to those covenants and because the percentage of freemen usually ran as high as 60 to 70 per cent of the adult male population in most towns, the potential for political participation was — by English standards — extraordinarily high. Most of the time, however, they willingly deferred to the magistrates, who assumed the dominant role in establishing political institutions, allocating land, making laws, dispensing justice, and reinforcing the position of the clergy and churches.[7]

A comparatively slow pace of economic development was also an important element in enabling the Puritans to succeed in their socio-religious goals in New England. Many immigrants, including even some of the clergy, certainly had economic as well as religious and social reasons for coming to New England and, although the economy of the region seems to have been reasonably prosperous and even to have enjoyed a considerable rate of economic growth over much of the seventeenth century, neither the soil nor the climate were conducive to the development of staple agriculture. Very early, fish, timber, furs and shipping brought some people more than ordinary returns, and in seaboard towns the proportion of the population engaged in fishing was substantial. But most settlers had no alternative source of income than cereal agriculture and animal husbandry, which yielded only modest profits. Hence, except in the emergent port centers of Boston and Salem, the wealth structure of the New England colonies, at least down to 1660, remained far more equitable than in other colonies. Nor, except perhaps in the fishing industry, did New Englanders have either the need, the incentive or the resources to recruit a large force of unfree laborers. The labor of family members and perhaps a few servants who resided in the nuclear family households was all that was either necessary or profitable for most economic enterprises in the region.[8]

---

7   Greven, *Four Generations*, 41-99; James Axtell, *The School Upon a Hill: Education and Society in Colonial New England* (New Haven, 1974), 166-244; Robert Emmet Wall, Jr., *Massachusetts Bay: The Crucial Decade, 1640-1650* (New Haven, 1972), esp. 21-40; Foster, *Solitary Way*, 67-98, 155-72; T.H. Breen, *The Character of the Good Ruler: A Study of Puritan Political Ideas in New England, 1630-1730* (New York, 1970), 1-86.

8   Terry Lee Anderson, *The Economic Growth of Seventeenth Century New England: A*

Along with the strong cohesive force exerted by the church, family, school and visible and authoritative leadership structures that characterized the New England villages, the absence of exceptional economic opportunities inhibited the urge to scatter that was so powerfully manifest among the settlers in the Chesapeake. The early colonists moved about a lot during the first two decades of settlement, and people who either had tenuous ties to the community or lived in the economically most active areas tended to be highly mobile. But those with close economic, family, political and religious involvement seem to have developed a deep emotional attachment to their communities, an attachment that in turn seems to have fostered a degree of persistence and spatial immobility that may have been lower even than in most established village populations in England.[9] These same conditions also helped to produce several decades of "relative social peace." Notwithstanding the well-known theological controversies between Bay Colony magistrates and religious rebels such as Roger Williams and Anne Hutchinson, the challenges presented by the arrival of the Quakers in the mid-1650s, and the presence of considerable controversy in the churches and contention in the courts, major social discord was rare and conflict restrained throughout most of the seventeenth century. As Timothy Breen and Stephen Foster have aptly observed in regard to Massachusetts, this characteristic of New England society

---

Measurement of Regional Income (New York, 1975); Anderson and Thomas, "White Population," 661; Bernard Bailyn, *The New England Merchants in the Seventeenth Century* (Cambridge, 1955), 1-111; Daniel Vickers, "Work and Life on the Fishing Periphery of Essex County, Massachusetts, 1630-1675," in Hall and Allen, ed., *Seventeenth-Century New England*, 83-117; William Cronon, *Changes in the Land: Indians, Colonists, and the Ecology of New England* (New York, 1983), 127-56; Charles F. Carroll, *The Timber Economy of Puritan New England* (Providence, 1973); Darrett B. Rutman, *Winthrop's Boston: A Portrait of a Puritan Town, 1630-1649* (Chapel Hill, 1965), 164-201; William I. Davisson and Dennis J. Dugan, "Commerce in Seventeenth-Century Essex County, Massachusetts," *Essex Institute Historical Collections*, CVII (1971), 113-18; Davisson, "Essex County Wealth Trends: Wealth and Economic Growth in 17th Century Massachusetts," *ibid.*, CIII (1967), 291-342; Donald W. Koch, "Income Distribution and Political Structure in Seventeenth-Century Salem, Massachusetts," *ibid.*, CV (1969), 50-71; Terry L. Anderson, "Wealth Estimates for the New England Background of the First Generation of the New England Clergy," *Historical Magazine of the Protestant Episcopal Church*, XVIV (1975), 473-88; Breen, "Transfer of Culture," 3-17; Stephen Innes, "Land Tenancy and Social Order in Springfield, Massachusetts, 1652 to 1702," *WMQ*, 3d ser., XXXV (1978), 33-56.

9 Breen and Foster, "Moving to the New World," 209-13; David Grayson Allen, "Both Englands," in Hall and Allen, eds., *Seventeenth-Century New England*, 77-80; Linda Auwers Bissell, "From One Generation to Another: Mobility in Seventeenth-Century Windsor, Connecticut," *WMQ*, 3d ser.,XXXI (1974), 79-110; W.R. Prest, "Stability and Change in Old and New England: Clayworth and Dedham," *Journal of Interdisciplinary History*, VI (1976), 359-74; John M. Murrin, "Review Essay," *History and Theory*, XI (1972), p. 231.

placed it in contrast not only to the Chesapeake but to virtually the whole of the contemporary civilized world and constituted perhaps the single "most startling accomplishment" of the orthodox Puritan colonies of Massachusetts, Connecticut and New Haven.[10]

The picture that emerges of the Puritan colonies during the first generation of settlement then is of a self-conscious and successful effort to recreate a traditional society in the New World. With low mortality, rapid population growth, a benign disease environment, and a far more fully and rapidly articulated old-world style society, the intensely religious colonies of Massachusetts, Connecticut and New Haven, moved by powerful millennial and communal impulses, exhibited rapid community and family development. With strong patriarchal families, elaborate kinship networks, and visible and authoritative leaders, localities quickly developed vigorous social institutions, including many schools, and deeply rooted populations. Mostly involved in cereal agriculture and with no generalized source of great economic profit, the Puritan colonies displayed a relatively egalitarian wealth structure and an extraordinarily low incidence of social discord and contention.

Increasingly after 1660 and in a few places even before, this carefully constructed and coherent social and cultural order began to change. To many contemporary Puritan settlers, in fact, these changes seemed to portend failure, and they interpreted them as evidence of social and moral declension, a pervasive and steady turning away from the original goals of the founders by their descendants. The explanatory structure they articulated to make this development comprehensible to themselves still provides the basic framework for the declension model that modern historians have conventionally employed to characterize the process of historical change in colonial New England. Positing a largely linear process of change from *gemeinschaft* to *gesellschraft*, from community to individualism, from traditional to modern, this model has come under sharp attack in recent years.

Among the most important of the conditions pushing the orthodox New England colonies into social patterns that suggested declension to contemporary inhabitants was their rapid demographic growth. Immigration continued low, in all probability amounting to no more 10,000 to 12,000 for the last half of the seventeenth century and never averaging more than a few hundred per year before the American Revolution. Yet

---

10 See David Thomas Konig, *Law and Society in Puritan Massachusetts, 1629-1692* (Chapel Hill, 1979); Paul R. Lucas, *Valley of Discord: Church and Society along the Connecticut River, 1636-1725* (Hanover, 1976), 1-57; Carla Pestana, "The City upon a Hill Under Seige: The Puritan Perception of the Quaker Threat to Massachusetts Bay, 1656-1661," *New England Quarterly*, LVI (1983), 323-53; Breen and Foster, "Puritans' Greatest Achievement", esp. 5-6.

population grew rapidly in response to highly favorable conditions of life. With an abundant food supply, a relatively equal sex ratio, a low population density, and a low incidence of epidemic diseases, New England settlers, especially in the rural areas that were the homes of all but five to ten per cent of them, enjoyed low mortality and exhibited a high percentage of married women and a vigorous birthrate that, for most of the seventeenth century, produced completed families averaging in excess of seven children. Notwithstanding considerably less favorable conditions in seaport towns such as Boston and Salem, the number of people of European descent in Massachusetts, Connecticut, Plymouth, Rhode Island and New Hampshire soared from just over 30,000 in 1660 to over 90,000 by 1700.

During the eighteenth century, the rate of population growth slowed significantly in New England. For the quarter of a century beginning in 1690, one case study has shown, the age of marriage rose, while the number of children per completed family fell by nearly 40 per cent to 4.6 before rising again to around seven in subsequent decades. At the same time, mortality increased, partly as a result of periodic epidemics that were, in turn, to an important degree, probably a function of higher population density and closer ties with the outside world. Declining life expectancy seems by mid-century to have brought mortality figures closer to both those long characteristic of Britain and those recently achieved in the Chesapeake. Despite these developments, natural population growth remained vigorous, averaging between 26 and 28 per cent per decade through the first seven decades of the eighteenth century. Total numbers, surpassing 115,000 by 1710 and 215,000 by 1730, had reached nearly 450,000 by 1760.[11]

---

11 Henry A. Gemery, "Emigration from the British Isles to the New World, 1630-1700: Inferences from Colonial Populations," *Research in Economic History*, V (1980), 193, 195; James H. Cassedy, *Demography in Early America* (Cambridge, Mass., 1969), 40, 175; Clifford K. Shipton, "Immigration to New England, 1680-1740," *Journal of Political Economy*, XLIV (1936), 225-39; Philip J. Greven, Jr., "The Average Size of Families and Households in the Province of Massachusetts in 1764 and the United States in 1790: An Overview," in Peter Laslett and Richard Wall, eds., *Household and Family in Past Time* (Cambridge, 1972), 545-60, and *Four Generations*, 185-97; Anderson and Thomas, "White Population," 639, 647-8; Daniel Scott Smith, "The Demographic History of Colonial New England," *Journal of Economic History*, XXXII (1972), 165-83; Maris A. Vinovskis, "Mortality Rates and Trends in Massachusetts before 1860," *ibid.*, 195-202; Lockridge, "Population of Dedham," 324-6, 332-9; Susan L. Norton, "Population Growth in Colonial America: A Study of Ipswich, Massachusetts," *Population Studies*, XXV (1971), 433-52; Douglas R. McManis, *Colonial New England: A Historical Geography* (New York, 1975), 66-72; Robert Higgs and H. Louis Stettler, III, "Colonial New England Demography: A Sampling Approach," *WMQ*, 3d ser., XXVII (1970), 282-94; Stettler, "The New England Throat Distemper and Family Size," in H.E. Klarman, ed., *Empirical Studies in Health Economics* (Baltimore, 1970), 17-27; Rose Lockwood, "Birth, Illness, and Death in 18th Century New England," *Journal of Social*

The effects of this burgeoning population were profound. Intensifying an already powerful demand for land, it supplied the energy for the rapid expansion of settlement. Although King Philip's War in the mid-1670s and the first set of intercolonial wars between 1689 and 1713 operated as a temporary brake on expansion, by the early eighteenth century New Englanders had occupied a broad band extending 50 to 70 miles inland and from New York to southern Maine. Driving out the Indians or shunting them off to marginal areas, settlers were rapidly replacing the forests with a European-style landscape of farm buildings, fields, orchards, pastures and fences. By 1700, the four New England colonies of Massachusetts, Connecticut, Rhode Island and New Hampshire contained about 120 towns. This expansive process accelerated after 1713. Over 100 new towns were founded during the next 50 years, and the area of settlement both became far more compact in areas of older occupation and spread over all of southern New England and north and east into New Hampshire, Maine and Nova Scotia.[12]

Already by the 1660s within the oldest settlements, population growth had led to the dispersal of people out from the early clusters of settlement. In the few places that had been initially settled as nucleated villages, this process sometimes resulted in the physical and social disintegration of the original village centers. Instead of settling together in close proximity, people tended more and more to establish their families on individual farmsteads, while some people moved so far away from the original meeting houses that they found it desirable to form new semi-independent and sometimes antagonistic settlements. Contrary to the designs of the original Puritan leaders, they thereby helped to destroy the prescriptive unity of the towns and perhaps to weaken the bonds of neighborhood and the authority of political and social institutions. Despite this dispersion, second and even third generation settlers may have been more rooted and less mobile than those of the first generation. When they moved, they did

History, XII (1978), 111-28.

12 McManis, *Colonial New England*, 46-66; Douglas E. Leach, *Flintlock and Tomahawk: New England in King Philip's War* (New York, 1966); Charles E. Clark, *The Eastern Frontier: The Settlement of Northern New England 1610-1763* (New York, 1970); Bruce C. Daniels, *The Connecticut Town: Growth and Development, 1635-1790* (Middletown, Conn., 1979), 8-44, and *Dissent and Conformity on Narragansett Bay: The Colonial Rhode Island Town* (Middletown, Conn., 1983), 23-47; Eric H. Christiansen, "The Emergence of Medical Communities in Massachusetts, 1700-1794: The Demographic Factors," *Bulletin of the History of Medicine*, LIV (1980), p. 66; Jere R. Daniell, *Colonial New Hampshire: A History* (Millwood, N.Y., 1981), 133-64; David E. Van Deventer, *The Emergence of Provincial New Hampshire, 1623-1741* (Baltimore, 1976), 62-82; Andrew Hill Clark, *Acadia: The Geography of Early Nova Scotia to 1760* (Madison, 1968), 330-69. Cronon, *Changes in the Land: Indians, Colonists, and the Ecology of New England*, 54-81, 127-70, suggestively discusses the changing social landscape of New England during the colonial era.

not usually leave the political jurisdictions in which they had been born and even then often stayed within 15 to 30 miles of the places of their birth. With growing population, however, land in the older agricultural communities was by the third and fourth generations usually all taken up, and young people coming into their maturity found that they either had to go into non-farming occupations or move to new towns to the north, west or east. Outmigration from old communities and the founding of new towns proliferated after 1715, as New Englanders became increasingly more mobile. Although a significant proportion of long-distance migrants consisted of middle-aged people who moved with their children only after the death of their parents to what they hoped would be better lands, many others were young, unmarried adults who, by the 1730s and 1740s, displayed little resistance to moving away from their homes and families. This willingness to migrate by young adults, in turn, seems to have weakened parental authority and pushed children more and more towards the imperatives of autonomy and independence that had been so powerfully manifest everywhere else in the English American world throughout the seventeenth century.[13]

Even before population growth had helped to accelerate the general processes of dispersion and mobility, the intense spiritual energies and utopian impulses that had been so central to the founding generation of Puritan colonists began to attenuate. Relative to population growth, church membership seems to have declined from about 1650 until 1675. Although absolute numbers remained fairly steady and there was even a revival of spiritual interest and church membership during the last quarter of the seventeenth century among the third generation, the clergy throughout these years decried the decay in Godliness and the growth in worldliness among the laity. In response to this situation, many ministers

---

13 Wood, "Village and Community in Early New England," 333-46; Greven, *Four Generations*, 41-71, 175-221; Lockridge, *New England Town*, 79-118, and "Land, Population, and the Evolution of New England Society 1630-1790," *Past & Present*, No. 39 (1968), 62-80; Bissell, "From One Generation to Another," 79-110; Thomas R. Cole, "Family, Settlement, and Migration in Southeastern Massachusetts, 1650-1805; The Case for Regional Analysis," *N.E. Hist. & Gen. Reg.*, CXXXII (1978), 171-81; John W. Adams and Alice Bee Kasakoff, "Migration and the Family in Colonial New England: The View from Genealogies," *Journal of Family History*, IX (1984), 24-44, and "Migration at Marriage in Colonial New England: A Comparison of Rates Derived from Genealogies with Rates from Vital Records," in Bennett Dyke and Warren T. Morrill, eds., *Genealogical Demography* (New York, 1980), 115-38; Darrett B. Rutman, "People in Process: The New Hampshire Towns of the Eighteenth Century," *Journal of Urban History*, I (1975), 268-92; Douglas Lamar Jones, *Village and Seaport: Migration and Society in Eighteenth-Century Massachusetts* (Hanover, N.H., 1981); John J. Waters, "Patrimony, Succession, and Social Stability: Guildford, Connecticut in the Eighteenth Century," *Perspectives in American History*, X (1976), 131-60; Charles S. Grant, "Land Speculation and the Settlement of Kent, 1738-1760," *New England Quarterly*, XXVII (1955), 51-71.

sought to broaden the base of church members beyond merely the visible saints. Though it was never adopted by all congregations, the half-way covenant of 1662 permitted baptized but unconverted children of church members to be "half-way" members and to have their children baptized. By the 1680s and 1690s, a few clergymen like Solomon Stoddard of Northampton advocated even further liberalization of membership requirements. Discovering "that a pure membership was a flimsy foundation on which to construct an ecclesiastical system, and that the restraining influence of the church on the entire community was more important than the preservation of a [pure] congregation of saints," the churches opted to sacrifice purity to community.[14]

Problems involving church membership were compounded by dissension within and among churches. By the 1660s, the search for a single orthodox and uniform way in theology and church government to which the emigrants had been committed had already been revealed to be a chimera. While the autonomy of individual congregations rendered any attempt to achieve regional religious uniformity impossible, disagreements — among the Godly — over baptism and other sacraments, predestination and the proper form of church government revealed deep fissures and contradictions within the Puritan movement. Whether or not, as Paul Lucas has argued, these disputes "made dissension a way of life" in New England during the last half of the seventeenth century, they certainly unleashed "a continuing struggle for control of church government." By seriously eroding "the community's power to suppress dissent," they also eventually forced colony and community leaders into a grudging acceptance of it.[15] Nor did ministers of the second and third generations enjoy the stature and immediate influence of those of the first. Although it is

---

14 Robert G. Pope, *The Half-Way Covenant: Church Membership in Puritan New England* (Princeton, 1969), 128-36, 210-11, 233-5, 276; Gerald F. Moran, "Religious Renewal, Puritan Tribalism, and the Family in Seventeenth-Century Milford, Connecticut," *WMQ*, 3d ser., XXXVI (1979), 236-54; Moran and Maris A. Vinovskis, "The Puritan Family and Religion: A Critical Reappraisal," *ibid.*, XXXIX (1982), 32-42; David M. Scobey, "Revising the Errand: New England's Ways and the Puritan Sense of the Past," *ibid.*, XLI (1984), 3-31; Charles E. Hambrick-Stowe, *The Practice of Piety: Puritan Devotional Disciplines in Seventeenth-Century New England* (Chapel Hill, 1982), p. 242; Selement, *Keepers of the Vineyard*, 43-59; Perry Miller, "Declension in a Bible Commonwealth," in *Nature's Nation* (Cambridge, Mass., 1967), 25-30, and *The New England Mind: From Colony to Province* (Cambridge, Mass., 1953); Joseph J. Ellis, *The New England Mind in Transition: Samuel Johnson of Connecticut, 1696-1772* (New Haven, 1973), 11.

15 E. Brooks Holifield, *The Covenant Sealed: The Development of Puritan Sacramental Theology in Old and New England, 1570-1720* (New Haven, 1974), 169-230; Scobey, "Revising the Errand," 19, 30; Lucas, *Valley of Discord*, 205; Lilian Handlin, "Dissent in a Small Community," *New England Quarterly*, LVIV (1985), 193-220; Sydney V. James, "Ecclesiastical Authority in the Land of Roger Williams," *ibid.*, LVII (1984), 323-46; Pope, *Half-Way Covenant*, 260.

certainly an exaggeration to speak of the "collapse of clerical authority," strife among the clergy, disputes between the clergy and the laity, and what David Hall has called the "diminished charisma" of the ministers who replaced the first occupants of the pulpits of New England combined to undermine clerical authority. It may be true that "the clergy's involvement with the mental images of the laity was as intense as ever after 1660" and that "the ministry remained the most important calling in New England," but the clergy no longer exerted such a profound influence in defining life in the Puritan colonies, and many congregations even revealed a growing reluctance to support their ministers in the style to which their predecessors had been accustomed. By the early decades of the eighteenth century, it was a general lament among ministers that they "did not enjoy the prestige, influence, and social status" of their seventeenth century predecessors.[16]

All of these developments stimulated the clergy to articulate a broadly diffused sense of religious decline. Increasingly after 1660, declension became the omnipresent theme in sermons, and the jeremiad, which publicly reviewed the "shortcomings of society" and called on the people to renounce their sins and return to the primitive religious and social purity of the emigrants, became the standard form of sermon on all "the great occasions of communal life, when the body politic met in solemn conclave to consider the state of society." Few modern historians accept these contemporary laments at face value. They recognize that New England was not declining but only changing, merely undergoing a series of intellectual and institutional adaptations to reflect the changing needs of the churches and society. As, more and more through the middle decades of the century, hope fell victim to experience and the "ideal of community" dimmed before "the shortcomings of community life," the original New England way, in Stephen Foster's words, simply dissolved "into unrelated, often irreconcilable parts." In the process, as Perry Miller noted nearly a half-century ago, it became "something other than it had started out to be, in spite of the fact that many...still desired with all their hearts that it remain unchanged."[17]

If the jeremiads of the late seventeenth century cannot be read as literal indications of New England's declension, they certainly revealed a widespread discontent with contemporary religious and social behavior

---

16 Foster, "Godly in Transit," in Hall and Allen, eds., *Seventeenth-Century New England*, 237; Lucas, *Valley of Discord*, p. xiii; James W. Schmotter, "Ministerial Careers in Eighteenth-Century New England: The Social Context, 1700-1760," *Journal of Social History*, IX (1975), 249-67; Hall, *Faithful Shepherd*, 181.

17 Miller, "Declension in a Bible Commonwealth", pp. 23, 43; Sacvan Bercovitch, *The American Jeremiad* (Madison, 1978), p. 16; Foster, *Their Solitary Way*, pp. xiv-xv; Pope, *Half-Way Covenant*, pp. 261, 275-76, and "New England Versus the New England Mind: The Myth of Declension", *Journal of Social History*, III (1969-70).

that gripped the laity as well as the clergy. By the 1660s, in fact, few colonists any longer had any very vivid sense of the urgency of the original mission that had brought their parents and grandparents to New England. As the "formulations of the first two decades" lost "their near monopoly position as the fulcrum for their members' imaginative lives," New Englanders seemed — to themselves — to be irresistibly carried "away from the original dedication to holiness and the will of God." The Crown's assumption of control over New England in 1684 effectively shattered "any lingering sense among the colonists that they formed a special, divinely chosen community." By that action, the Crown at once destroyed the old government that had theoretically "bound the whole community in Covenant with God," rendered impossible any further efforts to enforce a religious orthodoxy by requiring toleration of all Protestant religions, and "left the third generation of settlers with no clear definition of the status" to which their grandparents and even parents had aspired "as the chosen children of God." Subsequently, the founders' prophetic vision of establishing God's city upon a hill became little more than "a pious memory, faithfully recorded by Cotton Mather [and other clergymen] but [largely] exotic to the religious life of the province" as a whole. During the first six decades of the eighteenth century, the idea of New England's special place in God's plan for human kind increasingly lost force and was gradually merged with the more general conception of the whole Anglo-American Protestant world as the bulwark against popery.[18]

Especially during the late seventeenth century, this declining sense of mission, this pervasive feeling of having fallen away from the faith of the fathers, may have contributed to alter still other aspects of the religious landscape of New England. By stirring "severe feelings of inadequacy and insecurity," it may have been largely responsible for driving people more and more "into the terrible wilderness of their own inner selves" and into an excessive preoccupation with the internal strife of the local communities in which they lived. Certainly, the ancient corporate religious impulse was no longer sufficiently strong to provide a vehicle through which communities could join together to contain the astonishing degree of contention and aggression that was so vividly manifest in the rise in criminal prosecutions for deviance and in the various witchcraft episodes,

---

18 Foster, Godly in Transit, in Hall and Allen, eds., *Seventeenth-Century New England*, 214; Miller, "Declension in a Bible Commonwealth," 25; Breen and Foster, "Puritans' Greatest Achievement," 20; Pope, "New England Versus the New England Mind," 105; Kai T. Erikson, *Wayward Puritans: A Study in the Sociology of Deviance* (New York, 1966), 157; Maclear, "New England and the Fifth Monarchy," 258; Bruce Tucker, "The Reinterpretation of Puritan History in Provincial New England," *New England Quarterly*, LIV (1981), 481-98, and "The Reinvention of New England, 1691-1770," *ibid.*, LIX (1986), 315-40.

especially the one that occurred at Salem in 1692-93.[19]

Although, as Perry Miller has emphasized, New England religious culture remained vital and adaptable throughout the years from 1670 to 1730, it no longer held its former pre-eminence in New England life. Despite some occasional local revivals, the spiritual life of new England seemed to the clergy throughout the first three or four decades of the eighteenth century to have become ever more "shamelessly secular." The continuing diminution of religious concern seemed to be indicated by further declines in both the proportion of the population who were full and active church members and in the authority and status of the clergy, as well as by the persistence of religious discord in many communities. For the first time, moreover, the Anglican church began to make significant inroads among the formerly almost wholly Congregational population. Already by the 1720s, some prominent ministers had defected to the Anglicans, who by 1770 had 74 congregations in New England and numbered as many as 25,000 adherents drawn from all segments of the population.[20]

Even more subversive of the old New England way was the moderate acceleration and changing character of the economy during the last half of the seventeenth century. Economic goals had never been absent from the Puritan settlements. Despite some religious scruples against excessive profiteering, the colonists had been responsive to economic opportunities from the beginning. If, throughout the seventeenth century, most of them were involved in agriculture, they successfully sought not simply to produce enough food to feed their families but a surplus to exchange for tools and other finished goods that they were unable to produce efficiently themselves and that had to be imported from England or some other major processing center. This surplus, at first consisting primarily of grains but increasingly composed of meat, dairy and orchard products, served both to

---

19 Emory Elliott, *Power and the Pulpit in Puritan New England* (Princeton, 1975), 8; Erikson, *Wayward Puritans*, 157-59, 163-81; John Demos, "Underlying Themes in the Witchcraft of Seventeenth-Century New England," *American Historical Review*, LXXV (1970), 1319-22, "John Godfrey and His Neighbors: Witchcraft and the Social Web in Colonial Massachusetts," *WMQ*, 3d ser., XXXIII (1973), 242-65, and *Entertaining Satan: Witchcraft and the Culture of Early New England* (New York, 1982). See also David D. Hall, "Witchcraft and the Limits of Interpretation," *New England Quarterly*, LVIV (1985), 253-81.

20 J. William T. Youngs, Jr., *God's Messengers: Religious Leadership in Colonial New England, 1700-1750* (Baltimore, 1976); Laura L. Becker, "Ministers vs. Laymen: The Singing Controversy in Puritan New England, 1720-1740," *New England Quarterly*, LV (1982), 77-96; Ellis, *New England Mind in Transition*, 55-122, and "Anglicans in Connecticut, 1725-1750: The Conversion of the Missionaries," *New England Quarterly*, XLIV (1971), 66-81; Bruce E. Steiner, "New England Anglicanism: A Genteel Faith?" *WMQ*, 3d ser., XXVII (1970), 122-35.

sustain a growing non- or semi-agricultural population in the coastal seaports that developed to handle the exchange but also acted as "a primer for overseas trade." Nor, in contrast to most other early British colonies, was agricultural produce the principal item of trade. Already by the late 1630s and the early 1640s, Boston, Salem and Charlestown were also developing a vigorous trade in furs, fish, and timber products, including planks, barrel staves, shingles, oars, naval stores, and masts. With the rapid dwindling of the fur supply at mid-century, the fur trade had declined to insignificance by the mid-1670s. But the fish and lumber industries expanded to meet the demands of new markets in the West Indies, the Wine Islands and the Iberian peninsula. Far and away the most important export industry, fishing, employed large numbers of people throughout the colonial period, perhaps never less than 10 per cent of the population, and by the early eighteenth century in Salem fishing exceeded the value of timber exports, "the second most valuable export," by twelve to one. Because most exports in all these areas had to be processed and packed in barrels, they all generated significant local processing industries that provided a livelihood for substantial numbers either in the localities where they were produced or in the points of export, while a growing shipbuilding industry emerged along the coast to produce the vessels that carried these products across the seas.[21]

Never a purely subsistence society, the New England colonies were thus from early in their histories, and increasingly during the seventeenth century, heavily involved in trade. By 1660, it was already clear that, to an important extent, the emerging economy of New England, as Terry Anderson has observed, would "be centered around" its "shipping sector and that many institutions" would have "to be developed or changed to meet the needs of a commercial society." The merchants who presided over this process of commercialization became leading agents of change. Aggressively seeking out new markets in North America, the West Indies, England and Europe, they first acquired and then supplied the capital and managerial expertise needed to link the "producers and consumers of [the] interior towns" of New England to "the larger world economy" and, when the resource base of the region proved insufficient to support continuous long-term economic growth, they increasingly began to supply "shipping services to major parts of the Atlantic world." By the second and third decades of the eighteenth century, they had thereby "created a well-integrated commercial economy

---

21 McManis, *Colonial New England*, 86-122; John J. McCusker and Russell R. Menard, *The Economy of British America, 1607-1789* (Chapel Hill, 1985), 91-110; Davisson and Dugan, "Commerce in Seventeenth-Century Essex County," 113-42; Allen, *In English Ways*, 228; Bruce C. Daniels, "Economic Development in Colonial and Revolutionary Connecticut: An Overview," *WMQ*, 3d ser., XXXVII (1980), 429-34; Carroll, *Timber Economy of Puritan New England*, 57-128; Van Deventer, *Provincial New Hampshire*, 93-106.

based on the carrying trade."[22]

Nor were the economic activities of this rising commercial elite limited to trade. Especially after King Philip's War in the mid-1670s, they were among the heaviest land speculators and developers, many of them acquiring several thousands of acres which they hoped eventually to sell for a profit to those segments of a burgeoning population eager to move to new lands. In the rich Connecticut River valley, the Pynchon family, as Stephen Innes has recently shown, turned Springfield into a company town by engrossing a large proportion of the land and exerting a near monopoly of the region's trade. Owning the only store and all the town's corn and saw mills, and employing a significant proportion of the adult male population as workmen in their various agricultural, processing, and trading enterprises, the Pynchons presided over a process of progressive social and economic stratification in which by 1680 at least one-half of the adult males in Springfield lived as tenants, renters and dependents in a socio-economic system that contrasted sharply with the egalitarian villages envisioned by the first settlers.[23]

As an ever enlarging circle of towns became involved in producing foodstuffs and other items for export during the last half of the seventeenth century, the hinterlands of both the larger ports and commercialized towns such as Springfield seem to have enjoyed substantial economic growth, to have become far more diversified in terms of occupational structure and to have experienced substantial economic stratification. Some experts have suggested that economic growth may have averaged as high as six per cent per annum in some of the more dynamic areas. At least in Connecticut, Jackson Turner Main has recently shown, opportunity to acquire wealth actually seems to have declined for several decades after 1660 before it began to rise again in 1690. But for New England as a whole during the second half of the century, this commercially- and demographically-driven economic growth, it has been estimated, contributed between 1650 and 1710 to a substantial rise in per capita real income at an annual rate of about 1.6 per cent and to a 295 per cent increase in real aggregate economic output. Over the same period, these same areas supported a growing number of artisans and craftsmen, many of whom continued to engage in farming, and exhibited growing concentrations of wealth in the hands of its richest inhabitants. In Salem, for instance, the amount of inventoried wealth owned by the most affluent ten per cent of the population rose from

22 Anderson, *Economic Growth of Seventeenth Century New England*, 21, 23; McCusker and Menard, *Economy of British America*, 107; Bailyn, *New England Merchants*, is the classic study of the role of the merchants in the developing New England economy.

23 Theodore B. Lewis, "Land Speculation and the Dudley Council of 1686," *WMQ*, 3d ser., XXXI (1974), 255-72; Stephen Innes, *Labor in a New Land: Economy and Society in Seventeenth-Century Springfield* (Princeton, 1983) and "Land Tenancy and Social Order," 33-56.

21 per cent before 1661 to 62 per cent thereafter.[24]

A far cry from the closed, cohesive and contained villages originally envisioned by Puritan leaders, Boston, Salem and other ports and commercial towns thus became prosperous mercantile centers with relatively large, concentrated, heterogeneous populations, many new economic opportunities in non-farm occupations, significant concentrations of wealth in the hands of their leading merchants, marked social and economic distinctions, considerable contact with the outside world, and a rising spirit of enterprise that gradually spread outward to the surrounding countryside. The growing intensity of economic activity and the emerging complexity of social patterns in these more dynamic areas of New England operated to undermine the communal unity, corporate and religious orientation, and social goals of the first settlers. In these dynamic areas, the old religious-based corporatism began to give way to the atomistic pursuit of wealth and self-interest.[25] As Bernard Bailyn has written, the ethos of the mercantile groups which dominated these commercial centers "represented the spirit of a new age. Its guiding principles were not social stability, order, and the discipline of the senses, but mobility, growth, and the enjoyment of life." Among this strategic segment of the population, the desire to "succeed in trade" and to emulate the lives of their London trading associates was far "stronger than any counterforce the clergy could exert." Increasingly after 1670, successful merchants and farmers comprised a new *economically*-based elite which exerted an influence greatly disproportionate to their numbers in the public life of Massachusetts and to a lesser extent in Connecticut, New Hampshire, and Rhode Island. Certainly at the provincial and, in many areas, also at the local level wealth and property, rather than piety, became the basis for political leadership and participation. Moreover, as rival groups among the elite vigorously competed with one another within the political arena for profits, land and influence, the old consensual politics gave way to division, conflict and discord.[26]

---

24 Innes, *Labor in a New Land*, 72-122; Jackson Turner Main, *Society and Economy in Colonial Connecticut* (Princeton, 1985), 68-9; Anderson, *Economic Growth of Seventeenth Century New England*, pp. 114-9; "Economic Growth in Colonial New England: 'Statistical Renaissance'," *Journal of Economic History*, XXXIX (1979), 243-7; and "Wealth Estimates for the New England Colonies," 151-76; Davisson, "Essex County Wealth Trends," 291-342; Koch, "Income Distribution and Political Structure," 50-71; Richard P. Gildrie, *Salem, Massachusett 1626-1683: A Covenanted Community* (Charlottesville, 1975), 155-69; James M. Henretta, "Economic Development and Social Structure in Colonial Boston," *WMQ*, 3d ser., XXII (1965), 75-92.

25 See, in this connection, Paul Boyer and Stephen Nissenbaum, *Salem Possessed: The Social Origins of Witchcraft* (Cambridge, Mass., 1974), 60-109; Gildrie, *Salem, Massachusetts*, 145-69; Innes, *Labor in a New Land*, 123-50.

26 Bailyn, *New England Merchants*, 139-42; Innes, *Labor in a New Land*, 151-70; Breen,

Accompanying this contention and discord in public life was a rising volume of litigation, most of it concerning economic issues involving property and debt. Denounced by many contemporaries in the orthodox Puritan colonies of Massachusetts and Connecticut as an indication of creeping *"Rhode Islandism,"* the acrimony and divisiveness produced by these developments certainly revealed the long-term ineffectiveness of religious and social communalism as devices to preserve social harmony in communities undergoing substantial demographic and economic growth and social diversification. "The force of ideological commitment alone," Stephen Foster has noted, "could [not] maintain a system of political and social subordination for which the traditional material and institutional bases were lacking." As David T. Konig has recently emphasized, however, the founders of New England had never expected to achieve their social vision without viable legal institutions, which they carefully incorporated into the governmental structure during the 1630s. As the force of that original vision continued to attenuate in the face of continued economic growth and the "intensified resentments of compact town life," Konig shows in his analysis of patterns of litigation in Essex County, Massachusetts, individuals increasingly found it useful "to turn to the outside authority of extra town institutions like the courts" to resolve their differences. Such legal institutions, he persuasively insists, "were to [a] large degree responsible" for the fact that Essex County continued throughout the seventeenth century to be a "remarkably stable society." If, in their passage from "communalism to litigation," the residents of Essex County had become a contentious and disunited people, they were still fundamentally a "well-ordered people." So far from being an indication of social disruption, increasing litigation, Konig contends, was "an agent of orderly social change and economic growth."[27]

Existing largely on the margins of — if by no means entirely cut off from — this increasingly bustling economic and social world, much of rural

---

Character of the Good Ruler, 87-202; "Who Governs," p. 473; and "War, Taxes, and Political Brokers: The Ordeal of Massachusetts Bay, 1675-1692," in Breen, *Puritans and Adventurers: Change and Persistence in Early America* (New York, 1980), 81-105; Richard P. Gildrie, "Salem Society and Politics in the 1680s," *Essex Institute Historical Collections*, CXIV (1978), 185-206; Robert deV. Brunkow, "Officeholding in Providence, Rhode Island, 1646-1686: A Quantitative Analysis," *WMQ*, 3d ser., XXXVII (1980), 242-60. Richard R. Johnson, *Adjustment to Empire: The New England Colonies 1675-1715* (New Brunswick, N.J., 1981), provides an excellent account of the imperial context of these developments.

27 Daniels, *Dissent and Conformity on Narragansett Bay*, 22; Foster, *Solitary Way*, 7; Konig, *Law and Society in Puritan Massachusetts, 1629-1692*, xii-xiii, 89-116, 188-89. That the enforcement of law itself became less exacting during the 17th century is suggested by R.W. Roetger, "The Transformation of Sexual Morality in 'Puritan' New England: Evidence from New Haven Court Records, 1639-1698," *Canadian Review of American Studies*, XV (1984), 243-57.

New England was relatively untouched by these social and economic developments during the seventeenth and early eighteenth centuries. Many inland towns, places described by Edward M. Cook as "small, self-contained farming villages," remained comparatively isolated, economically underdeveloped, socially egalitarian and religiously homogeneous. Certainly during the seventeenth century, all but a few Connecticut towns seem to have belonged to this category: in Jackson Turner Main's words, they were "not very flourishing, predominantly agricultural and middle class, with few large property holders." In these "peaceable kingdoms," traditional institutions of community, family and church continued to display a vitality that was considerably less evident either in the bustling market centers and seaport towns of New England or in the other Anglo-American colonies, and the corporate impulse probably remained strong.[28]

With the further acceleration of the economy as a result of rapid internal population growth and the increasing integration of the New England economy into the larger Atlantic economy during the early decades of the eighteenth century, and especially after 1720, more and more of New England was drawn out of a relatively isolated existence and pushed in the direction of greater social differentiation, geographical and economic mobility, and individualism. The vast majority of New Englanders continued to live on farms, but recent scholarship has effectively challenged the ancient myth that these farms were self-sufficient and independent units of production on which yeomen families, concerned with little more than their own security, produced all that was required to meet their needs without the help of additional labor. As Bettye Hobbs Pruitt has recently shown in the case of the agricultural society of mid-eighteenth century Massachusetts, "interdependence rather than self-sufficiency" is the concept that best describes that society. Although local communities were often self-sufficient, at least in foodstuffs and other primary services, most individual units were not. Only those few farms with relatively large amounts of both labor and land under cultivation did not have to involve themselves in local networks of exchange in which they traded products, labor and skills simply to meet the subsistence requirements of their families. In this situation, Pruitt emphasizes, "production for home consumption and production for sale or exchange were complementary...objectives."[29]

---

28 Edward M. Cook, Jr., *Fathers of the Towns: Leadership and Community Structure in Eighteenth-Century New England* (Baltimore, 1976), 179; Main, *Society and Economy in Colonial Connecticut*, 87-8; Michael Zuckerman, *Peaceable Kingdoms: New England Towns in the Eighteenth Century* (New York, 1970); Christopher M. Jedrey, *The World of John Cleaveland: Family and Community in Eighteenth-Century New England* (New York, 1979).

29 Carole Shammas, "How Self-Sufficient Was Early America?" *Journal of International*

If virtually all New England agricultural communities were thus "not atomistic but integrated" into a series of "local networks of exchange involving all sorts of goods and services," they were also increasingly "linked either directly or through...dealings with others" to the larger provincial and Atlantic worlds. New England's rapid demographic growth not only generated dozens of additional rural settlements but also produced significant urbanization. New England had only two major cities: Boston, which, despite a decline in its population and relative importance as a commercial entrepot after 1740, continued to be the region's primary urban center, and Newport, which developed impressively after 1710. As the second largest city in New England, Newport had more than two-thirds as many people as Boston by 1775. After 1715 and increasingly during the boom years of the 1740s and 1750s, however, a large number of towns, many of which had been little more than hamlets through most of the seventeenth century, developed into important secondary commercial centers. These included seaports — Portsmouth in New Hampshire; Salem, Marblehead and Gloucester in Massachusetts; Providence in Rhode Island; and New Haven, New London and Norwich in Connecticut — and inland commercial and administrative centers — Worcester and Springfield in Massachusetts and Hartford and Middletown in Connecticut. Perhaps as many as another two to three dozen places were distinctly urbanized by 1770.[30]

To a significant extent, this urbanization was a function not merely of growing population but also of a steady expansion of external trade. Although New England's exports were relatively unimpressive compared to those of all of the other regions of colonial British America, they were nonetheless substantial and underwent "an enormous expansion" during the century from 1660 to 1760. Not including the coastal trade, which may have accounted for as much as 40 per cent of the value of its total trade, New England annually exported products worth almost £440,000 by 1770.

History, XIII (1982), 247-72; Bettye Hobbs Pruitt, "Self-sufficiency and the Agricultural Economy of Eighteenth-Century Massachusetts," *WMQ,* 3d ser., XLI (1984), 333-64; Winifred B. Rothenberg, "The Market and Massachusetts Farmers, 1750-1855," *Journal of Economic History,* XLI (1981), 283-314.

30 Pruitt, "Self-Sufficiency and the Agricultural Economy," p. 349; Gary M. Nash, *The Urban Crucible: Social Change, Political Consciousness, and the Origins of the American Revolution* (Cambridge, 1979), 111-8, 172-6, 180-97, 244-7; G.B. Warden, "Inequality and Instability in Eighteenth-Century Boston: A Reappraisal," *Journal of International History,* VI (1976), 585-620; Lynne Withey, *Urban Growth in Colonial Rhode Island: Newport and Providence in the Eighteenth Century* (Albany, 1984); Daniels, *Connecticut Town,* 140-80, and "Emerging Urbanism and Increasing Social Stratification in the Era of the American Revolution," in John Ferling, ed., *The American Revolution: The Home Front* (Carrolton, Ga., 1976), 15-30; Cook, *Fathers of the Towns,* 172-9; Jones, *Village and Seaport;* Christine Leigh Heyrman, *Commerce and Culture: The Maritime Communities of Colonial Massachusetts 1690-1750* (New York, 1984).

Fish accounted for around 35 per cent of the whole; livestock, beef, and pork for 20 per cent; wood products for 15 per cent whale products for 14 per cent; potash and grain products each for five per cent; rum for four per cent; and a variety of other items for the remaining two per cent. Far and away the largest proportion of this trade — 63 per cent — went to the West Indies. Britain and Ireland with 19 per cent and Southern Europe with 15 per cent were, respectively, second and third, while Africa with only three per cent to four percent was a distant fourth.[31]

Though the growing populations that inhabited New England's increasing number of urban places produced some of their own food and necessities, they all required significant supplements of both food and timber products and, together with the additional demand for those products for export to the West Indies and elsewhere, these requirements inevitably acted to produce a lively commercial exchange between town and country, which were more and more linked together by a proliferating network of roads, bridges and ferries. This exchange in turn helped to raise levels of agricultural production and to stimulate timber industries in the countryside, first in the immediate vicinities of the towns and then in areas farther away. By the mid-eighteenth century, as Pruitt has remarked, few New England "communities existed wholly beyond the reach of [these] market forces," while most were inextricably tied into, and deeply affected by, not just the local regional markets with which they had long been associated but also "the larger provincial and Atlantic economies of which they were a part."[32]

Compared with their counterparts elsewhere in colonial British America, eighteenth century New England farmers were, perhaps, "not highly commercialized." Yet the commercialization of agriculture and the expansion of the fishing, timber and whaling industries in response to growing internal and external demand had a significant impact upon the social landscape of the region. That impact can be seen clearly in the development of regional specialization. Of course, fishing and whaling had always been confined to the coast, the former concentrated in the area north of Boston and the latter in the coastal and island area along the southeastern coast of Massachusetts. During the seventeenth century, most other products had been diffused throughout the region. As time went on, however, the timber industry came to center in New Hampshire and Maine, grain production tended to concentrate in the breadbasket areas of the Connecticut River valley and in Middlesex and eastern

---

31 McCusker and Menard, *Economy of British America*, 107-10; James G. Lydon, "Fish for Gold: The Massachusetts Fish Trade with Iberia, 1700-1773," *New England Quarterly*, LIV (1981), 539-82; David C. Klingaman, "The Coastwise Trade of Colonial Massachusetts," *Essex Institute Historical Collections*, CVIII (1972), 217-33.

32 Pruitt, "Self-Sufficiency and the Agricultural Economy", 362, 364; Rothenberg, "Market and Massachusetts Farmers."

Worcester County in Massachusetts, grazing and livestock production in hilly and rocky regions and along the southern coast of New England, and dairying in areas near to urban centers. The Narragansett region of Rhode Island was particularly noted for its large estates, which concentrated upon stock, especially horses, and dairy farming.[33]

Although a few farmers in eighteenth century New England — the Narragansett planters and the owners of the larger farms in the rich Connecticut River valley and along the southern coast of New England — seem to have "crossed a line where commercial production brought sufficient returns to warrant a preponderant investment" in large landed estates and market crops, the principal beneficiary of the growing commercialization of New England seems to have been the expanding service sector of society. To an important extent the result of the population's strenuous and purposeful efforts to wrest economic returns from disadvantageous circumstances as well as an indication of the growing economic and social diversity of the region, this development led to an increasingly complex occupational structure that provided new opportunities for young men who did not inherit land or did not want to stay on the farm. Most numerous of these service occupations were the artisans and craftsmen ranging, in status and wealth, from shoemakers, tailors, and weavers at the bottom through coopers, carpenters and joiners in the middle up to millers and tanners at the top. The last two often operated comparatively large-scale enterprises. Representatives of all these occupations could be found in rural as well as urban areas. But some more specialized artisans — ship-wrights, distillers, silversmiths, printers, and rope and iron manufacturers — rarely resided outside the larger towns. Out of this proliferating body of skilled artisans derived the well-known New England penchant for mechanical ingenuity that during the closing decades of the eighteenth century would make such a powerful contribution to the beginnings of industrial change in the new American republic.[34]

Two other groups, merchants and professionals, also expanded in

---

33 Pruitt, "Self-Sufficiency and the Agricultural Economy," 359-61, 364; Van Deventer, *Provincial New Hampshire*, 93-106, 159-78; Bruce C. Daniels, "Economic Development in Colonial and Revolutionary Connecticut," 429-50; Elinor F. Oakes, "A Ticklish Business: Dairying in New England and Pennsylvania, 1750-1812," *Pennsylvania History*, XLVII (1980), 195-212; Karen J. Friedmann, "Victualling Colonial Boston," *Agricultural History*, XLVII (1973), 189-205; William D. Miller, "The Narragansett Planters," *American Antiquarian Society Proceedings*, XLIII (1934), 49-115; Christian McBurney, "The South Kingstown Planters: Country Gentry in Colonial Rhode Island," *Rhode Island History*, XLV (1986), 81-93.

34 Richard L. Bushman, "Family Security in the Transition from Farm to City, 1750-1850," *Journal of Family History*, VI (1981), 240; Main, *Society and Economy in Colonial Connecticut*, 151, 241-56, 381; Daniels, "Economic Development in Colonial and Revolutionary Connecticut," 438-43.

numbers, wealth and influence in the increasingly diverse society of eighteenth century New England. The mercantile group, consisting of large overseas traders, shipowners, ship captains, shopkeepers and peddlers, was increasingly complex and prosperous. The large overseas merchants who organized and presided over the region's commerce with the outside world and, as in the case of Rhode Island slave traders, provided freight and shipping services for other areas of the Atlantic commercial world were usually the richest people in the region. Professionals — ministers, doctors and lawyers — were far fewer in number. But the last two became far more numerous during the eighteenth century, while lawyers were more and more often also among the wealthiest and most influential inhabitants. Together with some prominent officeholders, the wealthier lawyers, overseas merchants and inland traders played an entrepreneurial role in New England's economic development and profited disproportionately from it. Often among the investors in industrial enterprises such as shipbuilding, distilling and iron production, they were also frequently involved as land speculators in the development of new towns on the eastern, northern and western frontiers.[35]

The acceleration and growing complexity of the economy during the eighteenth century also helped to produce and to reinforce a more typically British social structure. The comparative economic equality that had characterized much of early New England had never obtained in Boston, where from the late seventeenth century onwards the concentration of wealth remained relatively high and relatively stable over time, with the wealthiest 30 per cent of property holders possessing around 85 per cent of the town's private wealth. By contrast, during the eighteenth century, rural

---

35 Main, *Society and Economy in Colonial Connecticut*, 262-65, 278-313, 370, and "The Distribution of Property in Colonial Connecticut," in James Kirby Martin, ed., *The Human Dimensions of Nation Making: Essays on Colonial and Revolutionary America* (Madison, 1976), 64-70; Withey, *Urban Growth in Colonial Rhode Island*, 123-32; Elaine F. Crane, *A Dependent People: Newport, Rhode Island in the Revolutionary Era* (New York, 1985), 16-46; Jay Coughtry, *The Notorious Triangle: Rhode Island and the African Slave Trade, 1700-1807* (Philadelphia, 1981); Alison Jones, "The Rhode Island Slave Trade: A Trading Advantage in Africa," *Slavery and Abolition*, III (1981), 226-44; Van Deventer, *Provincial New Hampshire*, 78-82, 174-8, 215; Christiansen, "Medical Communities in Massachusetts," 64-77; John M. Murrin, "The Legal Transformation: The Bench and Bar of Eighteenth-Century Massachusetts," in Stanley N. Katz, ed., *Colonial America: Essays in Politics and Social Development* (Boston, 1971), 415-49; David H. Flaherty, "Criminal Practice in Provincial Massachusetts," *Publications of the Colonial Society of Massachusetts*, LXII (1984), 191-242; McManus, *Colonial New England*, 132-9; Grant, "Land Speculation and the Settlement of Kent," 51-71, and *Democracy in the Connecticut Frontier Town of Kent* (New York, 1972), 55-65; Richard L. Bushman, *From Puritan to Yankee: Character and the Social Order in Connecticut, 1690-1765* (Cambridge, Mass., 1967), 73-82; Julian Gwyn, "Money Lending in New England: The Case of Admiral Sir Peter Warren and His Heirs 1739-1805," *New England Quarterly*, XLIV (1971), 117-34.

areas experienced a slow but steady growth in the concentration of property until by the 1760s and 1770s the richest 30 per cent owned between 65 per cent and 75 per cent of total wealth. In urban areas, this trend toward wealth consolidation was even more pronounced, with towns like Portsmouth, Salem, Newport, Providence, New Haven and Hartford already moving powerfully towards Boston levels by the early decades of the century. While it is undoubtedly true that, in comparison with most of the rest of the British American world, the wealthiest men in late colonial New England enjoyed only "moderate rather than large fortunes," had fewer servants and slaves, lived less genteelly, and had to share political office with men "entirely lacking in family connections and large estates," some individuals, especially in the towns, managed to accumulate impressive wealth. In New Hampshire, for instance, David E. Van Deventer has found that only two people whose estates were probated before 1740 had estates valued at more than £3,000 in New Hampshire old tenor currency, whereas 21 people who went through probate between 1741 and 1760 and 27 between 1761 and 1770 had estates exceeding that amount. Indeed, the wealthiest decedents after 1740 greatly exceeded that amount. The estate of Ebenezer Smith who died in 1764 was valued at just over £90,000, that of John Gilman in 1751 at nearly £48,000 and that of Nicholas Gilman in 1749 at just under £34,000. Three other decedents had estates valued at over £20,000, and twelve others at over £10,000.[36]

If few New Englanders enjoyed such impressive wealth, those who did aspired, as did rising elites elsewhere in colonial British America, to recreate the genteel culture of contemporary Britain. To that end, they built larger and more commodious houses and filled them with English and continental furnishings and other fashionable consumer items, made charitable bequests, filled their towns with impressive public buildings, created a host of urban voluntary associations, and otherwise sought to

36 Main, *Society and Economy in Colonial Connecticut*, 122, 132-3, 278-366, 368, 381, and "Distribution of Property in Colonial Connecticut," in Martin, ed., *Human Dimensions of Nation Making*, 77-90; Bruce C. Daniels, "Long Range Trends of Wealth Distribution in Eighteenth Century New England," *Explorations in Economic History*, XI (1973-74), 123-35; "Defining Economic Classes in Colonial New Hampshire, 1700-1770," *Historic New Hampshire*, XXVIII (1979), 53-62; "Money-Value Definitions of Economic Classes in Colonial Connecticut, 1700-1776," *Histoire Sociale*, VII (1974), 346-52; and "Defining Economic Classes in Colonial Massachusetts 1700-1776," *American Antiquarian Society Proceedings*, LXXXIII (1973), 251-9; Alice Hanson Jones, "Wealth Estimates for the New England Colonies about 1770," *Journal of Economic History*, XXXII (1972), 98-127 and *The Wealth of a Nation To Be: The American Colonies on the Eve of the Revolution* (New York, 1980), 50-194; G.B. Warden, "The Distribution of Property in Boston, 1692-1775," *Perspectives in American History*, X (1976), 81-128, and "Inequality and Instability in Eighteenth-Century Boston: A Reappraisal," 585-620; Withey, *Urban Growth in Colonial Rhode Island*, 123-32; Crane, *Dependent People*, 25-9; Van Deventer, *Provincial New Hampshire*, 173-8.

reproduce the urban amenities of British provincial cities. The elite of Newport, where the old Puritan sanctions against conspicuous consumption were less powerful, could carry this process farther than its counterparts in either Boston or smaller cities in the orthodox Puritan colonies of Massachusetts and Connecticut. Everywhere, however, elite behavior in New England was calculated to reinforce the traditional prescriptive association among wealth, social status, and political authority.[37]

To an increasing extent during the eighteenth century, New England's wealthy inhabitants, as Edward Marks Cook has shown in his study of political leadership in a large sample of towns, also monopolized public office. To be sure, patterns of officeholding in many small agricultural towns remained relatively egalitarian throughout the century. But towns with more developed economic structures all showed a powerful tendency towards oligarchy, with a handful of wealthy and prominent families, often as few as one to three, dominating both appointed and elective offices. In most towns, these family political dynasties were based, to an important degree, upon long association with the town's history. But in a few towns, those in which a coherent and continuous elite had been slow to develop — Marblehead provides one example and, perhaps, Portsmouth, New Hampshire another — a significant number of relative newcomers could be found among the eighteenth century elite. In large towns like Boston and Newport, the structure of local elites was too complex, too open, and too broadly based and economic power too often independent of political power to permit such heavy concentrations of political power in a few families. Whatever the local variations, however, most commercially-oriented towns displayed a strong correlation between wealth and officeholding. The growing number of Anglicans who held political office in communities where they were numerous testified to the diminishing importance of Congregational church membership in New England public life.[38]

---

37 See Robert J. Dinkin, "Seating in the Meeting House in Early Massachusetts", *New England Quarterly*, XLIII (1970), 450-64; Anthony G. Roeber, " 'Her Merchandize...Shall Be Holiness To The Lord': The Progress and Decline of Puritan Gentility at the Brattle Street Church, Boston, 1715-1745," *N.E. Hist. & Gen. Reg.*, CXXXI (1977), 175-91; Christine Leigh Heyrman, "The Fashion among More Superior People: Charity and Social Change in Provincial New England, 1700-1740," *American Quarterly*, XXXIV (1982), 107-24, and *Commerce and Culture*, 143-81, 330-65; Withey, *Urban Growth in Colonial Rhode Island*, 13-50; Crane, *Dependent People*, 47-62; Van Deventer, *Provincial New Hampshire*, 217-25; Main, *Society and Economy in Colonial Connecticut*, 278-366.

38 Cook, *Fathers of the Towns*; Michael Zuckerman, "The Social Context of Democracy in Massachusetts," *WMQ*, 3d ser., XXV (1968), 523-44; Van Deventer, *Provincial New Hampshire*, 218-23; Main, *Society and Economy in Colonial Connecticut*, 317-66; Bruce C. Daniels, "Family Dynasties in Connecticut's Largest Towns, 1700-1760," *Canadian*

Increasing concentrations of wealth and the solidification of an economic and familial elite were also accompanied by the spread of both slavery and poverty. Slavery was a direct function of growing wealth. From early on in the settlement of New England, there had been a few Indian and black slaves. As late as 1690, however, there were fewer than 1,000 blacks — about one per cent of the total population — in the entire region. Over the next three decades, they increased slowly if steadily to over 6,000 — or about three per cent of the total population. Though their numbers continued to increase to over 15,000 by the early 1770s and though slavery was still an expanding institution in all the New England colonies on the eve of the American Revolution, the proportion of blacks in the population remained steady at around three per cent for the rest of the colonial period. These aggregate figures mask much greater concentrations of slaves in the more commercialized areas, particularly in the port towns, where they served as domestics, artisans, watermen, dock workers and emblems of conspicuous consumption for urban elites. Although Jackson Turner Main is certainly right to point out that there were few incentives to develop a plantation-style agriculture with a large servile labor force in most parts of New England and although most rural slaves were distributed in small numbers of one or two among farm families for whom they performed agricultural or household labor, they were present in more substantial numbers on many of the commercial plantations in the Narragansett country of Rhode Island, where some estates employed as many as 20 slaves as stockmen and in the dairy industry. Indeed, as Louis Masur has recently emphasized, "slavery flourished in eighteenth century Rhode Island." Slaves comprised as high as 18 per cent of the population of Newport in 1755, and as many as 30 per cent of white households in several Rhode Island towns in 1774 "contained slaves or blacks bonded in some manner." For the colony as a whole, 14 per cent of households owned slaves. Without dispute, these figures represent "a substantial commitment to the institution." If New England as a whole was not, like colonies farther south, heavily dependent on slave labor, it was certainly a society that condoned slavery, and it contained a few areas that had concentrations of

Journal of History, VIII (1973), 99-110, "Large Town Officeholding in Eighteenth-Century Connecticut: The Growth of Oligarchy," *Journal of American Studies*, IX (1975), 1-12, and "Democracy and Oligarchy in Connecticut Towns: General Assembly Officehlding, 1701-1790," *Social Science Quarterly*, LVI (1975), 460-75; Withey, *Urban Growth in Colonial Rhode Island*, 9-111, 130-31; G.B. Warden, "Officeholding and Officials in Boston, 1692-1775," *N.E. Hist. & Gen. Reg.*, CXXXI (1977), 267-90; Robert M. Zemsky, "Power, Influence, and Status: Leadership Patterns in the Massachusetts Assembly, 1740-1755," *WMQ*, 3d ser., XXVI (1969), 502-20, and *Merchants, Farmers, and River Gods* (Boston, 1971); Heyrman, *Commerce and Culture*, 143-81, 330-65; Bruce E. Steiner, "Anglican Officeholding in Pre-Revolutionary Connecticut: The Parameters of New England Community," *WMQ*, 3d ser., XXXI (1974), 369-406.

slaves roughly comparable to those in the Chesapeake during the early period of its transition to a slave plantation system after 1680.[39]

If the increasing social stratification of New England during the eighteenth century provided some families with the wherewithal to live a genteel life and to own slaves, it does not seem to have resulted in a manifest proletarianization of the population. To be sure, as Charles Grant, Kenneth Lockridge and several other historians have observed, by the third and fourth generations in most towns vigorous demographic growth rendered existing land resources inadequate to enable many families to provide a viable farm for each of their male offspring. As a result, there was a sharp increase in the number of young adult males with minimal levels of property. By the mid-eighteenth century, as many as a third of the adult males in most communities were landless laborers. As Jackson Turner Main has shown in the case of Connecticut, however, this development was very largely a function of age. Typically, laborers were young men who were either waiting a few extra years until they inherited land from their fathers or preparing themselves to enter a craft, a profession or trade, while those who found inadequate opportunity within their own communities simply joined the stream of immigrants to new settlements or to urban areas. Whichever of these choices they made, Main has found, laboring was, for the vast majority of whites, only "a temporary line of work." If more and more young men began adult life with few assets, almost all of them could expect to obtain property "as they passed through the life cycle," and the "great majority of Connecticut's people fared as well in 1774 as in 1700 or 1670." "By contrast with most pre-industrial societies," Main concludes, "virtually all of the married men and their families...did not simply escape poverty but enjoyed real plenty." Main's findings have been reinforced by recent work on the changing diet of colonial New England by Sarah F. McMahon, who has found that

---

39 Robert C. Twombly and Robert H. Moore, "Black Puritan: The Negro in Seventeenth-Century Massachusetts," *WMQ*, 3d ser., XXIV (1967), 224-41; "Estimated Population of the American Colonies: 1610-1780," in Jack P. Greene, ed., *Settlements to Society 1584-1763: A Documentary History of the American Colonies* (New York, 1966), 238-9; Daniels, *Dissent and Conformity on Narragansett Bay*, 57-9; Withey, *Urban Growth in Colonial Rhode island*, 71-73; Crane, *Dependent People*, 76-83; Miller, "Narragansett Planters," 67-71, McBurney, "South Kingstown Planters," 81-93; Main, *Society and Economy in Colonial Connecticut*, 129-30, 176-82, 309, 378; Louis P. Masur, "Slavery in Eighteenth-Century Rhode Island: Evidence from the Census of 1774," *Slavery and Abolition*, VI (1985), 140-50; Van Deventer, *Provincial New Hampshire*, 113-14. On conditions of slavery in New England and the Black response to it, see Robert C. Twombly, "Black Resistance to Slavery in Massachusetts," in O'Neill, ed., *Insights and Parallels*, 11-2, and Lorenzo J. Greene, *The Negro in Colonial New England* (New York, 1942). On the decline of slavery in Massachusetts after 1770, see Elaine MacEacheren, "Emancipation of Slavery in Massachusetts: A Reexamination 1770-1790," *Journal of Negro History*, LV (1970), 289-306.

changes in land use and improvements in food production and preservation over the course of the colonial period meant that the region produced enough food so that few families could fail to enjoy a "comfortable subsistence."[40]

This is not to suggest that eighteenth century New England was without poverty. Poor relief had been a feature of New England life from the beginning, and it increased visibly during the eighteenth century as population growth, personal misfortune, the typically high loss of males in a seafaring economy, and other factors arising out of the increasingly complex character of New England society produced, in both city and country, an expanding class of both transient poor in search of employment and impoverished people unable to care for themselves. The towns dealt with this problem either by "warning out" non-residents or providing public relief for residents. But the costs of placing poor people in families or caring for them in almshouses became so high in major urban centers that several of them — Newport in the 1720s, Boston in the late 1730s, Providence and other towns in the 1750s and 1760s — built workhouses in an effort to make the able-bodied poor pay for themselves. The extent of this problem is easy to exaggerate. A close examination of people in the ranks of the poor reveals that they contained a small number of adult male heads of households. Rather, the vast majority seem to have fallen into one or the other of two principal categories: first, young unemployed single men and women who, if Main's findings for Connecticut can be extended to the rest of New England, presumably eventually found employment and rose out of the ranks of the poor and, second, members of traditionally dependent groups — widows, the aged, the sick, the disabled and orphans, only the last of whom could usually be expected ever to escape their dependence upon the community for their support. Yet, while transiency and poverty were increasing all over New England in the eighteenth century, they were still far below levels exhibited by contemporary British or European cities. With never more than five to seven per cent of a given locality's population receiving poor relief — and in most rural areas the percentage was much lower — New Englanders, as David Flaherty has observed, "had only limited experience with poverty in comparison with their fellow country men in Great Britain," where as "much as one-third of

40 Grant, *Democracy in the Connecticut Frontier Town*, 83-103; Lockridge, "Land, Population, and the Evolution of New England Society," 62-80; Main, *Society and Economy in Colonial Connecticut*, 149-51, 377-78, and "Standards of Living and the Life Cycle in Colonial Connecticut," *Journal of Economic History*, XLIII (1983), 159-65; Gloria L. Main, "The Standard of Living in Colonial Massachusetts," *ibid.*, 101-8; Jones, *Village and Seaport*, 103-21; Nancy R. Folbre, "The Wealth of Patriarchs: Deerfield, Massachusetts, 1760-1840," *Journal of International History*, XVI (1985), 208; Sarah F. McMahon, "A Comfortable Subsistence: The Changing Diet in Rural New England, 1620-1840," *WMQ*, 3d ser., XLII (1985), 26-65.

the...population may not have been able to feed and clothe themselves adequately."[41]

Along with the continuing internalization of Puritan religious constraints and a "high standard of law enforcement," students of legal records have cited this relative lack of poverty as at least part of the explanation for a low incidence of serious crime in New England. Throughout the last half of the seventeenth century, Roger Thompson has found in his study of sexual misbehavior in Middlesex County, Massachusetts, "New Englanders in general...were markedly more law-abiding" than English people in the home islands. Although crimes involving fornication, "by far the largest part of the criminal business" of local sessions courts, were being progressively and "effectively decriminalized" during the eighteenth century, the "rate of prosecution for crimes of violence, sexual offenses, and miscellaneous crimes," David Flaherty has found in the case of Massachusetts, was far higher than in England. But a much lower incidence of crimes against property, traditionally associated with poverty, meant that the per capita crime rate in Massachusetts was 43 per cent less than that in Essex County, England, and far below that in London.[42]

A low crime rate did not necessarily betoken inactivity on the part of the courts. At least in Massachusetts, civil litigation increased dramatically throughout the eighteenth century. Though inhabitants of some more isolated communities continued to eschew the courts and to try to resolve differences through the church or the town government, litigation rose steadily, and at a much faster rate in rural areas than in towns, and there was a marked increase in the number of cases involving disputes across town boundaries. An indication of the penetration of the commercial economy into the countryside, the growing interdependence between urban and rural areas, and the further attenuation of the consensual communalism of the founders, these developments, together with low

41 Charles R. Lee, "Public Poor Relief and the Massachusetts Community, 1620-1715," *New England Quarterly*, LV (1982), 564-85; Douglas Lamar Jones, "The Strolling Poor: Transiency in Eighteenth-Century Massachusetts," *Journal of Social History* VIII (1975), 28-54, and "Poverty and Vagabondage: The Process of Survival in Eighteenth-Century Massachusetts," *N.E. Hist. & Gen. Reg.*, CXXXIII (1979), 243-54; Daniels, *Dissent and Conformity on Narragansett Bay*, 57-9; Withey, *Urban Development in Colonial Rhode Island*, 51-71, 133-36; Nash, *Urban Crucible*, 71-74, 88, 125-27, 185-89, 217, 245-46, 253-55, 263, 310, 326-28, 337; Allan Kulikoff, "The Progress of Inequality in Revolutionary Boston," *WMQ*, 3d ser., XXVIII (1971), 375-412; David H. Flaherty, "Crime and Social Control in Provincial Massachusetts," *Historical Journal*, XXIV (1981), 352-53.

42 Roger Thompson, *Sex in Middlesex: Popular Mores in a Massachusetts County, 1649-1699* (Amherst, 1986), 194, 198; Flaherty, "Crime and Social Control," 339-60; Hendrik Hartog, "The Public Law of a County Court; Judicial Government in Eighteenth Century Massachusetts," *American Journal of Legal History*, XX (1976), 282-329.

crime rates and high prosecution rates for criminal offenses, provide powerful testimony to the public acceptance and efficacy of the courts as "instruments of social control."[43]

Increasing civil litigation may have been linked to a general "withering of traditional parental and community control." The first generation of rural New Englanders founded remarkably stable and closely integrated communities around a base of strong patriarchal families, while the second generation put down even deeper roots and developed a series of complex and overlapping extended kinship networks within the community. However, already by the third generation, which came to maturity in the early eighteenth century, and certainly by the fourth generation, which reached adulthood beginning in the 1730s and 1740s, the pressure of population growth, the decreasing availability of land, the opening up of new towns, and the emergence of many new opportunities for young men outside agriculture in an increasingly varied occupational structure all contributed to a significant diminution of patriarchal authority and loosening of family ties. As evidence of these changes, historians have noted a rising proportion of impartible inheritances, a tendency to convey land to sons at earlier ages, a steady increase in the out-migration of sons, a sharp drop in the age of marriage among both men and women, a major rise in daughters marrying out of the birth order, a diminution of parental control in marriage and a corresponding rise in the importance of romantic love in mate selection, a surge in pre-marital pregnancy, a shift away from parent-naming and Bible-naming, the provision of more space — and, hence, more privacy — for individual members of households and perhaps even a rise in female offenders in the courts. Along with an apparent improvement in the status of women as suggested by "their more frequent petitions for divorce and their greater success in obtaining it," all of these developments have been interpreted as indications that the circumstances of eighteenth century New England life were forcing fathers and husbands to redefine their roles, changing the character of the family, and helping to accelerate a powerful process of individuation among children and young adults.

The effects of these changes upon the basic character of New England

---

43 William E. Nelson, *Dispute and Conflict Resolution in Plymouth County, Massachusetts, 1725-1825* (Chapel Hill, 1981), 13-75, and *Americanization of the Common Law: The Impact of Legal Change on Massachusetts Society, 1760-1830* (Cambridge, Mass., 1975), 13-63; Murrin, "Review Essay," *History and Theory*, XI (1972), 250-1; David Grayson Allen, "The Zuckerman Thesis and the Process of Legal Rationalization in Provincial Massachusetts," *WMQ*, 3d ser., XXIX (1972), 456-9; L. Kinvin Wroth, "Possible Kingdoms: The New England Town from the Perspective of Legal History," *American Journal of Legal History*, XV (1971), 318-27; Flaherty, "Crime and Social Control," p. 355; Bruce H. Mann, "Rationality, Legal Change, and Community in Connecticut, 1690-1760," *Law and Society Review*, XIV (1980), 187-221.

life were profound. No longer "patriarchs grandly presiding over an ancestral estate and minutely controlling the lives of their sons and heirs," fathers now tended to act as "benefactors responsible for the future well-being and prosperity of their off-spring." At the same time, the tendency for parents to find fulfillment "in the success of their children" has been alleged to have produced a "new and different type of family life...characterized by solicitude and sentimentality towards children and by more intimate, personal, and equal relationships" among members. Finally, this new "organization of family life contributed to the emergence of a liberated individual, a person who was exempt from all except voluntary ties to the family of his birth and free to achieve his own goals."[44]

Increasing population growth and the changing character of religious, economic, social and familial life provided, as Richard L. Bushman has argued, the necessary preconditions for nothing less than a behavioral revolution that stretched over, and had a transforming effect upon all but the least dynamic areas of New England. Far from playing merely a passive role, people became active agents in this process. Increasingly ignoring traditional ideological and social restraints, they turned energies formerly devoted to religious and community endeavors to their own private pursuits of personal and individual happiness. By encouraging competitive behavior, this behavioral revolution also provided identity models and standards of personal conduct for the society at large that stood at marked variance with the original values of the leaders of the founding generation.

---

44 Greven, *Four Generations*, 125-258; John J. Waters, "Family, Inheritance, and Migration in Colonial New England: The Evidence from Guilford, Connecticut," *WMQ*, 3d ser., XXXIX (1982), 64-86; Jedrey, *World of John Cleaveland*, 58-94; Daniel Scott Smith, "Parental Power and Marriage Patterns: An Analysis of Historical Trends in Hingham, Massachusetts," *Journal of Marriage and the Family*, XXXV (1973), 419-39, and "Child-Naming Practices, Kinship Ties, and Change in Family Attitudes in Hingham, Massachusetts, 1641 to 1880," *Journal of Social History*, XVIII (1985), 541-66; Smith and Michael Hindus, "Premarital Pregnancy in America, 1640-1966," *Journal of International History*, VI (1975), 537-70; David H. Flaherty, *Privacy in Colonial New England* (Charlottesville, 1972), 26-27, 34-35, 38; Nancy F. Cott, "Divorce and the Changing Status of Women in Eighteenth-Century Massachusetts," *WMQ*, 3d ser., XXXIII (1976), 586-614, and "Eighteenth-Century Family and Social Life Revealed in Massachusetts Divorce Records," *Journal of Social History*, X (1976), 20-43; Folbre, "Wealth of the Patriarchs," 199-220; C. Dallett Hemphill, "Women in Court: Sex-Role Differentiation in Salem, Massachusetts, 1636 to 1683," *WMQ*, 3d ser., XXXIX (1982), 164-75; Lyle Koehler, *A Search for Power: The Weaker Sex in Seventeenth-Century New England* (Urbanna, Ill., 1980), 345-46, 361, 366; James A. Henretta, *The Evolution of American Society, 1700-1815: An Interdisciplinary Analysis* (Lexington, Mass., 1973), 30-1; Winnifred B. Rothenberg, "Markets, Values and Capitalism: A Discourse on Method," *Journal of Economic History*, XLIV (1984), 175-76. Thompson, *Sex in Middlesex*, 190-200, has recently persuasively questioned the coerciveness of patriarchical authority in late 17th century Middlesex County, Massachusetts

No longer was the moral and psychological necessity of obedience to the authority of the community and its traditional leaders — magistrates, pastors and fathers — automatically assumed. Rather, contemporary models of behavior emphasized the authority of self rather than the authority of community; individual economic achievement and success rather than ascriptive criteria for political leadership and social status; the fulfillment, privacy and comfort of the individual rather than self-denial in favor of the common good; and the "capacity of the individual to direct his own existence rather than...an unquestioning response to public morality." With this behavioral revolution, the pursuit of wealth and gentility became as important as the pursuit of salvation and even more important than the pursuit of consensus and community.[45]

If all of these developments combined to push New England in the direction of greater individualism, personal autonomy and social fluidity, the revolution in behavior exemplified by these developments was by no means universal. Nor did it produce a social environment that could be exclusively characterized in terms of "fluid, unstable social relations [that were] conducive [only] to individual mobility and a competitive ethos." Not just rural areas like those described by Michael Zuckerman and Christopher Jedrey but also urban communities continued, throughout the colonial period, to show remarkable stability in family life and to exhibit many other powerful residues of their Puritan cultural inheritance. "Rather than being at odds with the ideals of Puritanism or the ends of communitarianism," Christine Heyrman argues in her recent study of eighteenth century Salem and Marblehead, "commercial capitalism coexisted with and was molded by the cultural patterns of the past." As Heyrman shows, New England communities could become more populous, stratified, complex, diverse and mobile without lapsing into social disorder. In Salem and Marblehead, at least, civic consciousness, deference to leaders and institutions, church membership, "traditional patterns of association" and, perhaps, family authority remained strong. The abiding power of these traditional elements of the old Puritan social order, Heyrman plausibly contends, testifies to both the resilience of that order and the enduring authority of inherited beliefs and values.[46]

---

45 Bushman, *From Puritan to Yankee*. See also, Richard S. Dunn, *Puritans and Yankees: The Winthrop Dynasty of New England 1630-1717* (Princeton, 1962). The quotation is from Fred Weinstein and Gerald M. Platt, *The Wish to be Free: Society, Psyche, and Value Change* (Berkeley, 1969), 31.

46 Toby L. Ditz, *Property and Kinship: Inheritance in Early Connecticut 1750-1820* (Princeton, 1986), 159; Zuckerman, *Peaceable Kingdoms*; Jedrey, *World of John Cleaveland*, 58-94; Heyrman, *Commerce and Culture*, 15-9, 407-14. Laurel Ulrich, *Good Wives: Image and Reality in the Lives of Women in Northern New England 1650-1750* (New York, 1982), emphasizes the role of women in sustaining the communal impulse in New England communities.

Certainly, the revolution in behavior suggested by the growing evidence of increasing individuation had not yet been accompanied by a revolution in values. In their quest for land and wealth, men might challenge traditional leaders and established institutions. What they could not challenge so easily, however, was the old system of values which deplored both self-oriented behavior and resistance to authority. Notwithstanding the continuing strength of so many aspects of the old social order, the increasingly palpable divergence between the values attached to that order and individual behavior produced a gnawing guilt that was evident in persistent demands, especially from the clergy, for a return to the traditional imperatives of community and obedience to authority. The fear that excessively atomistic behavior would lead to social chaos and loss of control and the belief that man could not tolerate freedom without strong societal restraints were still too deeply embedded in cultural consciousness and too easily activated to permit the development of an alternative morality that would more accurately reflect the new modes of behavior.

Although the old millennial impulses of the founders had been severely attenuated by the latter decades of the seventeenth century, they had been "replaced by a conservative determination to perpetuate the symbols and institutions of the colonial founders." Cotton Mather and others engaged in what Robert Pope has referred to as "an oppressive filiopietism that transformed the founding generations into paragons of social virtue, wisdom and saintliness" who were constantly held up as a model for later generations and as a contrast that provided a framework for the interpretation of American Puritan history as a process of steady declension. The guilt felt by later generations over this declension and the disjuncture between the values of the founders and their own behavior made men, as several scholars have suggested, peculiarly susceptible to the atavistic appeals of the mid-century Great Awakening, the first large-scale religious revival in American history.[47]

Though it helped those men most deeply affected by it to cleanse themselves of guilt by throwing off their worldly ambitions, the Great Awakening did not result in a return to the old communal mode and the old values. Instead, as Bushman and other scholars have shown, it intensified religious divisions. Although some communities managed to contain those divisions within the existing church, many others split into rival congregations, thereby shattering all hope of religious unity. Such

---

47 Maclear, "New England and the Fifth Monarchy," 259; Pope, "New England Versus the New England Mind," 107; Bushman, *From Puritan to Yankee.* See also Axtell, *School Upon a Hill,* on the role of schools in perpetuating puritan social ideology and Kenneth A. Lockridge, *Literacy in Colonial New England: An Enquiry into the Social Context of Literacy in the Early Modern West* (New York, 1974), on one of the unintended modernizing effects of the widespread schooling.

developments and the bitter enmity they engendered further undermined the authority of the church and the clergy and made it clear that "revivalism, the ministry's favorite panacea [for the restoration of the old Puritan social order], could no longer be counted on to preserve [communal] order and harmony." Because they inevitably spilled over into politics and brought into the open personal and factional animosities which had previously operated beneath the surface of public life, the religious disputes generated by the Awakening also helped to transform politics by legitimizing factionalism and contention in the public realm and thereby weakening the traditional deference accorded magistrates. The egoistical impulses and frank pursuit of self-interest set free by the Awakening seemed to New England leaders of all persuasions to portend only social and political chaos. Many of them demanded a return to the old social order and decried attempts by a few "worldly individuals" to develop a new conception of the social order that, by giving "self-interest...a free rein" and making "the satisfaction of human desires the main end of government," would once again bring values and behavior into harmony. At best, however, such people were only fighting a delaying action. Already by the mid-eighteenth century, the expansive impulses in New England economic and religious life had sufficiently "relaxed the restraints of men's feelings and actions and sufficiently sapped the authority of traditional social institutions that they had significantly altered both the character of life and the character of the inhabitants. That the spread of autonomous behavior did not immediately lead to social chaos did, however, enable New Englanders to live with the behavioral revolution even when they could not bring themselves to endorse it.[48]

Despite the enduring vitality of so many aspects of the original Puritan social order, New England, recent historiography thus reveals, had changed dramatically between 1660 and 1760. Far more populous and more densely settled and stretching over a far larger area, it had a much

---

48 Bushman, *From Puritan to Yankee*, ix, 276, 279; Harry S. Stout and Peter Onuf, "James Davenport and the Great Awakening in New London," *Journal of American History*, LXXI (1983), p. 577; Onuf, "New Lights in New London: A Group Portrait of the Separatists," *WMQ*, 3d ser., XXXVII (1980), 627-43; Stout, "The Great Awakening in New England Reconsidered: The New England Clergy," *Journal of Social History*, VIII (1974), 21-47; James Walsh, "The Great Awakening in the First Congregational Church of Woodbury, Connecticut," *WMQ*, 3d ser., XXVIII (1971), 543-62; James W. Schmotter, "The Irony of Clerical Professionalism: New England's Congregational Ministers and the Great Awakening," *American Quarterly*, XXXI (1979), 148-68; Robert D. Rossel, "The Great Awakening: An Historical Analysis," *American Journal of Sociology*, LXXV (1970), 907-25; James W. Jones, *The Shattered Synthesis: New England Puritanism before the Great Awakening* (New Haven, 1973); Patricia J. Tracy, *Jonathan Edwards, Pastor: Religion and Society in Eighteenth-Century Northampton* (New York, 1979); Gregory H. Nobles, *Divisions Throughout the Whole: Politics and Society in Hampshire County, Massachusetts, 1740-1775* (Cambridge, 1983), 36-106.

more complex economy. Less reliant on family agriculture and more heavily involved in trade, it had developed a number of important urban areas that were closely linked by an already well-articulated transportation and marketing network with the countryside, many parts of which were engaged in more specialized and market-oriented agriculture and small-scale processing and natural resources manufacturing. Except perhaps in some isolated rural areas, its society was considerably more differentiated with greater extremes between the richest and poorest inhabitants and a more complex occupational structure. That society was also far less cohesive and solidary as the social agencies of church, community and family had all become much less coercive while the individuation process had become considerably more powerful.

In the words of Perry Miller, this "progression of the communities from primitive simplicity to complexity and diversity...irresistibly" carried New England "away from the original dedication to holiness and the will of God." In the process, it not only, as Miller suggested, made religion less central to the lives of its people but also sapped the strength of the corporate impulse that had been so powerfully manifest during the first and even second generations of settlement and greatly loosened the old Puritan social order. As New England society became both more complex and looser, it also lost many of the distinctive features it had exhibited during the seventeenth century. While it may be an exaggeration to say, as have John J. McCusker and Russell R. Menard, that by the late colonial period the region's well-integrated agricultural and commercial society "resembled nothing so much as old England itself," through the long process of social change over the previous hundred years it had certainly become by the middle decades of the eighteenth century far more demonstrably English than it had been during the decades immediately after its establishment.[49] To the extent that these changes can be seen, as so many clerical leaders at the time saw them, as an attenuation of the original Puritan social order and can be represented as a decline from the radically traditional world envisioned and, to a remarkable degree, actually achieved, by the founding generations of orthodox Puritans, the declension model can still plausibly be used as a framework for describing the social history of colonial New England. The process of social change in New England during the century after 1660, however, involved considerable demographic and economic growth as well as social elaboration, stratification and consolidation, and such trends can be at best only partially and inaccurately comprehended within a declension model.

---

49 Miller, "Declension in a Bible Commonwealth," 25; McCusker and Menard, *Economy of British America*, 92.

J.B. Brebner and Some Recent
Trends in Eighteenth-Century
Maritime Historiography

G. A. Rawlyk
Winthrop Pickard Bell Professor of Maritime Studies
Mount Allison University, 1987-1988
Professor of History, Queen's University

J.B. Brebner, in so many ways, was a remarkable historian. Born in Toronto in 1895, he did his graduate work at Oxford and Columbia, and after teaching at the University of Toronto from 1921 to 1925 he went to Columbia where he spent the rest of his academic career.[1] He was an inspiring and concerned teacher. Moreover, he was able to digest quickly and carefully the work of others and to impose upon it a persuasively argued and often brilliantly executed organizational overview. Brebner was, as he convincingly demonstrated in *The North Atlantic Triangle* and *The Explorers of North America*, a master of penetrating synthesis and lucid, cogent writing. But, of course, he was much more than this. He was, as Donald Creighton once observed, "quite capable of a very high level of original research."[2] Brebner's *New England's Outpost* published in 1927 and *The Neutral Yankees of Nova Scotia* published ten years later were, according to Creighton, "without any doubt two of the most important books on the history of Canada that have appeared during the twentieth century."

It should not be surprising, therefore, that few scholars, since the publication of *The Neutral Yankees*, have been eager to rework Brebner's Nova Scotia world. Those who have are usually content to write about historical problems which did not really engage Brebner — Louisbourg, the Great Awakening and Scottish immigration. Those revisionists who have attempted to challenge Brebner's interpretation, on the whole, failed to transcend him, at least as far as their academic peers are concerned as well as in the opinion of some of the revisionists themselves. One of the latter has recently complained about his inability "to escape the long shadow cast by Brebner" as well and the remarkable sustaining power of Brebner's paradigm.[3]

Not only has Brebner's widely-perceived "classic" *The Neutral Yankees* discouraged, for half a century, other scholars from reassessing, in a

---

1   See my brief sketch of Brebner in *The Canadian Encyclopedia* (1985), 216.
2   D. Creighton, "Introduction to the Carleton Library Edition" of J.B. Brebner, *The North Atlantic Triangle* (Toronto, 1968), xiii.
3   See my "J.B. Brebner and *The Writing of Canadian History*," *Journal of Canadian Studies*, 13, 3 (Fall 1978), 92.

significant manner, the historical development of Nova Scotia during the 1760 to 1783 period, but the publication of the volume also encouraged Brebner to leave the field once and for all. There was, as W.S. MacNutt has observed, a "note of petulance in the Foreword" of the book as if Brebner had suddenly realized in 1937 that all his widely-praised work on Nova Scotia was, like the province itself, of marginal importance after all.[4] And in the Foreword he permitted his frustration and bitterness, for once, to break through the hard crust of his usual dispassionate prose style. He really wondered whether his *New England's Outpost* and *The Neutral Yankees* had been worth all the effort he had lavished on the research and writing of the two books. With reference to the 1760 to 1783 period of Nova Scotia history, and why it had not been examined in a scholarly manner before 1937, Brebner caustically observed:

> The reasons why this had not been done before was that it was properly questionable whether the result, even if fairly definitive, was sufficiently important to justify the necessary expenditure of time. It seems debatable, for instance, whether this book should not have been much briefer than it is, considering the relative colonial insignificance of Nova Scotia.[5]

His Columbia University colleagues had been right after all in arguing that Brebner was wasting his time, energy and ability in writing about a "marginal colony" of little real consequence. By 1937 Brebner had come to the conclusion that there would not be a third Nova Scotia volume dealing with the post-1783 Loyalist period. Instead, underscoring his bitter disillusionment with his two Nova Scotia volumes, Brebner found himself powerfully attracted to *The North Atlantic Triangle* and then in the twilight of his academic life with the mainstream of British history. Before he could make his scholarly mark in this area, he died in New York City, on 9 November 1957. "In his last years," it has been observed, "Brebner had become more continentalist, more engrossed with Canada as a curious collection of fragmentations by-passed in the march of American Manifest Destiny."[6]

The central thrust of Brebner's *New England's Outpost* was the contention that the "expanding energies" of New England had led "inevitably and naturally" to the expulsion of the Acadians in 1755.[7] And

---

4   W.S. MacNutt, "Introduction" to J.B. Brebner, *The Neutral Yankees of Nova Scotia* (Toronto, 1969), xiii.

5   "Foreward" to J.B. Brebner, *The Neutral Yankees*, xix.

6   MacNutt, "Introduction" to Brebner, *The Neutral Yankees*, xvii.

7   For a more detailed critique of this aspect of the Brebner thesis, see G.A. Rawlyk, *Nova Scotia's Massachusetts* (Montreal, 1973).

in *The Neutral Yankees* he argued that during the Revolution the Nova Scotia Yankees, most of the population of the "fourteenth colony," like their Acadian predecessors during periods of Anglo-French conflict, had resolved to walk the knife-edge of neutrality. Even though, of course, he warned his readers of the dangers involved in relying "on a single explanation for Nova Scotia behaviour," Brebner nevertheless concluded that the colony's "insulation from the rest of North America" provided the "principal clue" for the region's neutrality.[8] Thus Brebner stressed what he saw as the striking theme of continuity in Nova Scotia's eighteenth-century experience; he confidently threw the "straightjacket of neutrality forward, from the 1750s, to catch all the Nova Scotia residents during the American Revolution."[9] Yankees became Acadians and a kind of environmental deterministic framework was imposed upon what otherwise appeared to be a largely meaningless jumble produced by the complex overlapping of names, events and personalities.

The great and continuing influence of Brebner's work may be assessed in a variety of ways. One of these is to ascertain how the revisionists have fared in recent years with the scholarly community. The evidence suggests that in Canada, at least, Brebner's interpretations are still regarded as "classic" ones, while the work of the revisionists is pushed off into some dark corner of historiographical oblivion. This general conclusion seems to be supported by a careful reading of a number of widely used and recently published Canadian history texts.

In Barry Gough's *Canada* (Englewood Cliffs, 1975) the Acadian Expulsion is not even mentioned — no mean accomplishment for a Canadian historian writing a general textbook; and Nova Scotia's reaction to the Revolution merits only one paragraph. According to Gough:

> Nova Scotia colonists also rejected revolution, but unlike the Quebec case, theirs was an instance of how a region on the fringes of the Revolution was torn by conflicting forces, and in the end remained passively neutral. Of the seventeen or eighteen thousand settlers, three-quarters were New England by birth. But though they knew of the complaints across the waters in Boston and Philadelphia and had close family ties there, they were part of the British colonial system of mercantilism. In Halifax, the capital, a cautious oligarchy maintained close ties with London merchants, and this same group maintained a dominance in the provincial assembly at the expense of

---

8 See the historiographical discussion of this point in G. Stewart and G. Rawlyk, *A People Highly Favoured of God* (Toronto, 1972), xviii-xix and also G.A. Rawlyk, "Revolution Rejected," *Emerging Identities*. ed., D.W. Bennett and C.J. Jaenen (Toronto, 1986), 133-57.

9 Rawlyk, "J.B. Brebner and *The Writing of Canadian History*," 92.

the rural areas. They looked on the war as advantageous for war contracts and good for trade. And, with the naval base for Royal Navy ships in the North Atlantic and Caribbean situated in Bedford Basin adjacent to Halifax, how could a revolution be got up anyway? It was only in the out-settlements such as in Cumberland county that the fervors of revolution ran high. Outbursts against the Crown did occur and indicated the sympathies of the rural or outport majority. But as the Revolution progressed, the Nova Scotians found themselves cut off from their former New England homelands, and they were divided from one another by the roadless Nova Scotian wilderness. Occasionally Yankee ships made raids on the coastal ports and this tended to weaken pro-revolutionary support. Thus, somewhat ironically, the Yankees who had conquered Acadia and expelled the Acadians now found themselves torn between revolutionary and reactionary forces. In the end, they became, as one historian called them, "The Neutral Yankees of Nova Scotia."[10]

In Kenneth McNaught's *The Pelican History of Canada* (Markham, 1975), New England imperialism, as personified in Governor William Shirley of Massachusetts, was responsible for "the ruthless device of expelling the Acadians from Nova Scotia."[11] And as far as Nova Scotia neutrality during the Revolution was concerned, it could be directly traced to the merchant oligarchy of Halifax. These men, many of whom were recently arrived Yankees, ensured that the residents of the outsettlements were at least neutral. And George Washington observing "the almost cynical attitude of Nova Scotia to the continental cause... decided to leave the province strictly alone."[12]

Brebner's influence certainly shines through the books by Gough and McNaught and there is no evidence of any post-Brebner scholarship. It is as though nothing had been written, since 1937, about eighteenth-century Nova Scotia. This same criticism cannot, however, be levelled against the 1984 version of J.L. Finlay and D.N. Sprague, *The Structure of Canadian History* (Scarborough, 1984), or Desmond Morton's *A Short History of Canada* (Edmonton, 1985). Yet, despite this disclaimer, the influence of Brebner is still to be found in these two volumes. As far as Finlay and Sprague are concerned, the "British launched a massive round-up of the entire French-speaking population in Acadia in 1755" and thus the "Acadian landscape was cleared for occupancy by British settlers from New England."[13] These Yankees, during the Revolution, because of

---

10 Gough, 38-39.

11 McNaught, 38.

12 McNaught, 52.

13 Finlay and Sprague, 61.

"situational pressures" adopted "neutrality."[14] Indeed, Finlay and Sprague are willing to go beyond Brebner by stressing that Yankee society "had not yet crystallized" in Nova Scotia:

> To the extent that the events of the period were a source of anxiety, that psychological energy was discharged in religious revival fostered by Henry Alline rather than in political slogan-shouting from the south. Then, too, it should be mentioned that Halifax was a naval base.[15]

Some academics might argue that these authors probably inserted material about Alline into the text because of the presence of Alline's biographer in their history department and also because a reader of the original manuscript for Prentice-Hall had also written extensively about Alline and Revolutionary Nova Scotia.

It has already been noted by John Reid that Morton's superficial treatment of pre-1713 Acadia is characterized by "inaccurate or misleading statements" and his discussion of the post-1713 period is "only marginally better."[16] Perhaps, Morton is guilty of the unpardonable sin in Canadian historical writing — he has not read J.B. Brebner. There is also some evidence to suggest that for the pre-1776 period he did not read anything written since 1937. For the Revolutionary period, however, he obviously had done more research but his descriptive-analysis was all summed up in one short paragraph:

> Like the Acadians, the American settlers who took their place and who spread themselves along the southern and western shores of Nova Scotia largely ignored the self-important little government of merchants and officials at Halifax. They sent home grim corrections of the glowing propaganda which had enticed them to "Nova Scarcity," but, while New Englanders' minds turned to revolution, Nova Scotia's Yankees turned their few leisure thoughts and moments to the "New Light" movement, a passionate religious revival. With a British fleet and garrison in Halifax, the few sparks of revolt in the 1770s were swiftly extinguished, and the missionaries of the "New Awakening," alarming though they seemed to Halifax Anglicans, sought revolutions in morals, not governments. Merchants in

---

14 Finlay and Sprague, 73.
15 Finlay and Sprague, 74.
16 See J. Reid, "Towards the Elusive Synthesis: The Atlantic Provinces in Recent General Treatments of Canadian History," *Acadiensis*, XVI, 2(Spring 1987), 115.

Halifax and other ports made too much money from the war to feel rebellious.[17]

What is particularly striking about how these recently published general histories of Canada treat eighteenth-century Nova Scotia is not necessarily their Brebnerite twist but rather their pronounced lack of interest or concern. Usually there is a short paragraph or two, at most, devoted to the Acadians in the 1713 to 1755 period and in this brief section there is sometimes a sentence about the Louisbourg Expedition of 1745. This is followed, perhaps a little later on in the text, by another paragraph about the founding of Halifax, the coming of the Yankees, the Revolution and neutrality. Then come the Loyalists and "Canadian" history can begin. Most recognize the Hartz thesis now, which is post Esther Clark Wright. As far as the 1713 to 1783 period is concerned, two or three paragraphs are regarded as more than adequate. This latter criticism could not, however, be applied to those contemporaries of Brebner's who wrote general history texts — men like W.L. Morton, Donald Creighton, Arthur Lower, J.M.S. Careless and Edgar McInnis. For example, Morton in his *Kingdom of Canada* devoted some thirteen pages to Nova Scotia's historical development during the 1713 to 1783 period and the Brebnerite bias was explicitly obvious. Arthur Lower even included a paragraph in his *Colony to Nation* on the "Planters":

> This little extension of New England into New Scotland brought up a vigorous and wide awake group of people, among the best immigrants that Canada has ever received...From the first, they gave the province weight and ballast and the reality of a democratic tradition. They insisted on the rights of Englishmen, one of which...was an elected Assembly. This they demanded even before they came, and in 1758, the authorities in England ordered the unwilling...Governor...to summon one.[18]

Lower described post-Planter Nova Scotia as "an extension of New England: but not new England over again": and as "the outpost of New England."[19] As far as Lower was concerned Brebner's neutrality thesis explained perfectly Nova Scotia's response to the Revolution. And Lower, moreover, explicitly argued that Nova Scotia was not in fact "a Loyalist province." Rather, it was "primarily pre-Revolutionary New England" in character, as demonstrated by the "appearance of its houses and villages and by the energy of its people, their avidity for higher-education and their

17 Morton, 54.
18 (Toronto, 1977), 107.
19 Lower, 65, 97.

religious denominations."[20] For Lower, the Loyalists were indeed the "dancing beggars" but he had a far more positive view of their predecessors.

It seems clear and obvious that Canadian history texts published during the past decade treat Nova Scotia in the eighteenth century far more superficially and far more inadequately than do texts published thirty or forty years ago. Brebner's declining influence may be one reason for this development and the presentist and Central Canadian obsession of so many Canadian historians may be another. Yet the point should be underscored that when there is a paragraph or two written in the 1970s and 1980s about eighteenth-century Nova Scotia these still very much reflect the Brebner bias. And when they do not it is often the case that the authors have not, in fact, read Brebner.

Another way of ascertaining Brebner's influence on eighteenth-century Nova Scotia historiography is to examine how recently-published collections of key articles have dealt with Nova Scotia in the 1713 to the 1783 period. In recent years three different two-volume collections have been published; the first volume of all three deal with the pre-Confederation period. P.A. Buckner and David Frank's *The Acadiensis Reader: Atlantic Canada Before Confederation: Volume One* (Fredericton, 1985) contains three articles largely about pre-1783 Nova Scotia and one about Prince Edward Island. Four articles out of a total of eighteen, from the best in *Acadiensis*, is both noteworthy and encouraging, for the eighteenth-century historian at least. And all of these articles, it should be observed, move beyond Brebner. Gisa Hynes, "Some Aspects of the Demography of Port Royal, 1650-1755," is certainly suggestive, however flawed her evidence might be; Naomi Griffiths, "Acadians in Exile: the Experiences of the Acadians in the British Seaports," points in the direction of her much anticipated two volume study of the Acadians. Also included in this volume of the *Acadiensis Reader* is Graeme Wynn's "Late Eighteenth-Century Agriculture on the Bay of Fundy Marshlands," a cogently original study somewhat influenced by A.H. Clark and J.M. Bumsted's "The Origin of the Land Question on Prince Edward Island, 1767-1805," a preliminary thrust for Bumsted's recently published important monograph *Land, Settlement and Politics on Eighteenth-Century Prince Edward Island* (Montreal, 1987). This book, together with Bumsted's *The People's Clearance 1770-1815* (Edinburgh, 1982), have established the author's position as, among other things, the leading authority on the Scots impact on the Maritimes in the last quarter of the eighteenth century. By concentrating on the Scots, the Celtic fringe of Nova Scotia and Prince Edward Island, Bumsted has succeeded admirably, in my view, in escaping the long shadow cast by J.B. Brebner. And, in the process, he has

---

20 Lower, 108.

compelled all students of late eighteenth-century British emigration and North America to take his work seriously indeed.

In his *Interpreting Canada's Past*, Volume I (Toronto, 1986), Professor Bumsted includes in his pre-Loyalist eighteenth-century section only Mason Wade's often neglected "After the *Grand Derangement*: The Acadians' Return to the Gulf of St. Lawrence and to Nova Scotia," originally published in 1975. This is, Bumsted contends, an example of "the best and most innovative work of the past few years."[21] For R.D. Francis and D.B. Smith, in *Readings in Canadian History: Pre-Confederation* (Toronto, 1986), two other articles about pre-1783 Nova Scotia are the "best and most innovative." These are Naomi Griffith's "The Golden Age: Acadian Life 1713-1748," originally published in 1984, and G.A. Rawlyk, "The American Revolution and Nova Scotia Reconsidered," written some twenty-five years ago. The inclusion of the Griffiths article — though it breaks little new research ground — may certainly be defended, but the Rawlyk study is now largely irrelevant apart from its very limited historiographical importance. The *Acadiensis Reader*, contains the best post-Brebner collection of articles about pre-Loyalist Nova Scotia. Yet the point should be made that the *Reader* is strangely silent about the Planters and the Yankee impact on Nova Scotia, apart from a very brief discussion of their agricultural methods in the brief Wynn article. Since *Acadiensis* has shown exemplary sensibility to new trends in eighteenth-century Nova Scotia historiography, this silence is testimony to the widespread Canadian neglect of Planter history.

It is ironic, maybe it is more than ironic, that five books published in the United States since 1982 reveal a far greater degree of perceptive awareness about recent trends in eighteenth-century Nova Scotia historiography than have most Canadian scholars. In 1982 Stephen Marini's much revised Harvard Ph.D. dissertation was published under the title *Radical Sects of Revolutionary New England*. In this most suggestive and ground-breaking study, Marini attempts to show how and why the "New Light Stir" of 1780, a religious revival triggered by Nova Scotia's Great Awakening, encouraged the fragmentation of the Whitefieldian Evangelical consensus and the growth of the sectarian folk religions such as the Shakers, the Free Will Baptists and the Universalists.[22] Though numerically insignificant, these three new sects showed how the traditional structures of Yankee society had crumbled under the hammering of the Revolution. And, as might have been expected, often bizarre yet satisfying ways of relating to the Almighty and to others became increasingly common as a growing number of northern New Englanders looked for a renewed sense of community-

---

21 Bumsted, *Interpreting Canada's Past*, I, x.
22 See my "Evangelicals, Patriots and Sectarianism," *Queen's Quarterly*, 91, 1(Spring 1984), 89-95.

belonging in order to neutralize the powerful forces of alienation then sweeping the region. It was a period when almost anything could be believed and almost everything doubted. Many Yankees found themselves in a state of spiritual tension torn by the contradicting forces pulling at them. Unlike the South, however, the sectarian centrifugal tendency was not effectively checked by the institution of black slavery and was therefore free, in the post-Revolutionary period, to spin off in a myriad of directions. Eventually the power of sectarian individualism would be such, especially in the Northeast, that the old Evangelical consensus would be seriously weakened and pushed to the periphery of the region's religious culture.

Marini traces the growth of the Universalists, Shakers and Freewill Baptists in northern New England during the 1780 to 1820 period. He places special emphasis on the roles played by the three key leaders of these movements, Caleb Rich, Benjamin Randel and Ann Lee. He then examines the theological basis of each of the sects, their polity and organization and in a particularly important section of his book throws much new light on what he calls "The Language of the Soul." What Marini is referring to in this finely-crafted chapter is the important role of hymnody in the ritual expression of these three sects. In their hymns, ordinary folk were able to express their peculiar theological views in a language which resonated with their experience.

One important feature of Marini's book is of special interest to the Canadian reader. Perhaps, for the first time in recent years, a serious American scholar has contended that an influential American social and religious movement — the "New Light Stir of 1780" — was triggered by Nova Scotian events and a charismatic Nova Scotian, Henry Alline. Marini argues quite persuasively that the Yankee revival owed a great deal to Nova Scotia's Great Awakening. Moreover, according to Marini, Alline, although he died in 1784, significantly affected the Freewill Baptist movement until at least 1800. Alline's theology was enthusiastically appropriated by Benjamin Randel, the Freewill Baptist founder, and by his followers, as were Alline's over 500 hymns and spiritual songs. Marini, making good use of recent Canadian work on Alline, is unusually sensitive to Alline's influence on unfolding events, locating it persuasively in its Nova Scotia-New England context.

John J. McCusker and Russell R. Menard, in their *The Economy of British North America 1607 to 1789* (Chapel Hill, 1985), have also been influenced by recent Canadian scholarship. The fact that McCusker began his teaching career at Mount Allison and St. Francis Xavier universities may help to explain this commendable clear-sightedness. In their much-praised book, they link in Chapter 5, "New England and Atlantic Canada," pointing out that Nova Scotia during much of the seventeenth and eighteenth centuries was "integrated into New England's economy through two processes," migration and the "aggressive commercialism" of the Yankee merchants:

> Attracted by market opportunities in fish, timber, and farm produce
> and pushed by the pressure of population on the land in more-
> densely settled regions, New Englanders flocked to Nova Scotia
> during the 1760s as part of the same migration that had earlier led
> them to New York, New Hampshire, Vermont, and Maine and that
> would later lead them to the Midwest. We know very little about the
> particulars of this migration or of the numbers involved, but they
> were sufficient to make Nova Scotia a "new New England" and help
> bring the region into Boston's expanding commercial orbit.[23]

McCusker and Menard have provided convincing evidence to support the
contention that "focussing on exports, on population growth, and on
settlement" they have, in fact, explained "more than just the narrowly
economic aspects of the British Americas in the seventeenth and eighteenth centuries."[24] And for them, of course, and this point needs to be
emphasized, British America included Nova Scotia, Newfoundland and
after the Conquest, Quebec.

D.W. Meinig has a similar broad view of North America in his *Shaping
of America: Atlantic America, 1492-1800* (New Haven, 1986). The book
has been described as "a post-Turnerian geography for the age of Fernand
Braudel and Immanuel Wallerstein." For Meinig, a leading historical
geographer, "the most important spatial relationships in early American
history are not the settlers' wrestling with fields and forest, but imperial
lines of authority stretched across the Atlantic determining the flow of
supplies and skills that made commercial expansion in North America so
implacable."[25] Meinig's picture of Acadian society in the pre-1760 period
has been significantly affected by Andrew Hill Clark's work, especially his
Acadia: The Geography of Early Nova Scotia to 1760 (Madison, 1968).
And Meinig's treatment of Nova Scotia from 1760 to 1783 owes a great
deal to Brebner and to *Nova Scotia's Massachusetts* (Montreal, 1973). His
description of the coming of the Planters captures some of the flavour of
his writing:

> In 1758 the British began their program for the recolonization and
> expanded development of an enlarged Nova Scotia. Much of the best
> land was soon in the hands of various officials and favorites, but
> there was a need for actual settlers and an obvious source lay nearby:
> New England, whose seamen had long been familiar with every little

---

23 McCusker and Menard, 113-4.
24 McCusker and Menard, 11.
25 See the Garry Wills review in the *Times Literary Supplement*, 17 April 1987.

harbour, whose merchants had long dominated the trade, whose soldiers had marched here against the French, and whose families had had more than a century of colonizing experience. Counties and townships were laid out, liberal land allotments offered, tolerance of Dissenters declared, and assurance given that local governments and courts were "constituted in like manner with those of Massachusetts, Connecticut and other Northern colonies." And so within a few years several thousand Yankees, drawn from coastal Connecticut, Rhode Island, and eastern Massachusetts, had taken over nearly all the former Acadian farms, filled in the Annapolis Valley and Minas townships far more thickly than the French had done, occupied every good harbour along the southerly coast, and were sprinkled here and there in the old contested borderland of the northern Fundy shore, as at Passamoquoddy and the lower St. John. And thus much of the domesticated landscape and social geography of Nova Scotia — its busy seaports, its closest villages with their greens and Congregational or Baptist churches, its farmer-forester-fishermen, its many cultural and commercial connections with Boston and many other ports — displayed the unmistakable mark of Greater New England.[26]

It is interesting to note that Meinig argues strongly that the "Neutral Yankees of Nova Scotia" were, in fact, Loyalists. For him, as for Professor Bumsted, their British allegiance "cannot be dismissed as simply on untested routine commitment" but rather was their response to a "great imperial crisis."[27] As far as Meinig is concerned, Brebner was absolutely correct in linking Yankee and Acadian neutrality and in generalizing from the December 1775 Yarmouth petition: "We were almost all of us born in New England, we have Fathers, Brothers & Sisters in that country, divided betwixt natural affection to our nearest relations, and good Faith and Friendship to our King and Country, we want to know if we may be permitted" to be neutral.[28] From his vantage-point at the University of Syracuse, Meinig has brilliantly succeeded in integrating Canadian scholarship into what he calls his "idiosyncratic" overarching thesis concerning the interplay of North American localities and regions, "networks and circulations," and "national and intercolonial systems."[29]

26 Meinig, 273-4.
27 Meinig, 312. See also J.M. Bumsted, *Understanding the Loyalists* (Sackville, 1986).
28 Quoted in Meinig, 314.
29 Meinig, xv-xvi.

Bernard Bailyn's prize-winning book *Voyagers to the West* (New York, 1986) also superbly integrates scholarship on pre-Revolutionary Nova Scotia. While researching for this volume, Bailyn kept in close touch with Canadian historians about British emigration to Nova Scotia in the 1770s. His research associate, Barbara De Wolfe, moreover, diligently combed through various relevant theses and other studies. In this impressive first installment of a proposed multi-volume series — *The Peopling of America on the Eve of the Revolution* — Bailyn presents a comprehensive and detailed picture of British immigration to North America in the years 1773-1776. Bailyn sets out to synthesize and reorganize the available information about population movements between the Old World and the New. To make sense of the migration of thousands of individuals across the ocean, he searches for patterns to explain their actions and for individual accounts to determine the character of the peopling process. The result is a masterful work of historical interpretation which successfully transports the reader back in time and allows one to sense the thinking and mentality of the early immigrants.

Bailyn's approach in *Voyagers to the West* is obviously much indebted to the tools of social history. He relies heavily on quantitative data, made intelligible with the aid of an adept human research assistant and the newest non-human aid to historians, a computer. As well, Bailyn's interpretation concentrates on the experiences, not of the elite, but of ordinary farmers, artisans and laborers. Both techniques are advantageously combined, as Bailyn, in the first half of the book, uses quantitative analysis to create an overview of the migration process, identifying its participants, their backgrounds and motivations. From this panoramic view, Bailyn zeroes in on the experiences of individual immigrants and promoters in different regions of British North America, including Nova Scotia, and by using literary documents recreates their multifarious experiences.

Before presenting the quantitative data he has analyzed, Bailyn begins by setting the scene for the British-American migration. The movement of people across the Atlantic is portrayed, within a "push-pull" framework. Bailyn considers both the pressures pushing potential emigrants away from England and forces attracting people to North America. The New World, by 1775, had become attractive both as a refuge and as a land of opportunity for many Britons, he convincingly argues. Many people believed that one could achieve a better situation in British North America than ever was possible in Britain. With the increase in popularity of this belief, North America began to have a growing influence on British life. At the same time, the pool of potential emigrants from Britain was increasing, as a result of a number of factors. Bailyn argues that farmers had been hard hit by the conversion to commercial agriculture, which had encouraged rent profiteering, enclosures and absentee landlords. Economic distress was further evident as a result of the structural changes in the linen and other textile industries. The effects of these events were compounded in the Scottish Highlands by the collapse of social organization due to the change in cultural role of the clan chieftain from warlord to landlord. Given these conditions, it is not surprising that a considerable number of people wished to leave their situation, but it is noteworthy that many of them decided to go to North America. The New World, Bailyn argues, was considered in the 1770s as "the best poor man's country in the world" and thus became a positive attraction in itself. Bailyn interprets the movement of the immigrants across the ocean as a continuing link between the Old World and the New. The American destination is considered, not only in itself, but on a continuum of options open to potential British emigrants.

The changing Anglo-American relationship, Bailyn notes, merited increasing critical attention in Britain. Officials and landlords became convinced that depopulation would fuel a radical social disturbance in the Old Country and that it posed as well a serious demographic, economic and cultural loss. In an effort to curb emigration from Britain, the government, under heavy pressure, altered the process of land distribution, so it could restrict and regulate land grants. As well, it undertook a statistical assessment of the extent of emigration.

The Register of emigrants, compiled between December 1773 and March 1776 listed 9,364 individuals who departed from England and Scotland for British North America. This documentary collection, gathered by customs officials, constitutes a detailed and comprehensive body of immigration data, which has never before been systematically analyzed in such a sophisticated manner by a historian. Bailyn's analysis of the data contained in the Register provides the statistical basis of his overview of the migration process. Before outlining the results of his analysis, Bailyn enumerates the shortcomings of his information source. Large areas of coastline were beyond the range of effective customs surveillance and, moreover, there was no legal requirement for vessels carrying emigrants to register with customs, and many ships picked up additional passengers after they had registered. Furthermore, it was up to local officials to decide who was and who was not an emigrant, a judgement coloured by class distinctions, and resulting in the coverage for the "gentle" occupations being indeed erratic. The accuracy of social data was also compromised when customs officials used vague terms and estimated personal information such as age.

Despite these shortcomings, the Register data provides a most revealing survey of British emigration in the 1770s. For Bailyn the movement of British people to North America was a dual migration. The "metropolitan" pattern, firstly, represented migrants from central and southern England. Emigrants were typically young men, in their early twenties, who travelled alone to the New World on ships carrying a few passengers for extra profit. Usually single and trained as artisans or craftsmen, these individuals could not find regular employment in England and thus had no prospects at home. Most were drawn to North America for positive purposes, as their chances seemed better across the Atlantic. With hope for a better future in mind, these young men commonly indentured themselves to serve an American employer for four or five years in exchange for their passage. Bailyn also identifies a second pattern of emigration, which he characterizes as a "provincial" one, set in northern England and Scotland. Migration from this region was usually undertaken, not by single individuals, but by family units moving intact, including small children. The family character of emigration meant that the age and sex of emigrants was more evenly balanced than in the metropolitan pattern and that heads of households were typically older than the English average. Occupationally, Scottish emigrants represented two groups, a traditional labour force of farmers and labourers and a semi-industrial work force of artisans, mainly in textiles. The move across the Atlantic was typically a carefully planned step by Scottish families searching for personal betterment or security, often in the form of their own land, and it involved the selling of the family's assets in the Old World to pay for passage to the New in large ships chartered specially for that purpose.

The two emigration patterns that Bailyn identifies were distinctive, not only in their characteristics in Britain, but also in their experiences in North America. The quantitative data shows that the central colonies of Pennsylvania, Virginia and especially Maryland were the destinations of the majority of immigrants in the "metropolitan" stream. The newcomers, Bailyn argues, represented a specific kind of work force. The labour market in the central colonies favoured young workmen, mostly artisans, whose services could be bought by individuals in advance. The high degree of economic specialization in the region meant that specific skills were highly in demand. Since the backcountry was being opened and established communities were growing quickly, the labour needs centered on men skilled in construction trades. The experience of the "provincial" family migration, however, was markedly different. Most of these newcomers settled in New York, North Carolina or Nova Scotia. They represented, not a specific labour force, but a patterned social movement of often substantial families. They sought destinations where land was available for their resettlement and where they could thus recover lost security.

In his discussion of the quantative data contained in the Register of emigrants, Bailyn identifies clear, coherent patterns in the seemingly random movement of individuals and families from the Old World to the New. He then proceeds to transfer the figures into human experience by recreating the career lines of both emigrants and emigration promoters in the central colonies, Nova Scotia, North Carolina and New York. Bailyn concentrates first on the experiences of immigrants representing the "metropolitan" pattern. He focuses, in particular, on the large number of workers gathering in London. London, as the largest urban centre in the world, was a powerful magnetic force for migrant workers. As the economic centre of the nation, it was also the main source of recruitment for the American work force. Bailyn identifies the emigrants as coming from the newly arrived, mobile, disoriented segment of London's population. Migrant workers without connections in the city often had difficulty finding work. Even for resident skilled workers, unemployment was a constant condition of life. Emigration was thus a rational option for workers facing low wages or periodic unemployment or both. It represented "the specific expression of a general search by the labour force for stability in an unstable economy." Aside from skilled and migrant workers, North America also became a viable option for textile industry artisans who were being made redundant, for laborers and farm workers for whom agricultural employment had become highly unreliable, and for convicts whose death sentences were commuted to banishment.

The mobilization of British metropolitan workers on their way to America was undertaken by merchants and agents whose transactions were impelled by the search for profit. The profit motive is, for Bailyn, the root cause of the pattern of movement across the Atlantic. The merchants sought to enlist the indentees skilled in high-demand trades who would fetch the highest prices for their talents. Lined up on the ships like cattle, the indentees were carefully inspected by single potential buyers in America. The most valuable young men were sold individually and quickly and the rest were sold together for a lump sum, to be distributed by an American buyer. The immigrants were thus absorbed separately into the organization of life in America, their final destinations often being miles inland in the isolated backcountry.

The career lines of emigrants representing the "provincial" pattern reflected the different characteristics and motives of family groups, and another type of profit. Their motivation, Bailyn states, was both a search for security and for resettlement on their own land. In Britain, farmers and artisans were being dislodged by shifts in the organization of the economy, which threatened to debase their settled way of life. Ambitious for greater security and prospects for the future and eager to escape the progressive constriction of life taking place around them, they looked to North America as a land of opportunity. Many Yorkshire and Cumberland Methodists, for example, were also attracted to Nova Scotia by their desire for religious freedom. The immigrants felt their goals could be reached by taking advantage of the unclaimed land still available in North America to rebuilt the family farm. On the American side, land speculators promoted colonization projects and migration schemes to entice settlers who would subdue the wilderness and render the land profitable. Again, the profit motive was a strong force shaping the pattern of human movement.

Bailyn retraces the histories of immigrants to Nova Scotia and the American South in some detail. In both areas, settlers were drawn by the advertised prospect of land ownership or cheap rentals in a world free of the power of the landlords. For immigrants to Nova Scotia, the claims of the speculators misrepresented the real-life hardships they actually faced. The typical story was that of the family's assembled resources being exhausted in the process of transplantation and the family being involved in a struggle for mere survival. Eventually, after years of labour in often harsh conditions, they would establish a secure position in the frontier world.

In the last section, Bailyn concentrates further on the individual experiences of entrepreneurs and immigrants, outlining their hopes and motivations, successes and failures in the New York region. Again, land speculation was interpreted as the driving force behind the opening of new lands and the expansion of American settlement. Each promoter and emigration organizer worked independently and Bailyn illustrates the variety of processes by which transfer and relocation of people was accomplished, as well as the range of experiences the immigrants endured. He concludes by characterizing British North America as "a poor man's country in which some grew rich" and which, most importantly, offered the opportunity to become "independent."

In his *Voyagers to the West* Bailyn has, without question, masterfully recreated the process of immigration from Britain to North America on both a general and individual level. In so doing, he has outlined both the significant influence of the migrants on American life and the historical fact of America's considerable and growing impact on life in Britain. Bailyn argues, for example, that there was no typical New World community, but that the different character of migrants to various areas produced regional discordances in the evolving culture. On the other hand, the fact of emigration made Britain painfully aware of the changing nature of its relationship with its formerly insignificant colony.

There are some flaws, however, in Bailyn's important study. Bailyn seems overwhelmed by detail and does not entirely succeed in imposing a tight organizational framework on his material. He also surprisingly makes no mention of the role of political ideas in the lives of the new immigrants. Although the reader gains a general sense of the possible response of certain specific individuals to Revolutionary ideas, their political thought remains obscure. Given Bailyn's great interest in evolving Revolutionary ideology, it is surprising that there is so little stress placed on ideology in his new book. Although Bailyn concludes with an expression of the settlers' wish for personal independence, this statement is neither given meaning nor substance in any ideological sense.

It is certainly noteworthy that Bailyn has made such excellent use of recently-published and unpublished Nova Scotia and Prince Edward Island immigration studies. For example, he has sensitively integrated into his own book the descriptive analysis provided by Professor Bumsted's articles on Scots emigration to Prince Edward Island as well as Donald MacKay's *Scotland Farewell: The People of the Hector* (Toronto, 1980), Graeme Wynn's article "Late Eighteenth Century Agriculture on the Bay of Fundy Marshlands" (*Acadiensis*, 1979) and E.C. Wright's *Planters and Pioneers* (Hantsport, 1978). Furthermore, Bailyn has underscored some of the real scholarly merits of James Snowdon's 1974 University of New Brunswick M.A. thesis, "Footprints in the Marsh Mud: Politics and Land Settlement in the Township of Sackville, 1760-1800." Bailyn has also, it should be pointed out, made excellent use of Brebner's *Neutral Yankees.*

Thus Bailyn in his *Voyages to the West* has accomplished two things with respect to the Maritimes in the 1770s. First, he has pulled the region into the mainstream of American scholarship. And, second, he has shown an exemplary awareness of some of the recent scholarship concerning Nova Scotia and Prince Edward Island, a greater awareness than most Central Canadian historians have shown in recent years.

Without question, the American book which has made the best and most effective use of the new and post-Brebner eighteenth-century Nova Scotia scholarship, and the Louisbourg Archives in particular, is John Robert McNeill's *Atlantic Empires of France and Spain: Louisbourg and Havana, 1700-1763* (Chapel Hill, 1985). McNeill's *Atlantic Empires* is a boldly conceived study in comparative history; some reviewers have described it as brilliantly innovative and a model for other historians to emulate. McNeill selected Havana and Louisbourg for comparison, as he put it, "not because their internal histories are especially similar — they are not — but because their assigned roles within their respective imperial systems were nearly identical, as were the problems of economic and defense policy." Their similar assigned imperial roles were affected by what is referred to and a fundamental "similarity in their geographic positions."[30] According to McNeill — and this is the central thesis of his study:

> Both faced numerous, energetic, and generally hostile British neighbors. Both were well situated for a lively entrepot trade within their imperial systems, and an equally lively smuggling trade without. Both served as the military, commercial, demographic, and administrative centre of a strategic island. Both fulfilled administrative responsibilities in adjacent settlements. Each was nominally subject to a higher authority (the Viceroy of New Spain and the

---

30 McNeill, xv.

Governor of New France, respectively), but both found themselves largely autonomous in practice. Both were heavily and expensively fortified and thus became symbols of the might of their colonial empires. And last, but far from least, both channelled the production of highly valuable hinterlands to Europe. Of course, important differences existed. Europeans found Cuba a most unhealthy place and Louisbourg comparatively salubrious. Louisbourg's population never exceeded 5000 while Havana's approached 35,000 by 1760. But despite these and many other differences, imperial dilemmas and responsibilities in Havana and Louisbourg were very much the same. In comparing the two port cities I compare the ways in which different imperial systems responded to the same sorts of problems.[31]

Although there might have been some serious conceptual and evidentiary problems endured along the way, McNeill has been remarkably successful in bringing to fruition his scholarly ambitious and groundbreaking volume. There is, in my view, a ring of truth and perhaps muted frustration in McNeill's concluding paragraph:

The history of Louisbourg and Havana in the eighteenth century represents the interplay of imperial policy — conservative policy based on traditional methods — with colonial conditions. The population, geography, and natural resources of Cape Breton and Cuba, together with financial and naval limitations, defined the boundaries within which imperial policy could determine colonial history. Historians who have ignored these local factors in favour of imperial policy alone have misunderstood the importance of these island colonies, seeing their military roles as paramount. Other historians who have ignored imperial policy in order to concentrate on social and economic patterns in the new colonies (and precious few among these newer generation of historians have turned their attention to Cape Breton or Cuba) have failed to see the critical impact — often unintended — of imperial policies in shaping colonial destinies.[32]

I am sure that McNeill is not, in any way, suggesting that younger scholars should turn their attention to Louisbourg and Havana as the centers of a crucially important unfolding historical dramas. Rather, with some justification, he is implicitly and explicitly suggesting that comparative history which cuts across national boundaries is both significant and

31 McNeill, xvi.
32 McNeill, 208.

suggestive. And his work, in my view, points in the direction in which, at least, some of the new eighteenth-century Nova Scotia scholarship, as well as American scholarship, should move.

McNeill's *Atlantic Empires*, owes a great deal — as his footnotes underscore — to what has been recently called "the Golden Age of Louisbourg historical scholarship."[33] It is scholarship that has been significantly encouraged by the ongoing "Louisbourg Project" and also by the fact that, being on the periphery of the Brebner paradigm, it has a great deal of freedom for growth and experimentation. During the past two decades, scores of historical researchers have worked on the "Louisbourg Project." But it has not been until recent years that their work has resulted in major monographs. The evidence suggests that the so-called "Golden Age" of Louisbourg historical scholarship is only beginning. At its best, this scholarship is absolutely first-rate, even within the general context of eighteenth-century North American and Anglo-French historiography. At its worst, it is second or third rate, even within the far more narrow confines of eighteenth-century Nova Scotia studies.

The best of these books, by far, is Christopher Moore's *Louisbourg Portraits: Life in an Eighteenth-Century Garrison Town* (Toronto, 1982). His imaginative reconstruction of Louisbourg's social life is both innovative and brilliantly executed. He has made remarkable use of the available primary sources, fleshing into two-dimensional perspectives often obscure personages from Louisbourg's eighteenth-century historical record. And he has done so by locating them and their lives firmly within the framework of recent historiographical developments. With good reason Professor James Axtell has contended that Moore's book "with deceptive ease" has "set new standards for scholarly and popular history." According to Axtell, "Moore has crafted a personalization of the past that, if it could be widely emulated, would do much to bring back a deserting audience to history."[34] *Louisbourg Portraits* is therefore perceived as a most unusual Canadian book; it is historical writing which American scholars not only emulate but also "envy."

This same point, however, cannot be made concerning A.J.B. Johnston's two books, *The Summer of 1744: A Portrait of Life in 18th-Century Louisbourg* (Ottawa, 1983) and *Religion in Life at Louisbourg, 1773-1758* (Montreal, 1984) or of Bernard Pothier's *Course a L'Acadie: Journal de campagne de François Du Pont Duvivier en 1744* (Moncton, 1982), each of which, for different reasons, is a disappointing study. B.A. Balcom's slim 88-page *The Cod Fishery of Isle Royale, 1713-1758* (Ottawa, 1984), on the other hand, though not as significant or as suggestive as Moore's study, is nevertheless very well researched and on the whole cogently and lucidly

---

33 See my "Louisbourg Revisited," *Acadiensis*, XIV, 1 (Autumn, 1984), 117.

34 *William and Mary Quarterly*, XLI, 1(January 1984), 154.

written. It is a noteworthy addition to eighteenth-century North American economic history. Balcom is particularly impressive in his discussion of the economics of the fishery and its major participants. He convincingly argues that the Isle Royale cod fishery was of greater value to the Mother Country than the fur trade of New France. Moreover, "dried fish exports formed a crucial link in the establishing of a triangular flow of goods between France, Isle Royale and the French West Indies."[35] Balcom has succeeded, in a rather understated manner, in questioning the central role given to the fur trade in any discussion of France's involvement in North America. This is no mean achievement.

Another historiographical project, this one funded by the United Baptist Convention of the Atlantic Provinces and not Ottawa, has also significantly affected the historiography of eighteenth-century Nova Scotia and New Brunswick. And, like the recent outburst of Louisbourg studies, the Baptist Heritage in Atlantic Canada series is located on the outer edges of Brebner's organizational framework. Thus far seven volumes have been published and each of these throw considerable light on the Yankee-Planter religious heritage, especially during and immediately following the American Revolution. The series, together with other studies associated with it, have, it has been correctly observed, resulted in the "Transformation of Maritime Baptist Historiography," and the confident locating of these studies on the so-called "cutting edge" of the discipline of religious history in Canada.[36] In 1979 G.E. Levy's *The Diary and Related Writings of the Reverend Joseph Dimock (1768-1846)* was published, followed in 1980 by B.M. Moody's collection of essays entitled *Repent and Believe* which contained among other things a long article on Harris Harding, "From New Light to Baptist." The following year witnessed the publication of B.C. Cuthbertson's valuable *Journal of the Reverend John Payzant (1749-1843)* and in 1982 *The Life of and Journal of the Rev. Mr. Henry Alline*, as edited by James Beverley and Barry Moody. In 1982 G.A. Rawlyk's *The New Light Letters and Spiritual Songs* was published and in the following year D.G. Bell's *The Newlight Baptist Journals of James Manning and James Innis*. In my view, this last book is the most important study published thus far about religion in pre-Confederation New Brunswick. The most recent volume in the series, *The Sermons of Henry Alline*, was published in 1986.

It should also be kept in mind that Gordon Stewart's Champlain Society's edition, *Documents Relating to the Great Awakening in Nova Scotia, 1760 -1791*, was published in 1982, followed two years later by Rawlyk's *Ravished By The Spirit* (Montreal, 1984). In addition, there has

---

35 Balcom, 65.

36 D. Bell, "All Things New: The Transformation of Maritime Baptist Historiography," *The Nova Scotia Historical Review*, 4, 2 (November 1984), 70-81.

been a basic reassessment of the immediate post-Revolutionary impact of Methodism on Nova Scotia in Rawlyk's 1985 article on "Freeborn Garrettson and Nova Scotia,"[37] and in A.B. Robertson's suggestive "Charles Inglis and John Wesley: Church of England and Methodist Relations in Nova Scotia in the Late Eighteenth Century."[38] David Bell, moreover, has continued his ground-breaking work on religion in early New Brunswick with his "Charles Inglis and the Anglican Clergy of Loyalist New Brunswick" also published in 1987.[39]

There have been a significant number of other articles dealing with the immediate Loyalist impact on New Brunswick and Nova Scotia. In fact, the evidence is overwhelming that Loyalist Maritime historiography is far more sophisticated and richly textured than is Upper Canadian Loyalist historiography. In the last few years very little of consequence has been written about the Upper Canadian Loyalist experience. According to Norman Knowles, writing in 1987, Upper Canadian Loyalist scholarship, despite the Loyalist Bicentennial celebrations "had not really progressed far beyond earlier studies by such historians as J.J. Talman, Adam Shortt, S.F. Wise and Gerald Craig."[40] Perhaps the only exception to this general rule is Jane Errington's recently published volume *The Eagle, the Lion and Upper Canada: A Developing Upper Canadian Ideology, 1784 to 1828* (Montreal, 1987).

On the other hand, Maritime Loyalist historical writing has taken a giant step forward in recent years. Black Loyalists, for example, have had two volumes published about their collective experience: E.G. Wilson, *The Loyal Blacks* (New York, 1976) and James Walker, *The Black Loyalists* (New York, 1976). In 1983 Brian Cuthbertson published *The Loyalist Governor: Biography of Sir John Wentworth*, a book criticized because of the "simplified version of Nova Scotia," presented and the "excessive claims about Wentworth's influence,"[41] as well as the lack of research on the New Hampshire background. The same criticism about the lack of American background cannot be levelled at Cuthbertson's second Loyalist biography, *The First Bishop: A Biography of Charles Inglis* (Halifax, 1987). In this study, as was the case with his 1986 article "Faithful Missionary: The Young Charles Inglis,"[42] Cuthbertson convincingly argues that while in New Jersey Inglis was a Methodist Evangelical. This

---

37 In R.P. Heitzenrater, ed., *Reflections upon Methodism During the American Bicentennial* (Dallas, 1985), 105-21.

38 *The Nova Scotia Historical Review*, 7, 1(June 1987), 48-63.

39 *The Nova Scotia Historical Review*, 7, 1(June 1987), 25-47.

40 See N. Knowles, "The Loyalist Tradition and the Adolphustown Centennial Celebrations of 1884," M.A. thesis, Queen's University, 1987, 2.

41 See D. Wilson, "The Ambivalent Loyalists," *Acadiensis*, XIV, 1(Autumn 1984), 125-6.

42 See Nova Scotia Historical Society *Collections*, 42 (1986), 99-120.

fact may tell us a great deal about his subsequent intensely negative attitude towards Methodists and New Lights in Nova Scotia and New Brunswick. Two other major books about the Nova Scotia Loyalist experience have been published during the past four years: Marion Robertson's *Kings Bounty: A History of Early Shelburne Nova Scotia* (Halifax, 1983) — a much neglected volume — and Neil MacKinnon's *This Unfriendly Soil: The Loyalist Experience in Nova Scotia, 1783-1791* (Montreal, 1985), a mature and persuasively-argued study.

Even though E.C. Wright's "landmark work"[43] *The Loyalist of New Brunswick* was published in 1955, it did not discourage two recent scholars from reassessing the Loyalist impact on New Brunswick. In 1983 the thoroughly researched and cogently written *Early Loyalist Saint John: The Origin of New Brunswick Politics, 1783-1786* (Fredericton, 1983) by David Bell appeared, and in 1984 Ann Condon's much revised Harvard Ph.D. dissertation was published under the title *The Envy of the American States: The Loyalist Dream for New Brunswick* (Fredericton, 1984). Condon's work was history from the top down while Bell's was history from the bottom up even though his concluding section attempted to thrust the concept of Loyalty into the mainstream of nineteenth- and twentieth-century New Brunswick political culture. There is also, of course, Bumsted's valuable treatment of the Loyalists and Prince Edward Island to be found in his *Land, Settlement, and Politics on Eighteenth-Century Prince Edward Island* (Montreal, 1987). This book's treatment of Loyalism should be carefully viewed through the revisionist prism provided by Bumsted's *Understanding the Loyalists* (Sackville, 1986), a fleshing out of the central thesis of his 1979 article "Loyalists and Nationalist: An Essay on the Problem of Definition."[44]

Is it merely a coincidence that where there is little evidence of Brebner's influence on eighteenth-century Maritime historiography, significant advances have been made in recent years? Perhaps not and perhaps it is unfair to blame Brebner for discouraging further research in a field that he had mined so thoroughly. Indeed it might also be argued that a basic reassessment of the Yankee immigration into Nova Scotia in the 1760s and 1770s did not take place because of Andrew Hill Clark. For at least a decade, in my view, Clark's declaration at the beginning of his magisterial *Acadia: The Geography of Early Nova Scotia to 1760* (Madison, 1968) frightened historians, especially those interested in historical demography, from this area of study. Clark underscored the fact that his *Acadia* was only "the first" volume of "two which will be devoted to an exposition of geographical change in the lands of Nova Scotia before that province,

---

43 See the very positive assessment of E.C. Wright's work in Bumsted, *Understanding the Loyalists*.

44 *Canadian Review of Studies in Nationalism*, VI (1979), 218-32.

rather painfully evolved out of Acadia and Isle Royal in the eighteenth century, joined most of the other units of British North America in the later nineteenth to form the Dominion of Canada.[45] I must confess that I discouraged not a few graduate students from moving into what I considered to be Clark's field. I was told in 1969 and the early 70s that the sequel would be imminently published — that all the maps were completed and that it was only a matter of time before the page proofs were returned to the publisher. When Clark died in 1975 the manuscript was still not close to being completed. By that time, most graduate students and other scholars interested in the eighteenth-century Maritime experience were being drawn to other areas, away from what J.S. Martel once called "the Boston-Bay of Fundy axis,"[46] to religion, Loyalism, Cape Breton and Prince Edward Island. And in the process they have helped to reshape the contours of eighteenth-century Maritime scholarship, even though most mainline Central and Western Canadian historians seem to be oblivious to the fact. And, moreover, because of the way in which the so-called leading edge of scholarship has in recent years cut through the century, the Planter period beckons the venturesome and the brave.[47]

---

45 Clark, vii.

46 MacNutt, "Introduction" to Brebner, *The Neutral Yankees*, xvi.

47 There is a good overview of the 1750s and 1780s in J.G. Reid's recently published *Six Crucial Decades: Times of Change in the History of the Maritimes* (Halifax, 1987).

New England Planters
at the Public Archives of Nova Scotia

Barry Cahill
Manuscripts Archivist
Public Archives of Nova Scotia

One of the more constructive results of the Loyalist bicentenary a few years ago was the rekindling of scholarly interest in archival sources for the writing of Loyalist history. Curiously, the Planter bicentenary over two decades earlier failed to evoke similar scholarly interest. My purpose here is to survey the holdings of one provincial archives for material relating to that group of pre-Loyalist immigrants who are now entrenched in the *Nova Scotia Subject Headings Authority* as "New England Planters." Anyone who has tried in a general way to research their history at PANS soon realizes that Planters have never been quite so popular with historians as Loyalists. The unexceptioned use of the term "pre-Loyalist," for example, presupposes a view of the history of Nova Scotia in which the coming of the Loyalists was the decisive event. The same cannot be said of the various groups of pre-Loyalists. If one checks the Miscellaneous card file in the Manuscripts Reading Room under "New England Planters" one finds only two cards. Obviously, that does not give an accurate indication of Planter sources at PANS — several, in fact, are entered under "Miscellaneous Townships"; nor does it mean that no one, apart from John Bartlet Brebner, has been interested enough in Planter history to have done sustained archival research on the subject. Quite the opposite is the case: distinguished contributions have been made by non-professional township and county historians and, more recently, by historical geographers, beginning with Andrew Hill Clark in the 1950s.[1] It does mean, however, that New England Planters have not been researched with the same enthusiasm and sophistication as either Loyalist or other pre-Loyalist immigrants easily identifiable as a group, such as the "foreign Protestants." A biased scholarly coinage, which the term "pre-Loyalist" is, at the very least implies that no distinction need be made among pre-Loyalist immigrants, where in fact there were three clearly defined groups, of which the New England Planters were the third, the latest and the largest.

The arrival in Nova Scotia of thousands of New Englanders, towards

---

1   See Andrew Hill Clark, *The Geography of Early Nova Scotia to 1760* (Madison, WI, 1968); and Graeme Wynn, "W.F. Ganong, A.H. Clark and the Historical Geography of Maritime Canada," *Acadiensis*, 10, 2(Spring 1981), 5-28. An outstanding recent example of the genre is Debra Anne McNabb, "Land and Families in Horton Township, N.S., 1760-1830," MA Thesis, University of British Columbia, 1986.

the end of the French and Indian War and the declaration of peace among the European powers, was the fourth great demographic event in the history of British Nova Scotia — the first being the founding of Halifax in 1749; the second the immigration of German and Swiss Protestants in the early 1750s; the third, the expulsion of most of the indigenous Acadian population in 1755, which created both the need and the opportunity for emigration from New England. Given the breadth and diversity of the subject, I shall confine my attention to the period when the Planter townships came into being, i.e., 1759 to 1764; to those townships located in peninsular Nova Scotia or in the trans-border area; and mainly — though not exclusively — to contemporary original documents which are available either as hard copy or on microform at PANS.

The New England Planters were not an accidental phenomenon, but a deliberately planned result of official British government policy for Nova Scotia. This policy was initiated in Halifax; agreed to and encouraged in Whitehall; and executed mostly in Massachusetts, Connecticut and Rhode Island. The very nature of the case seems to require a heavy dependence on government records to research Planter history. In his newly published biography of Bishop Charles Inglis, Brian Cuthbertson makes the point that a common problem which confronts those who attempt to write the history of the Loyalist and post-Loyalist years in Nova Scotia is the necessary over-reliance on official correspondence which results from the scarcity of personal papers.[2] What is true for the later period is truer still for the pre-Loyalist. The farther back in Nova Scotia's history one goes, the fewer documents of a non-governmental nature one is likely to encounter. It is just possible, however, to lessen the harmful effects of this over-reliance on government records by making allowances for the bias inherent in them. Authors of documents, whether writing as private individuals or as government officials, had vested interests or axes to grind, and their point of view is reflected in which subjects they addressed; what they said about them; how they said it; and whom they said it to.

Planter history may be considered to have begun in October 1758, when Governor Charles Lawrence issued a proclamation soliciting proposals from would-be settlers and providing a description of the lands. A copy of this document was forwarded by Lawrence to the Lords of Trade, and is among the Colonial Office Papers in the Public Record Office.[3] This first proclamation has always been overshadowed by the longer and more detailed second proclamation of 11 January 1759, which was issued in response to the various questions raised by the first, and which prospective settlers had been asking of Lawrence's agents at Boston and New York —

---

2   Brian Cuthbertson, *The First Bishop: A Biography of Charles Inglis* (Halifax, 1987), 282.

3   CO 217/16/311, Public Record Office (hereafter PRO).

concerning "particular encouragement," the bounty of provisions, quantity of land, quit rent, form of government, taxes and religious toleration. Copies of the second proclamation are to be found among Colonial Office Papers;[4] among House of Assembly papers collected and bound by the Records Commission,[5] predecessor of the Public Archives of Nova Scotia; and in a volume of miscellaneous proclamations collected by the Records Commission.[6] Both proclamations, of course, were entered *verbatim* in the minute-book of the Council at Halifax.[7] The number of copies of this document which are available at PANS indicates both its contemporary administrative value, and its perceived importance by archivists conversant with history — not only the province's, but also their own family's. Thomas Beamish Akins (1809-1891), the Records Commissioner, was himself the grandson of an original grantee of one of the Planter townships.[8]

Governor Lawrence's plan called for thirteen townships of 100,000 acres, twelve square miles, each to be settled over a period of three years with 2,550 families or 12,750 individuals.[9] The township was a quintessential New England concept which had been introduced into Nova Scotia by emigrants from Massachusetts soon after the founding of Halifax. It was a model which could not altogether be dispensed with — the farthest thing from Lawrence's mind, of course, was that public officials in the new townships might be elected at a meeting of freeholders rather than appointed by himself — because the township was the fundamental institution of local government in New England, and was therefore a necessary inducement to prospective settlers.[10] Such a structure generated its own types of record: not only the township grant, but also the township book, which was both the minute-book of meetings, and the official register of vital statistics, proprietors, lots, cattle marks, etc. It is understandable, therefore, that Planter history has traditionally been studied township by township within a county, and family by family within a township.

PANS holdings of Planter township books include Annapolis, Barrington, Chester, Cornwallis, Cumberland, Falmouth, Granville, Horton,

---

4   CO 217/16/315, PRO.

5   RG 1, Vol. 310, doc. 3, Public Archives of Nova Scotia (hereafter PANS).

6   RG 1, Vol. 346, doc. 10, PANS.

7   RG 1, Vol. 187, pp. 30ff., PANS.

8   Stephen Akin was a grantee of Falmouth Township in 1761. The genealogy is in John V. Duncanson, *Falmouth: A New England Township in Nova Scotia* (Belleville, Ont., 1983), 161-2.

9   Lords of Trade to the King, 20 December 1759, CO 218/5/195-200, PRO.

10 On the subject generally, see D.C. Harvey, "The Struggle for the New England Form of Township Government in Nova Scotia," in Canadian Historical Association *Report* (1933), 15-22.

Liverpool, Newport, Onslow, Sackville, Truro and Yarmouth.[11] Several of these documents go back to the very beginning of Planter settlement, and indeed beyond — into New England, whence the Planters themselves came; others date from the 1770s or later. PANS holdings consist for the most part of microfilm copies or transcripts; the originals often are held either privately or in the custody of a town or municipal office or the county court-house — or at a national or local repository other than PANS. The Granville and Newport township books, for example, are at the National Archives in Ottawa;[12] the Cumberland township book is at Fort Beausejour National Historic Park. The originals of six Planter township books are at PANS: Cornwallis, Falmouth, Liverpool, Truro and Yarmouth in MG 4,[13] and Onslow in RG 1[14] — the only such document to be preserved in that collection. Though for purposes of archival arrangement, the township books are now considered to be non-governmental records, and have thus been placed in a "manuscript group" rather than a "record group," they are public records within the meaning of the Act, which has stood on the statute-book in one form or other since 1914. In that year, the Legislature passed "An Act in respect to the Preservation of Court Records."[15] According to section 1 of the Act, which comprises section 6 of today's Public Records Act:

> All the papers, documents and record books of the Court of Sessions, of the Inferior Court of Common Pleas, and also of the old townships constituted about the year 1760...are hereby vested in the Province, which is hereby empowered to take possession of the same, and also to take proper measures for their permanent preservation and for placing them where they will be available for investigation and students of history.[16]

The passage of this Act preceded by some fifteen years the formal establishment of the Public Archives of Nova Scotia, an aspect of the mandate of which is to collect and preserve the public records of the province. "[T]he old townships constituted about the year 1760" are the Planter townships, of course, and I shall be focusing on their records and papers both sessional and judicial.

The thirteen original townships projected by Governor Lawrence in 1759 were Horton, Cornwallis, Falmouth, Onslow, Granville, Annapolis,

---

11 These are divided between "Micro. Places." and MG 4, PANS. For precise references, see the finding aid concerned.

12 MG 9, B9, No. 20, National Archives of Canada (hereafter NAC).

13 MG 4, Vols. 18; 218; 180; 150A; 167, PANS.SFB

14 RG 1, Vol. 361 1/2, PANS.

15 4 Geo. 5, C. 6 (1914).

16 *Revised Statutes of Nova Scotia*, 1967, C. 253.

Cumberland, Amherst, Sackville, Tinmouth, Liverpool, Barrington and Yarmouth.[17] Omissions from the list rather beg the question of whether, for the sake of definition, a New England Planter had to be a native of New England. Onslow, and then Londonderry and Truro — the Cobequid Townships — were settled by Ulstermen who had been brought out to New England by Alexander McNutt. Tinmouth, moreover, was stillborn, though to be resurrected in 1762 as (New) Dublin Township and settled, again, by Northern Irish whom Colonel McNutt had this time brought over directly from Ulster. Also to be added to the list of those Planter townships which were erected after 1759 are Chester (or Shoreham), Newport (or East Falmouth) and Wilmot. Among the oversize manuscript documents in PANS are the original grants of all the Planter townships in peninsular Nova Scotia except Amherst, Barrington, Cumberland, Falmouth, Newport, Wilmot and Yarmouth.[18] The township grant *per se* describes the boundaries and names the grantees; registered or "effective" grants may be found in the Land Grant books, which are on microfilm at PANS,[19] the originals being at the provincial Crown Lands Records Centre in Dartmouth. Difficulties with filling up the number of grantees, or with processing the township grants, meant that there were often two grants, and, in the case of Cumberland, as many as three. Elsewhere in the Crown Lands papers at PANS are brief statistical reports for the early 1760s of Cornwallis, Falmouth and Horton Townships.[20]

In terms of the sheer survival of records, pride of place undoubtedly belongs to Horton Township, which is better represented in PANS holdings than any of the other Planter townships. The original grant of Horton Township was dated 22 May 1759. A copy of this document was sent by Governor Lawrence to the Lords of Trade, who subsequently appended it to their long and detailed "Representation" to the King on the subject of filling vacant Acadian lands with settlers from New England.[21] RG 1, Volume 362, for example, is a register of grants for the township, arranged by the grantee, in 197 folios, with a contemporary index at the beginning. Volume 177 is a seventy-page book of abstracts from the registrar's office at Horton, between 1765 and 1775. It gives the date of registration; the names of the parties and the date of the deed; the lands conveyed, and for what price: an arrangement made all the more accessible

---

17 Lawrence to Lords of Trade, 20 September 1759, CO 217/16/345, PRO.

18 O/S No. 209 (Annapolis), 212 (Granville), 217 (Onslow), 223 (Truro), 239 (Cornwallis), 246 (Horton), 258 (Shoreham [Chester]), 263 (Liverpool), 267 (Sackville).

19 Micro. Places. Nova Scotia. Land Grants, PANS.

20 RG 20, Series C, Box 89, doc. 1, 2, PANS; cf. "A List of the Proprietors of the Township of Liverpool With Their Number In Family Respectively" [1761], RG 20, Series C, Box 43, doc. 1 (I am grateful to Elizabeth Mancke for bringing this item to my attention).

21 See Note 9 above.

by a contemporary index at the beginning by name of conveyor. The Horton township book is extant, though apparently in private hands. PANS has both a microfilm copy of the original, and a nineteenth-century transcription.[22]

Elsewhere in RG 1 are documents which concern the Planter townships, among others, more or less as a group. Pre-eminent among them are the "General Return of Townships," made in 1767, and the Census of 1770, both in Volume 443. The former covers thirty townships in Nova Scotia and what is now New Brunswick, including all the Planter communities. Cumulative statistical data is given for each township in six principal categories, which are then divided and subdivided. Under the subject heading "Numbers in each Family" is entered how many males and females. Under "Religion," Protestant and Roman Catholic. Under "Country of Origin," English, Scotch, Irish, Americans, German and other foreigners, and Acadians. Under "Stock and Substance," cattle, mills and vessels. Under "Produce of the last Year," the various grains, etc., in bushels, hundredweight and barrels. Under "Alteration of Inhabitants since last year," the number born, died, arrived and left the province. Apart from the necessary addition of the "Name of master or mistress of the family," the subject headings for the Census of 1770 are nearly identical to those on the General Return of 1767. There are fewer statistical subdivisions, however, especially as regards the composition of households. The seventeen extant returns for 1770 include all the Planter townships except Chester, Cornwallis, Liverpool, Newport and Wilmot. The return for Yarmouth, however, is dated 1773. The General Return of 1767 and the Census of 1770 notwithstanding, the "return" or "state" is probably the most frequently occurring type of semi-official record which documents the early history of the Planter townships.

Volumes 221 and 222, two of a long series in RG 1 entitled "Manuscript Documents of Nova Scotia," run from 1751 to 1791, and from 1757 to 1781, respectively, and contain diverse material on most of the Planter townships. Volume 222, with more than ninety Planter-related items, is especially valuable. There are lists of proprietors and lots; memorials, reports, returns, warrants and writs of partition. Each of these volumes has been fully calendared.[23]

Volume 359 contains lists of grantees, draft grants, memoranda, memorials and petitions dating from 1759 — relating to Horton, Cornwallis, Granville, Cumberland, Onslow, Truro, Liverpool and Chester. The second part of Volume 360 is a fifty-page register of grantees arranged alphabetically by township. Compiled in 1760 or 1761, the register gives the proprietor's name, the township and, in some cases, the

22   MG 4, Vol. 74; Micro. Places. Horton, PANS.

23   The calendars are in RG 1, Vol. 250, pp. 115 and 160, respectively.

number of shares. All but three of the original thirteen townships are represented.

Volume 361 is made up of papers connected with the partition of the townships of Falmouth, Horton, Newport, Yarmouth, Chester and Onslow. There are lists of grantees; writs of partition issued out of the Supreme Court at Halifax; and petitions requesting them. Of particular interest is an undated document in the handwriting of Isaac Deschamps entitled, "A List of the Grantees in the Township of Falmouth with the Numbers and Contents of the Respective Lots drawn by, or allotted to them, in the Several Divisions agreed on by the Proprietors." Precise information about the size and distribution of the lots is given under eight different headings.[24]

Volume 374, a so-called "Land Book" of about three hundred pages, covers the years 1760 through 1767 and gives both the names of proprietors and descriptions and boundaries of township grants. There is an alphabetical list by name of township at the end. Unfortunately, the first fifty pages or so are missing.

Volume 473 1/2 is a two-hundred-page alphabetical and chronological index to Crown grants of land in Nova Scotia from 1725 to 1768. Though neither contemporary nor original, this document is a finding aid appropriately limited in scope and handily divided into five parts, each part having its own alphabetical arrangement with the names in chronological order. The second, third and fourth parts, which cover the years 1759 through 1763, are especially useful to Planter historians. The information given includes the name of the grantee; number of acres and district; date of grant or conveyance; and book and page where recorded. The cumulative Crown land grants index for 1730 through 1937, on the other hand, which researchers normally consult, distinguishes only among the names of the grantees; there are no periodic subdivisions.

Volume 204 contains the minutes of Council from May 1761 to September 1763 relative to Crown grants of land. Though not specifically concerned with Planters, this volume nevertheless contains much useful information about them, often in the form of petitions presented to the Council and summarized or abstracted in the minute-book. The latter part of it may be used in conjunction with the land papers in the first box of RG 20, Series A. These commence in 1763, and consist of petitions, warrants of survey, draft grants, etc.

Of continuous importance and interest, especially for establishing the broad historical context from an official or quasi-official perspective, are not only the Halifax and Whitehall dispatches in CO 217 and 218,[25]

---

24 There is no document number.

25 Micro. Miscellaneous. Colonial Office, PANS.

respectively; but also the Executive Council minutes,[26] "inland" letter-books,[27] and miscellaneous Assembly Papers in RG 1 and RG 5, Series A.[28] Halifax dispatches for the years 1759 through 1764 frequently describe in detail the progress of the Planter townships and enclose documents, such as returns, which are concerned with specific townships. A dispatch from Lieutenant-Governor Jonathan Belcher to the Lords of Trade in September 1762, for example, enclosed returns of inhabitants and livestock for Yarmouth Township, Barrington Township and the area in between.[29] The names of householders and numbers in each family were given, together with a "General Return of the Inhabitants in the Several Townships Settled at Cape Sable." A dispatch in January of the same year enclosed an eighteen-page "Description of the Several Towns in the Province of Nova Scotia...," which had been drawn up by Surveyor-General Charles Morris in 1761. This work concluded with an abstract showing the number of inhabitants and acreage of cleared upland marsh in each township.[30] Comparable with this is a statistical return from 1763, which analysed each of the nineteen townships — fourteen were Planter — under number of families; and acreage of marshland, cleared upland and woodland.[31]

Despite limitations of space, and my declared emphasis on government records at the various levels — imperial, provincial and township — it would not be possible to leave the subject of the Planters at the Public Archives of Nova Scotia without mentioning the unique "Chipman Papers" in MG 1, Volumes 181-218. The title of this collection may not perhaps be the best guide to its provenance, as the papers are by no means confined to the Rhode Island Planter, Handley Chipman, and his descendants — many of whom were prominent in the official life of Kings County. The collection seems to have originated with the Connecticut Planter Robert Denison, whose name is first among the grantees of Horton township.[32] Denison was a judge of the Common Pleas and was elected MHA for Kings County in 1761; already an elderly man when he came to Nova Scotia, his brief official career is well documented in the Chipman Papers. This magnificent collection covers a century of Planter

---

26   RG 1, Vol. 188 covers the years 1757 through 1766.

27   RG 1, Vol. 136 covers the years 1760 through 1784.

28   The Assembly Papers have all been calendared, those in RG 1, Vol. 301ff. twice: by T.B. Akins and Margaret Ells. The calendars are available in the Manuscripts and Public Records reading room on the third floor of PANS.

29   CO 217/19/134ff., PRO.

30   CO 217/18/246-263. PRO.

31   "State of the Settlements in the Province of Nova Scotia 1763," RG 1, Vol. 219, doc. 118, PANS.

32   CO 217/16/334, PRO.

history, articulated through different townships and families and types of record. Represented are not only the Kings County townships of Horton and Cornwallis, but also, at least until 1781, two of the three townships which were joined together to create the new county of Hants: Falmouth and Newport. Thematically, the papers range over the whole gamut of official life in the Planter townships on Minas Basin. So numerous are the examples of the various types of record generated in the 1760s and 1770s by local government — the Court of Sessions — and the administration of justice, whether by the Inferior Court of Common Pleas or by the Supreme Court on circuit, that the distinction between government records and family papers is effectively blurred. In the Chipman collection are the papers, both public and private, of individuals who held government office in Kings County; the collection very precisely documents their activity as office-holders, because it often contains the records of the bodies in which they served. Indeed, one might even say that the Chipman Papers preserve the records of township government in Horton, Cornwallis, Falmouth and Newport in the first two decades of their existence. Facilitating access to the thirty-seven boxes of documents is a two-volume content report, which has itself been indexed, in three parts, by the Kings Historical Society. What is undoubtedly the most important collection of its kind has therefore been made easily accessible.

On a much smaller scale than the Chipman Papers — they require only a single box — are the Deschamps Papers in MG 1, Volume 258. Isaac Deschamps, of course, was not a New England Planter, but rather a "foreign Protestant" who came to Halifax in 1749. He nevertheless was one of the original grantees of Newport Township in 1761; represented Falmouth and then Newport in the House of Assembly for over twenty years; and was intimately involved in Planter affairs in Kings County in the 1760s and 1770s. Like Robert Denison, he was made a judge of the Common Pleas in 1761, and held "numerous minor offices in the administrations of several townships."[33] Appointed a judge of the Supreme Court in 1770, Deschamps continued to travel regularly to Horton, which, as the seat of government for Kings County, was one of the original stations on the Supreme Court circuit. Several Planter townships are represented in the Deschamps Papers, just as Deschamps himself appears in the voluminous Chipman Papers. Of particular value is a "Return of the families settled in the Townships of Horton Cornwallis Falmouth & Newport...together with the Numbers of persons said families consist of and their Stock of Cattle and Grain and Roots raised the present year 1763."[34] Statistical information is given here under twelve different

---

33 Grace M. Tratt, "Deschamps, Isaac," *Dictionary of Canadian Biography*, V (1983), 251.

34 MG 1, Vol. 258, p. 125 [doc. 23], PANS.

headings.

Allowing for the official or at least semi-official nature of both the Deschamps Papers and the Chipman Papers, it is necessary to consider two further collections of government records in conjunction with which the latter, especially, can be used. I refer to the General Court of Quarter Sessions of the Peace (RG 34) and to the Inferior Court of Common Pleas (RG 37).[35] In no county, even Halifax, have the sessions records survived more extensively than Kings. There is a complete run of proceedings from 1760 to 1890, which includes fees of the clerk of the peace, subpoenas, warrants, assessments, etc. In no county except Halifax, moreover, have the original papers of suits brought before the Inferior Court survived from an earlier period than Kings. The earliest document in the collection is dated 1762; the latest, a docket of judgments, 1780. There is a long run of cases, especially for the years 1764 and 1765, and these have been arranged by year and then alphabetically by plaintiff. There are a few documents from the later 1760s and 1770s, but the major part of what has survived from those years appears to be in the Chipman Papers. The records of the Kings County Court of Sessions and Inferior Court of Common Pleas, not to mention the Supreme Court — after 1774, when the law establishing the circuit was enacted — are therefore complemented by the Chipman Papers. These three collections are all the more important in the 1760s and 1770s, because they comprehend four townships instead of two.

Finding aids at various levels of description facilitate access to most of the collections dealt with thus far. Other useful access points to Planter material in PANS are the "Biography" and "Genealogy" card files, which reference documents or collections of documents concerning both individuals and families. Useful, too, is the "Communities" card file, the main entry being the name of the township — whether or not it corresponds to a contemporary place-name. This file provides quick access to records and papers, especially in MG 4 — churches and communities. Worth mentioning here are the registers of St Paul's Church, Halifax, which include early records for Newport, Falmouth, Horton and Cornwallis. A special "rolodex" card file, arranged alphabetically by place-name and then by denomination or name of church, greatly facilitates access to church records. The registers of deeds and wills, moreover, which include all the Planter townships, are available on 3,282 reels of microfilm in the PANS Library. Though the extent, condition and organization of these records varies widely from registry to registry, they are a vital research tool — access to which is provided by a descriptive finding aid for both deeds (RG 47) and wills (RG 48).

The greater number and variety of archival sources for the Planter townships around Minas Basin, than elsewhere in the province, may be

---

35 RG 34-316, Series P, Vols. 1-12; RG 37, Series KI, Box 1, PANS.

reflected in the fact that the first work of academic scholarship in Planter history was a study entitled "Pre-Loyalist Settlements Around Minas Basin. A History of the Townships of Cornwallis, Horton, Falmouth, Newport, Windsor, Truro, Onslow and Londonderry, 1755-1783." Written in the early 1930s as an MA thesis by James Stuart Martell, a future Assistant Archivist of Nova Scotia, and under the direction of Professor Daniel Cobb Harvey, then Archivist, more than fifty years after its composition this work could still be described by a leading historical geographer as "a sound study."[36] With the exception of CO 217, and other materials available at PANS only on microfilm, the sources used in the preparation of Martell's thesis are the same as those mentioned above.

The fact that Planter sources are less diverse, less numerous and less well-known than Loyalist sources may account for their comparative underuse by professional historians. One does not speak of "pre-Planter" Nova Scotia or the "Planter" period in Nova Scotia history — though indeed there was one, between 1759 and 1783 — because it was the American Loyalists not the New England Planters who were considered the watershed migration. Nevertheless, it would perhaps be more satisfactory to regard the Planters as a culmination of the ten-year process of peopling — and depeopling — Nova Scotia, which had begun with the founding of Halifax and continued with the expulsion of the Acadians, than as mere prolegomenon to the immigration of the Loyalists. Planter history need not be viewed exclusively, if at all, from the Loyalist perspective in order to be understood and appreciated. Hindsight is anachronistic.

A survey of archival sources for Planter history rather begs the question of the types of use to which they can be put by historians. Statistical data such as one finds in census returns obviously lends itself to quantitative analysis. The data may be incomplete and inaccurate, however, and there is often no means by which it can be checked — or by which disagreements among contemporary original sources can be resolved. The categories in which statistical data is presented are subjective, moreover, and difficulties arise when evidence derived from such a source is analysed as if it were purely quantitative. The method of presentation is as important as the data itself, and the latter cannot be analysed except in relation to the former.

The use to which government records may have been put in their own time, in other words, their administrative value, is necessarily quite different from the use to which they must be put by historians, who are concerned with their evidential or informational — in other words, historical — value. To interpret or analyse a government record, however, involves understanding the nature and purpose of its creation; the

36 Graeme Wynn, "A Province Too Much Dependent on New England," *The Canadian Geographer*, 32, 2(Spring 1987), 111.

presuppositions and expectations of its creator; and whether it efficiently discharged its administrative function. The record cannot be taken out of context and treated as if its life-cycle had nothing to do with its historical significance. Whether evidence derived from government records is more or less impressionistic and biased than evidence derived from other contemporary original sources, it is the historian's responsibility to classify the evidence — regardless of its origin — and interpret it accordingly. The business of the archivist, on the other hand, is to identify and preserve the source materials and to facilitate access and retrieval. If the documents no longer exist, then they cannot be used. If they are known to exist, however, but cannot be identified, located or accurately described, then they still cannot be used — at least not to their full potential. By implication, therefore, archivists, whether they manage contemporary records or advise on how they were generated and managed in centuries past, are helping the historian do justice to the evidence. This paper has attempted to show the extent to which the historiography of the New England Planters depends on the sensitive interpretation of government records concerning them.

Genealogy, Migration and the Study of the Past

Terrence M. Punch
Chairman, Genealogical Institute of the Maritimes

The historian and the genealogist were once the same person, until specialization and professionalization of the former took the two along separate paths. While the specialist wrote and lectured in universities mainly of politics, the genealogist's work was discounted as snobbery or antiquarianism. In recent years we have witnessed the collapse or at least the weakening of the rather artificial walls among the several disciplines. Most of the territory claimed for history is being worked on by those using the techniques of anthropology, geography, economics, demography and sociology. So much has this been so that people sometimes speak of economic, political or social history as though these were fundamentally distinct, rather than being differing aspects of the study of humanity through time. I believe that genealogy as a system of research offers a further useful perspective for the study of past generations and their worlds.

It is no secret that some family historians conduct their research in a disorganized fashion. An examination of several "finished" family histories will reveal that their compilers had no particular idea of how to relate family or individual to some economic, social or political context. People lived within a milieu or setting in which families, events, even the actions of individuals, were related through cause and effect.

Historians supply information and interpretations in their writings, and one would expect that family historians would gather a knowledge of context from such literature, but all too often they do not profit from the written histories. One of several reasons for this failure may be that much of the best historical writing is not directed to the so-called general reader. Much of this literature seems to have been written by authors who have despaired of involving the common person in the study of the past. In doing so those historians may have misread the contemporary situation. Winthrop Bell's study of the settlement of foreign Protestants in Nova Scotia is a heavy, almost an encyclopedic, work; yet scores of family historians are clamouring for copies, almost at any price.

The psychological and sociological considerations which have propelled millions of North Americans into a quest for ancestry have also created a potential readership for works of history. This new audience wants to see how the society and the family reacted one on the other. These readers expect that those who possess the advantages of education and opportunity for research will both reveal and interpret the events of the past.

Recently we have experienced the emergence in our region of the genealogical historian. Usually, though not necessarily, university-trained, such people have been imbued with or have naturally had an interest in the community as a whole and in explanations that go beyond the obvious. Such genealogists want context and information beyond the skeletal family tree. They want to know how and why, as well as who and when. They practice macro-genealogy, a form of cooperative data extraction that arranges the information about all the people rather than merely one family. This person cares about methodology and has even developed a methodology that could be of service to social scientists. As a writer of research articles and guides I have found that one cannot simply produce a collection of lists, but one must present a methodology as an integral part of the work; otherwise one is writing an inventory and not a guide.

Since it is impractical for the academic historian to carry out detailed nominal record linkage for hundreds of families, it is the province of genealogical historians to educate family researchers in the techniques and methods of analysis and organization of information. By improving the critical standards of genealogical research and by drawing historical literature to the attention of family historians, the genealogical historian serves as a useful intermediary between some of the public and some of the valuable work being produced from within the university community. The academic world has much to offer to the family researcher, if only it is kept in mind that the audience may be unsophisticated in the arts of scholarship, but nonetheless seeks adequate information and logical explanations. In short, I am not urging anyone to write down to people, but simply to write for people whose lives are lived outside the academic milieu.

I began a few moments ago to speak of methodology and it is only right that I define genealogical methodology as a way of organizing information and of conducting research and trying out ideas. The emphasis is upon planning in the gathering of information, as well as observing an order and sequence in research. This method seeks for context and historical setting. People lived their lives within several communities (a farm, a fishing hamlet, a regiment, a factory, an extended family, a congregation, or any of the array of groupings within which one might have been found.) Each new setting wherein one finds an individual in the past will have left its traces or records. Explanations for many of the things that happened, for what people did, will emerge from an examination of many sources.

We can begin by considering genealogy as being, firstly, a motivation that will draw people into research of a more general nature, including the reading of sound historical literature. Secondly, it offers a methodology which can be utilized to generate new bodies of information designed to help in the investigation of specific questions about past generations. In compiling the record of even one family, the family historian performs a service. Marc Bloch observed that "one of the most difficult tasks of the historian is that of assembling those documents which he considers necessary." Has the family historian perhaps been doing this for us, all unawares? Because so many family historians have a pack-rat approach, they will look at anything if there is a chance they will find the family name mentioned therein. The British scholar, Alan Macfarlane, recognized this when he spoke of classes of records that were "little used by historians until a few years ago. Genealogists, however, were fully aware of their value."

Have I perhaps hinted that historical genealogists and the researcher in the social sciences at universities have something in common? If university faculty and students bring fresh points of view to the archival evidence and offer new interpretations of the recorded past, they require that there be conservation and preservation of that documentation, that inventories, catalogues and indexes be prepared to expedite research. If genealogists seek evidence for their specific projects, they also have these needs.

The genealogists tend to go further, however, by the particular nature of their endeavours, and bring into the repositories much documentation that might otherwise not have arrived there and become available to all, academics and amateurs, alike. In Nova Scotia I can cite as examples of this truth the discovery of the 1851 census for Pictou County, about two dozen sets of church records, hundreds of Bibles, pictures and maps, and copies of documentation in private hands. Of course, one's notion of history must involve an attempt to gain a progressively more thorough understanding of the human past for one to see the exciting challenge posed by new evidence becoming available.

If one common interest shared by amateur and academic is the identification, collection and preservation of documentation; another might be projects of a more or less demographic character. When we know the pattern of fertility, marriage and mortality among a people and have tried to identify and classify the factors which explain the emergent patterns, we may be able to explain more about past society than so far we have been able to do. Naturally we are not concerned simply with data quantification but also with the relationships of one group or community to others. We want to know, for instance, whether the patterns of family life and vital activity in colonial Nova Scotia were merely a continuation of the model in the former home, or whether the change in environment overcame the traditional forms. I think it is rather an indictment of our priorities that we know more about the evolution of buildings in this region than we do about the history of the family here. Was the family essentially a biological or an economic unit, or did this change from place to place, time to time, and if so or if not so, why did the evolution follow the patterns it did? Genealogists, or some of us, ask those sorts of questions; so do many scholars in other fields of study.

The contribution that genealogy might offer to the solution of these problems could be significant if we distinguish between family reconstitution and genealogy. In the former the rules of linking one record to another are relatively few and at some points arbitrary. Consequently demographers must accept a small level of error, much as statisticians allow for in political polling. Genealogists cannot accept such a rate of error, because familiar linkage can only be made on the basis of complete identification. Unless a precise linkage can be established among individuals, no reputable genealogist would consider the connection as having been made. In family reconstitution fewer records are used than in family history, hence the resultant linkages cannot be considered as being so firmly established in the former as in the latter.

Sound genealogical studies may open up new perspectives for the social sciences. As gradually we supplement demographic data by using other documentation we have at our disposal four sets of data concerning the development of a family: (a) its demographic behaviour (especially its fertility); (b) its geographic mobility; (c) its matrimonial alliances; and (d) its social standing, related to the accumulation of wealth, inheritance and changes in occupation. If we had scores of well-documented representative genealogies, we might solve some of the problems which continue to concern scholars who are too often obliged to limit the scope of their studies either to narrow topics or to further development of existing studies.

The study of migration such as that of eight thousand people from New England to greater Nova Scotia in the generation before the outbreak of the American Revolution offers possibilities for cooperation and mutual assistance. The demographer or the scholar practicing family reconstitution is particularly handicapped here, due to a shortage of banks of data which contain complete information of the migrations of large numbers of families or individuals. If one studies a single city or township, its records rarely contain specific references to the origin or the destination of the people who come and go. The evidence needed to follow people beyond the specific jurisdiction will be found scattered in many records in many locations, and no simple reconstitution based on a few sources will gather sufficient data.

In these circumstances a complete and accurate picture can be obtained only through a tedious process of piecing together the several family histories one by one. This is the area where the genealogical investigator is most experienced because the migration of families and the proving of their identity as they move along is one of the problems that a genealogist most often faces. I suggest that when a scholar wants to study a problem in migration and finds the usual statistical methods or the technique of family reconstitution to be inadequate, he/she consider designing a new genealogical study to meet the needs of the particular migration problem being studied. The demographer could accomplish this by enlisting the help of one or several experienced genealogists.

Assume for a moment that seventy-five Planter families settle within a Nova Scotian township between 1759 and 1772, and that it is generally known that the first eighteen families among them came from a specific New England town. How reliable is a generalization about the date and cause of migration if it is based purely on the circumstances affecting the first eighteen families? For anyone who has not yet tried the experiment, may I suggest they take a random list of two dozen New England names from among those reaching Nova Scotia in those years and then to attempt to find out *from which* place in New England each family came. After all, knowing the place from which they came may have a considerable bearing on the when and the why of the migration. Was each following neighbours and kindred to Nova Scotia, thereby serving as a link in a chain migration? Did the particular settler bring a skill or craft with him which may have been valued enough that his coming was solicited? Were those who came eldest sons, second sons, youngest sons, children of landowning families, whatever? Some of the work of finding answers to such questions might be alleviated by recourse to published genealogies or to the methods of enquiry commonly employed by sound genealogical historians.

The genealogist may produce studies of large numbers of families that would assist others in answering questions about the family cycle or life course and its wider relationship to social and historical movements, because the genealogist habitually covers a wider and more eclectic range of documentation than does the typical researcher who is carrying out family reconstitution.

I would like to set forth a synthesis of the concerns we have in doing genealogical research on a basis of migration. I think most will agree that the questions we ask and about which we attempt to collect data in a search for answers are not very different from those the academic scholars have been asking themselves. Bear in mind that such an investigation may involve reconstruction of the family story across several jurisdictions over several generations. A not unimaginable path might be that taken by a family from southwestern Scotland to northern Ireland about 1690, and from thence to New Hampshire about 1725, and from thence to Minas Basin after 1760.

First, we seek to identify the economic, social, political or religious reasons contributing to each major migration of some or all family members. Political factors might include war (flight from conscription, from enemy occupation, or being posted or discharged from a regiment abroad), revolution (e.g., Loyalists), government policy in the homeland. Economic and social reasons might have to do with exhausted carrying capacity of land; natural misfortunes such as crop failures, severe winters, forest fires; industrialization or urbanization; mineral discoveries; receipt of word from successful earlier emigrants; or serious changes in major markets for one's produce. Religious reasons include persecution or the desire of a sect to establish a new community stamped with their vision of a godly "new Jerusalem."

Secondly, was the migration of the family unique, or was it part of a larger movement of population? How many people were involved and over what length of time?

Thirdly, what documentation exists in which the details of the migrating families may have been recorded (e.g., passenger lists, naturalization, travel documents, newspaper notices, customs returns, governmental correspondence, land or church registers, and so forth.)?

Fourthly, what human resources are available to us? Are there official records, genealogical societies or descendants of the migrating families to be found in the place of origin?

The arts and sciences change and grow. Good genealogy offers techniques and information that will assist scholars in finding answers to some questions that are not easily answered through the methods of family reconstitution or statistical analysis. Together with other methodologies, genealogy might offer its contribution to our insights into what Peter Laslett termed "The World We Have Lost." If the immigration historian is not involved in the human dimensions of the past, he has begun to lose his *raison d'être*. Likewise, if genealogical historians do not show a regard for methodology and study their families within the wider contexts of community, country, ethnicity and culture, they will indeed be dismissed as "mere antiquarians."

It is time that genealogists and the academic humanists embarked upon a dialogue aimed at enhancing their mutual cooperation and awareness. Because of the remarkable character of genealogical progress in the Atlantic Provinces and Quebec, our area has one of its infrequent opportunities to show leadership. Let us embrace the opportunity to help Canada to catch up at least with Germany, France and the British Isles in this important respect.

REFERENCES

Anderson, Robert C. "The Genealogist and the Demographer," *Genealogical Journal,* 9, 4(December 1980), 182-97.

Burkhardt, Geoffrey. "Methodology and Research Techniques for the Family Historian," *The Ancestral Researcher*(Canberra), IX(1986), 3-10.

Dupâquier, Jacques. *Introduction à la demographie historique.* Paris, 1974, 43-52.

Imhof, Arthur E. "Sozialgeschichtliche Familienforschung," *Taschenbuch für Familiengeschichtsforschung,* ed. F. Wecken. Neustadt an der Aisch, 1980, 43-68.

Macfarlane, Alan. *Reconstructing Historical Communities.* Cambridge, England, 1977.

Punch, Terrence M. "Historical Genealogy, or Why Genealogy Must be Recognized," *Canadian Genealogist,* 9, 2(June 1987), 89-92.

Taylor, Robert M. Jr. and Ralph S. Crandall. *Generations and Change: Genealogical Perspectives in Social History.* Macon, Georgia, 1986.

The Geography of the Maritime Colonies in 1800: Patterns and Questions[1]

Graeme Wynn
Associate Professor of Geography
The University of British Columbia

To fully appreciate the importance of the New England (Planter) migrations into Nova Scotia during the 1760s, it is essential to consider them in context. By taking the broader view, we can better grasp the contribution that this relatively small group of settlers on the margins of colonial America made to the development of Nova Scotia; we can more fully appreciate the magnitude of their achievements in occupying the land, establishing societies, providing for themselves and their descendants, and creating communities. We can begin to identify common and unique elements in their experience, and we can hope to focus attention on those aspects of the Planter past that seem to warrant further inquiry. To these ends, this paper is comprised of two parts. The first — "Patterns" — briefly surveys the human geography of the British "Maritime" colonies in 1800. It is no more than a sketch,[2] but it provides a backdrop against which the "Questions" of the second part of the paper can be considered.[3]

PATTERNS

In 1800, approximately 75-80,000 people lived in the four British North American colonies of Nova Scotia, New Brunswick, Cape Breton and Prince Edward Island that would come to be called the Maritimes. Halifax, with one-fifth of Nova Scotia's population and Saint John, with a tenth of New Brunswick's were the only cities. Shelburne ranked third among the region's urban centres, but it was little bigger than Fredericton, a capital village of 120 to 150 houses, "scattered," according to the wife of a military officer, "on a delightful common of the richest sheep pasture I ever saw."[4] Despite their administrative functions as capitals of Prince Edward Island and Cape Breton, Charlottetown and Sydney were tiny places, and

---

1 I gratefully acknowledge the permission granted by the Canadian Association of Geographers to reproduce the illustrations and some of the text of the first part of this paper.

2 This sketch is elaborated in more detail in my article, "A Region of Scattered Settlements and Bounded Possibilities: Northeastern America, 1775-1800," *The Canadian Geographer*, 31, 4(1987), 319-38.

3 These questions bear, in turn, upon the discussion of Nova Scotian development between 1755 and 1775 contained in my essay "A Province Too Much Dependent on New England," *The Canadian Geographer* 31, 2(1987), 98-113 which reviews the foundation of the Planter settlements from a geographical perspective.

4 Mrs. Hunter to Elizabeth Bell, 7 August 1804, Provincial Archives of New Brunswick (PANB), MYO/H/76.

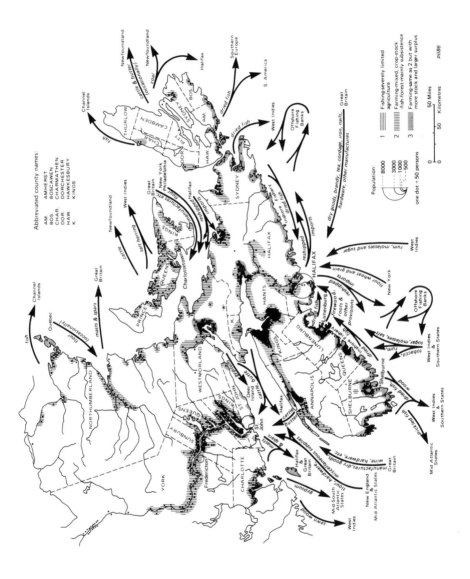

Figure 1

few other agglomerations were more than hamlets.

Along the rocky Atlantic shore of Nova Scotia and on the coast of Cape Breton (Type 1 areas in Figure 1) kitchen gardens and fish provided a meagre subsistence for residents of isolated fishing settlements. Life in these settlements was simple; a scattered group of merchants apart, their residents had little contact with the world beyond. There was little geometric order to these places whose accretive growth was shaped by beach room, topography and consanguinity. Dwellings were modest, their furnishings utilitarian. Sheds and flakes lined the strand, cabins were surrounded by irregular fences encompassing the acre or two of rockbound soil from which the families supplemented diets of fish.[5] Generalizing from fragmentary poll-tax returns of the 1790s, we can estimate that possibly three-quarters of the households in these communities owned cattle or horses.[6] Over half of those with cattle kept only one or two beasts; very few had more than five. Sheep were less numerous than cattle, and were kept by fewer people, a handful of whom had flocks of ten or more. Cattle numbers were less than double the numbers of taxable men in these communities, and most individuals paid the minimum head tax.

Away from the fishing ports, mixed farming was characteristic. Through most of the region, farms were the means and purpose of existence. Potatoes, a variety of grains, peas and turnips were grown. In those areas designated Type 2 in Figure 1, surpluses were generally small and sporadic; when they entered trade it was, first and foremost, to sustain relatively high levels of local self-sufficiency. Again poll-tax returns indicate something of the economies of these communities. On a per capita basis, livestock holdings were clearly more substantial than in the fishing settlements. In broad terms, cattle and horses exceeded the number of people on the tax lists by a factor of 3 or 4. In some areas, such as Windsor with an unusual concentration of relatively well-to-do settlers, horses accounted for almost 25 percent of this total; generally they were considerably less important. Several individuals kept eight or more neat cattle (and some twenty-five or more). Sheep numbers were substantial and in some areas exceeded the number of cattle; flocks of twenty and thirty were not uncommon, but as in the fishing settlements fewer households kept sheep than cows.

---

5   J.J. Mannion, *Point Lance in Transition* (Toronto, 1976) is suggestive of the pattern of these settlements, although it deals with Newfoundland.

6   Poll tax returns from the 1790s are in RG 1, Vol. 443, 444, 444½ [*sic*] in the Public Archives of Nova Scotia (PANS). They are available on microfilm and several have been reprinted [e.g., in *Genealogical Newsletter of the Nova Scotia Historical Society*, 15 (1976),14-23; *Canadian Genealogist*, 1(1979), 103-4]. All estimates from these returns are broad guesses. Best estimates have to be made in adjusting the records for extended family households and for taxable men living with their parents.

Only a few parts of the region (designated 3 in Figure 1) contributed regularly to the regional trade in foodstuffs. From older-settled districts on the productive Fundy marshlands, livestock went to Halifax and Saint John. From Lunenburg, roots and other supplies accompanied shipments of firewood to the provincial capital, and hay, at least, moved downriver from the immediate hinterland of Saint John. In the Fundy settlements, farmers grew a variety of grains and other crops on marsh and upland, but American flour was stiff competition in the region's urban markets, and these were mainly for local consumption. Livestock offered better returns, and large areas of dyked and undyked marsh were turned to hay as economic connection prompted product specialization. Numbers of cattle and horses exceeded the number of taxed individuals five or six fold in many parts of this district during the 1790s and William Trueman surely followed a familiar line of trade when he made two trips from Chignecto to Halifax in the summer of 1802, the first with thirty oxen and the second with twenty-four cattle for sale.[7]

Landscapes revealed rather more of the social geography of the area. Contrasts and incongruities were many: a few large well-established farms pointed up how little cleared land most settlers had; finely coiffed ladies in "pink and lilac high-heeled shoes" picked their ways over the "rugged rocky paths" of Saint John; hard-scrabble fishing settlements bore little resemblance to the well-cultivated marshland fringes of the Bay of Fundy; the social world of the Halifax elite was a vast remove from the humble settings of countless provincial lives.[8]

Through much of settled New Brunswick and southwestern Nova Scotia, building forms revealed the American origins of the settlers. The Cape Cod house was an established form on the Atlantic coast of Nova Scotia as it was along the shores of Maine and Massachusetts (Figure 2a).[9] "Loyalist" or "Georgian" dwellings were the second recognizably American house type common through the southwest of the region by 1800 (Figure 2b). Gravestones also revealed the cultural ties between New England and southwestern Nova Scotia. Traditional death head motifs, more fashionable in early than late eighteenth-century Massachusetts, decorated gravemarkers shipped from Boston to the South Shore communities between 1765 and the 1780s (Figure 2c).[10] Angelheads, or cherubim, carved on late eighteenth-century gravemarkers still stand in the graveyards of Liverpool, Chebogue and Halifax; many have close stylistic

---

7   Diary of William Trueman, 5 May 1802-April 1809, Mount Allison University Archives.

8   Mrs. Hunter to Mary Brydine [1804], PANB, MYO/H/76.

9   P. Ennals and D. Holdsworth, "Vernacular Architecture and the Cultural Landscape of the Maritime Provinces. A Reconnaissance," *Acadiensis*, X (1981), 86-106.

10 D. Trask, *Life How Short Eternity How Long: Gravestone Carving and Carvers in Nova Scotia* (Halifax, 1978) is a useful first study.

Figure 2

counterparts in Salem and neighboring Massachusetts towns (Figure 2d). Other symbols vied with cherubim in the 1790s. Angels sounding the trumpet of resurrection were perhaps most common in areas touched by the evangelical protestantism of many Planters and Loyalists (Figure 2e); urns — reflections of the neo-classical revival in the United States — appeared on imported and local stones by the turn of the century.

Elsewhere, distinctive cultural imprints on the landscape were less obvious. German inscriptions and simple floral designs distinguished the gravestones of Lunenburg. In Pictou, sandstone markers generally recorded the origins of the deceased but were rarely ornamented with more than a thistle or two. Yorkshiremen in Chignecto had begun to replicate in brick and stone, as well as wood, the Georgian and hipped roof forms of dwellings in their native country.[11] Through much of the Gulf Shore, Prince Edward Island and Cape Breton, however, the recency and economic marginality of settlement stamped a utilitarian similarity on the landscape. Crude cabins, hall and parlour dwellings, and simple log structures with two or three rooms were frequently home to returned Acadians and the first permanent shelters of immigrant families throughout the region (Figure 2f).

Still, the basic ethnic divisions that marked the region through the nineteenth century — an English/American south and west, a Scottish Gulf, Germans in Lunenburg, Irish in Halifax and the Cobequid area, and a cluster of Acadian enclaves in Madawaska, northeastern New Brunswick, western Prince Edward Island, southeastern Cape Breton and St. Mary's Bay — were already coming into focus at the end of the eighteenth century. So, too, were the associated patterns of religious differentiation.[12] And the essential and persistent patterns of economy and settlement in this overwhelmingly intractable region were clear: most people occupied modest farms or clustered in sea-girt villages; their distribution was basically peripheral; fingers of population followed the region's major valleys inland.[13]

In 1800, the Maritime colonies remained an unconsolidated amalgam of families and small communities. In most things, the reach of colonial institutions was limited. Although common backgrounds provided a measure of coherence among many groups of settlers, there had been little time for the settling of people into place. The considerable task of establishing, and maintaining, a subsistence threshold preoccupied the majority of the region's settlers. Yet economic, social and, above all,

---

11 Trask, *Life How Short...*, Ennals and Holdsworth, "Vernacular Architecture...."

12 A.H. Clark, "Old World Origins and Religious Adherence in Nova Scotia," *Geographical Review*, 50(1960), 317-44.

13 There are several published descriptions of the colonies early in the nineteenth century; fuller documentation is available in *The Canadian Geographer*, 31, 4(1987), 338.

geographical changes in this corner of the continent during the last half of the eighteenth century reflected broader patterns of North American development. The migratory fishery of Cape Breton shared a great deal with the trade that shaped landscapes and settlements in Newfoundland and much of the Gulf of St. Lawrence for better than three centuries. Essentially static in technology and organization, it turned "surplus" European labour to the extraction of New World resources. Closely controlled by powerful merchants, and integrating the western Atlantic littoral into a complex international trading network, it made that area a distant workplace for several thousand young men from the farms and villages of Ireland, southern England, France and the Channel Islands, but returned little to local, North American economies.

The essential characteristics of the region's resident fishery were repeated the length of the coast from Twillingate to Martha's Vineyard. Few prospered in this enterprise. In Nova Scotia, even more than in New England, the industry was "delicately balanced between profit and loss." Catches were variable, the cure unreliable, and as the American geographer Ralph H. Brown recognized long ago, those engaged at all levels of the trade were caught up in "a relentless battle on an economic front that included all countries of the North Atlantic basin."[14] For the individual fisherman, the results were all too often debt and impoverishment.

Although colonial rather than European merchants dominated the resident fishery, and although its connections to the West Indies were stronger than those of the Mediterranean-oriented migratory fishery, the commercial spheres of the two enterprises overlapped and interlocked. Together they sketched, in outline, the complex web that bound the North Atlantic into a triangle of trade. But with few forward, backward or final demand linkages, neither migratory nor resident fishery was an effective motor of local economic growth in the Maritime colonies. Even the profits and multipliers of Nova Scotia's resident fishery tended to concentrate in Halifax. Beyond, harsh toil on the rugged Atlantic coast yielded a meagre subsistence for scattered families.

In New Brunswick, Loyalist dreams of creating a stable, ordered, hierarchical society had faded through fifteen years of settlement.[15] Most colonists exhibited a sturdy independence while struggling to make their way in the new land. Few, indeed, shared the social conceptions of the elite. For most New Brunswickers, pedigree was a thin claim to privilege, and tenancy was unpalatable.[16] For Governor John Parr, such signs were

---

14 R.H. Brown, *Historical Geography of the United States* (New York, 1948), 111.

15 W.S. MacNutt, *New Brunswick, A History 1784-1867* (Toronto, 1963), 11, 17, 42, 92. A.E. Morrison, "New Brunswick: the Loyalists and the Historians," *Journal of Canadian Studies*, 3(1968), 39-49.

16 E.C. Wright, *The Loyalists of New Brunswick* (Moncton, 1972), 175-77. Ward Chapman

evidence that many Loyalists had inherited "a deal of that Liver, which disunited the [Thirteen] Colonies from their Mother Country."[17] But prevailing attitudes were as much the product of conditions in New Brunswick as they were of convictions shaped in the old colonies. In New Brunswick, as on countless New World frontiers, land had little intrinsic worth. Its value was created by the hard labour of forest clearance and cultivation. And where readily available land allowed men to work for themselves, they would rarely toil for others. Thus large land holdings brought few economic benefits. Gentlemen of education and refinement were obliged "to undergo all the drudgery of farming"; servants were hard to come by; hirelings insisted on sharing their masters' tables; and British soldier William Cobbett, who had never thought of approaching a "Squire without a most respectful bow" in England, found himself, "in this New World," ordering many "a Squire to bring me a glass of Grog and even take care of my knapsack."[18] Abhorred as they were by Loyalist leaders, the levelling democratic tendencies of North American settlement could not be excluded from New Brunswick. Around the indulgent islands of splendid houses, fine wines, and social pretensions sustained by military pensions and aristocratic conventions, most turn-of-the-century New Brunswickers inhabited an essentially egalitarian world. Recent and relatively remote, defined in opposition to the United States, and without a vigorous commercial outlet, their society bore a thin veneer of traditional English conservatism on its democratic New World core.[19]

Settlement in the Maritime colonies had proceeded largely by chance. For most settlers, the region had provided tolerable alternatives to unpromising or difficult circumstances in their old homelands; for some it had offered prospects of real advantage; to few had it yielded substantial wealth or comfort. Here and there newcomers had and might continue to find, for a time, a modest niche for themselves and their families. Whether that niche were in a narrow valley, along a rocky shore, or on an upland plateau, hard work, ingenuity and versatility — to say nothing of good fortune — were generally required to take advantage of it and to survive. And within a generation or two (at most) the limits of local resources would be met. As contexts changed so new adjustments were made. But always sons and daughters would move on, in the late eighteenth century to occupy new pockets of land and limited opportunity in the region, in the

Correspondence, Various items re. Kemble's Manor, Public Archives of Canada (PAC), MG 23 D1.

17 J. Parr to Nepean, 3 September 1784, PAC, CO 217. Vol. 59.

18 W. Reitzel, ed., *The Autobiography of William Cobbett* (London, 1933), 28.

19 E.C. Wright, "The Settlement of New Brunswick: An Advance Toward Democracy," *Canadian Historical Association, Report* (1944), 60 ff. R.C. Harris, "European Beginnings in the Northwest Atlantic. A Comparative View," in D.G. Allen, *Seventeenth-Century New England* (Boston, 1985), 119-52.

late nineteenth century to find work in Boston, and in the late twentieth century to seek their fortunes in Ontario and Alberta. Simply to recognize this reality is to conceive the experience of settlement in these provinces as an important variant of a recurrent facet of life in the Canadian archipelago.[20]

QUESTIONS

A fuller grasp of this complex territory and its significance to our understanding of the country as a whole will not be developed easily. Sources are scarce and intractable. Detailed community records, rich and complete enough to allow such revealing analyses as we now have for New England, are wanting. The usual types of literary evidence — sermons, diaries, letters — are equally limited in extent and, as always, in their representativeness. Yet the insights of a generation of detailed work on the communities of New England, coupled with a growing interest in the comparative study of new-settled territories, suggest a host of questions relevant to the eighteenth-century Maritime colonies that might be approached by work in the land-office records, with genealogies, wills and inventories, and on the newspapers and periodicals of the region. By combining the results of such inquiries with a re-examination of traditional sources and whatever can be recovered of material culture patterns in the area, we might yet learn a good deal about the ways in which late eighteenth-century inhabitants of this region shaped, and regarded, their land and their lives.

Demographic and economic questions are central. Although there was hardly time, in eighteenth-century Nova Scotia, for the development of a clear generational or cyclical pattern of community life, the observed tendency of New England towns to move through sequential stages — initiation in the first generation, consolidation in the second and disintegration in the third — is probably richly suggestive of the dynamics that moulded many communities in the Maritime region.[21] Close analysis

---

20 J.M. Bumsted, "Settlement by Chance: Lord Selkirk and Prince Edward Island," *Canadian Historical Review*, 59 (1978), 170-88; D.A. McNabb, "Land and Families in Horton Township, Nova Scotia, 1760-1830," MA thesis, University of British Columbia, 1986; R.C. Harris "Regionalism and the Canadian Archipelago," in L.D. McCann, ed., *Heartland and Hinterland: A Geography of Canada* (Scarborough, 1987), 532-59.

21 J.M. Bumsted and J.T. Lemon, "New Approaches in Early American Studies: the Local Community in New England," *Histoire Sociale/Social History*, 2 (1968), 98-112. J.P. Greene and J.R. Pole, eds., *Colonial British America: Essays in the New History of the Early Modern Era* (Baltimore, 1984), 14-5 also argue for a developmental framework that has three phases: social simplification; social elaboration; and social replication. For Nova Scotia, the records of the Registry of Deeds (RG47) and the Court of Probate (RG48), grouped by counties and (largely) on microfilm available at the Public Archives of Nova Scotia are the basic resources for such analysis. McNabb, "Land and Families..." effectively explores some of these important questions.

of land-holding patterns, the quantities of productive land held by individuals, and the patterns of inheritance and land transfer could tell us much about how the Planters of the 1760s "initiated" life in their new setting, how successful they were in building the foundations upon which their sons and daughters could consolidate, and when, if ever, disintegration set in. These are crucial issues in substantially rural societies, in which land generally constitutes the foundation of wealth, not least because they underpin any discussion of "class-structure," status and power-relationships within the community. But do they have any relevance to the fishing settlements?

Everywhere the course of development was surely affected by migration and the rate of population growth, and a systematic assessment of early Nova Scotian fertility rates, family sizes and marriage ages would yield important clues to understanding the pressures and tensions shaping communities. Fertility rates and family sizes affect (and are affected by?) patterns of landholding, and in colonial America variations (in space and time) of the average age at marriage seem to have been associated with economic factors. Perhaps one might even suggest that relatively youthful marriages reflect an optimistic appraisal of the future of both self and society, and vice-versa.[22] Furthermore we need to know more of the processes by and the degrees to which settlements on more — or less — remote frontiers were "simplified" by the selectivity of migration and the revised terms of access to land that prevailed in the new setting.[23] Detailed assessments of the circumstances of migrants in New England hearths and their subsequent fortunes in Nova Scotia would enhance our knowledge of the Maritimes and contribute to discussions of the settlement process, not least by revealing whether the migrations from New England were an essentially conservative escape from changing circumstances — a question relevant, in turn, to any discussion of the reasons for Nova Scotia's rejection of the American Revolution.[24]

The patterns of everyday existence in northeastern America also warrant attention. The daily routines, the range of contacts and experience, the hopes, the fears and the family lives of well-to-do immigrants,

---

22 The Nova Scotian data, largely township records and genealogies, are particularly fragmentary, but the wider questions that a systematic assessment might address are many. See P.J. Greven, Jr., "Historical Demography and Colonial America," *William and Mary Quarterly*, 24 (1967), 438-54; J. Potter, "Demographic Development and Family Structure," in Green and Pole, eds., *Colonial British America...*, 123-56 is an extended review of recent work.

23 Harris, "European Beginnings...."; R.C. Harris, "The Simplification of Europe Overseas," *Annals of the Association of American Geographers*, 67 (1977), 469-83.

24 c.f. G.A. Rawlyk, ed., *Revolution Rejected, 1775-1776* (Scarborough, 1968); G. Stewart and G.A. Rawlyk, *A People Highly Favoured of God: The Nova Scotian Yankees and the American Revolution* (Toronto, 1972).

outport merchants, and those scratching a subsistence from land or sea differed dramatically. Diaries, letters and recollections are the starting point for investigation of these matters, but careful reconstruction of the material circumstances of individual lives by the analysis of wills and inventories is at least as important. To establish the matrices and rhythms of everyday activity — including the size and lay-out of the dwellings occupied, the tasks conducted in and around the home, and the technology used by men and women of different stations — is to reveal the blocks out of which landscapes were built, and to clarify the settings in which lives were spent. More than this, it is a step towards the sort of imaginative and stimulating interpretation that John Demos has provided for Plymouth Colony.[25] Recognizing the absence of private space in seventeenth-century dwellings, Demos investigated family organization and child-rearing practices to conclude that Old Colony settlers strove to repress conflict within the home. Perhaps, then, the demands of what we would consider crowded living through the long months of northeastern winters worked in similar ways to foster social conformity and non-aggressiveness among early Maritimers. Did not Thomas McCulloch's "Letters of Mephibosheth Stepsure" published in the *Acadian Recorder* of Halifax in 1821-22, stress the importance of home comforts and domestic harmony? Were not the satirical barbs of Sam Slick, the Yankee peddlar, directed at Nova Scotians some fourteen years later for their lack of assertiveness and their failure to exploit the resources of their country as vigorously as possible?[26] Speculative as these hypotheses are, they raise fascinating questions that are potential springboards for the generation of new lines of inquiry.

According to Michael Zuckerman, the New England town meeting was the setting in which values of peace and harmony were articulated for public emulation; thus it framed the consensus by which communities existed.[27] But local government was exceedingly weak in the Maritime colonies, and the town was a far less important institution there than in New England. This raises intriguing questions. Addressed comparatively they might tell us much about the interpenetration of political and private spheres of conduct and about how these affect social organization and communal order.[28] Certainly any assessment of the cohesiveness, or otherwise, of community life in the eighteenth-century Maritimes would be most useful. Did the emasculation of the town meeting encourage the

25 J. Demos, *A Little Commonwealth: Family Life in Plymouth Colony* (London, 1970).

26 McCulloch's writings were reprinted as *The Stepsure Letters* (Toronto, 1960); Haliburton's as *The Clockmaker* (Toronto, 1958).

27 M. Zuckerman, *Peaceable Kingdoms: New England Towns in the Eighteenth Century* (New York, 1970).

28 Elizabeth Mancke will address some of these questions in her Ph.D. dissertation for Johns Hopkins University, focussing on Machias, Maine and Liverpool, Nova Scotia.

growth of individualism on the new frontier? Although most agricultural settlers of the 1760s chose to dwell on one of the larger parcels of their scattered holdings, rather than on their town plots, their dispersal is no certain reflection of community decline. Community, after all, is a social web; nucleated settlement may have been incidental to its development. An accessible focus of community activity was perhaps the minimum physical prerequisite for the continued vitality of community spirit in its fullest sense. Did such nodes exist in the settlements of maritime British North America? Contemporary maps and plans might provide answers. Were town boundaries marked and maintained? Might churches have been self-conscious community foci? Perhaps webs of social interaction crossed the lines of territorial administration. Did the coming of Loyalists, or the revival inspired by Henry Alline, divide local populations and create factional communities within the bounds of single townships? Ultimately, of course, community life has several facets. Economic communities of barter exchange involving goods and services were probably not congruent with communities of social interaction.[29] Nor does the expression of community consensus depend entirely upon the vitality of a town meeting or its equivalent. Early in the nineteenth century, published apologues and other prose writing had a clear didactic intent.[30] Earlier, a surprisingly extensive body of poems — satirical, didactic, religious, eulogistic and lyric — found in manuscript, and in the periodicals and newspapers of the period served to "articulate and make intimate cultural values" in the new communities. This work characteristically sets individual feeling against a background of basic communal concerns. It stresses public civility and defines the matrix of social, political, moral and religious propriety.[31] Thus it is an important reflection of the "special texture" of life in the region at the end of the eighteenth century, and should be an integral component of future attempts to understand the complex interrelationship of people and

29 D.C. Harvey, "The Struggle for the New England Form of Township Government in Nova Scotia," Canadian Historical Association *Report* (1933), 15-22; J.S. Wood, "Village and Community in Early Colonial New England," *Journal of Historical Geography*, 8 (1982), 333-46; T. Bender, *Community and Social Change in America* (New Brunswick, N.J., 1978); E.G. Nellis, "Work and Social Stability in pre-Revolutionary Massachusetts," Canadian Historical Association *Historical Papers* (1981), 81-100; J.T. Lemon, "Spatial Order: Households in Local Communities and Regions," and R.B. Sheridan, "The Domestic Economy," in Green and Pole, eds., *Colonial British America...*, 86-122 and 43-85; G. Stewart, "Socio-Economic Factors in the Great Awakening: the Case of Yarmouth, Nova Scotia," *Acadiensis*, 3 (1973), 18-34.

30 G. Wynn, " 'Deplorably Dark and Demoralized Lumberers'? Rhetoric and reality in early nineteenth century New Brunswick," *Journal of Forest History*, 24 (1980), 168-87.

31 T.B. Vincent, "Eighteenth Century Poetry in Maritime Canada: problems of approach — a research report," Atlantic Provinces Literature Colloquim: *The Marco Polo Papers*, I (Saint John, 1977), 13-23; T.B. Vincent, ed., *Narrative Verse Satire in Maritime Canada, 1779-1814* (Ottawa, 1978).

place in this corner of North America.

How, then, to proceed with the task of further reconstruction? Careful, detailed community studies, manageable in scale, and allowing exhaustive use of the available documentation, promise insight into many of the questions about which we know least. We cannot proceed without them. But nor can we assume that a series of community studies will define the framework of a new synthesis. Local studies are inevitably moulded by the sources from which they are hewn; they reflect the particular circumstances of their individual foci. Although their replication would provide great detail about particular settings and probably yield agreement on some substantive issues, it would likely leave us with a collection of largely unassimilable case studies. Only with difficulty have the many local studies from New England been integrated into more general statements about the evolution of that society, and the problems of generalization are likely to be even greater for the Maritimes, where populations and circumstances differed so considerably.

Rather than building from the bottom up, the most productive answer, at this juncture, may be to identify two or three unifying themes and to sharpen and refine them by reading down to the record of individual settlements. This probably implies, at least in part, that we move beyond the emphasis on spatial patterns that has constituted the recent orthodoxy of historical geography, and abandon the blinkers of traditional historical scholarship to seek a fuller knowledge of the past interrelations of people with their environments, and heighten our understanding of the evolving character of societies *and* places. With such a focus comes the prospect of engaging in a challenging interdisciplinary debate that illuminates human experience, and promises to generate essentially humanistic inquiries that contribute to our understanding of ourselves by offering a perspective on "the interwoven phenomena of the world of man."[32] And this is a prospect that is enormously appealing as we seek to forge new and important insights from a fragmentary archival record and the disparate inquiries of several disciplines, in pursuit of a fuller grasp of this northeastern corner of America, where settlers wrestled to establish themselves and their institutions in a tough environment.

---

32 A.H. Clark, "First Things First" in R.E. Ehrenberg, ed., *Pattern and Process: Research in Historical Geography* (Washington, D.C., 1975), 12-3.

The Role of the Land
in the Development of Horton Township,
1760-1775[1]

Debra McNabb
Geographer, Halifax

The New Englanders who colonized the Nova Scotia township of Horton in the 1760s were drawn to the area by the promise of free land and easy settlement terms. They came to get ahead by exploiting the opportunities of the frontier. For many, it represented a chance to gain security and prosperity through a sizeable family farm, an opportunity no longer available in the overcrowded land of eastern Connecticut from which they had come. For others, land became the tool by which they could obtain profit and status in the new community. Clearly, land was the most powerful dynamic underlying the settlement process. An investigation of the first generation of New England settlement at Horton reveals that this interplay of people and land resulted in a closing off of opportunity within the first generation.

Unlike their Puritan forefathers who proceeded cautiously in developing a new town to ensure that local society was structured to foster community, the Horton grantees immediately focused on exploiting the opportunities of the frontier. A deep-seated desire to own land of one's own and an impulse to acquire as much of it as they could, led the proprietors to divide the entire township into individual holdings in the first decade.

The township was surveyed in typical New England form. Divisions of land of different types were laid out in lots of various sizes around a compact town plot. To ensure that all proprietors shared equally in the dykeland, marsh, upland and woodland of the township, grantees did not receive a contiguous block of land; rather, holdings were scattered around the township. The amount each received varied according to distinctions of status, family size and "ability to cultivate." Grants ranged from .5 to 2 shares. One share equalled 500 acres.

All of the township's land except the "size"[2] lots and the remote wildlands were laid out and distributed within the first four years of settlement. By 1770 virtually all lands were allocated and the settlement

---

1   For a more detailed discussion of the New England settlement of Horton Township see Debra A. McNabb, "Land and Families in Horton Township, N.S., 1760-1830," M.A. thesis, University of British Columbia, 1986.

2   To compensate for variable soil quality appraisers assessed each lot against the highest prized lot, A No.10, and awarded proprietors pecuniary tickets to be exchanged for "size" lots of equal value at the recipient's leisure. In this way, proprietors pitched one or more lots on the residual marsh, dykeland, intervale and woodland of the township.

pattern was established. No land reserve or communal property remained; even the so-called town "common" was privately owned. Providing land for future generations — which once had been a community responsibility — became the private duty of each landowner.

Even as the property surveys of the 1760s organized the land for settlement, proprietors restructured and used their assigned holdings according to their individual aspirations. Land changed hands quickly and often during the first decade of settlement. In the 1760s, 80% of all Horton grantees participated in the land market; more than 53,000 acres changed hands through 480 deeds.[3] Although more than three quarters of the grantees registered fewer than six deeds for the decade,[4] in many instances more than one and as many as ten lots changed hands in a single transaction. Consequently, the land trade was probably busier than the figures suggest. In all, at least 777 parcels of Horton land changed hands.

Landowning behavior between 1760 and 1770 suggests that acquisitiveness, expressed both in the pursuit of immediate profit and in property accumulation, motivated landowners.[5] The land trade provided one of the few opportunities to raise capital on the Nova Scotia frontier and during the 1760s, one half of Horton's resident grantees engaged in transactions that brought them a profit.[6] Astute landowners capitalized on the land without reducing the size of their own shares by selling individually-purchased lots as a package deal. More often, though, immediate profit was only realized by the reduction of a shareholder's improvable acreage. Defined broadly, "improvable" acreage was land easily prepared for cultivation. In the 1760s this meant accessible township land rather than the undivided third division. Exclusive of "size" land, grants of .5 to 2

---

3 The following analysis of Horton landholding patterns uses all deeds recorded in PANS, RG 47, King's County, reels 1273, 1274. It should be noted that Horton's extant registered deeds are not a complete record of all land transactions. For example, in reconstituting individual landholdings it was discovered that there are deeds for the sale of one or more lots for which there was no record of purchase.

4 The average number of deeds recorded by grantees from 1760 to 1770 was 4.5. Non-grantees have been excluded from these calculations because otherwise they could have been included by making a single purchase in the late 1760s, which would skew the general trends.

5 The following discussion of landowning behavior is based on an analysis of the dates, locations, acreages and prices of all lots bought and sold by every known landowner in Horton between 1760 and 1770.

6 Resident and absentee grantees are examined separately because their landholding practices were markedly different. Net profit/deficit is calculated as the difference between the prices cited for lots purchased and those sold during the decade. It excludes the monetary values of that portion of the original grant still owned in 1770, and therefore it does not measure the cash equivalent of total wealth in land.

shares contained from 31 to 145 improvable acres.[7]

Three-quarters of the grantees who made money from their shares reduced their farm areas.[8] On average, this reduction amounted to 31 improvable acres. Clearly, some conceived of their land as a commodity of exchange in the cash-short economy of eighteenth-century Nova Scotia. They sold off some parcels to obtain funds necessary to improve and stock the remainder. For others, less committed to setting up a farm in Horton, emigration to Nova Scotia was temporary. Whether engulfed in debt, discouraged by pioneering hardships, or caught up in the speculative fever sweeping the colony,[9] 38 shareholders sold their rights by 1770, putting more than 17,000 acres up for sale. Most of those who departed early in the 1760s sold their land before leaving Horton, but by mid-decade the majority of grants sold were the property of settlers who had returned to New England.[10] The price varied according to whether a proprietor sold before or after leaving Horton, the buildings and improvements to be included, or if the grant was sold by a disinterested heir, but generally, one share of 500 unimproved acres could be purchased for approximately £100.

The willingness of many grantees to sell at least part of their shares made it possible for anyone with capital to buy land in Horton. A few Halifax businessmen who invested heavily in the outsettlements took advantage of this opportunity. But these were not typical newcomers. Of 35 non-grantees who purchased land in the 1760s, most owned less than 25 acres; as a group they acquired only 15% of the township's improvable acreage.

Most of the lands sold in the 1760s became the property of proprietors eager to augment their original shares. One quarter of the resident grantees invested substantial sums in the local land market to increase their holdings by an average of 66 improvable acres. A trend towards concentrated land ownership developed. By 1770, the top 20% (40) of Horton landowners controlled one half of the township's improvable acreage; 10 of these landowners owned three times the total acreage of the 78 smallest property holders. In effect, the balance of population and land was shifting in their favour. Future access to land would be severely limited

---

7 Documentary references to "size" are not included in calculations of "improvable" acreage in this discussion, although it may have been among the most valuable and frequently cultivated acreage any farmer owned.

8 The other one quarter are discussed above as that group of landowners who made a profit without reducing the size of their landholding.

9 That one quarter of the complete removals of Horton grantees occurred in 1760 and 1761 argues strongly for speculation as a motive behind some New Englanders obtaining Nova Scotia land grants.

10 Only two grantees who left Horton for good remained in Nova Scotia. Amos Fuller moved to Cumberland and Benjamin Woodworth settled in Cornwallis.

if these few individuals were not inclined to sell. Only six ranked in the top 20% without purchasing any land. They had been given the larger 1.5 and 2-share rights and by not selling any land, owned some of the largest holdings in 1770. All of them were non-residents. In 1770, seventy-five absentee grantees owned one third of Horton's improvable acreage. Most never ever lived in Horton and their shares were subsequently sold by heirs.[11]

And yet, non-residency did not have to mean inactivity. In 1770, Horton's largest landowner was Halifax merchant and government servant, Joseph Gray. A shrewd businessman, Gray not only consolidated several substantial farms, he purchased a large chunk of third division wildland, perhaps speculating on the future value of the properties as tenant estates.[12] By 1770 he had increased his original 1-share grant of 517 acres to 21,494 acres.[13]

Gray's closest rival as a Horton landowner was local resident, Charles Dickson. In 1755, Colonel Dickson led a company of New Englanders to Nova Scotia to fight at Beausejour. Five years later he returned with his wife and five children to claim 1.5 shares at Horton. There he became a prominent merchant, politician and landowner. Unlike Joseph Gray, Dickson's land dealings favoured Lower Horton. By 1770 he owned almost 1500 improvable acres, more than four times Gray's improvable acreage and more than three times the improvable property of Horton's third-ranked landowner. By the time he died fifteen years later, Dickson had made twice as much money as he had invested in local land and still owned 5418.25 acres, although by that time primarily in the third division.[14]

---

11 There is no evidence to suggest how non-residents might have contributed their required share of capital and labour needed to establish the infrastructures of settlement. Perhaps, as in Sackville Township, N.B., local agents agreed to meet the obligations of non-residents (see James Snowdon, "Footprints in the Marsh Mud: Politics and Land Settlement in the Township of Sackville, 1760-1800," M.A. thesis, University of New Brunswick, 1975, 89).

12 Although the final disposition of Gray's Horton lands is unknown, he probably profited from this strategy; as early as the late 1770s, settlers were carving farmland out of the township's wooded interior. As well, Gray had tenants on his farms known as "The Pear Trees" and "Mud Creek."

13 For Joseph Gray's Horton deeds of the 1760s see PANS, RG 47, Reel 1273, Vol. 1: 8, 9, 12, 13, 16, 17, 19, 21, 36, 40, 42, 55, 64, 66, 68, 70, 72, 74, 76, 80, 82, 84, 105, 108, 110, 113, 114, 116, 117, 119, 120, 122, 123, 124, 126, 127, 133, 150, 159, 161, 167, 190, 196, 197, 199, 201, 203, 205, 207, 256; Vol. 2: 16, 19, 23, 25, 26, 27, 28 (2), 30, 31, 32, 54, 63, 64, 65, 67, 68, 71 , 77, 130, 131, 274; Vol. 3: 269, 359.

14 For Charles Dickson's Horton deeds see PANS, RG 47, Reel 1273, Vol. 1: 2, 21, 35, 38, 40, 53, 60, 61, 86, 92, 152, 173, 180, 181, 182, 195, 212, 215, 217, 218, 231, 232, 234, 235, 236, 242, 247, 251, 268, 269; Vol. 2: 3, 4, 7 (2), 8, 22, 31, 47, 51 (2), 79, 102, 106, 140, 167, 182, 185, 187, 191, 211, 212, 213, 214 (2), 234, 241, 246, 247, 249, 273, 303; Vol. 3: 7, 66, 148, 150, 153, 154, 168, 199, 200, 227, 264, 352, 486, 519, 521, 530, 532; Reel 1274, Vol.4: 5, 8, 154; Vol. 5: 104.

Few of the others who accumulated land emulated Joseph Gray and Charles Dickson. In fact, there seems to be no general pattern to the property acquisitions of the 1760s. Some grantees purchased one or two pieces adjoining, or near one of their other lots, but few attempted to acquire the most fertile land or to consolidate their holdings into contiguous fields. Land seemed to be acquired for the sake of owning it. As a result, the dispersed land system that had been initiated by the township survey, became entrenched on the landscape by 1770. Horton landowners left their farms spread over several miles, a few acres here, a few more there.

This acquisition pattern, in turn, affected the settlement pattern. To compensate for fragmented holdings or to concentrate on what remained of their grants, inhabitants began to build their homes on one of their upland lots. Even in the 1760s settlement began to drift westward, drawing families away from a communal town plot to homesteads often widely separated from each other by the empty fields of absentee proprietors.

Simeon Dewolf's residential mobility illustrates how people moved around the township. A blacksmith from Lyme, Dewolf arrived in Horton between 1761 and 1764 and erected a dwelling, barn, smithy and assorted outbuildings on the town lot of his 1-share grant. By 1768, he had built a frame house on a piece of upland size adjacent to his first division farm lot and moved his family and forge to that site just west of town plot. Although he was not Horton's only blacksmith, Dewolf must have believed that his business would not suffer by moving away from the center of town and closer to his farmlands. In fact, his new location on the well-travelled "road to the lower bridge" may have made him more accessible to others who had moved out of town. In 1770, Dewolf moved again. He purchased a house and 100 acres in the second division along the king's highway to Annapolis. In 1779, five years before he died, Dewolf moved for the last time to a dwelling farther west along this road.[15]

There were others who shared Dewolf's wanderlust, but most inhabitants who moved probably did so only once or twice. Although the evidence is impressionistic, it appears that as soon as they could build frame dwellings, most settlers left the crude shelters they had hastily erected at town plot. If they rebuilt at another site, it is likely that their first dwelling was sold or rented, although occasionally the building was moved or torn down so that the lot could be used for agricultural purposes.

The demand for land in Horton in the 1760s did not reflect the state of agricultural development in the new farming community. An analysis of agriculture at the end of the first decade of settlement reveals that farmers did not adequately provide for their families' needs and the land was

---

15 For mention of Simeon Dewolf's houses, see PANS, RG 47, Reel 1273, Vol. 1: 56, 214; Vol. 2: 116; Vol. 3: 296; Reel 1274, Vol. 4: 97.

under-utilized. There is no data on production and consumption to estimate subsistence levels at Horton. The only source of nominal agricultural information before 1851 is the census of 1770.[16] To provide an interpretive framework for analyzing this agricultural data, those listed on the census were divided into three groups (top 20%, mid 40%, bottom 40%) according to the size of their landholding in improvable acres. Averaging farm size and crop yields for each of the three groups resulted in three distinct farm types. The characteristics of these "types" were compared to estimates of the minimum acreage required to produce a basic food supply found in James Lemon's study of eighteenth-century Pennsylvania.[17] Admittedly, this procedure is crude; however, it does make an attempt to correlate farm size and agricultural production and it provides at least an impressionistic statement of Horton's agricultural system.

According to Lemon's requirements, most families were still struggling to obtain life's basic necessities ten years after they arrived in Horton. For example, farmers in the bottom 40% of Horton landowners possessed on average, slightly less than the minimum acreage identified by Lemon as necessary for adequate subsistence, and their meager crop yields reflected their primitive agricultural practices. Generally, middling landowners did not fare much better. Farmers in the middle 40% of landowners owned three times the mean improvable acreage of their counterparts in the bottom two fifths of society, but their holdings differed only in the larger size of their second division farm lots. Crop yields were only slightly higher than those of the bottom 40% and they were still well below comparable American subsistence estimates.

Horton's most successful husbandmen were its principal landowners. Yet, on average, the agricultural output of the top 20% of Horton's landowners only barely met basic subsistence requirements although they held thirteen times the required minimum acreage. No rates of clearing Horton land have survived; yet even at the pace of farmers who levelled a thick Ontario forest to clear 5 acres a year,[18] sufficient acreage could have been cleared and prepared for planting in the first ten years to allow Horton farmers to produce more prodigiously. The reasons why they did not do so remain unclear. It is evident, however, that dispersed holdings, scarce labour, difficulties in obtaining stock and seed, poor markets and

16 "A Return of the State of the Township of Horton, 1770," PANS, RG 1, Vol. 443, 15; reprinted in PANS *Report*, 1934, 39-42.

17 James T. Lemon, *The Best Poor Man's Country: A Geographical Study of Early Southeastern Pennsylvania* (New York: 1972), 164.

18 The estimate of five acres a year is quoted in Kenneth Kelly, "The Impact of Nineteenth Century Agricultural Settlement on the Land," in J.D. Wood, ed., *Perspectives on Landscape and Settlement in Nineteenth Century Ontario* (Carleton Library, 1975), 103.

the problems of adjusting to farming a new land were common hardships of eighteenth-century Nova Scotia farmers. Together they stood in the way of efficient agriculture.

The steady increase in population in Horton during this time (described below) suggests that the inhabitants did not suffer unduly from low agricultural productivity, but there is no documentation to indicate how they sustained themselves. It is not unreasonable to assume, however, that they lived as pioneers do, by making the most of what the new land had to offer. Horton could provide both a river fishery and proximity to the rich Bay of Fundy fishery; hunting and trapping opportunities in the woods of South Mountain, and the fruits of former Acadian orchards. Similarly, how their standard of living may have been influenced by a well-established trading network between New England and the Bay of Fundy region is unknown.

The imbalance in the distribution of land resulting from the active trading of the 1760s, persisted for at least the next two decades. Those who had gained control of the best township lands kept them out of circulation; as measured by the number of deeds registered, land transactions occurred at little more than half the rate that marked the 1760s.

Between 1770 and 1791 access to land was further reduced by escalating prices, driven upward by a rising demand and shrinking supply of land. Any comparison of Horton land prices over time is risky because the impact of the type of sale (i.e., private or public auction), soil quality, improvements and location on price are impossible to determine, although they surely were felt; lots of equal acreage in similar parts of the township were sold for different sums at almost the same time. In absolute terms though, prices increased. With time and the progression of settlement, buying land meant paying for improvements such as clearing, fencing, cultivation and perhaps even a house, barn and outbuildings. Because less expensive unimproved properties were not often offered for sale, the price of land was pushed out of the reach of some.

As the threshold of access to land rose, the population of Horton increased. The number of inhabitants grew from 689 in 1763[19] to approximately 743 by 1770. By extrapolation from the number of adult men listed on the Poll Tax of 1791, the population of Horton in that year can be estimated at 1175; this was an increase of 63% over the 1770 total.[20] Such growth can be attributed in part to the high rate of persistence among the founding settlers and their families. Twenty-six of the 184 original Horton landholders are known to have died by 1790. Of the remaining 158,

---

19 "Return of the Families Settled in the Townships of Horton, Cornwallis, Falmouth, and Newport in King's County... 1763," PANS, MG 1, Vol. 471, 2.

20 "The Horton Poll Tax of 1791," in "Nova Scotia Poll Tax Lists, 1790-1795," PANS, RG 1, Vol. 444.

fully 123 certainly lived in Horton in 1791; the proportion may well have been higher because we do not know that some of the apparently missing 30 did not continue to live in Horton unrecorded.

Inmigration was another component of population growth. Horton attracted several newcomers in the 1770s and 1780s. Fully 117 of these appeared as new names (not on the 1770 Census) on the Poll Tax; a few were Loyalists, some came from Ireland and others moved from Cornwallis and Falmouth, but the origins of most are unknown. So too are the reasons that they came to Horton. Some (perhaps seven) men settled Horton land included in the dowries of their local brides.[21] Others may have had little choice but to move to Horton or one of the other settled communities in the colony. Between 1770 and 1783 Crown lands were available only by purchase; because prices were relatively high there was little settlement of unoccupied land and newcomers gravitated into established towns in search of other opportunities.[22] Even the relatively well-to-do British migrants of the 1770s came, as Governor Legge observed, not "with the expectation of having lands granted to them", but "to purchase, ... perhaps to become tenants" or "to labour."[23]

This was certainly the pattern followed by many of those who settled in Horton after 1770. Only one fifth purchased land in the next twenty years and only half ever acquired real property. In 1791 two thirds made their living as wage labourers. Revealingly, less than half of those registered as farmers on the Poll Tax owned land. To farm they had to rent land. Tenancy had become an important facet of the economic structure of the community.

As land grew scarce in Horton, everyman's opportunity to own a farm diminished. Between 1770 and 1791 the number of farmers in Horton decreased by one third. There were also fewer artisans and professionals on a proportional basis, and by 1791 labourers comprised almost half (47%) of the workforce.[24] They were not simply farmers' sons; Hortonians of the second generation accounted for only one quarter of this occupational group. Of the remainder, only one quarter had lived in Horton in 1770. Once landowners, they had sold their property for one reason or another, but continued to seek a living there. The rest were newcomers to

---

21 J. Noble Shannon, Samuel Avery, Ebenezer Fitch, James Fullerton, Moses Stevens, John Graham and Michael Wallace married daughters of Hortonians.

22 Margaret Ells, "Clearing The Decks For The Loyalists," Canadian Historical Association *Report* (1933), 43-58.

23 Letter, Governor Legge to Lord Dartmouth, May 10, 1774, in "Letter Books and Transcripts of Dispatches from the Governors," PANS, RG 1, Vol. 44, 32.

24 "The Horton Poll Tax of 1791", *op cit.* An increase in the number of labourers after 1770 is supported by an increase in the occurrence of the term "labourer" as an occupational identification in the Court of Quarter Sessions papers. For examples, see PANS, MG 1, Vol. 182, 38, 116-117, 228; Vol.183, 2-31, 79-81, 103-107, 267-270.

the community. Although it is difficult to tell what kinds of labour were performed, scattered references suggest that men were hired for a variety of unskilled and semi-skilled tasks, most of them farm-related.

When time came to pass on their land to the next generation, Horton testators faced difficult decisions. Forced to recognize even in the 1790s that the limits of good agricultural land had been reached in Horton and that the rising threshold of accessibility put land at a premium, they were conservative in subdividing their holdings. Some endowed all male offspring but only after most sons served lengthy apprenticeships as farm labourers, and then only with as much land as could be parcelled out without jeopardizing the viability of the family farm.

More importantly, almost one half (43%) of Horton testators bequeathed all of their real estate to one son. In some cases this represented the last of several disbursements that had begun many years before rather than a deliberate attempt to exclude all but one son. Even so, many of these testators had sizeable holdings, property which could have been divided among all of their offspring. By choosing to favour only one, these men preserved the integrity of the family farm in a way probably calculated to ensure the family's social and economic position in a farming community.

The incidence of impartible inheritance at Horton is high when compared to New England where it was rarely practised when settlements were new. There, characteristically large landholdings accommodated the first settlers who wished to distribute their land among all their sons. But after a few generations severely reduced the size of the family's landholdings by this practise, partible inheritance was no longer realistic. Still, rather than give land to some sons and not to others, men stubbornly clung to some form of partible inheritance long after it was a feasible method of transmission.[25]

Perhaps the attitudes of Horton testators signify a conservative reaction to their earlier experiences in Connecticut. There, as in all of older settled New England, growing population pressure on a limited land supply, aggravated by generations of partible inheritance, severely reduced family landholdings and left fathers incapable of providing adequate patrimonies for their grown sons. This dilemma provided at least part of the impetus for some of these sons to leave Connecticut for Nova Scotia. These were the men who became Horton landowners and later found themselves forced to make hard choices that affected the lives of their sons. Because their own youth had been unsettled, these men must have been sensitive to the situations their sons faced when they reached manhood. But, at the same time they were keenly aware of their struggle to establish a patrimony and what sub-dividing the farm into small parcels would mean for the

---

25 Philip J. Greven, *Four Generations: Population, Land and Family in Colonial Andover, Mass.* (Ithaca, 1970), 125-172.

family's chance of keeping a foothold in the community for future generations. As a result, decisions regarding the transfer of property to the next generation were influenced more by priorities of maintaining the family landholding and ensuring the patriarch's economic security in old age than by the affection testators may have felt for their children and their instincts to provide for them.

Some of the wider implications of the settlement experience at Horton seem clear. Acquisitiveness was the motor of colonization and formed the central tendency in the *mentalité* of the settlers who established the new community. It was best expressed in the accumulation of land for purposes of exchange and status-enhancement. More than anything else, this drive to accumulate shaped Horton's evolving character. The flurry of trading in land during the 1760s greatly outpaced agricultural development. Whether or not they wanted to participate in the drive to accumulate, all residents were affected by it. Few resisted re-shaping their landholding in some way. This process identified the leaders and lesser sorts and had ramifications for other aspects of community life. Economic differentiation, which was in place from virtually the beginning of settlement, was as important as the limitations of the Nova Scotia environment in determining the direction and extent of community development.

This discussion of Horton examines only the initial phase of the settlement process and ends with the deaths of the first generation of settlers. It reveals a society characterized by restricted opportunity, stratification and uncertainty. To fully understand the patterns of community development requires the investigation to be carried forward to determine how subsequent generations of Hortonians coped with the legacy left by the founding settlers. Perhaps the initial imbalance in land ownership levelled out and the significance of land as a commodity diminished as the importance of agriculture increased, the local economy matured and society grew more complex. As well, further study of Horton must place the township in its spatial context to understand its role in the economy and society of the Minas Basin area, its place in the hinterland of Halifax, and what the investigation of life and livelihood at Horton reveals about the colony of Nova Scotia in the much-neglected period of the Planters.

Corporate Structure and Private Interest: The Mid-Eighteenth-Century Expansion of New England

Elizabeth Mancke
Johns Hopkins University

As the French made their last defences of Canada in the late 1750s, New Englanders, who had long fought them in North America, quickly realized that the end of French influence would open a band of land stretching from eastern New York, across Vermont and New Hampshire, and out to the Atlantic in Maine. For over a hundred years the area had served as a buffer and battleground between English settlements in New England and French settlements in Canada. But with the end of French control in Canada the Anglo-French conflicts, which had blocked Euroamerican settlement in the region, ceased. The response from land-hungry New Englanders was almost immediate. A number of Massachusetts' soldiers rather than going home after being discharged from the French and Indian Wars settled on "some of the Lands they had Conquered" in Maine, reasoning in their petition for a grant of land, that as no English inhabitants had ever settled there that the land "would be as likely to fall to their share as to others."[1] A group organized in 1759 in the towns of Duxborough, Pembrook, Kingston and Plympton, Massachusetts, stated that "having small and very poor farms or Tenements...and some of us not one foot of Land in the world," they very much desired a grant on the Penobscot River in Maine.[2] Thomas Pownall, Governor of Massachusetts, advised the General Court in his January 1760 address "that now every other obstacle is removed" [i.e., the conflict with the French and Indians] it should resolve all title disputes in Maine so as to facilitate the orderly and legal settlement of the region.[3] New Hampshire's Governor Benning Wentworth busily granted dozens of townships in what is now Vermont and New Hampshire. And in 1759 Nova Scotia Governor Charles Lawrence circulated a proclamation throughout New England inviting settlers to immigrate to that colony, from where, only four years before, the Acadians or French Neutrals had been deported.[4]

---

1 Petition of Thomas Westgatt and others, 3 October 1763, *Maine Documentary History* (Portland, 1909-10), XIII, 315-16. See the petition of Ebenezer Thorndike and others, 2 January 1762, XIII, 242-43; and Petition of a Number of Soldiers, 1 April 1761, XIII, 232-33, for similar expressions.

2 Petition to the General Court of Massachusetts, November term 1759, *Maine Documentary History*, XIII, 180-81.

3 Speech by T. Pownall to the Council and House of Representatives, 2 January 1760, *Maine Documentary History*, XIII, 199.

4 Lawrence issued two proclamations, the first on 12 October 1758 when he described the

Between 1759 and 1775 approximately 200 townships were granted in Vermont, New Hampshire, Maine and Nova Scotia.[5] A conservative estimate of the number of grantees involved is ten thousand, assuming fifty men per grant, or one out of every ten men in New England between the ages of sixteen and sixty.[6] It was probably much higher since the two townships to be discussed here — Liverpool, Nova Scotia, and Machias, Maine — had 164 and 80 grantees respectively. The number of settlers involved was much greater. Between 1759 and 1764 approximately 7000 New England settlers went to Nova Scotia. During the 1760s New Hampshire's population increased by 22,000 or fifty-eight percent, most of which was in the western counties. By 1776 Vermont had 20,000 inhabitants, when in the early 1760s it only had a few dozen families. And in Lincoln County, Maine, there were over 15,000 souls, most of them recent settlers. Thus the migration into northern New England and Nova Scotia involved upwards of 60,000 people.[7]

Demographic conditions in lower New England encouraged this demand for land. By the mid-eighteenth century, many of the New England towns which had been settled in the seventeenth century had reached land to people ratios of one adult man to approximately forty acres.[8] While some towns did develop more diversified economies to absorb some of the displaced agricultural labor, many New Englanders preferred to move on in search of new land.[9] In addition to demographic pressure, massive forest fires burned across lower New Hampshire and southern Maine in the summers of 1762 and 1763, destroying the forests and livelihood of many timbermen, and thus intensifying the demand for

---

lands available for settlement, and a second on 11 January 1759 to respond to inquiries he had received. See D. C. Harvey, "The Struggle for the New England Form of Township Government in Nova Scotia," Canadian Historical Association *Report*, 1933, 15-22.

5 Graeme Wynn, "A Province Too Much Dependent on New England," *The Canadian Geographer/Le Geographe Canadien*, 31, 2 (1987), 100.

6 The percentage is based on the figures in Robert V. Wells, *The Population of the British Colonies in America before 1776: A Survey of Census Data* (Princeton, N.J., 1975), 69-89 passim. In 1767 New Hampshire's population was 52,700, in 1764 Massachusetts' was 245,698, and in 1762 Connecticut's was 145,590, or approx. 440,000 for New England ca. 1765. Using Well's sex and age ratios, half were male, and half the males were between the ages of sixteen and sixty, or approx. 110,000 adult men.

7 Wynn, "A Province Too Much Dependent on New England," 100; J. Potter, "The Growth of Population in America, 1700-1860," in *Population in History: Essays in Historical Demography*, eds. D. V. Glass and D. E. C. Eversley (Chicago, 1965), 638-39; and Charles E. Clark, *The Eastern Frontier: The Settlement of Northern New England, 1610-1763* (New York, 1970), 354.

8 Kenneth Lockridge, "Land, Population and the Evolution of New England Society 1630-1790," *Past and Present*, 39 (April 1968), 62-80.

9 Darrett B. Rutman, "People in Process: The New Hampshire Towns of the Eighteenth Century," *Journal of Urban History*, 1, 3(May 1975), 268-292.

land.[10] The collapse of French power and the opening of Nova Scotia explain the interest in the lands north and east of lower New England.

While demographic pressure and ecological catastrophe account for the expansion of New England in the mid-eighteenth century, these factors do not explain the pronounced group or corporate character of expansion. It was the corporate structure of New England expansion, both through the granting and settlement processes, which drew in so many so fast. The preference of New Englanders for group grants and settlements and the response of the governments involved is the major focus here. Two townships under different political jurisdictions — Liverpool, Nova Scotia, settled in 1760, and Machias, Maine, settled in 1763 — will be considered to explore the interactions of individual, group, and government, and how each influenced the resettlement process.

* * * * *

Land for resettlement became available in Nova Scotia before it became available through the governments of New Hampshire or Massachusetts, but New Englanders had always been wary of moving there and did not head north just because there was land. Commercially and militarily, Nova Scotia had long fallen within the orbit of the Bay Colony; Massachusetts merchants had traded with the Acadians in the Bay of Fundy and the French in Louisbourg, New England fishermen frequented its harbors and shores, and New England soldiers fought to bring the region under the British flag. Politically, though, the British retained control in Nova Scotia and for nearly a half-century they ran the colony as a military outpost, hardly a selling point for New Englanders with a strong commitment to local self-government. Finally in 1758, under pressure by the Board of Trade, a representative assembly was elected, and met for the first time on 2 October.[11] Ten days later on 12 October Governor Lawrence issued a proclamation inviting New Englanders to submit proposals for settling in the colony. He received sufficient inquiries about the nature of government in the colony to issue a second proclamation on 11 January 1759 stating:

That the Government of Nova Scotia is constituted like those of the neighbouring colonies, the Legislature consisting of Governor Council and Assembly, and every township as soon as it shall consist

10 Catherine Fox, "The Great Fire in the Woods: A Case Study in Ecological History," M.A. thesis, University of Maine at Orono, 1984.

11 D. C. Harvey, ed., "Governor Lawrence's Case Against an Assembly in Nova Scotia," *Canadian Historical Review* 13, 2 (1932), 184-94.

of Fifty Families will be entitled to send two representatives to the General Assembly. The Courts of Justice are also constituted in like manner with those of the Massachusetts, Connecticut and other Northern colonies.[12]

The proclamation appeared to be an about face to a long-standing British policy not to develop Nova Scotia as a "new New England." Whenever the British had considered initiating a more broadly based government, official opinion held that a centralized government, similar to Virginia's with appointed county magistrates and local officials, would be superior to the decentralized New England practice of town government and locally chosen officers. The proclamation, however, convinced many prospective settlers, and some merchants resident in Halifax, that the British intended to allow New England-style town government in Nova Scotia.[13]

The language of the proclamation allowed for generous interpretation, without promising more than what had been achieved with the establishment of the colonial assembly. Those who drafted the document almost certainly carefully chose the term "township" rather than "town." A township is a unit of land and could be defined by survey whether peopled or not. A town is the incorporated political entity within the territorial definition of a township. While the distinction between the two terms may have been lost on prospective settlers, it undoubtedly was not lost on British officialdom. But under the misimpression that town government would be allowed many New Englanders took up land in Nova Scotia, among them Captain John Dogget, who secured a grant for the township of Liverpool for himself and 163 other men from Massachusetts.[14]

The language of the Liverpool grant and the subsequent organization of the township's proprietors indicate how shrewdly the officials in Halifax used the cosmetics but not the substance of New England practice to disguise a centralized government. In style and organization the grant read as would one from Massachusetts. It noted the four primary organizers who had applied for the grant of a township on behalf of themselves and the within named grantees. Governor Lawrence stated his power and authority to make the grant. The location of the township was given in detail. And stipulations were made regarding the number of families to be settled and the amount of land to be cleared within a given time. In these details the grant is very much like any New England township grant of the

---

12 Quoted in Harvey, "The Struggle for the New England Form of Township Government in Nova Scotia," 18.

13 Report of Charles Morris and Richard Bulkeley, October 1763, Public Archives of Nova Scotia (PANS), RG 1, Vol. 222.

14 Liverpool Grant, 1 September 1759, PANS, MG 100, Vol. 176, 26 Q.

era. But some important differences existed which easily could have been overlooked by the grantees. The grant stated that the township was "given, Granted and confirmed...unto the Several Persons hereafter Named...," thus in severalty to each of the 164 men named and not to them as "tenants in common," the language used in the Massachusetts grants.[15] The grantees were to divide the land among themselves in 500 acre shares, though if a majority could not agree upon adequate procedures the Governor would appoint a committee to divide the land. Land could not be sold or alienated within ten years except by licence from the governor, lieutenant governor or commander-in-chief. And the grant remained conditional upon the settlement of "Forty One of the said Grantees with their Wives, Children, Servants and Effects..." by 30 September 1760 and another sixty grantees and their families within the following twelve months. In contrast, the grant for Machias required the grantees to settle the township "with Eighty good Protestant Families" within six years of the King's approval of the grant. It did not state that the grantees themselves had to be among the eighty families.

The Liverpool grant played upon the very strong corporate traditions in New England resettlement; the grant would become null or void if the grantees did not work together to assure the necessary numbers of settlers. At the same time the grantees were given no vested corporate rights as "tenants in common" or a proprietorship. The corporate responsibilities for organizing the resettlement of New Englanders in Nova Scotia had been retained while the corporate rights had been removed. Though the change initially may have escaped the notice of grantees, it was most assuredly intentional on the part of the government. Had the desire been to replicate faithfully a New England type grant then one could have been copied from the Massachusetts' *Acts and Resolves*, since as acts of the legislature grants were printed. And anyone drafting a grant would know that titles to land and the right to grant land had been long-standing sources of controversy between the British and the New England governments. Thus it is reasonable to conclude that subtle differences between a New England-style grant and the Nova Scotia grants had been constructed quite wittingly. Whether it was witting deception is less clear, but some New Englanders who went to Nova Scotia were indeed deceived.

In August 1761 the Council appointed a committee of five Liverpool settlers to divide the forfeited lands of the grantees who had not come.[16] The decision provoked a memorial from eight settlers who protested that

---

15 Liverpool Grant, 1 September 1759, PANS, MG 100, Vol. 176, 26 Q. For examples of Massachusetts grants see *Documentary History of Maine*, XIII, 322-30 and XIV, 80-82.

16 Order in Council, 15 August 1761, PANS, RG 1, Vol. 211, 210.

"we conceive we have right and authority invested in ourselves (or at least we pray we may) to nominate and appoint men among us to be our Committee," a right they perceived as theirs by virtue of being "born in a Country of Liberty." The appointed committee, they argued, created unease among the settlers, causing some to leave and others not to come. The memorial ended by the men reiterating their right to chose their own committee and other officers, a privilege they "must insist on as it belongs to us alone to rule ourselves."[17] The petition did not move the Council. In 1760 the assembly passed an act to "enable the proprietors to divide their lands held in common and undivided," but the King had disallowed the act.[18] Six years later a Justice of the Peace had issued a warrant allowing the settlers of Londonderry, Nova Scotia, to choose their own committee to divide the lands, which the Council in Halifax declared unlawful.[19]

In a 1763 evaluation of the status of the townships, Charles Morris and Richard Buckeley recommended to the Council that the New England settlers be allowed the political rights to which they had been accustomed. This had been, they believed, one of the conditions Governor Lawrence had used to induce New Englanders to come.[20] They did not persuade the Council. Lawrence's personal intentions are not known, and perhaps Morris and Buckeley were right when they argued that he had intended the townships to have local self-government. But the Board of Trade would not permit any governor much rein in granting settlers extra rights, whatever his personal predilections.

The settlement of Liverpool proceeded rapidly and was the most successful of the South Shore fishing townships. Seventy families with thirteen schooners and three sawmills settled the first year.[21] By 1762 ninety families (504 individuals) had settled, twelve families short of the 102 required by the grant but enough to pacify Halifax and give some assurance of the survival of the township. By the following year Liverpool

---

17 Memorial from Peleg Coffin, *et al.*, 8 July 1762, PANS, RG 1, Vol. 211, 250-51. This memorial is cited by D. C. Harvey as referring to rights of town government, though the incident which provoked the memorial was the appointment of a proprietors' committee and not town officers. When New England was first settled in the seventeenth century there was no distinction between the proprietorship and town, but by the eighteenth century they were two distinct incorporated bodies within a township. See Roy Hidemichi Akagi, *The Town Proprietors of the New England Colonies: A Study of Their Development, Organization, Activities and Controversies, 1620-1770* (1924; reprinted, Gloucester, Ma., 1963), 12-13.

18 Harvey, "The Struggle for New England Township Government," 18.

19 Council Minutes, 28 October 1766, PANS, RG 1, Vol. 212, 21.

20 Report by Charles Morris and Richard Buckley, October 1763.

21 John Bartlett Brebner, *The Neutral Yankees of Nova Scotia: A Marginal Colony during the Revolutionary Years* (1937, reprinted New York, 1970), 54.

had grown by another ten families (634 total inhabitants).[22] In 1764 the inhabitants of Liverpool gave up the 1759 grant and the government reissued it to conform to the families and individuals who had actually settled.[23] The 1759 grant had named 164 individuals, while the 1764 grant named 142. Only thirty-one names carried over from the one grant to the other. Though a small percentage of the original grantees (18.9%), the thirty-one provided a solid core of settlers. Many of the original grantees may have thought that they could sell their share or have someone settle in their stead, as may have happened since getting settlers to go to Liverpool did not seem to have been a problem. The government seemed willing to overlook the discrepancy by reissuing the grant, and indeed reinforced its position that there were not to be absentee proprietors. The language of the second grant is nearly the same as that of the first. Added, though, is a share for the first settled minister of the Church of England, and one share for the use of the school. The settlement stipulations changed slightly to require that each grantee settle himself or a family before 30 November 1765, reflecting a change in imperial policy on land grants in Nova Scotia.[24]

Throughout, the government retained the right to increase the number of grantees if it thought land was available, and it monitored the number of settled grantees through the reports of the appointed proprietors' committee. On 11 January 1771 an amending grant was issued to fifteen men, as agreed upon by the proprietors' committee at a 2 December 1770 meeting.[25] The 1784 proprietors' report noted another ten men who had been admitted as proprietors in 1771 but were not grantees since they had been absent at the time or could not raise the money to pay their share of the cost for petitioning the government.[26] Through Orders-in-Council the government granted another five shares, and nine men from Halifax received shares in Liverpool as political favors. Between 1759 and 1770, 172 individuals had received land as settlers with the explicit intention of settling (the nine men who received shares as political favors are not counted). The 1784 report noted that 132 of these had fulfilled their settlement obligations. Twenty-six others had settled and made some improvements but poverty and the difficulties of a new settlement had pushed them on. Another twelve had never settled their share and two had settled but made no improvements. Fifty-three families and seventeen

---

22 Nova Scotia Population, 29 October 1763, PANS, C. B. Fergusson Collection, Box 1897, F 2/3.

23 Grant of Liverpool, 20 November 1764, PANS, MG 4, Vol. 77.

24 Margaret Ells, "Clearing the Decks for the Loyalists," *Canadian Historical Association Report* (1933), 47.

25 Grant to John Godfrey, *et al*, 5 January 1771, PANS, MG 4, Vol. 77.

26 Return of the Township of Liverpool, 19 March 1784, PANS, MG 4, Vol. 77.

single men had taken up residence in the township, some for nearly twenty years, but were not grantees. In the 1784 report the proprietors' committee recommended they be given land from those shares which might be escheated from grantees who had not fulfilled their settlement requirements.

One welcomed deviation from New England practice was the willingness of the Nova Scotia government to subsidize the new settlements, primarily for transportation and food. In the fall of 1760 the government shipped 360 rations to Liverpool to be distributed among the township's indigent population.[27] The following March thirteen barrels of pork and thirty barrels of flour arrived, supplemented in April with another ten barrels of pork and forty barrels of flour.[28] John Dogget, the primary organizer for the township of Liverpool, received some governmental monies for his expenses in transporting settlers to Nova Scotia.[29] In the spring of 1761 the government requested him to hire a ship to transport twenty families and their livestock from Nantucket to Liverpool.[30] After the first two years Halifax assisted Liverpool upon reported incidents of need. In December 1762 Dogget requested assistance for a poor family of three and seven other indigent children in the settlement.[31] The following summer a committee surveyed the condition of the new settlements and reported that 1000 bushels of Indian corn might be needed for the sea coast communities of Liverpool, Barrington, and Yarmouth to be distributed from Halifax upon reported need.[32]

The government subsidies had numerous effects, not the least and most immediate of which was to assist in the speedy settlement of the colony. But they could also serve to foster a sense of local obligation to government largess. As well, the committees which oversaw the distribution of food stuffs were appointed out of Halifax and not chosen locally, thus creating a precedent for the intrusion of the central government into local affairs, however benign or necessary it might have been. And lastly, as a very minor form of political patronage, it shifted some of the allegiance of local leaders from the township to the government in Halifax.

* * * * *

The circumstances leading up to the grant in Machias in 1770 are more

---

27 Letter from Richard Buckley, Halifax to John Dogget, Liverpool, 29 October 1760, PANS, RG 1, Vol. 136, 2.

28 Council Minutes, 4 March 1761, PANS, RG 1, Vol. 204, 163; and Council Minutes, 14 April 1761, PANS, RG 1, Vol. 211, 173.

29 Council Minutes, 4 March 1761, PANS, RG 1, Vol. 204, 163.

30 Council Minutes, 22 May 1761, PANS, RG 1, Vol. 211, 192.

31 Council Minutes, 31 December 1762, PANS, RG 1, Vol. 211, 288.

32 Report on the Counties of Nova Scotia, October 1763, PANS, RG 1, Vol. 22.

complex. During the summers of 1761 and 1762 drought plagued New England. In the timber cutting areas of New Hampshire and southern Maine forest fires broke out, probably ignited by lightening. Fuelled to enormous size by the refuse left by wasteful cutting practices, the fires destroyed the timber industry of the region, and drove men eastward down the coast of Maine.[33] Among the first to leave were thirteen men from Scarborough, Maine, who, in 1763, loaded a sawmill onto a boat, sailed downeast and planted their mill on the falls on the West Machias River.[34] The following year their families and others from Scarborough reinforced the nascent settlement. Thinking themselves on the Nova Scotia side of the border they applied to Halifax for a grant of a township encompassing the upper end of the Machias Bay, and the West, Middle and East Machias Rivers. Learning they had settled within the jurisdiction of Massachusetts, they petitioned the Massachusetts General Court for a grant in 1767, but their petition was rejected.[35] In 1768 they applied again; the House of Representatives gave them a grant, but the Council rejected it.[36] In 1770 they applied yet again. This time the grant received the approval of the House of Representatives, the Council and Governor Hutchinson.[37] It was subsequently sent to London for the King's approval, where it was tabled. Only in 1784, after Massachusetts had gained uncontested jurisdiction over Maine, was the grant confirmed and the township's inhabitants were incorporated into the town of Machias.

Machias became the most well-known settlement in the dispute between Massachusetts and Britain over which government had the right to initiate grants in the area of Maine between the Penobscot and St. Croix Rivers. Massachusetts claimed that its title to the area lay in the 1691 charter of William and Mary which had established the Province of Massachusetts Bay. In that charter William and Mary gave Maine to the Bay Colony in gratitude, Massachusetts claimed in 1762, for exertions in driving out the French. In the following seventy years the area east of the Penobscot remained unsettled due to hostilities between the French and the British, but during that time Massachusetts had continued as the area's main source of British defence. Prior to the 1760s the British government had twice challenged the legitimacy of Massachusetts' title to the Territory of Sagadehock, as it came to be known, but both times the Attorney and

---

33 Fox, "The Great Fire in the Woods."

34 "The Proprietors Book of Records of Machias," copy of the original in the Washington County Court House, Machias, Maine, 3.

35 Petition of Machias Inhabitants for a Township Grant, 4 June 1767, Commonwealth of Massachusetts Archives, Vol. 118, 290-91.

36 Petition of the Inhabitants of Machias for a Grant, 7 January 1768, Mass. Archives, Vol. 118, 314-16.

37 Act of the House of Representatives, 4 April 1770, Mass. Archives, Vol. 118, 446.

Solicitor General had found in favor of Massachusetts.[38] Then in the 1760s the British challenged the title again, arguing this time that William and Mary had not possessed the territory in 1691 and therefore could not have granted it legitimately. Specious at best, the argument was part of a British attempt to restructure its North American colonies and especially those in New England.

The conflict also created tension between the Massachusetts General Court and the royally appointed governors. When the General Court began to receive petitions for land in Maine in 1759, Governor Thomas Pownall urged it to resolve all outstanding claims of private parties so that the area could be settled. In the seventeenth century various sections of Maine had been granted to individuals and over the course of the next century a few of the heirs continued to assert their claims to the region. Among them were the heirs of Brigadier Samuel Waldo. In 1762 the Massachusetts General Court granted them a township on the Penobscot River in return for releasing and quiting claim to all right and title to the area between the Penobscot and St. Croix Rivers.[39] This arrangement freed the General Court to grant land in this area, and within a short while it granted twelve townships. By this time Francis Bernard had succeeded Thomas Pownall as governor of Massachusetts, and it fell upon him to decide whether or not to sign grants in territory of disputed jurisdiction. He did and then had to explain his action to the Board of Trade.

In a lengthy letter to the Lords Commissioners for Trade and Plantations written on 8 April 1763,[40] Bernard acknowledged the dispute between Massachusetts and the King over who had owned the area of Maine between the Penobscot and St. Croix rivers and therefore who had the right to initiate grants. He felt, though, that the exigencies of settling the area speedily and the good intentions of the Massachusetts government in achieving this end, overrode any serious complaints that the Lords Commissioners might raise. To demonstrate the good intentions of the General Court he made three points. One, the sole purpose of the grants was to further settlement, and to this end the government had given away and not sold the land. Two, the grants conformed to the restrictions in the 1691 charter, including the requirement that the grantees gain royal approval for all grants in the area. Thus, Bernard saw the grants as "recommendations" to the King, which if not signed would cease after the eighteen months the General Court had allowed for the grantees to gain royal approval. As it happened, the King had it within his power to

---

38 For the 1762 Massachusetts' defense of its claim to the land between the Penobscot and St. Croix Rivers see, *Maine Documentary History*, XIII, 296-302.

39 Grant to S. Waldo and others, 6 March 1762, *Maine Documentary History*, XIII, 264-66.

40 In *Maine Documentary History*, XIII, 308-11.

withhold his signature, and the General Court had it within its power to continue to extend the time allowance for receiving it. From 1762 to 1784 the grants of thirteen townships in Maine (including that of Machias), existed in a legal limbo. But in 1763 when Bernard wrote his justification of the grants he did not reckon with the great stubbornness of both the King and the Massachusetts government. Bernard's third point was that the Massachusetts government required each grantee to give a fifty pound bond against fulfillment of the settlement requirements, therefore reinforcing the point that the grants were for immediate settlement and not long-term speculation. Reckoning that the dispute over the right to land would take a number of years to resolve, Bernard thought it nevertheless worthwhile to open the area to settlers. Massachusetts had proceeded in good faith to achieve just this end and he saw no reason not to give his approval to the grants.

The first six grants, of which Bernard wrote, had been passed in the House of Representatives on 20 February 1762, though he did not write his letter to the Lords Commissioners until 8 April 1763, probably after he learned that there was some resistance in London to approving them. A week after he sent off his explanatory letter he received a strong reprimand from the Lords Commissioners, written on 24 December 1762, for giving his approval to the grants.[41] Thus, by the time the men from Scarborough settled in Machias in the spring of 1763 the conflict over land grants in Maine had reached an impasse beyond which neither Massachusetts nor Britain would move until the resolution of the American Revolution.

The dispute did not keep settlers from continuing to move downeast. In 1768 the House of Representatives and the Council approved a grant to the settlers at Machias, but it had not received gubernatorial approval. In 1770 the same grant passed again and this time Governor Thomas Hutchinson approved it. And like his predecessor Bernard, he had to explain his actions to the Lords Commissioners. For Hutchinson the dilemma was that by 1770 the area between the Penobscot and the St. Croix Rivers had 500 to 1000 settlers, and by barring grants there was no effective way to organize government or resolve differences between settlers. Fearing the complete collapse of law and order in the region, and the emergence of groups similar to the Regulators in North Carolina, he thought it best to sanction the grant of Machias, the site of the largest settlement in the region.[42] From the point of view of the Lords Commissioners, there should have been no settlers in the area, but, as Hutchinson noted, measures to

---

41 Gov. Bernard to the Lords Commissioners, 25 April 1763, *Maine Documentary History*, XIII, 311-15.

42 There are numerous letters in the Massachusetts State Archives written by Hutchinson concerning affairs downeast and his actions in signing the grant for the township of Machias. Some of the more important are found in Vol. 26: 493-94 and Vol. 27: 26, 57-58, 59-60, 60-61, 79.

eject the settlers would have had to originate in either the Massachusetts Council or the House of Representatives, a move which neither body would initiate. Lawrence felt that unless Parliament was willing to take unilateral action and remove Maine from the jurisdiction of Massachusetts then he had to accept the reality of settlement, and under the laws of the Bay Colony provide for civil governance. Like Bernard, Hutchinson defended his action in terms of the immediate exigencies to be met; for Bernard the benefit of settling British subjects in Maine; for Hutchinson the need to have some semblance of order among those settlers. Hutchinson saw the short-term benefits of recognizing grants as having greater primacy than the long-term controversy between London and Boston over who had ultimate jurisdiction in Maine. And like Bernard, Hutchinson was strongly reprimanded by the Lords Commissioners.

Hutchinson, in signing the grant to the Machias settlers, reinforced the hand of the Massachusetts government. So long as the settlers' petition stalled at the level of the General Court, then discontent would focus there or be diffused, rather than be focused explicitly on the King's refusal to sign the grant. But more importantly, Hutchinson reinforced New England patterns of social and political organization. And that was the real issue. Hutchinson thought it best for the grant to go through so that institutions for the maintenance of public order could be established, but his superiors in London probably thought the opposite judging from their condemnation of Hutchinson's action and their position on the Nova Scotian settlements. In Nova Scotia the Board of Trade blocked any move to allow autonomy at the local level, whether in the form of the quasi-public proprietorship or incorporated town government. It is unlikely that the same board would have seen the settlements in Maine in a different light. In Boston the General Court had no intention of letting the settlements develop on the Nova Scotian model. From London's position, the only immediate ploy to maintain some control over settlements in Maine was to keep the governor from signing any grants passed by the House of Representatives and the Council. Withholding the King's signature blocked clear title to land, and incorporation of the town, but it did not prevent the incorporation of the proprietorship which served to replicate and legitimate New England patterns of corporatism and local autonomy. And here the case of Machias is useful.

Once the grant received Governor Hutchinson's signature, the grantees applied to a Massachusetts Justice of the Peace, Samuel Danforth, to issue them a warrant to call the first meeting of the proprietors.[43] (This is also what the settlers in Londonderry, Nova Scotia, had done and which the Council overturned.) The grantees did not first act to receive the King's approbation. Nor was that detail on their agenda when they met on 11

---

43 The Proprietors Book of Records of Machias, 29 June 1770, 1-4.

September 1770 as a proprietorship. Rather they elected their officers: a proprietor's clerk, a committee for calling future meetings, a collector of proprietary taxes, a treasurer, a committee to examine the expenses involved in getting the grant and a committee of lot layers. (These types of offices were common for proprietorships and the ones which the settlers of Liverpool thought were their right to have.) At the first meeting the proprietors also acted to assure the mill rights of the first sixteen settlers to Machias, and to pass a bye-law which would allow them to confiscate and sell the property of proprietors who failed to pay proprietorial taxes. Only at their second meeting, held on 8 November 1770, seven months after the grant was passed, did they arrange to hire an agent to obtain the King's approbation.

The sequence of events is significant. First, the Massachusetts government did not itself act to obtain the King's signature. Rather the grantees had to assume the responsibility, and they sought it not as a group of individuals, in the way they had approached the General Court to receive the grant, but as an incorporated body. The lack of the King's signature did not keep the Justice of the Peace from issuing a warrant for the grantees to meet, elect officers and to vote to tax themselves. This part of the replication of New England society did not depend on the King's signature. It did block the settlers from obtaining unencumbered title to property, but with a large number of resident proprietors, as were present in Machias, that too only provided a minor block to orderly development. The proprietors proceeded to divide the land and define individual lots, thus avoiding or resolving disputes over property boundaries. Division of land became a matter controlled at the level of the township and not the colony. And defined property boundaries, even though the title was not clear, meant that land could be sold on quitclaim deeds. Hutchinson's signature produced the situation of vested corporate rights at the local level which the Board of Trade had guarded against in the Nova Scotia settlements.

The Revolution ended group grants in New England, the last one in Maine being Machias. The Commonwealth of Massachusetts, faced with a large war debt, initiated a program to sell land in Maine to repay its loans. On 28 October 1783, the General Court appointed a committee to dispose of the unappropriated land of Lincoln County, Maine, by settling squatter rights and selling the vacant lands. In 1784 the Eastern Lands Committee circulated a notice throughout Lincoln County for those with claims to submit a statement to the committee either individually or as a group. Most people submitted their claims as part of a group petition, with individual claims tendered almost exclusively for specific islands along the coast.[44] While Machias was the largest settlement east of the Penobscot

---

44 The 1784 petitions for land in Lincoln County are found in the Massachusetts State Archives, Eastern Land Papers, Box 14.

River numerous smaller settlements had developed in the region in the late colonial period. As a rule, people in these settlements petitioned as groups. These petitions either explicitly or in tone acknowledged the changes in land policy wrought by the war, but it is also clear that these settlers knew that their only chance of persuading the government to give them more than 100 acres in squatter rights was to petition as a group and ask for the colonial-style grant. And since most settlements did not have enough adult men to constitute a proprietorship, these petitions had a number of non-resident signators.

For example, eighteen people petitioned for Bucks Harbor, a small peninsula adjoining Machias, and included a detailed summary of their individual claims. Calculating that the whole peninsula would yield approximately 170 acres for each petitioner, and noting that much of the land was rocky, broken and unfit for cultivation, they asked for the whole to be granted to them in common, and they would divide it among themselves. The Eastern Lands Committee rejected the petition, and included Bucks Harbor in the sale of Plantation No. 22. In the deed the five Bucks Harbor petitioners who were residents were named and were to be allowed 100 acres for every five Spanish milled dollars paid within six months of notice.[45] The claims of the other thirteen, many of them by proprietors in Machias, were not acknowledged.

Another sixty-one men, twenty-five of them settlers, petitioned for the land around the settlement at Chandler's River. Since the tract included great sections of barren heath the petitioners reasoned that the useable land would allow "but a moderate share" to each of them. But the Eastern Lands Committee sold this land, together with Bucks Harbor, as Plantation No. 22 for 6120:17:5 pounds to eleven men from Boston. And the twenty-five settlers received the same consideration for land as did the settlers at Bucks Harbor.[46] Unlike colonial petitioners, post-revolution petitioners felt it necessary to justify their request for extensive tracts of land. In both the Bucks Harbor and Chandler's River petitions the justification was the poorness of the land, a very reasonable claim, though surveyors from Boston who had assessed the potential of the region had waxed eloquent about the agricultural prospects.[47] Other petitioners mentioned their steadfast loyalty to the patriot cause in the late war, hoping it would give them greater claim to the grant of a township.[48] And

45 The petition for Bucks Harbor is in the Eastern Land Papers, Box 14. A copy of the deed for Plantation No. 22 can be found in the Washington County Land Deeds Office, County Court House, Machias, Maine, Vol. 1, 129-31.

46 The petition from Chandler's River is found in the Eastern Lands Papers, Box 14.

47 Report of the Commissioners on Machias, 12 September 1771, *Maine Documentary History*, Vol. XIV, 137.

48 See the petitions from Plantation Nos. 4, 6, and the back section of 6, for these sentiments. Eastern Lands Papers, Box 14.

all mentioned the labor and money they had expended in settling the land. In the level of justification there had been a marked shift in the manner of petitioning. But like their colonial counterparts, these post-revolution petitioners, most persons of modest means, knew that their best chances for a substantial grant lay in petitioning as a group.

While these settlers did not gain the privilege of a township grant, they did have the right to meet to discuss plantation concerns, tax themselves for needs such as roads and a minister, and eventually to petition for incorporation as a town. Although one part of the colonial resettlement practice was lost after the war, the rights of local autonomy and self-regulation were retained. In this respect the corporate patterns of New England resettlement remained strong and intact.

* * * * *

Why the New England commitment to corporate behavior in the process of resettlement? First, it allowed many middling and probably some quite poor people access to land. A group had a voice strong enough to be heard in positions of power which the individual of modest circumstances lacked. Second, the group gave the individual greater flexibility, for in Machias, and other towns within the New England colonies, not every grantee had to settle for the terms of the grant to be met. The corporate structure reinforced private individual interest by protecting one's share of land even in one's absence, provided enough of the group settled. It is significant that the British eliminated this practice in Liverpool, and required actual settlement to claim a share of land. Some absentee landholding persisted in Liverpool, but with the chance that the government would escheat the land. The resident proprietors in Liverpool could provide only limited protection to absentee landholders, and only by not reporting or rationalizing the person's absence. In Machias, the group provided greater and legitimized protection to the absentee's property claims.

Group settlement also promised the more rapid extension of political rights through the incorporation of a town than did individual settlement. In New England political rights were extended through one's inclusion in town. Thus to settle without benefit of a group, which could soon be incorporated as a town and send a representative to the assembly, was to choose to be disenfranchised for an indeterminate period of time. Most New Englanders resisted this situation. When the Northwest Territory was opened the provisions for temporary government included in the 1787 Ordinance were put there to attract New England settlers, who were leery of resettling without clear promises of law and order and protection of political rights.[49]

In Nova Scotia, and subsequently throughout British North America, the British eliminated vested corporate rights, whether in the form of proprietorships or incorporated town government. It is significant that before the 1830s only one urban concentration in British North America — Saint John, New Brunswick — had incorporated status. All others, including the major centers of Halifax, Quebec City and Montreal, were run as parishes through the colonial governments. Vested corporate rights concerned the British as much or more than individual rights as they set about to reshape colonial policy. By restricting corporate rights they could restrict alternate focuses of authority, as well as the organized discourse on governmental policy which played such a large role in town meetings in places like Boston. On 14 April 1770 the Nova Scotia Council ordered that the Attorney General notify all concerned that "Town Meetings for debating and resolving on several questions relating to the Laws and Government of the Province ..." were "Contrary to Law" and concerned parties could be prosecuted.[50] Assemblage was not a right, but a privilege given to designated corporate bodies. The protest submitted by the grantees of Liverpool over the appointment of a proprietorial committee indicates that in the minds of many New Englanders assemblage had come to be understood as a "right" of corporate bodies, though not necessarily a right of individuals, with governmental sanction being largely perfunctory, rather than a "privilege" extended by the central government.

While the British could, with the stroke of the pen or lack thereof, severely restrict local corporate rights, changing behavior could not be accomplished so speedily. Thus, in the case of Nova Scotia, it is important to examine how much the New England commitment to local autonomy and corporate behavior continued to shape Nova Scotia development. How much is the resistance of the outports to the control of Halifax a legacy of New England local autonomy? How much and how long did New England behavior persist in the absence of sanctioned structure, and how much did it effect the long-term institutional structure of the province?

Finally, the corporate behavior of New Englanders was functionally specific. The Machias proprietorship regulated the division of the commonly held land and provided some ancillary development such as roads. While it gave some structure to the township before its incorporation, it never presumed to function as the town government. At the end of the Revolution the proprietors moved quickly to have the grant confirmed and the township's residents incorporated as the Town of Machias. Town government was the preserve of another and separate corporate body.

49 Peter S. Onuf, "Settlers, Settlements, and New States," in Jack P. Greene, ed., *The American Revolution: Its Character and Limits* (New York, 1987), 172-73.

50 Council Minutes, Province of Nova Scotia, PANS, RG 1, Vol. 212, 136.

Functional specificity undercut corporate communalism and enhanced private rights. The proprietorship existed to provide and protect individual access to land. The town protected an individual's political rights within the larger political unit of the colony. Neither existed to regulate all or most aspects of a person's life. The corporate structure existed to enhance the protection of private interest rather than to be an end in itself. It is tempting to go one step further and say that if the corporate structure was subservient to private interest then it was basically individualism and little else. But this misses the point that private interest finds protection and enhancement in many different forms and expressions, including corporatism and individualism. If the first priority of New Englanders in search of land in the 1760s had been clear titles, then they would not have been dissatisfied with the policies in Nova Scotia. The government was willing to give clear title to land held in severalty if a person settled, which was more than Massachusetts could promise to settlers in Maine. But many New Englanders chose questionable title to land and a hope for localized corporate rights in Maine, over clear title in Nova Scotia. With resettlement New Englanders had come to associate the protection of private rights with localized corporate rights, rather than through the protection of a centralized government. The retention of them in Maine and their suppression Nova Scotia would have a great impact on the social and political development of the two areas.

Methodism Among Nova Scotia's Yankee Planters

Allen B. Robertson
Queen's University

During the 1770s two revivalist evangelical sects gained a following in Nova Scotia; one, Newlight Congregationalism — with both Predestinarian and Free Will variants — grew out of the religious and social heritage of the colony's dominant populace, the New England Planters. The other sect, Wesleyan Methodism, took root among transplanted Yorkshiremen who moved between 1772 and 1776 to the Isthmus of Chignecto region where it was initially propagated among the faithful in local prayer groups. Ordained and lay preachers of both movements promoted a series of revivals in the province which drew an increasing number of followers into the evangelical fold.[1] The first of these revivals was the Newlight-dominated Great Awakening of 1776-84. In general, Newlightism's greatest appeal was in the Planter townships even though it mutated by 1800 into a Baptist polity. Methodism, which had a fluctuating number of adherents among the visiting military forces at Halifax, had its stronghold in areas settled by British-born colonists, and increased in numbers with the successive waves of Loyalists coming to the province after 1783.[2] Methodism was not confined, however, to segregated geographical areas of Nova Scotia. By the early nineteenth century, there were significant Methodist congregations composed primarily of Planters located throughout the Annapolis Valley and along the province's South Shore. Interesting questions are posed for historians when we consider why New Englanders and their descendants were attracted to what appeared to be essentially a foreign hierarchical religious-cultural movement which had broken from

---

1   Gordon Stewart and George Rawlyk, *A People Highly Favoured of God: The Nova Scotia Yankees and the American Revolution* (Toronto, 1972); J.M. Bumsted, *Henry Alline 1748-1784* (1971; reprint Hantsport, 1984); a valuable early study is Maurice W. Armstrong, *The Great Awakening in Nova Scotia 1776-1809* (Hartford, Conn., 1948); George A. Rawlyk, "From New Light to Baptist: Harris Harding and the Second Great Awakening in Nova Scotia," in *Repent and Believe: The Baptist Experience in Maritime Canada*, ed. Barry M. Moody (Hantsport, 1980), 1-26. For the Yorkshire migration, see W.C. Milner, "Records of Chignecto," *Collections* of the Nova Scotia Historical Society, 15 (1911), 40-46, 61-64, 80.

2   An early, though still standard work on the New England migration to Nova Scotia is J.B. Brebner, *The Neutral Yankees of Nova Scotia: A Marginal Colony During the Revolutionary Years* (1937; reprint Toronto, 1969); see also C.B. Fergusson, "Pre-Loyalist Settlements in Nova Scotia," *Coll* NSHS, 37 (1970), 5-22. For special attention to Methodist centers consult T. Watson Smith, *History of the Methodist Church within the Territories embraced in the late Conference of Eastern British America....*2 Vols. (Halifax, 1877-1890).

rigid predestinarianism. Methodism, moreover, was strongly associated with the Church of England, an institution that had been abhorred by generations of Rhode Island, Connecticut and Massachusett's colonists.[3] An examination of the similarities and differences between Newlightism and Methodism goes far to illuminate the various elements which made it possible for some Planters to make the transition to Methodism.

It is obvious to even the most casual observer that there were many similarities between the two sects and one of the noticeable peculiarities of Nova Scotian colonial religious history is the difficulty which faced sectarian preachers as they tried to gain individual followings. Planters, Yorkshiremen and Loyalists — all were willing to listen to any visiting preacher, contribute to his expenses and donate funds for the erection of more than one place of worship within a community. As a result, a settlement might be described as Methodist or Newlight depending on who happened to be evangelizing. Since, as David Bell has pointed out, Newlights, Wesleyans and Baptists placed emphasis on the 'New Birth' as a demonstrative conversion experience and preachers from the three sects relied on highly charged language to instill their audiences with vivid, emotional imagery, it is little wonder that the lay community often found it confusing to distinguish between Newlight and Methodist preaching.[4] Combined with these shared characteristics were sermons, hymns and exhortations containing a similar message which further clouded the differences between the two sects.[5]

About 1780, for example, John Payzant (in-law of the charismatic Newlight preacher Henry Alline), reported that Alline had gathered a mixed Newlight-Methodist congregation in Cumberland. William Black, who had corresponded with John Wesley prior to embarking on a career as an itinerant preacher, was said to have been associated with this meeting.[6] Although this union only lasted a short time before doctrinal differences arose, it was indicative of the laity's confusion over the sects. Indeed, it took ministerial leadership to point out the differences which lead to the eventual division of this congregation. Payzant provides another example

3   E. Arthur Betts, *Bishop Black and His Preachers* (Sackville, 1976); Allen B. Robertson, "Charles Inglis and John Wesley: Church of England and Methodist Relations in Nova Scotia in the Late Eighteenth Century," *Nova Scotia Historical Review*, 7, 1(1987), 48-63.

4   D.G. Bell, *Newlight Baptist Journals of James Manning and James Innis* (Hantsport, 1984), 4.

5   An examination of comparable American revival techniques is found in William H. Williams, *The Garden of American Methodism: The Delmarva Peninsula 1769-1820* (Wilmington, Del, 1984). Cf. "The Anatomy of Revival" in Stewart and Rawlyk, *A People Highly Favoured*, 121-39; G. A. Rawlyk, *Ravished by the Spirit; Religious Revivals, Baptists and Henry Alline* (Montreal, 1984), 58-69.

6   Brian C. Cuthbertson, ed., *The Journal of John Payzant* (Hantsport, 1981), 28.

from Liverpool in 1783. Liverpool was a town primarily inhabited by Massachusetts and Connecticut Planters. The Newlight Payzant wrote that:

> The people received [him] [Black] as one of Mr. A[lline's] preachers. Mr. Chipman at that time came to Liverpool and found Mr. Black and preached with him. At the same time Mr. B[lack] was drawing a party of[f] from the others. Mr. Jos. S. Baily who was from the Bay of Fundy w[h]ere Mr. B[lack] was well known, he acquainted the people that Mr. Black was not Sound in his principles and was not owned by the people called newlight — which made a Separation. Some said that Mr. Black preached the Same Gospel that Mr. A[lline] preached. But the[y] soon found a Radical difference between the two, so that the[y] made two congregations which were ever after continued.[7]

It is little wonder that Liverpudlians were bewildered. There was already tension among the Newlights over Free Will and Predestinarianism, and Methodist William Black sounded much like Henry Alline when he espoused Arminianism and a 'New Birth.' Those attracted by the new birth theology therefore could be forgiven for believing that the two great preachers offered the same message. During the 1780s and 1790s, however, churches became more institutionally formalized and leaders aimed both for a core congregation composed of loyal members and increased conversions. In the competition for followers, greater attention was paid to the laity and the explication of doctrinal differences as well as the similarities between the sects.

Many of Nova Scotia's first-generation Yankee Planters could remember the upheaval caused by New England's Great Awakening. It too had left a legacy of divisions between 'Old Light' Congregationalists and the 'New Lights'; however, both groups had continued to adhere to orthodox reform Protestant doctrine and the peculiar New England version of Calvinist predestination.[8] Under the charismatic influence and teaching of Henry Alline from 1776 to 1784 these old splits were renewed in Nova Scotia. Alline rejected the deterministic theology of New England for Free Will soteriology; yet it is evident from the subsequent success of the Baptists that few of Alline's followers went on to perpetuate their leader's more extreme heterodox cosmological pronouncements.[9] Nonetheless,

---

7 Cuthbertson, 31.

8 See Williston Walker, *A History of the Congregational Churches in the United States* (New York, 1894); William G. McLoughlin, *Revivals, Awakenings, and Reform: An Essay on Religion and Social Change in America, 1607-1977* (Chicago, Ill., 1978).

9 Armstrong, *Great Awakening in Nova Scotia*, 88-107; Rawlyk, *Ravished by the Spirit*, 6-9; Bumsted, *Henry Alline*, 77-96.

sufficient numbers embraced Free Will theology to sustain Newlight Congregationalist (Allinite) and Free Will Baptist churches. From that number of Free Will adherents, some were convinced of the correctness of Wesleyan Arminianism as preached by William Black, Methodist missionaries from the United States and English missionaries directed by John Wesley and his successors.

The years of Alline's preaching and the sixteen years following his death in 1784 were marked by turbulent sectarianism in the Maritimes. Alline had been indifferent to church discipline, sacraments and denominational labels — for him the 'New Birth' was everything. His evangelical message is succinctly summed up in a journal entry at the time of his conversion:

> O the infinite condescension of God to a worm of the dust! for though my whole soul was filled with love, and ravished with a divine ecstacy beyond any doubts or fears, or thoughts of being then deceived, for I enjoyed a heaven on earth, and it seemed as if I were wrapped up in God.[10]

Even if Alline's understanding of his own experience deviates from the orthodox norm, such lines put him in the tradition of the Christian mystics, among whom Richard of St. Victor may be singled out for the similarity of his descriptions of Divine Love.[11]

Similar depths of ecstatic response or at least profound pietistic expressions could be found among Methodist adherents as well. The Methodist Reverend William Jessop of Delaware, a brother-in-law of a leading Loyalist merchant, Robert Barry, himself a lay exhorter at Shelburne and in Planter Liverpool, made extended missionary tours of New Brunswick and Nova Scotia. His journal was replete with passages in this vein:

> This has been a day of peace to my soul; when I awoke I was favored with some precious gales of the spirit from Pesgath's top. I was also made to drink of those streams which make glad the city of our God. O! Lord where shall I begin to praise thee for if I had ten thousand

10 Rawlyk, *Ravished by the Spirit*, 5.
11 F.C. Happold, *Mysticism: A Study and an Anthology* (1963; reprint Harmondsworth, England, 1970;), 245: "The third degree of love is when the mind of man is ravished into the abyss of divine love so that the soul, having forgotten all outward things, is altogether unaware of itself and passes out completely into its God....In this state, while the soul is abstracted from itself, ravished into that secret place of divine refuge, when it is surrounded on every side by the divine fire of love, pierced to the core, set alight all about, then it sheds its very self altogether and puts on that divine life, and being wholly conformed to the beauty it has seen passes wholly into that glory...." Richard of St. Victor (d. 1173), *The Four Degrees of Passionate Charity* [Love].

tongues they would not be sufficient, for thou hast done great and marvellous things for me; thy precious blood hath purchased my pardon and salvation; all I enjoy comes from thee.[12]

Planters who expected enthusiastic religious language were certainly able to find it in both Jessop and Alline, for there was no insurmountable boundary between the sects on this issue.

Nova Scotia's Yankee settlers also endeavored to duplicate their New England models of church and state. The Congregational church, with its heavy emphasis on individuality, perpetuated the concept of a church as a voluntary association of 'saints.' The church called and dismissed its ministers, and the ministers themselves formed a kind of Puritan brotherhood which worked out doctrinal questions, sought consensus on disputed theological points and ensured that the laity were properly instructed in the steps to conversion.[13] The Great Awakening of the late 1730s had introduced demonstrative, emotional conversions as a required rite of passage into the company of Newlight saints. It had also added the danger of community upheavals that often accompanied vigorous revivals. The Allinite Awakening revived the New England Awakening heritage.[14] Congregational churches in Nova Scotia continued to be democratic associations which regulated their own internal affairs while preachers held churches together through a loose organizational network.

By the 1780s and 1790s, problems existed in the religious and cultural life of Congregational communities which made Methodist alternatives more attractive to the populace. Although historical elements drawn from the New England past brought about difficulties in the new churches, Alline was to blame for many of the insurmountable obstacles facing the Planters. Concerned almost solely with bringing the message of the 'New Birth' to all who heard him, Alline's preaching tours agitated congregations, made divisions in previously consolidated church bodies and left the converted to organize and attempt to govern themselves.[15] The 'ravager of souls' failed to provide the leadership which might have prevented sectarian splits. The abdication of such responsibility and Alline's indifference to the sacraments, together with the emphasis on the Holy Spirit's renewal of souls, led in the years following his death (as it had

---

12 "Journal of William Jessop," 1 January-11 March 1788, 18 January, PANS: MG 100: Vol. 169 #274; For more information on Jessop see, Smith, *Methodist Church*, Vol. 1, 196-98, 310-11.

13 A discussion of the New England Puritan ministerial brethren and their relationship to the laity can be found in Darrett Rutman, *American Puritanism* (Philadelphia, 1970).

14 McLoughlin, *Revivals*, 8; Rawlyk, *Ravished by the Spirit*, 8-9.

15 Allen B. Robertson, "Legacy of Henry Alline: The Antinomian Challenge to New Lights in Nova Scotia," B.A. Hon. thesis, Acadia University, 1982, 21-23; Bell, *Newlight Baptist Journals*, 14-19.

done, indeed, even during his life) to serious outbreaks of antinomianism. The most widespread variant was labelled the "New Dispensation" in which private revelation took precedence over Scripture, Church authority and ministerial control.[16] The 1790s were a chaotic period for Newlights and Newlight Baptists, a time in which several prophets (male and female) declared themselves, some ministers were led in New Dispensationalism and each church seemed to have become almost an island without any overruling authority to whom it could appeal for guidance.

It was against this background, then, that Wesleyan Methodism offered comforting security to the Planters without overthrowing evangelical revivalism. John Wesley had institutionalized and integrated laity-led prayer groups within the structure of a highly regulated hierarchical ministerial association based, in part, on Anglican ecclesiastical precedent. His Nova Scotian followers used this system to foster Methodist respectability in areas devoid of ordained ministers and fostered the faith throughout the province.[17] Classes, composed of seekers after conversion and perfection and led by a designated elder, formed Methodist 'cells' at Cumberland, Shelburne, Liverpool, Halifax, Guysborough and in several smaller centers. These mini-congregations provided a ready audience for itinerant preachers and were used as the basis for evangelical efforts in these localities. Like the Newlights, late eighteenth-century Methodists used a mix of ordained men and trainees, as well as local men gifted as preachers, to spread the Word. Added to this array were the exhorters who enlarged on and re-emphasized pertinent points drawn from the sermons. When numbers warranted, trustees were selected from the Methodist converts. These men — exemplars of Wesleyan teaching — served as elders, raised funds for the construction of meeting houses and salaries for missionaries and concerned themselves with other aspects of institutional church organization. In all cases, the local 'societies' — as the churches were termed — were governed by the District Meeting of Ministers of the New Brunswick-Nova Scotia circuits.

It is necessary at this point to summarize the unique composition of the Nova Scotia Methodist mission field. Following his entrance into a career of itinerant preaching, William Black had called on John Wesley to take responsibility for the fledgling church and to assist it with missionaries. Loyalists at Shelburne had among their numbers Wesleyan leaders from the John Street Chapel in New York city and two of their number, James and John Mann, joined Black on the itinerant circuit. Meanwhile Robert Barry in Liverpool and Philip Marchington in Halifax added their appeals

---

16 'Prophets' included Lydia Randall and Sarah Bancroft; one may also cite Rev. Harris Harding, as a spokesman/prophet for New Dispensationalism, see, Robertson, "Legacy of Henry Alline," 38-39; 55-67.

17 French, *Parsons & Politics*, 8-11; Betts, *Bishop Black*, 5-6, 26-27.

for aid from England.[18] In 1785, the American Methodist Episcopal Church responded to Wesley's and Black's representations by sending Freeborn Garretson and James O. Cromwell to the province, the first two foreign missionaries to be sent to Nova Scotia. Until the mid-1790s the province was nominally a mission of the Methodist Episcopal Church, though in reality it existed as a semi-autonomous District led by a Superintendent (or 'bishop') and his ministerial colleagues. At the same time, Wesley also sent missionaries to the colony, as did his successors, through the English Conference. Although the American/English over-lapping of responsibility created problems, it can be said that in general the result was a coherent Maritime structure which resisted the fractionalizing tendency of Newlightism.

Planters troubled by the confusion inherent in Newlight divisions found refuge in the Wesleyan Methodist fold. Those who cared to learn the doctrinal basis of Methodism could do so through the writings of John Wesley,[19] a trained theologian whose body of writings stood out in marked contrast to the convoluted heterodoxical insights in Henry Alline's theological-metaphysical works, *The Two Mites* and *The Anti-Tradition-alist*.[20] Further, the often-felt sense of isolation in the ultra-independent Newlight congregations was absent from the Methodist societies which from 1785 fostered a sense of regional identity through the District Meetings. Ties to both the Methodist Episcopal Church and the English Connection provided an international fellowship in which Nova Scotia Methodists found themselves part of a dynamic and growing 'global' religious movement.[21] Methodism in the province, at least prior to 1800, was an expanding religious body in marked contrast to Newlight

---

18 D.A. Sutherland, "Marchington, Philip," *Dictionary of Canadian Biography*, Vol. 5; Robertson, "Charles Inglis and John Wesley," 53-54; Nellie Fox, "Loyalist Brothers: John and James Mann," *Nova Scotia Historical Review*, 4, 2(1984), 83-89.

19 A standard stipulation in deeds for sites of Wesleyan chapels included reference to Wesley's works; eg.: Robert Gray to Robert Barry, Thomas Smart, Thomas Ridgeway, Isaac Enslow and Alexander McKay [Trustees], 19 Sept. 1804: "...to the intent that they and the Survivors of them and the Trustees...for ever permit such Person or persons as shall be appointed by the Yearly Conference of the People called Methodists and no others...to preach and expound God's Holy word Provided always that the said Person or persons preach no other Doctrine than is contained in Mr. Wesley's Notes upon the New Testament and Eight Volumes of Sermons...": Registry of Deeds, Shelburne, N.S.: Book 5, 459.

20 Henry Alline, *Two Mites on Some of the Most Important and Much Disputed Points of Divinity....* (Halifax, 1781); Henry Alline, *The Anti-Traditionalist* (Halifax, 1783). For commentary, see, Rawlyk, *Ravished by the Spirit*, 56-58; Bumsted, *Henry Alline*, 78-90.

21 Frank Baker, The Trans-Atlantic Triangle: Relations between British, Canadian, and American Methodism during Wesley's Lifetime, *The Bulletin* (United Church of Canada), 28 (1979), 5-221.

factionalism.[22]

Planters who continued to value baptism and communion found a strong sacramentalism in the Wesleyan fellowship. It perpetuated, in Planter eyes, the Congregationalist practice of admitting only the converted to the communion table, a contrast to Anglicanism's all-inclusive call. In essence, Methodism was that 'Puritan' church sought by Nova Scotia's Yankee ancestors rather than being a mere variant of the suspect Church of England.[23] Combined with sacramental observance, evangelical piety and structure, the Methodist societies with their classes and selection of trustees gave the Planters a degree of democracy which made the Wesleyan association less 'foreign' than it first might have appeared to them.

The Methodist road to conversion and its subsequent pursuit of perfection was not a narrow one. Enough variation in individual conversions was permitted to accommodate a variety of temperaments. By contrast, the Newlight tradition as exemplified by Alline was far more rigid. Alline, who had undergone an intensely emotional conversion, took his rebirth as the norm by which the validity of other such conversions were tested.[24] Anyone who could not match this experience was left to endure great psychological distress. Methodism provided the evangelical alternative to this situation and John Payzant, commenting on a Horton township revival in 1786, disdainfully alluded to the desertion of Newlightism by Planters:

> The Baptists Insist that Mr. Payzant Should Preach in their meeting House, which accordingly he did and continued until the reformation was over. Then they Refused him the House. At almost the conclusion of the Reformation the Methodist came to Horton, and preached there. In a reformation there are always some that our Churches cannot receive. They were a pray [prey] for the Methodist, which caused a division, for they took all such into their Class, So that the opposers, to vital religion, opposed more than ever. They said that the Methodists were more favorable than the new lights....[25]

---

22 Smith, *Methodist Church*, Vol. I, 332-44, provides a review and summary of Wesleyan progress at the end of the 1790s on such matters as church buildings, seating capacity, general sizes of congregations and numbers of the congregations who were full members of the Methodist churches — for example, Halifax [Zoar Chapel] c.900 capacity, 1798 membership 120; Liverpool c. 500-600 capacity, 1798 membership 130; Shelburne-Barrington circuit 1798 membership 158.

23 Cf. Williams, *Garden of American Methodism*, 90-104.

24 Rawlyk, *Ravished by the Spirit*, 5.

25 Cuthbertson, *John Payzant*, 41; Robertson, Legacy of Henry Alline, 30-32.

The Methodist perspective of the same event, as recorded by William Black, is of a decidedly different cast:

> We had some very happy times...during the winter, especially at Horton, where there was a powerful awakening among the people. Fifteen witnessed a good confession; I doubt not but more would have found the love of God, had it not been for the great opposition they received from the Antinomian Mystics.[26]

As we can see, it was difficult in a predominantly Planter area to go over to a minority religious position. Nonetheless, there were converts to Methodism at Horton, an indication of the powerful attraction that the Wesleyan path offered.[27]

Besides its purely religious aspects, Methodism was attractive to Planters in other ways. As with traditional Congregationalism, Wesleyan Methodism favoured an educated clergy. Of course, few native Maritimers could proceed by any path other than private study. Their English counterparts, who came from Anglican backgrounds, had better educational opportunities and were respected for their intellectual training. This is not to say that the leadership eschewed employing gifted men who lacked formal training. There never was, however, the deep seated suspicion of education which existed among the Newlights.

Squire Simeon Perkins of Liverpool was a shrewd businessman and discerning worshipper. His diary chronicled the comings and goings of all the denominational preachers in his community from the 1760s to 1810. Won over by Methodism in the early 1790s through the instruction of William Black and the friendship of business acquaintances Robert Barry and John Kirk (both Loyalists), he had no objections to hearing a read sermon.[28] As trustee of Liverpool's first Methodist chapel, Perkins also tried to evaluate the orthodox content in the preacher's delivery, as he did when Rev. Cooper spoke in town in 1801:

> Mr. Cooper is an Orator, and uses very Good Language, his Observations Very pertinent, and his doctrine Strictly according to the General Doctrines Preached by the late Mr. John Wesley, and, to my weak apprehension, Scriptual.[29]

---

26 Matthew Richey, *A Memoir of the late Rev. William Black, Wesleyan Minister* (Halifax, 1839), 164.

27 Smith, *Methodist Church*, Vol. 1, 164-66.

28 Charles Bruce Fergusson, ed., *The Diary of Simeon Perkins 1804-1812* (Toronto, 1978), 16: 4 March 1804: "Mr. Barry Read one of the late Mr. Charles Wesley's Sermons in the afternoon...."

29 Charles Bruce Fergusson, ed., *The Diary of Simeon Perkins 1797-1803* (Toronto, 1967), 313.

Perkins, like many of his day, was a reader of religious works and following his conversion he continued with Wesleyan tracts. A man of business, he readily recognized the need of education and became part of that mercantile leadership element in colonial Methodist society which promoted such values.

It has been persuasively argued that the Great Awakening of 1776-1784 helped prepare Nova Scotia's Yankees to cope with the political-social outcome of the Revolution.[30] Residents of the British Empire, they had found consolation in the Newlight message and concept of themselves as special people. Those Planters who adopted Methodism were likewise given reassurance. Outreach by the Methodist Episcopal Church enabled Nova Scotians to continue close ties with their former New England home land and expanded those ties to the middle states which formed the heart of American Methodism. Though such relations created some problems for elements among the Loyalist Methodist groups still resentful of the political outcome, it nonetheless proved the means by which animosities were lessened.[31] At the same time, orientation toward England was facilitated by correspondence with John Wesley and as a result of the increased numbers of English missionaries coming to the province. The English tie of Methodism appealed to Planters eager to acknowledge that they had a new role to play in a royalist colony and enabled the 'neutral Yankees of Nova Scotia' to become full participants in the Second British Empire.[32]

Finally, Methodism facilitated the integration of both Planters and Loyalist settlers in Nova Scotia. As already mentioned, there was a core group of Methodists at Shelburne in addition to a presence at Halifax — both the result of the refugee influx. This bolstered the Methodist numbers in the province, provided new preachers and leaders, and introduced an active mercantile class which increased the sect's respectability. Planter Liverpool was the most important south Shore community outside Halifax. Its proximity to Shelburne meant that contact was inevitable. William Black and subsequent missionaries made Halifax, Liverpool and Shelburne a regular part of their circuit so that news of the faith's growth

---

30 Stewart and Rawlyk, *People Highly Favoured*, 179-92; Rawlyk, *Ravished by the Spirit*, 16-17, 88-89.

31 "I made bold to open matters to Mr. Wesley, and begged of him to send one preacher from England as a number of people would prefer an Englishman to an American. Many have refused hearing me on this account." Freeborn Garrettson to Francis Asbury, 1786, quoted in Nathan Bangs, *The Life of the Rev. Freeborn Garrettson*, 5th ed. (New York, 1847), 11.

32 Neil McKinnon notes the reestablishment of ties to the United States by the Loyalists but does not consider how they reoriented themselves in their Nova Scotia residency vis-a-vis the crown: Neil McKinnon, *This Unfriendly Soil: The Loyalist Experience in Nova Scotia 1783-1791* (Montreal, 1986). Cf. Robertson, "Charles Inglis and John Wesley."

was passed along to both Planter and Loyalist followers. The relocation of a few Loyalist labourers, artisans and merchants to Liverpool was eased through the support of the Planter Methodist society. John Kirk, Captain Samuel Man and Doctor Daniel Kendrick were three noteworthy members of this Society as was Robert Barry who, prior to moving to Liverpool in 1810, was already an active supporter of Methodism in the town.[33] When the trustees were chosen in 1793 to oversee the Society in Liverpool the group included Loyalist John Kirk and Planters Simeon Perkins, Samuel Hunt, William Smith and Captain Bartlett Bradford. These men spoke for the Society in the absence of ministers, while Hunt and later Barry (who became trustee in 1815) led the services when no missionaries were present.[34] While Liverpool is only one center, it is a fine example of the blending of peoples into Nova Scotians — a process aided in part by the sharing of belief in the tenants of Wesleyan Methodism.[35]

The year 1800 is important in the history of both Nova Scotia's Newlight Baptists and Wesleyans. This was the year that the Baptist Association was organized, marking a breakaway from Newlight theology.[36] Methodists recall this as the year that William Black sailed to England to appeal for Wesleyan missionaries to replace the Methodist Episcopal missionaries who had been redirected to aid the rapidly expanding movement in the United States.[37] Those few years in the 1790s when Methodist manpower was depleted marked a time for Baptists to regain lost ground and build up a foundation from which they were to remain numerically superior to

---

33 John Kirk: Loyalist grantee Shelburne Twp.; trader, merchant, ship-owner at Liverpool, N.S.; medical consultant. Capt. Samuel Man (1753-1833): Loyalist grantee Shelburne Twp.; sea-captain and fisherman at Liverpool; removed c. 1807 to Gabaruse, Cape Breton Island. Dr. Daniel Kendrick: Loyalist refugee at Shelburne; physician 1790 at Liverpool; 1793 in Cornwallis Twp., 1800 surgeon to Royal Newfoundland Regiment.

34 For initial discussion to build a Methodist meeting house and subsequent developments, see, Charles Bruce Fergusson, ed., *The Diary of Simeon Perkins 1790-96* (Toronto, 1961), 215-16, 233.

35 PANS, MG 4, Vol. 79, Records of the Methodist Church, Liverpool, Nova Scotia. The class lists and pew-subscribers provide information and offer a way to identify which Planter families converted to Methodism and help locate Loyalist settlers in the town and vicinity. Pre-1800 records for the Annapolis-Granville Circuit, an area of Planter and Loyalist settlement, are not extant; however, a check of baptismal and marriage records post-1800 offer a source comparable to Liverpool's records: PANS, Mfm, Churches, Bridgetown: Methodist/Presbyterian/United. Planter settler lists, Loyalist grantee lists and genealogical records would have to be drawn on to provide percentage statistics of Planters-Loyalists in either the South Shore or Annapolis Valley circuits (and elsewhere in the province). Even a cursory check, however, reveals both immigrant groups in the Annapolis-Granville Circuit as Methodists and increased intermarriage between Planters and Loyalists.

36 Cuthbertson, *John Payzant*, 78-83.

37 Smith, *Methodist Church*, Vol. 1, 369-73; Betts, *Bishop Black*, 51-55.

Methodists throughout the nineteenth century.[38] Though the ratio would be about three to one for Baptist congregations over Methodists in the 1800s, Yankee Planters did not drop away from the latter.[39] They continued to find comfort in the spiritual and institutional alternative of Wesleyanism and would remain, as had their Methodist parents and grandparents of the eighteenth century, Planters with a difference.

38 George A. Rawlyk, *New Light Letters and Songs* (Hantsport, 1983), 35-37.
39 Smith, *Methodist Church*, Vol. 1, 332-44.

From Disunity to Integration: Evangelical Religion and Society in Yarmouth, Nova Scotia, 1761-1830

Daniel C. Goodwin
Acadia Divinity College[1]

In recent years there has been a resurgent interest in the New England Planters. However, little serious attention has been given to Planter settlements as they evolved into the nineteenth century. Even the works which ably interpret the religious awakenings of the Planters have failed to probe the role of religion in the development of specific settlements.[2] In response to this gap in the field of Planter Studies, this paper charts four phases of religious development in Yarmouth Township from 1761 to 1830. These phases include disunity, identity, structure and integration. Although economic and political factors were undoubtedly important in the development of Yarmouth Township during these years, the focus is confined primarily to the role of Planter religion.

DISUNITY

The early years of settlement in Yarmouth Township, 1761-1779, marked a period of disunity and strife as the newly settled Planters tried to create a society comparable to that of their former New England homeland. The first major problem for the struggling immigrants was the actual settlement process. Because the procedure for relocating had not been planned in detail for Yarmouth Township, families which settled in the township came from as many as twenty different towns and villages in Massachusetts and Connecticut.[3] Hence, large numbers of Yarmouth settlers were not linked together by shared life experiences or family relationships which had been the case in other Planter settlements such as Falmouth, Horton and Cornwallis.[4] Since the church was the only visible public institution in Yarmouth society during the early years, it is not surprising that it reflected the tensions of this period. Although most of the

---

1 I would like to express my thanks to Dr. Barry Moody, Department of History, Acadia University, who acted as my M.A. supervisor when the material for this paper was collected.

2 The following represent the most important works on Planter religion: G.A. Rawlyk, *Ravished by the Spirit: Religious Revivals, Baptists and Henry Alline* (Montreal, 1984); G.T. Stewart and G.A. Rawlyk, *A People Highly Favoured of God: The Nova Scotia Yankees and the American Revolution* (Toronto, 1972); J.M. Bumsted, *Henry Alline, 1748-1784* (Hantsport, N.S., 1984).

3 George S. Brown, *Yarmouth, Nova Scotia: A Sequel to Campbell's History* (Boston, 1888), 159-161.

4 A.W.H. Eaton, *The History of Kings County, Nova Scotia* (Salem, Mass., 1910), 71-72; John V. Duncanson, *Falmouth Township, Nova Scotia* (Belleville, Ont., 1983), 11.

Yarmouth settlers were Congregationalist, the religion which they had in common was unable to provide societal stability because New England Congregationalism itself was far from being uniform by 1760. In spite of religious differences among the township residents, two churches were established in 1767; one in Cape Forchu and the other in Chebogue, the larger of the two communities. The Congregational church in Cape Forchu was organized on 2 September 1767, under the leadership of the Reverend Nehemiah Porter.[5] Signs of dissatisfaction soon erupted, however, as Porter was not thought by some to be "friendly to the revival of Religion" and doctrinally unsound because he "did not so well agree with the Doctrines of Grace in some Particulars."[6] The evidence suggests that doubt was cast upon Porter by some, not for theological reasons but because of the way in which he preached the doctrines. He did not preach in the intensely emotional style which was characteristic of New Light preachers and popularized in America by George Whitefield. By 1771 the hostile opposition towards Porter had reached unacceptable proportions and caused a division within the congregation. As a result, Porter was forced to return to New England, discouraged, distraught and impoverished. For the next twenty years this church went without a full time pastor.[7]

The Chebogue church, which was officially organized on 18 December 1767, chose John Frost, a lay preacher from Argyle, to be its minister. Like the congregation in Cape Forchu, there were divisions from the very beginning in Chebogue. One cause of division was the fact that many individuals were not eligible for full membership because they were unable to obtain letters of dismissal from their churches in New England. Therefore, only a small percentage of residents were eligible to covenant together to form the 'church' proper. Those who were not members but attended were known as the 'society.'[8]

The second cause of division, became evident when many in the congregation (church and society) thought that Frost "had not an entertaining and easy Way of delivery in his publick discourses."[9] Given the importance that New Light's placed on preaching style, the church invited Frost to resign from his position as pastor. To this request he replied, "he was chosen or elected to the Sacred Office, and had not forfeited his Right by any Scandelous Behaviour," and was, therefore,

---

5   Public Archives of Nova Scotia [hereafter PANS], MG 2, Vol. 770A, No. 1, Letters and Papers of Reverend Nehemiah Porter.

6   G.T. Stewart, ed., *Documents Relating to the Great Awakening in Nova Scotia, 1760-1791* (Toronto, 1982), 20.

7   Stewart, *Documents Relating to the Great Awakening*, 20.

8   Stewart, *Documents Pertaining to the Great Awakening*, 18.

9   Stewart, *Documents Relating to the Great Awakening*, 13.

"bound in Conscience not to give Way."[10] Since a covenant relationship, which bound together pastor and church under God, was a solemn and serious oath, the church did not dismiss Frost from his position.

These divisions led to a separation in the congregation, primarily along the lines of church and society. Since the society was under no convenant obligations to remain in fellowship with the congregation, it sought the leadership of a Baptist preacher, the Reverend Ebenezer Moulton, who lived in Yarmouth Township.[11] In a desperate attempt to heal the separation, the church ordained Frost on 21 September 1769. Contrary to accepted practice, the ordination took place without the assistance or representation of any other church body or association. It had been assumed, erroneously, that those who had separated would return when it was known that the church possessed a valid minister who was ordained. The plan failed. The irregular ordination of an unwanted, stubborn pastor who had questionable talents for the ministry did little to unify the congregation. If anything, it widened the gulf between the two groups.[12]

In one final attempt to bridge this separation in the congregation, the church petitioned a number of churches in Massachusetts for assistance. In response to this desperate plea for help, the Massachusetts brethren sent the Reverends Sylvanus Conant and Solomon Reed of First and Third churches, Middleborough, Massachusetts, respectively, to Yarmouth Township to assess the situation. After their evaluation was completed the New England pastors made the following suggestions: first, that Frost and Moulton cease all Sunday preaching activities; secondly, that Jonathan Scott, a lay preacher and church member, assume the role of interim pastor until such time that a full time minister could be obtained. Both recommendations were followed and the congregation was unified once again.[13]

Since Scott's preaching and pastoral gifts were found to be acceptable by the congregation, and the likelihood of engaging a settled pastor from New England was slim, the Chebogue congregation invited Scott to be its permanent pastor. Sensitive to the instability of the congregation and the disastrous effects of Frost's irregular ordination, Scott requested that he be examined and approved for ordination by the churches in Middleborough, Massachusetts. Scott's request was granted and he was ordained 29 April 1772.[14]

The congregation now looked to a future of unity and solidarity as Scott appeared to be able to meet the expectations of the different factions. He

10 Stewart, *Documents Relating to the Great Awakening*, 18.

11 G.T. Stewart, "Ebenezer Moulton," *Dictionary of Canadian Biography*, Vol. 5, 564-5.

12 C.B. Fergusson, *The Life of Johnathan Scott* (Halifax, 1960), 25.

13 Stewart, *"Documents Relating to the Great Awakening*, 23-8.

14 Stewart, *Documents Relating to the Great Awakening*, 30-1.

preached in the accepted tradition and possessed a legitimate claim to the pastoral office, having been affirmed by the Chebogue church and ordained through proper channels. However, congregational or township unity was not to be realized under Scott's direction. Soon after he assumed his responsibilities as permanent pastor, Scott introduced and enforced a rigid church discipline. During his first decade as pastor, people were admonished for "Dancing and Frolicking with losse company," breach of sabbath, family disputes, giving children too much freedom, failing to attend worship and cursing. Discipline was often carried out in the face of great opposition because people were asked to confess their sin publicly and repent of their wayward behaviour.[15] If some persons regarded the behavioural code upheld by Scott to be too rigorous and too strict, others such as Cornelius Rogers regarded Scott to be lax in his duties in this area.[16] Squabbles on both sides erupted around the discipline issue, indicating that the congregation was far from being uniform in its expectations of Scott and what constituted proper church practice.

Further doubt was cast upon Scott's ability and sincerity when in the fall of 1778, prior to his visit to the Congregational church in Cornwallis, he complained to his parishioners that his income was far too small, and that he lived too far away from the bulk of his congregation and had little time to operate his small farm. During his absence, the congregation attempted to correct the problems he had presented to them.[17] Sensitive to their pastor's situation, the congregation secured land near the meeting house and funding to build Scott a new house. In addition, the congregation increased his salary to fifty pounds yearly. Upon return from Cornwallis, Scott was informed that his complaints had been addressed. However, legal difficulties resulted in the deed for his land being improperly registered. Responding unwisely, Scott remarked, "What you have proposed to give, will half support my family." The lasting impression was that "Mr. Scott was after Money" and wanted to leave his pastoral charge to go to Cornwallis.[18]

The division within the two congregations in Yarmouth Township were restricted to religious and ecclesiastical concerns; nevertheless, they reflect the disunity, vulnerability, fragility and growing pains of Yarmouth Township in the first decade of settlement. These divisions would soon be further widened when Henry Alline, the dreaded 'church wrecker' and catalyst for the Great Awakening in Nova Scotia, appeared in Yarmouth.

15 Stewart, *Documents Relating to the Great Awakening*, 45-64.

16 Stewart, *Documents Relating to the Great Awakening*, 128.

17 Stewart, *Documents Relating to the Great Awakening*, 80.

18 Stewart, *Documents Relating to the Great Awakening*, 86.

IDENTITY

On 20 October 1781, Henry Alline arrived on the Yarmouth scene with his unique gospel message. Having worked with the Congregational church in Cornwallis where Alline had caused discord, Scott immediately opposed Alline from a theological perspective, questioning his heterodox theology as found in the *Two Mites*.[19] Since the Yarmouth Planters assessed the validity of their ministers primarily by their preaching style, Alline was received with open arms. Their attitude was best expressed by deacon James Robbins who said that Alline was acceptable because he "was desirous to promote Reformation" and Amos Hilton who remarked that it "was no matter of any great Consequence to him what a Man's Principles were, if he was but earnest in promoting a good work."[20] It is ironic that the same standard which declared Jonathan Scott to be an acceptable minister of the gospel also affirmed that Alline was one sent by God to do a good work.

Scott failed to realize that his congregation placed 'Alline's reformation' clearly within the accepted bounds of their New England Congregational experience. By vehemently attacking Alline, both privately and publicly — and publishing his views in a 1784 tract entitled *A Brief View*,[21] Scott added great pressure to his already unstable congregation. Those who opposed Scott's position, formed a separate religious group in 1783. In the beginning this split in the congregation was not unlike that of 1771 when Ebenezer Moulton established a second group but there was one important difference. By forcing many in his congregation to define the Allinite movement as something distinct from New England Congregationalism, Scott reinforced the uniqueness of the Great Awakening in the minds of those who supported Alline. Ultimately they began to define their religious orientation as "Allinite." Although the evangelicalism held by those who separated was not significantly transformed by Alline, the Scott-Alline controversy consolidated the separated group's corporate sense of sharing in a significant religious experience under the direction of Alline.[22]

Henry Alline left Yarmouth in 1782 never to return but the Allinite group continued to flourish. Local lay leaders such as Cornelius Rogers and itinerant Allinite evangelists such as Thomas Handley Chipman, John Payzant, Joseph Dimock and Harris Harding gave direction to this

19 The most comprehensive one volume collection of Alline's theological works and other writings is G.A. Rawlyk, ed., *Henry Alline: Selected Writings* (New York, 1987).

20 Stewart, *Documents Relating to the Great Awakening*, 124.

21 Jonathan Scott, *A Brief View of the Religious Tenents and Sentiments lately Published and Spread in the Province of Nova Scotia* (Halifax, 1784).

22 I have developed this in "Advancing Light: Evangelicalism in Yarmouth Township 1761-1830," M.A. thesis, Acadia University, 1986, 66-73.

Allinite following,[23] and helped to maintain the unique identity held by the separated group which the Scott-Alline controversy had caused in Yarmouth. This leadership prevented any possible reconciliation which might have taken place between the Allinite group and the Congregational establishment in Yarmouth Township.

Of all the Allinite evangelists who continued to preach in the Yarmouth area, Harris Harding was by all counts the most influential. He not only assisted in forming the separated group into a Newlight Church, but also became its permanent minister in 1798. So strongly entrenched in the Allinite tradition was Harding that he tried physically to appear and preach as had Alline.[24] Only Alline himself would have been a more appropriate choice of a pastor at Yarmouth.

By 1800 the Newlight church embodied a distinct identity in that its evangelicalism, though remarkably similar to that of New England Congregationalism, was regarded as Allinite. Implicit in this orientation was an evangelistic zeal which greatly increased its numbers and influence in the Yarmouth area. Since the Newlights had established their meeting house in Cape Forchu, now the larger of the two township communities, they were in the best location for influencing the area with their religious orientation.[25] For the first time, a significant number of people in Yarmouth township shared a common religious identity which was the direct result of having experienced in a dramatic way the Great Awakening and subsequent more localized revivals led by Allinite preachers such as Harding.

STRUCTURE

Despite the growth in Allinite followers, a well-defined structure within the Yarmouth Newlight church was slow in coming. It was not until 1820 that the Allinite body had developed structurally into a Baptist church. The beginning of this development may be traced to a series of revivals which took place between 1790 and 1810. These 'religious outpourings,' which occurred throughout the western end of the colony, are often referred to collectively as the Second Great Awakening in Nova Scotia.[26] An outpouring of evangelical zeal coupled with baptism by immersion 'en

---

23 Stewart, *Documents Relating to the Great Awakening*, 138; I.E. Bill, *Fifty Years with the Baptists in the Maritime Provinces* (Saint John, 1880), 184.

24 G.A. Rawlyk, ed., *New Light Letters and Spiritual Songs* (Hantsport, N.S., 1983), 147; G.A. Rawlyk, "From Newlight to Baptist: Harris Harding and the Second Great Awakening in Nova Scotia," in Barry Moody. ed., *Repent and Believe: The Baptist Experience in Maritime Canada* (Hantsport, N.S., 1980), 1-26.

25 John Davis, *Life and Times of the Late Reverend Harris Harding* (Charlottetown, 1866), 73-4.

26 Rawlyk, *From Newlight to Baptist*, 1.

masse' characterized this revival. This fusing of believer's baptism by immersion with the revivalistic orientation altered, slightly, the Allinite tradition but more so in Yarmouth than elsewhere in Nova Scotia.[27]

During the Yarmouth revival of 1799, James Manning baptised the Reverend Harris Harding by immersion.[28] By 1807 Harding had led his congregation to acceptance of much of the Baptist system of faith and practice. However, the church still maintained the practice of open communion, admitting to membership those who had not received believer's baptism by immersion.[29] This open communion practice was the main reason for the Yarmouth Baptist church's succession in 1809 from the Nova Scotia Baptist Association which insisted on closed communion.[30]

In 1807 Zachariah Chipman of Bridgetown, Nova Scotia, settled in Yarmouth. An active lay-person and promoter of the Regular Baptist position, as espoused by the Nova Scotia Baptist Association, Chipman was sensitive to the 'Newlight to Baptist' transition which had occurred in many churches in the colony. Having witnessed this transition in the Bridgetown Baptist church, Chipman played a crucial role in the development of the Yarmouth church as it evolved into the Regular Baptist fold.[31]

In 1814, the much neglected principle of "occasional communion," which had been embraced officially in 1807, was enforced under the influence of Zachariah Chipman. Thereafter unimmersed persons were denied full membership status in the church, although they were still permitted to receive the Lord's Supper.[32] Further structural advances made under Chipman's direction included the introduction of church discipline, an emphasis on regular church attendance and the appointment of deacons.[33] Although much effort was channelled into the development of internal church structure, social responsibility was not ignored. In fact, the Baptists became the most socially active denomination in the township by unanimously resolving to take a weekly collection to assist the poor and aged.[34]

By 1820, the Yarmouth Baptist church, under the careful direction of

27 Baptist Collection, Acadia University Archives (hereafter BCAUA), Manning Correspondence.

28 BCAUA, Manning Correspondence.

29 Davis, *Life and Times of the Late Reverend Harris Harding*, 85.

30 BCAUA, Minutes of the Nova Scotia Baptist Association, 26-28 June 1809.

31 *Christian Messenger*, 1 August 1860.

32 BCAUA, Zion Baptist Church Records.

33 BCAUA, Zion Baptist Church Records.

34 For an assessment of Chipman's crucial role in this transition consult Davis, *Life and Times of the Late Reverend Harris Harding*, 83-4.

Zachariah Chipman, developed a well-defined structure and had assumed a vital role within the society of Yarmouth. The Allinite identity of the church was maintained primarily because the implementation of church order and structure did not threaten the essence of the people's evangelicalism which was steeped in Allinite tradition.[35] If the church adequately reflected the society at large then these two decades may be seen as crucial for the development of the township. Its largest social institution, the Baptist church, established order and structure, perhaps out of necessity to accommodate its growing numbers and more likely as a reflection of a changing society.

UNITY/INTEGRATION

The most dramatic expression of the church's role in the development of Yarmouth Township is found in the massive revival of 1827-28. Whereas the church had often caused or at least reflected the instability of the township communities in the past, this revival proved to be the catalyst for the actual integration of Yarmouth society.

The developments leading up to the revival of 1827-28 placed the Baptist church in an excellent position to reap the benefits of this religious outpouring. By the mid-1820s the Baptist church had attracted a significant number of people to its fold while the other denominations of the township, including Methodists, Anglicans and Congregationalists, do not seem to have gained large followings.[36] At the same time, the Congregational church in Chebogue, the only real threat to the Baptists, suffered another period of disunity which prompted several of its prominent leaders to leave the church.[37]

In response to the needs of a growing township, the Baptist church began to hold extra meetings in some of the outlying areas. By 1826, monthly meetings were being held in Chebogue, the Ponds and Beaver River. Although this small network of mission posts, which were manned by Harding and a number of lay leaders, did not generate a rapid increase in the church's membership, it did ensure that Baptists in the out-lying areas of the township would not be swept into the folds of other denominations.[38]

---

35 For a discussion of church discipline in Maritime Baptist Churches see Charles W. Deweese, "Church Covenants and Church Discipline among Baptists in the Maritime Provinces," in Moody, ed., *Repent and Believe*, 27-45.

36 Holy Trinity Anglican Church, Yarmouth, N.S.: "Church Records;" United Church Conference Archives, Halifax, N.S., Wesleyan Methodist Missionary Society, Reel No. 1; PANS, MG 4: Vol. 12A, Records of the First Chebogue Congregational Church, 1790-1840.

37 Records of the First Chebogue Congregational Church, 282.

38 Zion Baptist Church Records, 1821-1826.

During the years that the church expanded its ministry into the smaller communities of Yarmouth Township, the Baptist Church began controversial discussions concerning the possibility of joining the Nova Scotia Baptist Association. Each time the question was raised it was deferred for further consideration because the association's statement of faith, to which member churches were required to subscribe, held to the principle of closed communion, which denied the Lord's Supper to all who were not baptised by immersion. The Yarmouth church was still not willing to deny the eucharist to unimmersed believers. To do so would have been to ignore the church's rich and varied Allinite heritage.[39]

In order to convince the church to accept closed communion and join the Nova Scotia Baptist Association, Zachariah Chipman invited the Reverend Thomas Ansley, an association minister/evangelist from Bridgetown, to supply preach while Harding itinerated in various areas of the province. Having been raised in the Episcopal tradition, and later converted to the Baptist position, Ansley's experience provided him with a sensitivity to Baptists who had emerged from a number of traditions, such as those in Yarmouth.[40] Therefore, he was able to preach, with great zeal and effectiveness, the salvation message of new life in Jesus Christ along with the polity and doctrinal position embraced by the Nova Scotia Baptist Association.

Ansley's remarkable success in Yarmouth as an evangelist and promoter of the regular Baptist cause, however, did not rest primarily on these factors. During this revival an acute and frequently fatal disease ravished the township. Writing on 14 April 1828, Zachariah Chipman provided the following background to the revival:

> Alarming Diseases still prevail viz, a resemblance of the cold Plague, Scarlet Fever, Cancer Rash, Arraipolis(?) with other uncommon Diseases. Some are first attracted in the fingers others in the legs, throat, and other parts of the Body when imperfect Health, and ends their existence here in some cases in the course of 2 to 10 days time, 9 funerals were attended in this town in 8 days[.] the Lord has in his great[?] prepared this people for his Judgements, out of 104 deaths there were but 4 persons that we can learn who gave no evidence of a saving Faith in the Lord Jesus Christ.[41]

In the midst of this epidemic, which Harris Harding defined as "the Judgements of the Lord by which people learn righteousness," Ansley

---

39 Zion Baptist Church Records, 1821-1826.
40 Bill, *Fifty Years with the Baptists*, 192.
41 Zion Baptist Church Records, 14 April 1828.

offered the people of Yarmouth Township meaning to life, security and comfort.[42] Although no examples of Ansley's sermons have survived, the evidence suggests that the message included the following themes: God's judgement graphically illustrated by the "plague," God's Love in the hope offered in Christ for eternal life, and a plea for the acceptance of the closed communion principles advocated by the Nova Scotia Baptist Association. This culminated in mass conversions, baptisms and reunions in the church.

The Planter revivalist tradition, which had indirectly precipitated divisions in the past, was the catalyst for a transformed and integrated township. People responded from all levels of society regardless of sex, age, social status and occupational standing. For example, among male respondents identified 61.6 percent were farmers, 19.8 percent seamen and 18.6 artisans. This is clearly in keeping with the township as a whole with 63.4 percent farmers, 20.1 percent seamen and 18.5 percent artisans. As well, this revival attracted equal numbers of men and women with 51.3 and 48.7 percent respectively. This was a marked contrast to the decade prior to the revival when for every male convert there were three females. The mean age of respondents by sex was higher than is usually assumed to be the case in nineteenth-century North America. The average age of women was 32 years while the men averaged 38.8 years.[43] Although these average ages in themselves do not indicate the breadth of age categories represented in the respondents identified, they do challenge the often-held assumption that the majority of converts in nineteenth-century revivals were young adults.

The effect of this revival on Baptist church organization in the township was significant. Six districts, each entrusted to the care of a deacon, were established in the area during and after the revival. While the main function of these districts was initially to raise church funds, they also provided a workable system whereby new members and adherents of the church could receive pastoral help and be kept informed of church activities.[44] Together with the network of religious meetings which had been established prior to and during the revival, this structure linked and integrated most of the significantly settled areas of the township in a way that they had never experienced before. People who may have had little or no personal contact with each other, living miles apart, were now drawn together as members and adherents of the Yarmouth Baptist church.

---

42 *Baptist Missionary Magazine of Nova Scotia and New Brunswick* 1(October 1828), 251.

43 For a fuller analysis of this revival consult chapter four of my "Advancing Light: Evangelicalism in Yarmouth Township 1761-1830."

44 Zion Baptist Church Records, Misc. papers.

Consequently, the township was drawn together not only religiously but socially, as well. This is not to suggest, however, that many Yarmouth people were not linked by marriage, occupation and location prior to the revival. In fact, it was probably these existing links that were the significant unseen factors in the revival itself and crucial to the integration process.

CONCLUSION

Although the process of societal integration was not fully accomplished during the 'Great Yarmouth Revival' of 1827-1828, it is clear that evangelical religion played an essential role in the development of Yarmouth society from its early years of hopeless disorientation to a more cohesive and unified community. Only as more studies emerge which chart the evolution of Planter religion in specific communities can the possible wider application of this four-phase model of societal evolution be tested. If, however, the findings of this case study are not atypical, the commonly accepted thesis that the New England Yankee Planters achieved a collective identity during the First Great Awakening may have to be re-evaluated.[45] Indeed, it may have to be conceded that a genuine Nova Scotia identity, an integration of society, only emerged in the early decades of the nineteenth century. Since this study deals only with one township, the implications are merely suggestive and point to the need for further research in the Nova Scotia Planter context. Regardless of whether the implications of this study are substantiated, it seems clear that evangelical religion played a crucial role in the societal development of Planter townships. It is to this point that future researchers of Planter history will have to address themselves.

---

45 This thesis is best expressed in Stewart and Rawlyk, *A People Highly Favoured of God.* For a different perspective on the interpretation of Planter society consult G.T. Stewart, "Charisma and Integration: An Eighteenth Century North American Case," *Comparative Studies in Society and History*, 16 (1974), 138-49.

Henry Alline: Problems of Approach and Reading the *Hymns* as Poetry

Thomas Vincent
Department of English
Royal Military College, Kingston

The cumbersome and rather vague title of this paper reflects a difficulty in reconciling its two focuses. Its primary concern is to discuss Henry Alline's verse in *Hymns and Spiritual Songs* (Boston, 1784) as poetry, but it begins by raising the broader issue of finding appropriate approaches to early colonial North American literature, particularly to the poetry of the eighteenth century. In studies of more contemporary Canadian and American literature, it would appear unnecessary, even pedantic, to precede interpretation with an extended discussion of approach. Readers are more aware of the broad social, cultural and intellectual contexts out of which this literature emerged. Good or bad, it is granted a place in a recognized socio-cultural landscape that we accept as our own. Early colonial literature, however, does not have the benefit of this kind of critical support. As a result, the writers who produced this literature often appear emotionally and intellectually facile; their work, scattered across a remote and confused cultural terrain. Their efforts are treated more as documents reflecting patterns of social or literary history than as imaginative works providing insight into the emergence and evolution of an indigenous literature. Not surprisingly, little effort has been made to find approaches that give full credit to the creativity of writers like Henry Alline and that recognize the literary integrity of their work.

To begin with an admission that ignorance and guess-work are major components of the critical frame of reference shaping our understanding of our earliest literature is salutary. It implicitly calls into question some widely-held critical assumptions about the literary nature, intention and value of these works. Because we know so little about the cultural character of eighteenth-century colonial North America (particularly British North America), there is a tendency to assume that its literature was "occasional," written in a cultural vacuum, or worse, that it can only be viewed as seventeenth- or eighteenth-century British literature "writ small." There is no question colonial writers were influenced by British models; the evidence for that is easy to observe. The challenge for the literary scholar — certainly for one interested in Alline — is to understand more fully the cultural intention of this apparently imitative literature and to explore the possibility that the character of these colonial creations was significantly shaped by the intellectual, moral and emotional dimensions of the colonial social environments in which their authors lived and which they knew best.

Regrettably, not much helpful work has been done on how diverse cultural influences were absorbed by emerging colonial societies and translated into a dynamic, integrative force that worked to shape a sense of cultural integrity. By "cultural integrity" is meant the emergence of a complex of critical values (moral, spiritual, social, intellectual, imaginative) which, though perhaps inherently contradictory in some aspects, is perceived to be coherent and is given assent and recognition even while some features are the focus of dispute. While such values function explicitly as instruments of judgement and valuation defining communal norms, the process by which they develop implicitly involves a degree of intellectual tolerance for the sake of a sense of cultural cohesion.

It is the pattern of creative inclusion, not the pattern of intentional exclusion, that most profoundly shapes the character of emerging colonial cultures. This is particularly true for Canadian cultural experience. But most studies of the cultural development of early North America are concerned with cultural identity, not cultural integrity, and are pursued with an eye to justifying incipient nationhood, creating the false impression that there was a kind of cultural manifest destiny in colonial American societies. To identify the development of a sense of cultural integrity with the pursuit of national identity, or to view it simply as a frame of reference in which the processes of social cohesion and national identity unfold, ignores the inherent complexity of cultural activity in emerging colonial societies and the different roles it plays in articulating coherent and meaningful visions of life on which a society may be credibly founded.

As a point of departure, it is helpful to recognize that, in early colonial society and literature, there are at least two major currents of cultural activity evolving simultaneously but quite different in intention. To understand the effect and function of the literary efforts of colonial writers like Henry Alline, it is necessary to distinguish between these two cultural imperatives. One works to identify the particular character of the emerging society and functions in an exclusive manner to distinguish it from other societies; the other is inclusive and integrative, and works to tie the emerging society to a larger, universal frame of reference whose values have a legitimacy necessary to that society's sense of its own integrity. While these currents of cultural activity are related and overlap, the evolution of the values that shape cultural integrity diverge frequently and significantly from the pattern of values promoted and pursued in the process of shaping a sense of national identity. The necessary and usually urgent accommodation of the latter to political and economic forces is incidental to the former. Again, this is especially true in early colonial Canada (or what is now Canada). Cultural forms, including literature, were sometimes pressed into the service of articulating national identity, but they generally functioned to interpret broader worlds of cultural civility to colonial contexts while at the same time projecting the particularities of colonial experience against universal patterns of life. In the process of expressing these relationships, a selective understanding and interpretation of both points of reference evolved, resulting in an assemblage of cultural values which suited the particular needs of that particular emerging society at that particular time without radically decoupling it from the cultural patterns, tradition, and heritage that gave it authority, validity and integrity. What we are lacking is a thorough understanding of the complexity of these colonial cultural assemblages and their subtle relationships to their sources. We simply do not understand how colonial cultural assumptions worked to tie colonial experience to a vision of universal civility while simultaneously acting as a resource to articulate the particular character of colonial life.

It means that, right from the start, there is a problem of finding appropriate cultural and literary contexts in which to read colonial literature. Out of necessity, we tend to latch onto whatever points of reference are most readily available. In Henry Alline's case, there is a significant body of historical and biographical information developed by historians over the last few decades.[1] It gives the reader much more secondary material than is usually available on a colonial writer, but the concerns and perspectives pursued by historians are not always helpful in approaching literary documents as literature. For example, the efforts of historians to come to terms with Alline's biography appear to have produced several versions of Henry Alline. There is the intense, complex, emotional personality, agonizing in the maelstrom of deeply felt religious conviction coupled with an equally strong sense of personal damnation. Then, there is the charismatic evangelical figure preaching a vision of religious life that had unintended political ramifications. On a less scholarly level, there is the dedicated church leader, a mythical, larger-than-life, proto-Baptist who could leap tall Anglicans and Methodists at a single bound, a veritable Paul Bunyan of revival enthusiasm. While these thumb-nail summaries of the historical Henry Alline may be somewhat unfair, there is not much in the prevailing biographical depictions of Alline that is very helpful in reading the *Hymns* as poetry.

A related, but more serious problem with historical studies is their tendency to treat Alline's verse as supporting documentation, adjuncts to the historical, biographical and/or theological hypotheses that are brought to it. Little effort is made to view the poems as imaginative documents with something to offer of their own. Such studies ignore the fact that the imaginative experience of poetry is not constrained by the limitations of historical opportunity or (in this case) even the logic of theology; it ranges beyond the literal and its insights must be sought there.

---

1 Of particular note are J.M. Bumsted, *Henry Alline* (Toronto, 1971) and G. Stewart and G. Rawlyk, *A People Highly Favoured of God* (Toronto, 1972).

Of course, interpretation of imaginative expression has its own pitfalls and, ideally, one would like to be able to test and confirm insights and observations in the light of a broader understanding of the literary and cultural contexts in which the works were written. Lack of such points of reference throws us back on the poems themselves and a search for the elements of experience that trigger the poet's imagination.

In Alline's case, it is the energy that flows from tension and struggle — emotional, intellectual and spiritual — that appears to stimulate imaginative response. In his verse, significant experience begins in perceived tension, which is recognized emotionally, depicted as spiritual, and therefore approached intellectually through a theological frame of reference. Alline's infelt struggle with that tension becomes the context in which it is explored and his poetry becomes the medium in which it is most fully known. As an eighteenth-century poet, Alline works to contain, control and articulate that struggle in language and image in order to give it objective meaning and to communicate his understanding of that meaning, simply and clearly. The source of his language and imagery is evangelical religious experience.

It is tempting at this point to proceed by comparing Alline's work and spiritual experience to that of similar religious poets, Isaac Watt and Charles Wesley, for example. But to keep the focus clearly on Alline's imagination, it seems more appropriate to stay with him and begin by looking briefly at his work as a whole. His non-poetic publications consist of a number of sermons and two theological treatises. Scholarly opinion of his theology is not flattering but the unresolved logical inconsistencies that bother theologians are helpful to the literary critic. There is a fundamental tension in Alline's work that flows from a contradiction at the heart of his view of religious life, a tension which affects both his theological and poetic writings.[2] Theologically, he was drawn, on the one hand, toward pietistical views of religious experience, particularly those of the English theologian William Law, and particularly to the mystical and ascetic elements he found there. At the same time, he was moved by the theology of enthusiastic evangelism which demanded active, personal involvement in the proclamation of the gospel of salvation. The broad picture of religious life that emerges from Alline's work is one that turns on an implicit tension between the private character of its pietism and asceticism and the public nature of its evangelism. In his theological writings, Alline was unable to reconcile this duality in his perception of spiritual life. His vision of grace and of divine purpose appears ambiguous at best, and at worst, intellectually inconsistent. In his religious verse, however, this tension becomes a source of dramatic energy as he struggles to balance the

---

2 Parts of the foliowing discussion are based on my "Introduction" to *Selected Hymns and Spiritual Songs of Henry Alline* (Kingston, 1982).

private introspective element of his poetry with its public evangelical purpose. The poems that most clearly draw vitality and energy from this effort are those where the tension is channeled into depictions of religious experience as an emotional and spiritual struggle. Religious experience here unfolds in a post-lapsarian world where the potential for good and evil co-exist and meet in the human condition: man is the image of God, yet fallen; man can perceive perfection but is always conscious of his separation from it because of his inherent sinfulness.

> Lord, what a wretched soul am I;
> In midnight shades I dwell;
> Laden with guilt, and born to die,
> And rushing down to hell.
>
> * * * *
>
> No hand but thine, O God of love,
> My wretched soul can save;
> O come, dear Jesus, and remove
> This load of guilt I have.
>
> * * * *
>
> Thy blood can wash my guilt away;
> Thy love my heart can cheer;
> O turn my midnight into day,
> And banish all my fear.[3]

The terms of expression are emotional, and dramatically so, but the level of consciousness is implicitly spiritual: man lives between the terrible misery of deserved damnation and the ecstatic joy of God's gift of salvation. The central image here which most fully expresses both dimensions of this spiritual dichotomy simultaneously is Christ on the Cross. In the image of the Crucifixion, Christ's agony is man's agony, and His triumph, man's salvation.

> As near to Calvary I pass,
> Me thinks I see a bloody cross
> Where a poor victim hangs;
> His flesh with ragged irons tore,
> His limbs all dress'd with purple gore
> Gasping in dying pangs.

---

3 "A Sinner Awakened," I:xxvi, stanzas 1, 3, 5, (p. 4). The Roman numerals identify the Book and Hymn numbers in the 1786 edition of Alline's *Hymns and Spiritual Songs*; the page reference in parenthesis refers to the 1982 *Selected Hymns and Spiritual Songs*.

Surpriz'd the spectacle to see,
I ask'd, who can this victim be
In such exquisite pain?
Why thus consign'd to woes? I cry'd.
"Tis I, the bleeding God reply'd.
"To save a world from sin."[4]

In the poetry that depicts religious experience this way, Alline draws heavily on seventeenth-century English religious verse for his conceptual frame of reference, for his imagery, for his tone and mood. This is familiar ground. However, when he moves from focusing on spiritual struggle to exploring resolution of that struggle, he moves into new and rather different territory, both emotionally and imaginatively. Resolution here comes through acceptance of God's grace as manifested in the loving personality of Christ.

Hark! is my Jesus passing by?
Methinks I hear him say:
"Awake, arise, thy friend is nigh:
"Rejoice and come away."

O is it, is it Christ the Lamb?
And does he call for me?
I come, dear Jesus, glad I come;
I long to be with thee.

Let others choose the chains of death
And tread the road to hell;
In wisdom's ways I'll spend my breath,
And with my Jesus dwell.

* * * *

Christ is my life, my joy, my love,
And everlasting peace;
He'll be my all in realms above
When mortal climes shall cease.[5]

Christ is always at the centre of Alline's best verse, but the image of the crucified Christ and the self-conscious inner struggle it symbolizes gives way at times to a vision of the expansive love of Christ (the Christ of the new dispensation) and the willing service it solicits from man. Implicit in the focus on the person and personality of Christ, is the knowledge that Christ is the medium in which man most clearly perceives God's grace and

4 "The Great Love of Christ Display'd in His Death," I:lix, stanzas 1-2 (p. 21).
5 "Delighted in the Lord," V:xxxvi, stanzas 1-3, 5 (pp. 9-10).

the means by which man most fully comprehends divine will. In Alline's poetry, the personality of Christ shapes the character of grace. In fact, Alline does not make sharp distinctions between God and Christ and grace. The theological complexities of the relationship between God and man are submerged in the personality of Jesus, a personality characterized by its openness, its approachability and its deep affection for man. The simple intimacy of man's relationship with Christ defines the character of God's love, God's grace, and inculcates a trust that invites simple resignation to the will of God. From acceptance of divine will flows peace, but it is a peace not easily attained and even harder to sustain once achieved. Doubt, willfulness, worldliness — all human weaknesses — undermine its stability and cast men back into the morass of mortal hopes and fears.

> There's none can tell, or yet conceive
> What diff'rent scenes I'm carry'd through
> But those who know the Lord believe,
> Are born, and know the travels too.
>
> Sometimes I think the Lamb of God
> Has spoke a word of peace to me,
> Has spent his life and spilt his blood,
> And bore my curses on the tree.
>
> Then leaps my soul with joys divine,
> Long as feel the heav'nly flame;
> I think the blessed Lamb is mine
> And find a sweetness in his name.
>
> But O how soon does unbelief
> Pretend it is too great for me!
> I never found that true relief
> Which real christians know and see.
>
> Cast down, and mourning then I go,
> And feel the borders of despair;
> My bleeding heart o'erwhelm'd with woe
> Is drove from place to place with fear.
>
> * * * *
>
> And thus I'm tossed from hope to fear,
> As faith or unbelief prevails;
> But still my God is always near,
> Though clouds so oft his face may veil.[6]

---

6 "The Strange Travels of A Doubting Christian," IV:lxiv, stanzas 1-5, 8 (pp. 12-13).

At this point, there is a great temptation to freeze the picture: to see man as doomed by the weakness of his will to cycles of struggle, and as being essentially passive in the face of Christ's love. But the strength and confidence of the poet's voice (reflected in the tone of the poetry) suggests a degree of spiritual consciousness which goes beyond passivity into a condition that is active and creatively so. There is a point at which the dramatic energy generated by spiritual struggle is translated through the vision of Christ's love and the poet's imagination into what might be called the "adventure of discipleship." It implies active service, but the poetic focus here is not on evangelizing (that is in the background). The focus is on the working environment of discipleship: on the sense of the immediate presence of Christ, the special openness and approachability of his personality, and on the easy intimacy and freedom of the relationship that exists between the disciple (the speaker of the poem) and Christ.

All this unfolds against a backdrop of service and purpose, but the immediate focus of the poem offers an imaginative vision of life inside the circle of discipleship.

> Should I be call'd to distant wilds,
> Or station'd on some foreign shore,
> If there I found my Saviour's smiles,
> And liv'd with him, I'd want no more.
>
> Tis all alike a heaven to me,
> If I might there enjoy my God;
> Cheerful I'd tread while Christ I see,
> O'er rocks and hills by feet untrod.
>
> * * * *
>
> The moss should be my downy bed,
> Through silent watches of the night,
> And Jesus guard my slumbering head,
> Till morning rays restore the light.
>
> Then should my sweet and morning lays
> Send echoes through the silent grove;
> Jesus would hear the notes I raise;
> My song should be redeeming love.[7]

It is as tangible and intimate as the love of Christ gets in Alline's poetry, and the confidence, the hope, and the faith that flows from it are reflected in the calm strength of the voice of the poet.

The ultimate reward of this "adventure of discipleship" appears to be the

---

7 "The Christian Happy in Any Place, if They Enjoy God's Presence," III:lxxxv, stanzas 1-2, 4-5 (p. 36).

attainment of "humility of spirit." It is a condition of being that is positive and active, yet without conflict, tension free.

> O for the spirit of the Dove,
> To bow this heart of mine!
> Lord let my soul enjoy thy love,
> And find a peace divine.

> O for the meekness of the Lamb,
> To walk with thee, my God!
> Then should I feel thy lovely name,
> And feed upon thy word.

> Jesus, I long to love thee more,
> And life divine pursue;
> I love thy worship, name adore,
> In songs forever new.[8]

This humility or "meekness" seems to imply an imaginative fusion of evangelism and pietism. It is the "pilgrim's" dream of becoming Christ-like through living the life of Christ in service to Christ. As such, it represents a reconciliation of both public and private religious imperatives. For Alline, his poetry itself was a part of this process, and in his best verse there is a "meekness" in the tone of the voice of the poet that the reader must hear for him or herself.

It is interesting to explore the patterns of Alline's religious experience and to see how in poetry he was able to resolve and articulate imaginatively aspects of experience that he was unable to express in theology. Moreover, to some extent, demonstrating something of the complexity of Alline's imagination and art elevates the dignity of early colonial verse. But what is missing from this reading is an insight into how Alline's imaginative patterns of tension, struggle and resolution in his religious verse reflect the broad character of colonial imaginative experience discernible in other dimensions of colonial cultural life. We sense a coherent vision of experience in the patterns we see, but we do not know how meaningful that vision may be. This is where our lack of a fuller understanding of the cultural dynamics of colonial life is crippling. We cannot judge how instructive Alline's poetic vision is in giving us insight into the conceptual nature and order of his cultural world. We know his verse performs a cultural function in his own time to the extent that it coherently interprets the relationship between particular experience in colonial Nova Scotia and universal reality as his readers perceive it. But we have no scholarly context in which to evaluate the sophistication and appropriateness of his vision. We also know that his art should perform a cultural function in our time to

---

8   "Longing for Meekness and Humility," II:lxxxviii (p. 18).

the extent that it offers particular insight into a continuum of human perceptions which is pertinent to our understanding of ourselves. In a real sense, our failure to understand Alline's poetry as fully as we might is a serious cultural deficiency for it is a reflection of our failure to understand ourselves as fully as we might.

Persona in Planter Journals

Gwendolyn Davies
Department of English
Acadia University

In *His Majesty's Yankees* by Thomas Raddall, the Planter merchant, Simeon Perkins, is depicted as "unheroic, uneasy, un-everything."[1] The portrait is anything but flattering, but the inspiration for it lies not in Raddall's creative imagination but in the private journals maintained by Perkins from 1766 to 1812, the year in which he died in his adopted home of Nova Scotia. A native of Norwich, Connecticut, Simeon Perkins had immigrated to Liverpool on the south shore of the province in May 1762 only three years after Governor Charles Lawrence had issued warrants to survey the township. Beginning as a dealer in lumber and fish, Perkins went on to become a prominent property owner, merchant, farmer, mill operator, shipbuilder and Atlantic trader, as well as a member of the Legislative Assembly, a Justice of the Courts, a Judge of Probate and a Colonel Commandant of the Militia for Queens County. By the time of his death, he was described as a "father" to the town of Liverpool, known as his obituary pointed out, for "great wisdom, general knowledge, piety and benevolence, and uncommon usefulness."[2]

"Uncommon usefulness" is an unsentimental attribution for someone to bear in death as in life, yet a reading of the five volumes of Simeon Perkins's diary published by the Champlain Society reveals a persona consistent with *The Weekly Chronicle's* assessment of Liverpool's leading citizen. Writing in his journal more frequently after war broke out in 1775 than before, Perkins records what he has seen and done and heard. There is nothing introspective or analytical about his entries. His journal is intended to document financial matters, ships leaving harbour, occurrences in the meeting house, weather conditions, or visitations of family and friends. However, it becomes something more because of the historical events in which Perkins is caught up. "Experiencing life as a graduated succession of changes is an absolute prerequisite for writing a journal,"[3] argues Robert Fothergill in *Private Chronicles : A Study in English Diaries*, and in Perkins's case, these changes were precipitated not so much by the domestic crises and financial transactions that punctuated his everyday life as by the political events between 1766 and 1812 that drew him willy-nilly into the fray, expanded his social and business horizons,

---

1   Thomas H.Raddall, *His Majesty's Yankees* (1942 repr. Toronto, 1977), 43.

2   C.B. Fergusson, ed., *The Diary of Simeon Perkins, 1804-1812* (Toronto, 1978), liii.

3   Robert A. Fothergill, *Private Chronicles: A Study of English Diaries* (London, 1924), 14.

and brought new stimuli to the town he had helped to nourish. Beginning as a personal recorder of mundane matters, Perkins was to become a self-appointed chronicler of his community in a period of enormous social change.

The catalyst for many of his observations came with his increasing role of responsibility within the township, for public affairs had become part of his private domain. Concurrent with Simeon's growing prominence within the town, however, was the outbreak first of the American Revolution, then of the Napoleonic Wars, and later of the War of 1812. In all of these cases, one senses that the Simeon Perkins of the journals shrinks from a breakdown of rational order and all that it implies. Thomas Raddall suggests Perkins's state of bewilderment when he compares him to "a sad little saw-whet owl" [4] when he is faced with the choices of the American Revolution. Yet, seemingly unhindered by any kind of active imagination, Simeon was able to initiate militia offensives and to document the social, economic and religious impact of the times on townspeople like himself living on the sea-lanes of the conflict. It is this unvarnished quality that Raddall recognized as a valuable resource in Perkins's journals when he first read them in the 1930s, and it is for this reason that Raddall's fictional treatment of Liverpool's Strang family in *His Majesty's Yankees* strikes true in idiom, domestic realism and historical detail.

While Simeon Perkins's journals grew out of his personal experience, they also represent part of the great impulse toward journal writing that flowered in the seventeenth and eighteenth centuries. Pepys' famous *Diary* maintained from 1660-1669 had set a standard as a personal record of the times and in the very year that Perkins removed to Liverpool from Connecticut, James Boswell had begun his *London Journal* by vowing to preserve the "many things that would otherwise be lost in oblivion." [5] Yet there was a marked difference between Boswell's journal and Pepys's, for Boswell was preoccupied less with events than with his self-conscious role in them. Boswell, as Fothergill points out, is more egocentric than is Pepys, who desires only "to cherish the events of each day, not because they are the theatre for his latest manifestation, but because they are what actually happened and as such deserve to be acknowledged." [6] Boswell creates a persona satisfactory to himself in a way unknown to either Pepys or Perkins. There are few revelations of self in Simeon Perkins's documentation of events, and when he does allow opinion to intrude into his record of wind and weather, the revelations are not inconsistent with the plain, blunt man who has been emerging: "I have been applied to for my approbation"

4   Raddall, *His Majesty's Yankees*, 61.
5   Fothergill, *Private Chronicles*, 78.
6   *Ibid.*, 71.

of a dance, he wrote on 12 January 1797; "I think it rather premature in such a Young Settlement, and Considering the late frowns of Providence in the death of several of our young men, & others missing, and the threatening aspect of public affairs, I think it highly Improper at this time, whether it might be in other Situations & Circumstances."[7]

Elsewhere, his observations can be more personal, focusing as he grew older as much on the affairs of his family as on the progress of the settlement. Typical of a rare glimpse into the sense of obligation he felt toward his children is the placing of his daughter Mary in a Halifax boarding school at the cost of £35 in October, 1804. "It is expensive," he notes, "but I think it my duty to give my children what Education I can, and this daughter acquiring Something may give the others an Opportunity to gain Something from her advantage."[8] Such insights into Perkins's character reveal enough of a persona to elevate the diary beyond the level of mere memoranda.

In this sense, Perkins's journal is far more interesting than are the Planter journals of the Reverend John Seccombe and his daughter of Chester with their litany of meals and visitations respectively. The Seccombe journals reveal life lead day-to-day in 1761, illustrating in the very narrowness of their references the limitations of dwelling in a community less strategic to the sea-lanes than was Liverpool. Moreover, the pattern of the Seccombe diaries suggests an exercise in personal documentation. On "Satterday," 21 November 1761, for example, the Reverend Mr. Seccombe noted: "Fair, cool — Pork & Cabbage Turnep &c for dinner — P.M. went wth Mr. Bridge to ye Mill, & to view a Lot. Supped on Moose Stakes, dry'd meat. Indians brought in wild Fowl. Bever &c."[9] In the Perkins's diaries, by contrast, there is the very real sense that Simeon is writing more of a record and from time to time will turn back to the pages of his journal to check an incident or date in the forty-six years of his recording. As Alan Young has noted in his book, *Thomas H. Raddall*, there are striking parallels between Perkins's diary-keeping and that of Sumter Larabee, a central figure in Raddall's *The Wedding Gift and Other Stories*. "The Diary of Sumter Larabee" was the "journal of a realist," he quotes Raddall, "written with an obsession for present facts and the deuce with past and future. Sumter seldom followed up an incident or looked back to compare anything but the weather or the date of last year's turnip planting."[10] Such seems to be the situation of Simeon Perkins whose sense

7   D.C.Harvey, ed., *The Diary of Simeon Perkins, 1780-1789* (Toronto, 1958), xxxviii.

8   C.B. Fergusson, ed.,*The Diary of Simeon Perkins, 1804-1812* (Toronto, 1979), 70.

9   "The Diary of Reverend John Seccombe," *Report of the Public Archives of Nova Scotia* (Halifax, 1959), Appendix B, 18-47, 240. See also: "Memoranda of Leading Events by a member of the Seccombe Family," PANS, MG 1, Vol. 797C, No. 2.

10 Alan Young, *Thomas H. Raddall* (Boston, 1983), 79.

of history was practical and whose future was always in the hands of God.

Of all the journals emerging from the Planter experience, it is those that probe the individual's relationship with God that best exemplify the qualities of introspection and analysis associated with the development of a persona in journal literature. As Steven Kagle has pointed out in *American Diary Literature: 1620-1799*, the spiritual journey occupied a central place in colonial America. Usually employing a standardized rhetoric and modelled after celebrated examples, the spiritual journey "allowed its author to find a pattern which could reveal the truth of the past and plan the direction of the future."[11] Particularly in Puritan diaries were the conventions of self-examination, self-abasement and dramatic conversion developed. For Puritans, salvation was an arbitrary thing dependent on the will of God, and the maintenance of a religious register was not only a way of justifying one's conduct but also a process of documenting one's path to election or grace. In a sense, then, the spiritual journal was a statement against despair, a form of confessional which the Puritan or Calvinist would construct in the spiritual isolation that went with his or her self-analysis. Casting back to his youth in his spiritual journey, Henry Alline of Falmouth, Nova Scotia, remembered in the 1780s that "God...gave me a sense of my lost and undone condition in a great degree: fearing almost everything that I saw, that it was against me; commissioned from God to call me away, and I unprepared: I was even afraid of trees falling on me, when I was in the woods, and in a time of thunder would expect the next flash of lightening would be commissioned to cut me off. Thus I was one of the unhappiest creatures that lived on earth; and would promise and vow, in time of danger, that I would leave all my carnal mirth and vain company, and that I would never rest until I had found rest in my soul."[12]

Alline's expression of fear and unworthiness is a stock convention in Puritan and Calvinist journals and finds repetition in the spiritual journals of two other Planter writers, Jonathan Scott of Chebogue and Mary Coy Bradley of Gagetown and Saint John. For both Alline and Bradley, this fear coloured their childhood years, so that Alline would pray even on his way to school "that this angry God would not send me to hell,"[13] and Mary Bradley would agonize, "how can I dwell in flames of fire and brimstone, through an endless eternity!"[14] Entering a covenant with the Lord

---

11 Steven E. Kagle, *American Diary Literature, 1620-1799* (Boston, 1979), 29.

12 Henry Alline, *The Life and Journal of the Rev. Mr. Henry Alline* (Boston, 1806), 29.

13 *Ibid.*, 4

14 Mary Bradley, *A Narrative of the Life and Christian Experience of Mrs. Mary Bradley* (Boston, 1849), 28.

dispelled that fear for both authors, but their pre-covenant terror is more rhetorical than chilling because of the retrospective nature of their journals. Alline's work was begun during his ministry in the late 1770s and, at the time of his death in 1784, was left to circulate privately in manuscript form, finally reaching publication in Boston in 1806.

Bradley's work was also destined for a public audience, becoming one of many Wesleyan-Methodist spiritual records published in the mid-nineteenth century in the wake of diaries by John Wesley, George Whitefield and others. While intensely focused on the routine events of Mrs. Bradley's Christian life, the *Narrative of...Mrs. Mary Bradley* does project into the litany of Methodist religious records the perspective of a woman who wanted to play anything but a passive role in the profession of her faith. "I always heard that women had nothing to do in public, respecting religious exercises," she noted early in her journal, "and that it was absolutely forbidden in the Scriptures for a woman to pray in public, or to have anything to say in the church of God. Under the consideration of those things, I felt much shame and confusion and knew not how to endure it."[15] Elsewhere in her journal she chafes under the social and marriage bonds that require sublimation of her opinions to those of her first husband: "But soon I found that, being his wife, I was bound by law to yield obedience to the requirements of my husband; and when he enforced obedience, and showed marks of resentment if his wishes were not met, I was tempted with anger and felt a spirit of resentment arise in my heart and retaliating expressions come into my mind...."[16] As Margaret Conrad has pointed out in an introduction to Mrs. Bradley's narrative in *Atlantis* in 1981, her authorship offers glimpses into the social and legal position of women in the Planter community and reveals something of the work patterns of such women in rural areas of the Maritimes.[17] However, the overall narrowness of Mary Bradley's interests restricts the emergence of a distinctive persona in her journal. Only when she recalls her childhood in Gagetown or describes the early years of her marriage is there a glimpse of the human being behind the stylized rhetoric of the spiritual diary. On the whole, Mary Bradley's journal conforms to established patterns and rarely offers those touches of domestic originality that emerge when she pauses in her weeding to compare herself to a good seed choked by weeds in the garden of Christ.[18]

It is in their inability to transcend the conventions of their genre that

---

15 *Ibid.*, 50.

16 *Ibid.*, 106.

17 Margaret Conrad, "Mary Bradley's Reminiscences: A Domestic Life in Colonial New Brunswick," *Atlantis*, 7,1(Fall 1981), 92.

18 Mary Bradley, *A Narrative*, 43.

many of the spiritual journalists fail in literary terms. The literary critic, as Robert Fothergill has pointed out, "is concerned with that work in which the impulsion to articulate the self has precipitated discovery of a fresh organization of the form's potential. The most remarkable displays of this discovery we call genius, and the diary indeed has its geniuses."[19] Amongst the spiritual journalists writing from the Planter experience, there seem to be few with this spark, for profession of faith rather than literary self-consciousness is both their intent and their preoccupation. The range is not wide, and even in the hands of so charismatic a figure as Henry Alline, the spiritual diary fails to reveal a persona so much as a vocation. This being said, it cannot be denied that Alline demonstrates a flair for dramatic presentation and an energy of phrasing that circumvent some of the limitations of the spiritual diary form. While honouring the same conventions as his spiritual colleagues (the terror of religion in childhood, the isolation of the unsaved soul, the revelation and covenant with God, the mission to carry the message), Alline can transform language into a powerful crescendo of euphony, rhythm, and harmony as he describes himself, "...groaning under mountains of death, wading through storms of sorrow, racked with distressing fears, and crying to an unknown God for help...."[20] As George Rawlyk has pointed out, Alline's power with language annoyed his Congregationalist opponent, Jonathan Scott, who saw Alline's work as "interspersed with Poetry calculated to excite and raise the Passions of the Reader, especially the young, ignorant and inconsistent, who are influenced more by the sound and Gingle of the words, then by solid Sentences and rational and scriptural Ideas of divine and eternal Things."[21] Moreover, as a journeyer as well as a journalist, Alline had an opportunity to meet new people, see new areas and hear new arguments. This range of constantly shifting sights, sounds and experiences enlivens the pace of his diary in a way denied the home-bound Mary Bradley or the congregation-tied Jonathan Scott. Steven Kagle has argued that it was often the diaries of itinerant Methodists that focused "outward to the world, giving a valuable picture of their world."[22] Alline's case is similar. The travel pattern of his journal expands it beyond the conventional structure of many spiritual records and enables Alline to explore religious questions within a wider and more interesting social context. In the main part of his journal, he is not isolated physically and spiritually as he was before he made his covenant with God. Rather, he functions on a broad geographical stage where his personal journey and his relations with others

19 Fothergill, *Private Chronicles*, 12.

20 Alline, *The Life and Journal*, 34-35.

21 George A. Rawlyk, ed., *The Sermons of Henry Alline* (Hantsport, 1986), 28.

22 Kagle, *American Diary Literature*, 51.

coalesce in a book designed to illuminate the lives of many.

As revealing as individual Planter journals can be about the social, political and religious lives of the speakers and their communities, there is little in the conventionalized language and format of most of these records to warrant their being called "literature" in the creative or imaginative sense. Thus, to speak of a Planter Literature is to speak of a Planter body of writing, for there is nothing of the development to be found later in nineteenth-century journals when literary self-consciousness made the persona assume a stance akin to that of a fictional character. In their dedication to fulfill their tasks, the Planter writers noted others as characters in the play of life (both Perkins and Bradley describe the visits of Alline, for example), but themselves only as vehicles (Alline wanted to be a mouth for God). It was to be left to the later generations of Thomas Raddall, Greg Cook and Douglas Lochhead, amongst the creative writers, and Michael Miller amongst the composers, to breathe imaginative life into the earnest personae who emerge from the Planter journals of Perkins, Seccombe, Alline and Bradley.[23]

---

23 As has been mentioned, Thomas Raddall adapted his knowledge of Simeon Perkins and his diary into literary dramatizations in *His Majesty's Yankees, At The Tide's Turn and Other Stories*, and *The Wedding Gift and Other Stories*. Maritime poets, Greg Cook and Douglas Lochhead, are currently working on long poems on Henry Alline. The first act of Michael Miller's opera-in-progress on Henry Alline was performed at Acadia University in October 1987.

A Planter House:
The Simeon Perkins House, 1766-7,
Liverpool, Nova Scotia

Allen Penney, Associate Professor
The Technical University of Nova Scotia

After twelve years of work unravelling the history of the Simeon Perkins House there is now a text of 330 pages,[1] but despite all attempts, some of the questions remain unanswered. When work began the key word was 'interpretation' and that word is used here as a central theme in this discussion of a single Planter house.

Our interpretation of any house is greatly influenced by the setting. The Simeon Perkins House (Figure 1) was built in 1766 in Liverpool, Nova Scotia.[2] By 1981 it had become severely compromised as a historic house because of the dramatic change in its context.[3] Visually overpowered by a new museum built too close beside it, Perkins house had become a cottage in the front yard of the museum.

Interpretation is also required in something as straightforward as the picture by which Simeon Perkins is usually recognized (Figure 2). There is only one known portrait of Simeon Perkins (Figure 3)[4] and this is a small profile painted in watercolour in an elliptical mount. The author was fortunate in tracking it down in York, Maine. As all the known published photographic representations appear to be reproduced from this one image, photographed and published in a book in 1895,[5] it is possible to reconstruct the sequence of retouching of the photographs over time. Whereas the latest reproductions show Simeon Perkins as a young man without a wrinkle or hair out of place,[6] the original watercolour shows him as a man with furrowed brow and wispy, greying hair which appears a trifle unruly. Interpretation of the latest and most heavily retouched photo-

---

1 Allen Penney, *The Simeon Perkins House, Liverpool, Nova Scotia*, Curatorial Report Number 60, Nova Scotia Museum, Halifax, N.S., 1988.

2 Dates are all derived from the Diary entries, usually footnoted as follows: Diary, I, 19 June 1766, for the start of construction and Diary, I, 18 April 1767, for the date on which he moved in and started to live there.

3 The Simeon Perkins Museum, now the Queens County Museum, was opened on 17 September 1980.

4 A watercolour portrait of Simeon Perkins is located in the Elizabeth Bishop Perkins Museum in York, Maine. There is no mention of either date or artist.

5 Mary E. Perkins, *Old Houses of the Ancient Town of Norwich, 1660-1800* (Norwich, Connecticut, 1895). At least three stages of re-touching of the photograph of Simeon Perkins have been used to illustrate the different volumes of the Diary and other publications.

6 *The Diary of Simeon Perkins 1780-1789*, Vol.2 (Toronto, 1958).

1. The Simeon Perkins House in 1982 with the new Queen's County Museum built beside it. The size and proximity of the latter are an aggressive and unfortunate intrusion, diminishing the house.

2. The original and only known portrait of Simeon Perkins now in the drawing room of the Elizabeth Bishop Perkins House, York, Maine. This small watercolour has no date.

(Courtesy of the Society for the Preservation of Historic Landmarks, York, Maine.)

graphic images would lean towards youthfulness, vigour and a slight arrogance brought on by success in business, whereas interpretation of the original painted image suggests a care-worn and harassed middle-aged businessman who was neither very astute nor successful, an interpretation one is likely to make from Perkins' writings.

Also located in York, Maine, is Simeon Perkins' grandfather clock. It has a maker's label glued to the inside of the door to the clock case to show that Simon Willard of Roxbury (who was born in 1753) was the manufacturer.[7] Below it is attached a handwritten provenance together with a type-written biographical sketch of the maker. If the provenance were true, then Simon Willard made the clock when he was just nine years old; an obviously suspect fact. Whoever wrote out the provenance made a primary error in interpretation. In the belief that Simeon Perkins owned the clock when he emigrated to Nova Scotia in 1762, it is easy to attribute too early a date for the manufacture of the clock. The author of the provenance had either no knowledge of Simeon Perkins' travels or failed to make the connection between the facts as existing, starting with the birthday of Simon Willard. According to his Diary, Simeon Perkins spent several months in New England in 1768 and probably in 1771 as well.[8] His diary for these two periods is missing but is believed to still be in the United States. Missing passages may contain references to the purchase date of the clock, but this is unlikely as Simon Willard would still have been too young. Other solutions may be found. For example, Simeon Perkins was forced into receiving goods instead of currency so often in his business transactions that the clock may not have been purchased by him directly from the maker at all, but came into his possession as part payment for goods or services.[9] But the solution found inside the clock case is the least likely of all: "This clock was probably made for Simeon Perkins after he returned to Norwich, Conn. from Nova Scotia where he spent the war years as a Loyalist." Also included on the label of Simon Willard is the location of his business, Roxbury. The type-written note which states that he started his business there in 1780 suggests the date of the purchase must be later than this.

How we interpret information may depend on the scope of our knowledge and how diligently we check out and order the facts. As we look at the house, the portrait or the clock, we exercise judgement, gathering as much data as possible to bolster our position and then we put it all together

---

7 Simon Willard, b. 3 April 1753, had his business at Roxbury, Massachusetts.

8 Diary, I, 24 February 1786. On the occasion of his birthday, Simeon Perkins refers to his family history. All portions referring to his life in the United States were removed by the Reverend Joshua Newton Perkins before repatriation of the bulk of the Diary in 1900.

9 See, for example, Diary, III, 27 October 1792.

3. Portrait of Simeon Perkins. A photographic copy hangs in the office of the house. Neither the date nor the artist are known.

to tell a story. This is always an interpretation of the facts as far as we can find and understand them. Fortunately Simeon Perkins left us more than a mere house. He put down on paper his own particular history covering a period of fifty years. His Diary and a collection of some of his letters have been published in five volumes by the Champlain Society.[10] These documents offer an excellent source of Planter knowledge and a significant source for the interpretation of the house.

A considerable quantity of other information relating to the house and its context is available; some interesting rather than relevant, and some interesting in its own right. For instance, the Charles Morris map of Nova Scotia from 1755,[11] and his town plan for Liverpool dating from 1759,[12] clearly show how planners are limited by other people interpreting their intentions. The actual development of Liverpool took place in an area which Morris had left undesignated as a white gap in the middle of the plan. This is precisely the area covered by the town centre today and over two centuries later the town still covers only a small area of that proposed by Morris. Having arrived after the initial land grants, Simeon Perkins had to wait two years before new land was freed for granting, when in 1764,

---

10 The Diary of Simeon Perkins has been published in five volumes, Vol. I, 1766 to 1780 in 1948; Vol. II, 1780 to 1789 in 1958; Vol. III, 1790 to 1796 in 1961; Vol. IV, 1797 to 1803 in 1967; Vol. V, 1804 to 1812 in 1979.

11 Map of Nova Scotia, dated 1755, Public Archives of Nova Scotia.

12 Map of Liverpool, dated 1759, from a dyeline print from the Nova Scotia Department of Lands and Forests.

from fish lots A & B, he drew lot B5 on which he began to build his house two years later.[13]

On 20 July 1817, John Elliot Woolford made seven sketches of Liverpool on the same day.[14] One of them shows the Liverpool lighthouse for which Simeon Perkins laid the foundation stone just before he died. Photographs are a valuable resource, yet few exist of the house before the 1940s, none show the back or the interior before 1947. Other interpretations of the house have been few and some have been quite inaccurate, suggesting, for example, that the windows have been replaced at some time.[15]

Before we can interpret the house, it is necessary to interpret the man. What of the man, the Planter Simeon Perkins? He was apprenticed to his cousin, Colonel Jabez Huntington,[16] who lived in a large house in Norwich, Connecticut, and who was a merchant and very obviously successful in business. Later he became a general on George Washington's staff. Simeon Perkins married Abigail Backus in 1762,[17] but she died soon after delivering a son named Roger. Abigail was a cousin of Governor Trumball of Connecticut, and therefore a cousin of the famous painter Jonathan Trumbull. As a young widower of twenty-eight Simeon Perkins wrote that he came to Nova Scotia a disconsolate man.[18] He nevertheless became a pillar of society, serving as magistrate, judge, town clerk and county treasurer, and Colonel in the Queens County militia during the American War of Independence.

The evidence suggests that we must interpret the builder of the house as a sad young man, a merchant, well-connected in Connecticut, but with limited resources from his trading in Nova Scotia: a Planter of limited success. In 1813, a year after the death of Simeon Perkins, a portrait was painted in Liverpool of his second wife, Elizabeth (Figure 4), wearing widow's grey.[19] All eight children born to her by Simeon Perkins were still alive in 1812, but within another nine years five of them had died. In 1822 she left Nova Scotia for New York with her two remaining unmarried daughters.[20]

---

13 Town of Liverpool, Proprietor's Book, Queens County Record Office.

14 The sketchbook of John Elliot Woolford is in the Nova Scotia Museum.

15 Parks Canada, Canadian Inventory of Historic Buildings, report by John F. Stevens, 1965.

16 General Jabez Huntington, b. 1719, d. 1786, graduated from Yale College in 1741.

17 Abigail Backus, b. 1742, d. 1760.

18 Quoted in Perkins, *Old Houses of the Ancient Town of Norwich*, 235, 236, quoting from the missing section of the Diary written before 1764 to which she had access.

19 A watercolour by J. Comingo painted in 1813 now in the Elizabeth B. Perkins Museum, York, Maine.

20 Public Archives of Nova Scotia, vertical mss. file, "Simeon Perkins," and Perkins, *Old Houses of the Ancient Town of Norwich*, 553.

4. Elizabeth Headley Perkins, the second wife of Simeon Perkins painted by J. Comingo in 1813. The original hangs in the drawing room of the Elizabeth Bishop Perkins House in York, Maine.
(Courtesy of the Society for the Preservation of Historic Landmarks, York, Maine.)

With this evidence of the owner's personal life, we can now attempt to interpret his house. Even the most ordinary descriptions of the architecture are confused by obscure terminology or mis-information. A standard design of house throughout New England is the so-called 'Cape Cod' or 'one-and-a-half storey' house, which are misleading terms and might be replaced with the more accurate 'floor-and-a-half' house, for the houses are externally single storey and internally are undoubtedly two stories high with an upper floor reduced in size by the lack of headroom at the eaves. These houses are typically built with a massive central chimney where several fireplaces are connected into one flue. Much less common is the house with end chimneys, though they can be found, including a brick house (Figure 5) in Uxbridge, Massachusetts, built the same year as Perkins House in 1766. It too has corner fireplaces.

Interpretation is made more difficult when there are few end chimney houses compared with central ones and very few published plans.[21] But if one travels far enough there are photographs to study as well as a few sketch books drawn by itinerant artists.[22] From these documents we can

21 It would appear that the ratio is about 4:1 in favour of central chimneys. In general there are few drawings published of single storey houses in New England, and very few plans of houses with end chimneys have been found.

22 Searches were made in the photograph collections and libraries of the American

see that the norm is a vernacular architecture of order, if not symmetry, and that additions often create their own form of naïve asymmetry. On the other hand there are few photographs of interiors and therefore meagre interpretations of the construction to be found. Visits to actual houses are necessary to discover their construction methods. Inside Perkins House the construction is still clearly visible today. The frame shows the state of development of the North American stud frame construction by the middle of the eighteenth century. Gone is the heavy European framing but remaining are widely spaced rafters and, spanning between them, horizontal purlins (Figure 6), a carry over from thatched-roof technology.[23] All there is to hold up the roof are the vertical planks in the perimeter wall (Figure 7). The house was built quickly. No time was wasted on grubbing out the tree stump under the parlour floor. The joint still shows clearly where the house was extended in 1781. Trim was not unnecessarily removed and replaced.

Other evidence suggests the sequence of alteration. The parlour door handle does not match the handle on the keeping room door. From the Diary we find that the keeping room door and wall were not built until October or November 1787, twenty years after the parlour was built. The builders were Mr. Grant and John Miles. The locks are of substantially the same pattern, but the style of handle varies; a carriage handle in the early one is replaced by a simple brass knob in the later one. In a photograph taken in 1947 (Figure 8) we find an entry without a stair, and might reasonably ask when it was removed. In a photograph taken in 1978 it had reappeared. Why? Today's stair is actually the fourth main stair in the house. The first dates from 1766 (original construction), and was replaced by the second in 1787 (recorded in the Diary); this was removed in about 1840 (based on oral tradition), and relocated at the back of the house; the fourth stair was the one reinstated at the front in 1949 (recorded by Raddall), which is the one we now see. Fortunately for the interpreter another person connected with the house also kept a diary. Thomas Raddall recorded all the activities of the Queens County Historical Society, including alterations to the house from 1935 to 1959,[24] so we have

Antiquarian Society, Worcester, MA., New Haven Colony Society, New Haven, CT., and the Society for the Protection of New England Antiquities, Boston, MA., where the search was time-consuming as the information was purely visual in nature and for which there is no easy index. The complete files were accessed. This obviously implies a great privilege and thanks are due to these organizations.

23 See R.W. Brunskill, *Illustrated Handbook of Vernacular Architecture* (London, 1978); J. Frederick Kelly, *Early Domestic Architecture of Connecticut* (New York, 1963); and N.M. Isham and A.F. Brown, *Early Connecticut Houses* (New York, 1965).

24 Thomas Raddall, "The Queens County Historical Society, 1929-1959," unpublished excerpts from his personal diaries. Copies can be seen in the Public Archives of Nova Scotia and the Queens County Museum.

5. The Moses Farnham house at Uxbridge, Massachusetts, built in 1766 and located about 65 km north of Norwichtown, Connecticut. Although built of brick, this house is remarkably similar to the initial phase of the Perkins house. There are end chimneys within the exterior wall, corner fireplaces in the main rooms and there is a central hallway with a staircase boxed in with vertical boards. Drawn from a photograph taken in June 1894, the original is in the collection of the American Society, Worcester, Massachusetts.

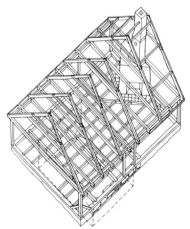

6. The frame of the Simeon Perkins House.
   Note the small number of vertical posts, the relatively few number of rafters and the use of purlins between the rafters. No evidence of a summer beam has been found but there has been no attempt at destructive investigation to make sure, so it cannot be entirely eliminated. The small cellar provides support in the centre, but when first built there were no walls under the sills except at the cellar.

an accurate date for the removal of the rear stair and the replacement of the front stair. But as with Simeon Perkins' Diary there are no drawings, photographs or sketches to show the architectural details, only words. This lack of visual proof so broadens the opportunity for inaccurate interpretation that it is at the same time both helpful to have a date, and frustrating to know the date and not have the details. The writings of Perkins and Raddall appear to cover the two main periods of building activity at the house. It is a remarkable coincidence that there is a written account of the major alterations, even if the information is incomplete.

In 1947 the main stair was at the back of the house.[25] Moving the stair from the front to the back is attributed to Caleb Seely,[26] who bought the house from Mrs. Perkins in 1822. The house remained in the same family until Seely's last grand-daughter died there in 1935, when it was sold by the heir to the Queens County Historical Society. Another support for the 1840 date of the stair removal comes from a snippet of wallpaper behind the plaster hiding the attic access hatch in the ceiling. The Gothic Revival pattern of the wallpaper dates from about 1840.[27] Of itself this evidence may appear insubstantial, but there is also some oral history to support the 1840 date.[28] The dates of the first, second and fourth changes to the stairs are therefore known to the day, while the third is only attributable to a date through oral history which links the removal of the stairs to a girl who died at the age of twenty-three in 1844.

We may find difficulty in our interpretation of the fabric of the house. The cellar walls appear ancient and long undisturbed. The mortar joints in the stone walls of the cellar are not original but were added to deter the rats.[29] An apparent lack of foundations can be interpreted from the deformation seen in a 1947 photograph (Figure 9). Apart from the cellar, the house had no foundations when it was first built. In 1982 it was found that the sill was lying directly on the sandy soil.[30] There remains a question about the foundations which is still too difficult to answer at present. Was there a foundation in 1766 and was it removed or destroyed in the alterations of 1949?[31] From the Diary we learn that the construction of the

---

25 Photograph by Hedly Doty, 1947.

26 Caleb Seely, b. 1787, Saint John, N.B., d. 1869, Liverpool, N.S., a well-known privateer captain and merchant.

27 Staff of the Nova Scotia Museum.

28 Thomas Raddall, "The Queens County Historical Society, 1929-1959," oral history by Mrs. John Day, 22 April 1949. In searching for the person who was the most likely cause for the stair to be moved, only Caroline Seely fitted the evidence and she died in 1844, aged 23.

29 Diary, II, 5 August 1788.

30 Verbal communications from an architect with Government Services.

31 There is no reference to the lack of foundations in Raddall only the description of the sills

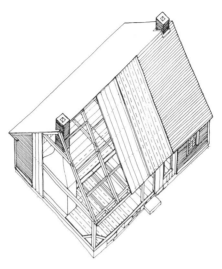

7. The cladding of the Simeon Perkins House.
   Both the roof slopes and the walls are covered with vertical boards. It is
   a single layer on the walls and a double layer on the roof, but thinner.
   The roof surfaces were shingled whereas the walls were clapboarded.
   The walls at the lower level were plastered from the start, but the upper
   level walls and underside of the roof sheathing appear to have merely
   been wallpapered; neither wall being good thermal insulation.

8. The entry in 1947. The space to the right is now occupied by the stair
   rebuilt in 1949.

extension was delayed when there appeared to be an imminent withdrawal of soldiers from the garrison.[32] Simeon Perkins used the soldiers as labourers to earn their keep.

It is not too difficult to interpret the architecture when the information is both written and the existing fabric can be examined, but how do we interpret the life which went on inside the house? It is this aspect of interpretation that is probably most required by society; yet is the most difficult to access.

On 11 January 1792 Simeon Perkins wrote: "...my Office room chimney took fire & Burn with great rage, and I was Very Apprehensive the chimney would Bust, in which case I expected the House would be in great danger. We put water & Salt into the fire & took out ye Pipe of the stove in the chamber and poured water in there which deadened the fire...."[33] Though covered over in 1978, the stove pipe thimble was still visible in a 1947 photograph,[34] which does strongly suggest the location of both the office, parlour and bedroom. Lucy Perkins fell into the kitchen fire at the age of three but lived to make a beautifully executed sampler at the age of twelve.[35] On 28 April 1800 the old brick domed bake-oven next to the kitchen fireplace was removed to make a closet.[36] The springing of the brick dome can still be seen to this day. Life in the late eighteenth century was remarkably like our own in that maintenance, accident, skill development in children and alteration are as common today as they were then. But there were also noticeable differences.

Once Simeon Perkins remarried, the household grew to seventeen people requiring more space and generating the first extension built in 1781.[37] The kitchen remained the same size and a keeping room was added along with two bedrooms.[38] The east chimney was entirely dismantled and rebuilt beyond the original end wall of the house. The joints in the floor boards upstairs still show the location of the original chimney. A previous interpreter was fooled by the appearance of the hood over the upstairs fireplace. He interpreted it to be of metal,[39] presumably from a photograph

---

being replaced. It is a shame that the sills were not better installed in 1949 as they are still susceptible to rot.

32 Diary, II, 29 June 1781.
33 Diary, III, 11 January 1792.
34 Photograph by Hedly Doty.
35 Diary, II, 27 March 1783. The Sampler is located in the Elizabeth B. Perkins Museum, York, Maine.
36 Diary, IV, 28 April 1800.
37 Diary, II, 20 June 1781 and following.
38 One bedroom was on the main floor and the other, initially called the garret, was only accessible through another bedroom.
39 Parks, report by John Stevens.

9. The north front in 1947. Note the horizontal window and plumbing stack on the east end, (left hand side) and the Victorian Gothic Chimney Pots. The overall deformation of the house can be seen by the drooping ends.

and because of its colour and shape, whereas it is merely painted plaster over brick. This example serves as a warning to first assess the accuracy of the facts and then check out the interpretation against all the available evidence.

Board cuts in the main roof show where the chimney was first positioned. Simeon Perkins wrote that he called in a "chimney doctor"[40] for this chimney, but later photographs suggest the "doctor" was unsuccessful in his cure because Gothic Revival style chimney pots were added during the latter half of the nineteenth century and were still in place in 1947.[41]

The corner post of the original house is visible in the north-east corner of the keeping room and the corner post in the extension of 1781 can be seen

40 Diary, III, 14 May 1792.
41 Photograph by Hedly Doty, 1947.

in the chamber, the former without diagonal braces but still showing mortise joints. The interpretation is that the original corner was braced, but as the extension required access, and the door opening conflicted with the corner brace, then the brace was removed. Unlike the outside of the house where no particular aesthetic concern was expressed over the showing of joints at the point of the addition, inside, the now redundant second diagonal brace was also removed for seemingly aesthetic reasons.

Interpretation may require physical effort, discomfort and diligence. A number of interpreters have looked at the house but failed to crawl into the eaves closet of the middle bedroom, where the inside of the original end wall can be viewed, or into the closet in the east bedroom where on the other side of the same wall can be found the original wall cladding from 1766 (Figure 10).[42] This portion of cladding suggests that the front of the house still retains its original clapboard finish after 220 years.[43]

Further subtle but important data may radically alter our impressions. The extension of 1781 included the new kitchen with its fireplace built the same year, whereas the staircase built in the same room dates from a year later, 1782.[44] It would be impossible to discern the different dates from the building alone, but from the Diary we learn both that it was built later and by whom. In his reference to it Simeon Perkins notes the name of the builder, Mr. Bangs, who not only built ships for Simeon Perkins, but also built the stair as though it were in a ship.[45] The remarkable comparison to a ship's companionway becomes understandable with the Diary references, and thus improves the architectural interpretation.

By 1792 Simeon Perkins decided the house was too small and a second extension was required. A large rock blocked development to the east so it was expedient to add the new wing on the south, turning the plan into a T-shape.[46] The extension is built virtually as a new building adjacent to the existing one with an unsatisfactory connection. From a careful inspection of a measured drawing of a section (Figure 11) the two buildings appear to be simply butted together, leaving a badly designed valley roof gutter, which is both a rain and snow trap.[47] The valley is remarkable for its state

---

42 Why this small area of clapboarding has remained is interesting, and must stem from the saving of unnecessary labour rather than from a need to leave historical clues.

43 Observation after comparing the materials and the dimensions of the two areas of clapboarding.

44 Diary, II, 6 August 1781 and following; 4 October 1782.

45 The rise of each step is higher than the going of each tread, it is narrow, and at the level of the floor above the girt in the end wall has been reduced in width to allow easier passage up the stair.

46 Diary, III, 5 June 1792.

47 Signs of consistent and considerable water staining are visible in the roofspace, as are traces of creeper which in 1947 covered the roof.

10. Clapboarded gable wall from 1767. This is definitely original as it was left untouched when the 1781 addition covered it over. The vertical boarded wall can be seen with mice holes gnawed at floor level. These original clapboards match those on the front or North elevation which supports the idea that the front is still the original cladding.

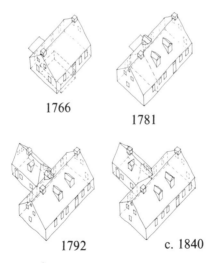

1766

1781

1792   c. 1840

11. Phases of construction:
    1766 Initial construction, completed in 1767,
    1781 First addition, at the near end, with new chimney,
    1792 Second addition at the rear,
    c 1840 South facing dormer window removed and the valley gutter filled in.

of preservation and shows that the roof valley was finally covered-over and also made water-tight at a later date.[48] What remains under the roof is the original roof slope from 1766 which has a few remaining shingles adhering to it, and the steep slope of the 1792 roof which has plenty of shingles still nailed in place. What is not initially visible to the casual observer is that the gaps between the horizontal sheathing boards are covered, not with birch bark, but with strips of thin canvas.[49] These appear to have been cut from somebody's discarded canvas trousers.

Interpretation of where people slept is difficult because the Diary is vague in this area. It is quite conceivable that Frank,[50] a black slave, might have lived in the attic over the kitchen, and the black couple, Anthony and Hagar,[51] might have lived there too. In either case, the thin walls meant the thermal comfort would have been similar to living in a contemporary tent and therefore a trifle rugged for everyday life. But thermal comfort was no better in the furnished part of the house where the owner and his family lived. On 28 January 1800 Simeon Perkins wrote: "My ink has been froze the most of the day on the table near the fire."[52]

Returning to the valley between the two roofs, why was it kept? The answer appears to have to do with the south facing dormer window which has since been removed from the middle bedroom. Cuts in the sheathing on the original roof slope can still be seen where the dormer was located.[53] We know from the Diary that in 1804, seven-year-old Mary was standing at the window when it was hit by scaffolding blown off the roof and chimney of the second extension roof and was in "Some danger." We do not know the date when the window was removed, except that if Simeon Perkins had it removed he probably would have recorded it. What is curious to the twentieth-century interpreter is that if the extension had been built just a few inches to the west, then the dormer need not have been in conflict with the extension roof, forcing the use of the valley, and the

---

48 No date can be given for the alteration. Few nails are visible but the saw marks in the wood sheathing are of later rather than earlier date. It is possible that the roof was completed in the 1840s along with the changes to the staircase position, but there is no particular connection between the two.

49 Although Raddall refers to finding birch bark under the shingles, this use of canvas suggests a different attitude to construction and possibly may relate to the use of soldiers to do the building work.

50 Diary, I, 12 July 1777. Jacob, aged 10 or 11 cost £35, and was renamed Frank. He died 22 June 1784.

51 Diary, Anthony and Hagar came to Liverpool from Shelburne, Diary, II, 20 December 1783.

52 Diary, II, 29 January 1780.

53 Visible in the space between the two early roofs, and also clearly visible from inside the bedroom.

resultant rain leaks, snow collection and water stains would have been prevented.

Hasty interpretation can cause long-lasting problems. When Thomas Raddall read the Diary to assist in the restoration work in 1949, he was presumably reading from the then existing typewritten manuscript. Four of the five volumes of the Diary had not yet been published. Where Raddall read "office"[54] he interpreted it as though there was only one 'office' and thought it was located in the house. In the comfortable to read, printed Diary, complete with introductions, indexes and so on, it is easier to come to the conclusion that at least four "offices" are being referred to, only one of them in the house. It also appears that there were two parlours, both of them in the house.[55]

Raddall appears to have incorrectly interpreted the Diary references and concluded the wrong room to have been painted green. But this does not preclude the room now painted green from having been that colour at some time during its lifetime; it simply suggests that the facts should have been interpreted differently in 1949.[56] It so happens that in the room next door a scrap of wallpaper was found which not only suggests that a different room should have been painted green but also that it should have been a different shade of green.[57]

It is easy to see when mistakes have been made if the original information is available for re-interpretation, but if the green paint is missing from the parlour, then also missing is the standard piece of eighteenth-century parlour equipment, the built-in corner cupboard. Which corner was it in and what did it look like? With so much alteration in the site and surroundings other questions might be put; for example, where were all the out-buildings located, and what was their size and shape, orientation and use? Although it is possible to be quite definite about the sequence of addition to the house (Figure 12), not all the dates are known for the individual stages. When were the shutters put on? The most likely date is after 1830, but there is no written data to help us here.

---

54 A number of references may be cited, but there are also a number of terms employed over the years, including, office, office room, and counting room, as well as a number of locations, including the waterfront, the store, an office on the street as well as in the house.

55 Perkins refers to both the "Parlour," "small Parlour," "back Parlour," and "great parlour," by which he refers to the original parlour and the conversion of the second kitchen into what we call a 'family room.'

56 Raddall, 14 June 1948.

57 Raddall refers to the colour as "queer dark green paint" and also as "Williamsbury blue" (sic). There is some confusion not only as to the colour and the room but also to whether it was woodwork or wall that was being painted. Perkins clearly states on 19 June 1793 that he was having the woodwork in the "small parlour and keeping room" painted blue.

Any interpretation can be altered in the light of new evidence. The present interpretive position has been arrived at after much help from others, especially those at the Nova Scotia Museum who have patiently taught an architect to begin to deal with history.

What was it really like to be a Planter? The furrowed brow in Simeon Perkins' portrait was come by honestly. In one year he lost no less than five ships, either to storm or privateer. He watched his boyhood friends become generals and state governors, and some just plain rich business-men, while he pioneered in Nova Scotia, dutifully carrying out his civic responsibilities, coping with the vagaries of war, and bringing up a family in a relatively isolated frontier fishing village. In 1947 a photograph (Figure 13)[58] of the outside of the house shows it to have been unpainted for a considerable time, with stains, rot, deterioration of window putty and collapsing foundations; in general appearance close to being derelict. In contrast we see the house today with its thick glossy bright white paint, pristine landscape and close cut grass. Which is the more accurate interpretation of the house in Simeon Perkins' time? The accurate interpretation has to be the shabby one. Perkins records for us the description of the house in 1803[59] when the shingles were falling off the roof, having never been painted in *thirty-seven* years.

We may not think this interpretation very nice, even if it is true. We may never have the courage to re-interpret the outside of this house to make it 'real shabby' because of the tourists, but we make a mistake if we fail to see the hardy, fallible, tough, courageous and often poor people that we now call Planters out of context. It seems that Simeon Perkins never knew he was a 'Planter,' but we can thank him for being one, for keeping a diary and for building a house and for the significant contribution he made to establish this Nova Scotia.

---

58 Photograph by Hedly Doty, 1947.
59 Diary, IV, 26 July 1803.

1792

After 1803

12. Cross Section.

Initially built in 1792, the valley gutter was formed by building simply and making the least effort. Retention of the south facing dormer window suggests that Bedroom 2 may have been divided at this time.

A cast iron stove was installed between 1803 and 1847, with the expectation that it was not put in before 1812 as there is no Diary entry for it, and it is unlikely that it was put in after 1900.

13. Perkins House. Government Services 1261.

An Examination of the Stephen Loomer House Habitant, Kings County, Nova Scotia[1]

Daniel E. Norris
Heritage Officer
Department of Tourism and Culture

INTRODUCTION

In Debra McNabb's study, *The Landscape of Eighteenth Century New England Settlement in Kings County* (1985), a large tract of land was identified as a culturally distinct element in the geography of the province of Nova Scotia. The tract of land encompasses a large number of sites which share one common feature: all of the sites were part of the eighteenth-century landscape of Kings County, and surprisingly, all remain today as part of the present twentieth-century landscape. Though many of the sites identified are part of the geographical district known as Horton Township, many are also found in the neighbouring historical district of Cornwallis Township. Such is the case with the Loomer-Goodwin house, a provincially registered heritage property located near Canning, Kings County, Nova Scotia.

A preliminary investigation of the Loomer-Goodwin House was conducted in July 1986 at the request of the owners, Olive and Ron Goodwin. The house is located in the present day community of Habitant approximately one half mile east of Canning (see Figure 1). The house displays many of the characteristics associated with an early New England Colonial form (the Dutch-Colonial House). It is a one and one-half storey gambrel-roofed house, low in the post, with a central chimney plan. The preliminary investigation of the house (see Figure 2) identified a number of interesting characteristics; notably, a fieldstone foundation, replete with a 6 foot by 8 foot chimney base; the use of post and beam construction with mortise and tenon joints; the location of the house on a well-established route within a Planter settled area; and two printed documents provided by the owners. The documents were particularly interesting because they identified two original owners who were both believed to have immigrated

---

1 I would like to acknowledge: first, the assistance of the Heritage Inventory Co-ordinators for Shelburne, Wolfville and Yarmouth, and my supervisor, Brian Cuthbertson; second, interested and informative members of the public, including David Burton and Art Pope, for technical assistance and access to information, drawings and genealogical research; third, the kind assistance of the Kings County Registry of Deeds, Kings County Museum, and Nova Scotia Department of Lands and Forests, Mapping Division; and most importantly, the home owners involved, especially Ron and Olive Goodwin, for their kind assistance and hospitality throughout my research.

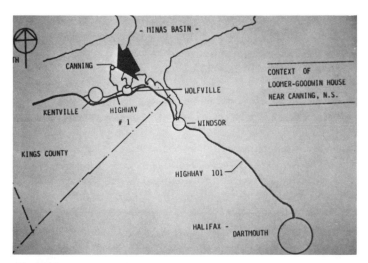

Figure 1

Figure 2 (a)

to Nova Scotia within the Planter period of settlement between 1760 and 1765.

Stephen Loomer is identified as the original owner by the present owners Ron and Olive Goodwin. They in turn based their opinions on that of the late Ira Cox, an early historian of Kings County. Mr. Cox maintained that the Loomer-Goodwin House was the oldest house in Cornwallis Township. According to Cox, the house was built by a Mr. Loomer, the materials being brought from New England by schooner and landed at the creek to the south of the property (Goodwin, 1986). A second possible owner/builder, a Mr. Hamilton, is noted in *Old Times: Canning and Habitant* (Bickerton, 1980, 172). According to this second source, Hamilton is believed to have immigrated to the area in 1761. Interestingly, this source also reports that the house was brought from New England to Kingsport.

To ascertain which of the two sources was correct, reference was first made to Esther Clark Wright's book, *Planters and Pioneers* (1982). Wright identifies Stephen Loomer as one of the two Loomers who immigrated to Cornwallis Township in the period between 1761 and 1765. No reference to any original Planter by the name of Hamilton can be found for Cornwallis Township (although a Mr. Hamilton is found in Horton Township). Deed research was subsequently conducted by Brian Cuthbertson, Head of Heritage, Department of Tourism and Culture, to attempt to determine the history of ownership and the original owner/builder of the Loomer-Goodwin House. According to the deed search undertaken, Mr. Hamilton is likely to be the second or possibly third owner while either Simeon (Stephen's son) or Stephen Loomer are likely to be the original owners. With preliminary deed sources exhausted, a secondary line of investigation was started, an examination of site, location and genealogy.

Figure 2 (b)

Figure 2 (c)

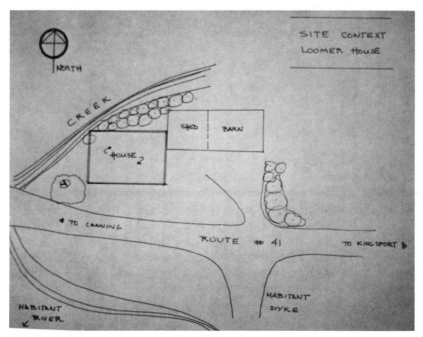

Figure 3

HISTORY OF OWNERSHIP

Loomer-Goodwin House
Habitant, Kings County, Nova Scotia

DATE	GRANTOR		*GRANTEE*	*Book:Page*
1812	Simeon and Mary Loomer	to	Oliver Hamilton (Shoemaker, Tanner)	5:309
1849	Charles Hamilton	to	John White Eaton (by mortgage)	_____
1873	J.W. Eaton	to	Frederick Eaton	33:493
1892	John Eaton	to	W.R. Porter	60:750
1900	W.R.Porter	to	George Morey	75:446
1918	George Morey	to	Fletcher McBride	19:650
1953	Fletcher McBride	to	Verge Porter	182:190
1967	Verge Porter	to	Ron and Olive Goodwin	260:695

SOURCE: Kings County Registry of Deeds, Kentville, Nova Scotia.

SITE, LOCATION AND GENEALOGY

The present-day site of the Loomer-Goodwin house is at the intersection of the Canning-Kingsport road immediately opposite the Habitant Dyke (see Figure 3). In the survey plan of Cornwallis Township (Eaton 1981) within the Subdivision of Lands to Grantees is noted a "S. Loomer" receiving lot #9, north of division #1 in 1762 in approximately the same location as the subject site. To determine if the S. Loomer identified by Eaton was either Simeon or Stephen Loomer, a genealogical search of the Loomer family was conducted. Kings County Courthouse Museum genealogy records (manuscript No. 91) traced the development of the Loomer family.

Stephen Loomer was born in Connecticut in May 1721, married in 1749 and removed to Nova Scotia about 1761. The exact date of removal is

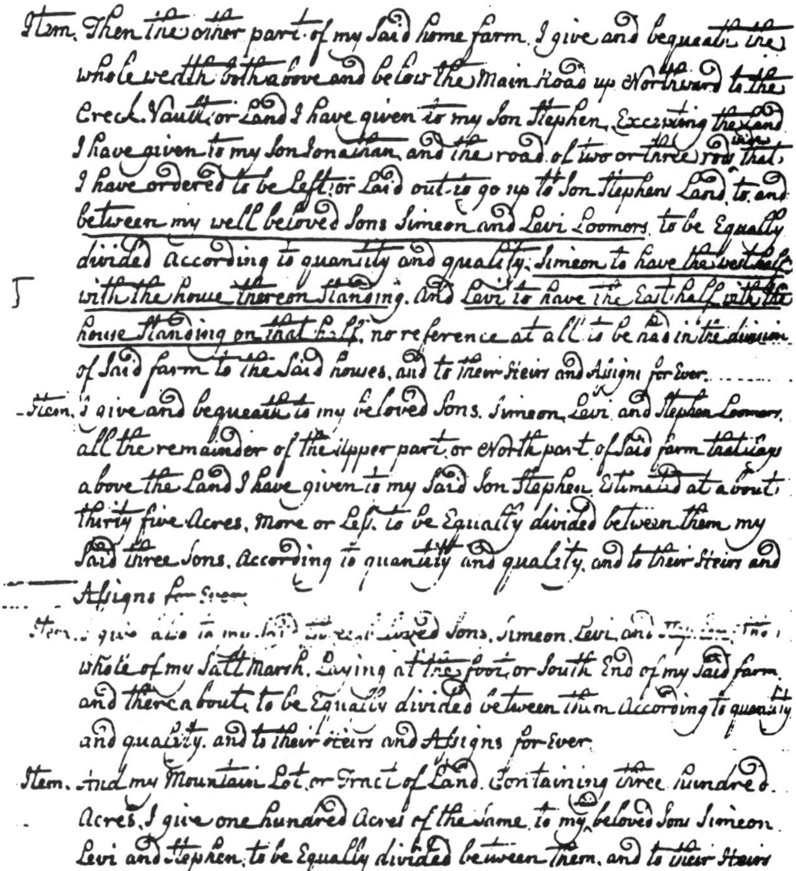

Item. Then the other part of my said home farm I give and bequeath the whole width both above and below the main Road up Northward to the Creek Vault, or Land I have given to my Son Stephen, Excepting the Land I have given to my Son Jonathan, and the road of two or three rod that I have ordered to be Left, or Laid out to go up to Son Stephens Land, to and between my well beloved Sons Simeon and Levi Loomers to be Equally divided according to quantity and quality; Simeon to have the west half with the house thereon standing. And Levi to have the East half with the house standing on that hill, no reference at all is be had in the division of said farm to the said houses, and to their Heirs and Assigns for Ever. ....

Item. I give and bequeath to my beloved Sons. Simeon, Levi and Stephen Loomer, all the remainder of the upper part, or North part of Said farm that lays above the Land I have given to my Said Son Stephen, Estimated at about thirty five Acres, more or Less, to be Equally divided between them my Said three Sons, according to quantity and quality, and to their Heirs and Assigns for Ever.

Item. I give also to my Said three beloved Sons, Simeon, Levi and Stephen, the whole of my Salt marsh, Lying at the foot, or South End of my Said farm and thereabouts, to be Equally divided between them according to quantity and quality, and to their Heirs and Assigns for Ever.

Item. And my Mountain Lot, or Tract of Land, Containing three hundred Acres, I give one hundred Acres of the same, to my beloved Sons Simeon Levi and Stephen, to be Equally divided between them, and to their Heirs and Assigns for Ever.

Item. And the other, or remainder two hundred Acres of my Said Mountain Lot or Tract of Land, I give and bequeath the whole thereof between my four dear and well beloved Daughters, namely Phebe Jackson, Hannah Pince, Easter West, and Mary Babcock. to be Equally divided between them, and to their Heirs and Assigns for Ever.

Item. I Will and require that all my just Debts and funeral Charges. be duly paid out of my personel Estate, by my Executor hereafter Named. And the remainder of my Estate if any, more or Less, I give to be divided Equally, between all my Said Children Sons and daughters, and to their Heirs and Assigns for Ever.   And

Figure 4

unknown; however, parish records note the birth of a Stephen Loomer child in Norwich, Connecticut, in 1760, and a subsequent birth of a child to Stephen and Hannah Loomer in Cornwallis in 1762. In the genealogical records a missing piece of the ownership puzzle was identified; the mention of a will probated by Stephen Loomer in 1790 (Kentville, N.S.). In this will Stephen Loomer makes note of the land parcels he gave to his children. Most kindly to present historians, he notes: "Simeon (b 1758) to have the west half with the house thereon Standing (see Figure 4)."

This parcel of land can be subsequently traced to Oliver Hamilton (in 1812) and then through subsequent owners continuously to Ron and Olive Goodwin, completing the history of the property ownership. Clearly, the process of deed searching and then seeking out property mapping, to return to deed and probate documents can be a profitable process.

One can, therefore, with reasonable certainty, conclude that the Loomer-Goodwin House was built between the time that Stephen Loomer arrived in Cornwallis (c. 1761) and the time that he passed on the land and house to Simeon Loomer in 1790. To arrive at a more precise date, our investigation turned to a third source of information, the architectural style and construction of the dwelling.

ARCHITECTURAL STYLE AND CONSTRUCTION

Peter Ennals in his article "The Yankee Origins of Bluenose Vernacular Architecture" (1982), argues that: "It is house form that provides the most evident landscape similarity between Nova Scotia and New England." The particular architectural style being examined here — the gambrel-roofed house — also reflects a similarity of style and form within both New England and Nova Scotia contexts. The gambrel-roofed house style, known to have largely developed in New England, was subsequently transported to Nova Scotia. It was my hope that by tracing the origins of the style in New England and its development in Nova Scotia, that I could narrow the potential dates of the construction of the Loomer-Goodwin House to a range of ten or fewer years.

The gambrel-roofed house style first came to this author's attention when illustrations were being selected for the publication of *A Nova Scotian's Guide To Built Heritage* (1985). This publication, produced by the Nova Scotia Department of Tourism and Culture, notes fifteen principal styles of architecture found throughout the province. The inclusion of a gambrel-roof house style, described in the guidebook as an example of the "Dutch-Colonial" style (see Figure 5) created a debate even before the guidebook was published. The style is known to occur in New England in areas settled by Dutch migrants, but is not typical of homes built by the Dutch in Holland (Embury, 1913; Kimball, 1966), nor typical of homes built by the Dutch who came to Nova Scotia. Our in-house debate of the definition and labelling of the style ended when no more appropriate title

DUTCH COLONIAL 1700-1800

Gambrel often called "Dutch" roof with handsplit shingles

Usually one and a half storey wood construction

Centered doorway with symmetrical 5 bay facade

Dormers absent or undersize

One large central or two end-wall chimneys

Figure 5

could be found; like other texts (McAlester 1984; Gowans 1986) the name Dutch-Colonial was then utilized in our text. Virginia and Lee McAlester (1984) suggest that there are three principal sub-types of the Dutch-Colonial style: the urban tradition; the rural tradition, unflared eaves; and the rural tradition, flared eaves.

The Loomer-Goodwin house is probably best described as part of the rural tradition, unflared eaves. The knowledge that the Loomer-Goodwin house matched a particular style category introduced a more specific approach for this study: that of isolating only rural tradition, non-flared eaved gambrel-roofed houses, in areas settled by Planters in Nova Scotia, and then comparing these houses (in terms of construction methods and dates of construction) to the Loomer-Goodwin house.

To isolate one single type of style within an entire province which contains many areas of Planter settlement is all but impossible without a comprehensive inventory. Fortunately, for historians and researchers, Nova Scotia is presently developing such an inventory. This inventory of built heritage, which contains architectural, historical, genealogical and contextual information for over 5000 properties province-wide proved to be an invaluable resource. All of the properties in the inventory date from before 1914, and a surprisingly large number are built before 1800. By referring to this information base, three comparable houses which fit the three independent criteria, eighteenth century, gambrel-roofed, in areas settled by Planters were identified: the de Gannes-Cosby house in Annapolis Royal, the Biggs house in the Gaspereaux Valley, and the Clements house in Chebogue, Yarmouth County.

CONSTRUCTION

With this pool of structures, an in-depth study of the Loomer-Goodwin house construction was conducted. The Loomer-Goodwin house is a 24 foot by 28 foot, 4 inch wood frame structure built on a fieldstone foundation with walls measuring approximately 4 feet in height, varying from 18 to 20 inches thick (these fieldstone walls are in turn capped by a 20 inch lift of quarried stone). A number of unusual framing features on the ground floor were noted. First, the beams supporting the eastern half of the house appear to be different in size and orientation from the western half. Second, it is unusual to see two major first floor beams that do not connect to a nearby chimney base. Third, and this is most unusual, there is a stone wall which exists midway through the cellar that does not support any overhead beams or walls (see Figure 6).

These three unusual construction features when taken singularly may simply indicate poorly carried out renovations; however, when these three observations are considered in the context of similar alterations in other eighteenth-century structures that I have observed, they suggest that the house has been constructed in two parts: an earlier eastern section with a later western addition. Additional structural information which might be used to support such a proposal, includes a variation in floor plank from the eastern (up to 20 inches) to western halves (up to 14 inches) and a variation in floor joint sizes from (4 x 5 inches) in the eastern half to (3 x 5 inches) in the western half of the structure.

These types of structural variations in the Loomer-Goodwin house can be compared to the structural variations we found in another eighteenth-century house in this region: the DeWolf house in Wolfville, Nova Scotia. The recognition of unusual structural variations in the DeWolf House led

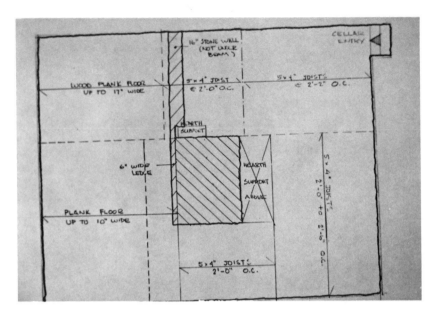

Figure 6

me to propose that the house was constructed in four stages, over time, each reflecting a particular configuration of dwelling and identifiable date.

To assess this evolutionary possibility with reference to the Loomer-Goodwin house, I first examined a number of texts which document early New England building configurations. In particular, the work of Martin S. Briggs (1932) is helpful here, because Briggs illustrates two common seventeenth-century New England house plans: the hall and parlour plan and the central chimney plan (see Figure 7). If one looks for a moment at the hall and parlour plan and then adds a similar living space on the right side of the chimney, the plan could evolve to look like the lower diagram, or a central chimney plan.

A two-bay plan with an addition can therefore look like a five-bay, central chimney plan. With these plan configurations in mind, I wondered if the Loomer-Goodwin house had indeed been built in two stages, each within an identifiable time frame? To assess the possibility I looked at three other rural traditional, gambrel-roofed houses with unflared eaves: the Biggs house in Gaspereaux, the Clements house in Chebogue and the de Gannes-Cosby house in Annapolis Royal.

The four houses identified thus far illustrate a number of basic similarities of construction: all are framed in post and beam construction; all share similarly styled gambrel-roofs; all buildings share similar five-bay

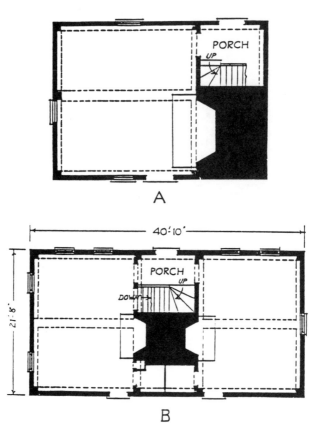

71. Plans of (A) Thos. Lee House, E. Lyme, Conn., before alteration, and (B) Older Williams House, Wethersfield, Conn. (Adapted by permission from J. F. Kelly's 'Early Domestic Architecture of Connecticut')

Figure 7

plans (two with central chimneys and two with end wall); and most interestingly, all three houses displayed varying degrees of structural evidence of being constructed in two stages, over time. That all four houses studied should exhibit similar variations in construction suggested to me that I was dealing with a rather homogeneous group of structures. Returning to the ownership information noted on the site forms, three quite remarkable findings could be noted: first, all four houses have deed evidence which suggests that they were built or enlarged between 1760 and 1769; second, three of the houses (Loomer-Goodwin, de Gannes-Cosby,

Biggs) show clear evidence of being built on or adjacent to Acadian cellars, and third, two of the houses (Loomer-Goodwin and Clements) have local documentary records that suggest that these houses were built in New England, dismantled, shipped to Nova Scotia and rebuilt.

SUMMARY

The comprehensive research approach taken here, which includes reference to deed information, mapping, probate records, genealogical notes *and* architectural evidence, suggests four conclusions. First, the Loomer-Goodwin house was probably built by Stephen Loomer, a Planter, between the years 1761 and 1769. This conclusion, based on documentary and structural evidence supports the local belief that the house was built in 1764. Second, the Loomer-Goodwin house style (gambrel) and sub-type (rural tradition, unflared eaves) appears to be associated with Planter settlement in Nova Scotia. Third, the method of construction (in a number of stages over time) parallels building practices in New England. This finding has significant implications for both our interpretation of eighteenth-century architectural forms in Nova Scotia and pioneer family forms. Fourth, there is a good deal of evidence which suggests that the gambrel-roofed Planter houses in Nova Scotia are built on or adjacent to pre-expulsion Acadian cellars. This finding is not particularly surprising given the small time period that elapsed between the two periods of settlement in Nova Scotia. Rather, the value of the finding rests with the new potential to examine and explore buildings and sites that bridged the material culture gap between Planter and Acadian societies.

The research conducted highlights the need for, and advantages of, a comprehensive approach for the study of built heritage. The comprehensive approach advocated here encompasses architectural, documentary and oral research, analysis and theory building. In particular, I would like to emphasize the importance of studying building construction. For far too long the value of Nova Scotia's built heritage resource has been underrated by the penchant of historical research to examine only documentary sources of information. The most obvious source of information, the building itself, has largely been overlooked. The building, analyzed in terms of its style, construction and design can help the researcher to discover the continuum of historical, architectural and cultural contexts; contexts not evident from documentary references alone. In conclusion, a comprehensive approach is advocated here, for all examinations of built heritage. Such an approach enables the researcher to develop a holistic understanding of a house, its inhabitants and their place in time.

BIBLIOGRAPHY

Bickerton, A. Marie. *Old Timers: Canning and Habitant*. Canning, Kings County, 1980.

Briggs, Martin S. *The Homes of the Pilgrim Fathers in England and America*. New York, 1932.

Crowell, F.E. "F.E. Crowell Scrapbook of New Englanders in Nova Scotia," Yarmouth Microfilm, Kings County Courthouse Museum, Kentville, Nova Scotia.

Eaton, E.L. "The Survey Plan of Cornwallis Township, Kings County," *The Nova Scotia Historical Review*, 1, 2(December 1981), 16-33.

Eaton, A.W.H. *The History of Kings County*. Salem, Massachusetts, 1910. reprint Belleville, Ontario, 1972.

Embury, A. *The Dutch Colonial House*. New York, 1913.

Ennals, Peter. "The Yankee Origins of Bluenose Vernacular Architecture," *The American Review of Canadian Studies*, 12, 2(Summer 1982), 5-21.

Goodwin, Olive. Miscellaneous notes, 1986.

Gowans, Alan. *The Comfortable House*. Cambridge, Massachusetts, 1986.

Heritage Section, N.S. Department of Tourism and Culture. *A Nova Scotian's Guide to Built Heritage*. Halifax, 1985.

Kimball, S.F. *Domestic Architecture of the American Colonies and of the Early Republic*. New York, 1966.

Loomer, Addie E. "Descendants of Stephen Loomer of New London, Connecticut," Iowa, 1959. Manuscript 91, King's County Courthouse Museum, Kentville, Nova Scotia.

McAlester, Virginia and Lee. *A Field Guide to American Houses*. Toronto, 1984.

McNabb, Debra. *The Landscape of Eighteenth Century New England Settlement in Kings County, Nova Scotia — A Geographical Study*. Halifax, 1985.

Wright, E.C. *Planters and Pioneers: Nova Scotia, 1749-1775*. Hantsport, 1982.

Private Lives from Public Artifacts: The Architectural Heritage of Kings County Planters

Heather Davidson
Acadia University

A study of the style of house constructed in Horton Township, Kings County, from 1760 to 1820 indicates a dramatic change from a simple rustic style which was easily adapted to changing needs to a sophisticated style which was rigid and stressed formality. This change in style paralleled a change in the focus of the society from the welfare of the community to the welfare of the family and the individual. This trend was demonstrated not only in the style and construction of the building but also in the changing use of interior space. Both dwellings and their extensions reflected this trend. What follows is a small part of a larger study which attempts to use surviving houses as a means of expanding our knowledge of the way of life of the Planters. The conclusions presented here are tentative and are subject to revision in the light of further research. The paper has several other limitations. First, it is unlikely that every style of house built during the period is represented by extant buildings. During the last 200 years many buildings have either been destroyed by fire or demolished. Some have been renovated; a few have been restored. In addition, it is difficult to determine the exact year of house construction. Deeds with their vague boundary references deal only with the transfer of land. Houses were rarely mentioned. Nevertheless, these houses are significant examples of Planter material culture.

Buildings have been recognized by historians as legitimate research material for more than sixty years. F. Frederick Kelly described houses as "human documents" and used them as resources in this early twentieth-century study of New England culture.[1] James Deetz regarded material culture as the "most objective source of information" and "most immediate" because it could be experienced directly.[2] In my research, I am indebted to scholarship on colonial New England material culture in general and Connecticut architecture in particular in my efforts to locate the antecedents of Horton houses. Also a valuable resource is the general chronology of Nova Scotia house styles which was developed by the Nova Scotia Department of Culture, Recreation and Fitness.[3] This document identifies

---

1 F. Frederick Kelly, *Connecticut's Old Houses — A Handbook and Guide* (Strougton, 1963), 34.

2 James Deetz, *In Small Things Forgotten: The Archaeology of Early American Life* (Garden City, 1977), 160.

3 *A Nova Scotian's Guide to Built Heritage: Architectural Styles, 1604-1930* (Halifax, 1985).

house styles and their periods of popularity. A few deeds, most of them found in the Kings County Registry of Deeds, mention dwellings. Wills and inventories of former owners often give specific information about the transfer of land with the dwelling and list its contents. Family histories supply invaluable information about its members.

Horton Township was one of four, known as the Minas Basin Townships, which were laid out along the south shore of the Bay of Fundy. A share averaged 500 acres and included town lot, dykeland, marshland and upland. Ownership of specific sections of land was determined by drawing lots. The amount of land an individual received varied from 250 to 2000 acres.[4] The majority of the settlers who laid claim to land arrived in Horton from Connecticut during the 1760s.

For this paper I selected four houses constructed in Horton between 1760 and 1820 either by the original grantees or their descendants. Each of these houses has a contribution to make to our understanding of the Planter way of life as it evolved during this period. Two of the houses are basically vernacular in style. This term implies that each was built using local materials by local craftsmen who combined tradition, individuality and utility to produce a graceful house. Form followed foundation and tradition in buildings constructed to provide living, working and sleeping quarters for the family. Built close to the ground, the house was generally asymmetrical and was freely adapted to meet changing needs. Individuality of the builder or owner was revealed in the pitch of the roof, the length of the roof and the location of the hearth. Exterior and interior decorative touches were minimal. Because its functions were to heat the house and to cook the meals, the massive chimney was the focal point of the interior. It was located in a large room or hall with a low ceiling. In this "great" room cooking, eating, entertaining and business dealings took place. The hall was the common shared space for family and visitors while the loft served as one large sleeping chamber.

The first house to be considered, the Calkin house (Figure 1), is located on its original foundations three miles south-west of the Horton town plot. It was built prior to 1768. The house, constructed of wood, has one storey and five bays including a central doorway on the facade. The asymmetrical bays are an external indication that the entire present structure is not original. This theory is supported by a study of the interior in general and the cellar in particular. In the cellar there is a marked difference in the type of stone used. Irregular fieldstone extends along the west end wall and approximately halfway down the north and south walls. The north wall abruptly changes to finished stone. There is a large stone chimney base along the west wall and a double wall along the south wall to the stairs

---

4 Arthur Wentworth Hamilton Eaton, *The History of Kings County* (1910, reprint Belleville, 1972), 86.

Figure 1: Calkin House, near Grand Pré.

leading outside. This area may have been an Acadian cellar. The original chimney has been removed at the first and second storey levels. Because several renovations have been made to the first storey, it is difficult to determine the original use of the interior space. Although the hearth was removed, the base of the chimney which is centrally located along the west wall indicates the existence at one time of one large open room on the ground floor. A staircase, now boarded in, led from the hall to the left. One interior wall is much thicker than the others and further supports the theory that the west section of the house is the elder.

The date of construction of the addition is unknown but its style indicates that it was prior to the end of the eighteenth century. The cellar is constructed of finished stone. The chimney located in the centre of the east wall has a unique triangular base and makes no contribution to the support of the structure. In most early houses the summer beam was placed through the chimney to give support to the frame. On the first floor, half of the east area was divided into two rooms, each with cornerposts, girts and a corner mantle. The antecedents of the triangular chimney and corner mantles are difficult to trace. They were not found in books dealing with New England or Connecticut hearths. Four houses built in Annapolis Royal dating from 1708 to 1763 and the Simeon Perkins House in Liverpool have this feature. The north-east room with its delicately moulded mantle was the "best" parlour and was opened only for special visitors. Although the south-east room was eventually converted into a kitchen, it was originally the second parlour. A central hallway which extends only half the width of the house leads from the present entrance and contains a staircase to the second storey. The fact that the summer beam — the major support beam for the addition — is located approximately five feet from the chimney and ends above the front entrance with the supporting timbers beneath it and the fact that the staircase treads show little sign of wear indicate that the present entrance is a later renovation. The second storey of the addition includes four bedrooms. The north-east one still contains the original mantle. Prosperity encouraged modest decoration and allowed privacy. Family members no longer slept together in a loft but were divided according to sex and ages into separate rooms. When the east addition was made, the loft above the original common room was divided into two bedrooms. The walls of the north-east bedroom, the walls of the existing stairwell and the walls of the upper hall are panelled with wide vertical boards which have bevelled edges.

The Calkin house is one of the few examples of a gambrel roof extant in Horton. The style which was employed in Connecticut may have been copied from buildings in seventeenth-century England.[5] According to many writers the style became popular because it allowed houseowners to avoid tax on the full second storey. In a simple one storey house, the steeply pitched roof limited storage and sleeping accommodations in the loft. By raising the pitch, the gambrel roof increased the utilization of the loft either for more storage space and/or for increased headroom. The style also enabled the builders to increase the breadth of the span without raising a higher steeper roof. The dormers which provide light for the half storey were constructed as part of the addition. The saltbox roof over the small addition to the west wall was traditional in England and New England. It provided the owner with a maximum use of continuous interior space without a major adjustment to the roof. Its date of construction is unknown but it has a low ceiling and a cupboard utilizes simple original iron hardware.

Ownership of the land on which the building stands is difficult to trace. The earliest deed at the Registry of Deeds in Kentville for any piece of land in the county is dated 8 April 1766. According to the *Horton Township Partition Book* which summarized grants to each settler in 1760, Jeremiah Calkin, Sr., was granted one share which included two First Division Farm Lots. When he purchased land in 1768 from Daniel Hovey, the lot was described as "lying west of the dwelling of said Jeremiah Calkin."[6] Calkin arrived in 1765 from Lebanon, Connecticut, with his wife Mary and three

---

5 Martin Shaw Briggs, *Homes of the Pilgrim Fathers in England and America, 1620-1685* (New York, 1932), 81.

6 Registry of Deeds, Kentville, N.S. Book 1, 221.

Figure 2: Atwell House, Wolfville

young sons.[7] By 1784 there were nine children in the family.[8] Between 1764 and 1777 he acquired nine parcels of land. As a prospering farmer and father of six sons and three daughters, Calkin was able to make a substantial addition to his dwelling and renovations to the original structure. Although wood was readily available, a carpenter or joiner was probably hired for the fine detail on the mantles and panelling. The division of interior space into many small rooms and the presence of decorative work indicate that privacy and style were increasing in importance for those who could afford them.

The second house, the Atwell house (Figure 2), was built c. 1770, approximately seven miles west of Horton town plot and in the western section of Mud Creek, or Wolfville. The house, built of wood, has two storeys and a five bay facade. Like the Calkin house, this one has an asymmetrical five bay facade and a central entrance. Interior evidence also suggests that this house gradually evolved to its present shape and size. The western portion of the cellar is older and may be Acadian. Along the west wall is the base of an enormous stone chimney. Although renovations made in the late eighteenth century divided the first storey into several rooms, the location of this chimney in the basement suggests that the first storey originally contained one large room. Evidence indicates that at least one addition was made, possibly by Edward or Elisha DeWolf.

7   Esther Clark Wright, *Planters and Pioneers* (Hantsport, 1982), 72.

8   Eaton, *History of Kings County*, 597.

In the basement of the additions is a massive vaulted chimney. The origins of this unique construction are unknown. On the first storey the end wall hearth in the original structure was relocated to the interior. The use of existing space was reorganized from a single common room to a north-west and a south-west room for use as parlours. A central hallway leads from the front to the rear of the house. Two new rooms were added to the first storey. The south-east room with its decorative mantle became the new dining-room. The north-east room with its large open hearth became the kitchen. Similarly the open loft of the original structure was converted into two bedrooms. A central hallway separated these rooms from more bedrooms over the addition. A later addition was made to the rear.

Because Elisha DeWolf was a prominent citizen, his activities were recorded extensively. He was High Sheriff of Kings from 1784 to 1789 and from 1818 to 1820. He was Assistant Judge of the Court of Common Pleas, Postmaster, Collector of Customs and Justice of the Peace.[9] He was a farmer, merchant and father of thirteen children. A large building was needed to house this family and to provide an office for this busy individual. DeWolf prospered and could afford the addition and renovations. The public offices which he held suggest that he would have a house appropriate to his position in the community.

This vernacular house developed according to the changing needs and increasing prosperity of the owner. On the facade, utility not symmetry was the primary concern. The side-lights at the front entrance are utilitarian and decorative, allowing sunlight through the hallway into the interior of the house. Small decorative details, including moulded mantles and bevelled edges, were incorporated into the interior when the additions were made. Gradually some houses began to combine vernacular with colonial or academic influences. (I prefer the term "academic" because it implies that the source of inspiration had changed from one in response to local ideas and traditions to one in reaction to international influences. The term "colonial" has vague generalized connotations.) This academic style was introduced, according to Abbot Lowell Cummings, when "functionalism was exchanged for expansive formality."[10] The elevated style resulted in a pretentious appearance. Function was subordinated to form. The house was built according to a definite plan in which form was the primary consideration. Builders were permitted variations in doors, windows and interior details. Harold Donaldson Eberlain characterized this style as "formality tempered with domesticity and common sense."[11]

9 Eaton, *History of Kings County*, 492-3.

10 Abbott Lowell Cummings, *Rural Household Inventories: Establishing the Names, Uses, and Furnishings of Rooms in the Colonial New England Home, 1675-1775* (Boston, 1964), xxii.

11 Harold Donaldson Eberlien, *Architecture of Colonial America* (Boston, 1927), 10.

Figure 3: Harris House, Town Plot

The front door opened into a long wide central hall. The house had two symmetrical interior chimneys each separating a front and rear room. Each of the rooms had a specialized function which included receiving formal company, entertaining informal company, and preparing and eating meals. The four rooms on the second storey which corresponded directly in size and shape to those below were bedrooms. Through the introduction of a central hallway and separate rooms for specific functions, the Planters were continuing to emphasize privacy, intimacy and isolation of family members and they were separating family members from visitors. Appearance triumphed over utility. Individuals no longer focused on their community but concentrated their attention on their families and themselves.

The third house, the Harris house (Figure 3), reflects the synthesis of the vernacular and academic styles. Although the two-storey building has been altered and renovated, there is evidence of the nature of the original wood structure built c. 1770. The original structure has a 18 by 14 foot basement. According to a former resident, the original kitchen and hearth were in the basement but today only the base of a large chimney is evident. The walls of the cellar which are built of stone and mortar have been renovated. The floor is dirt and rock. The original structure was a one storey dwelling with a three bay facade including two windows and a door. The present door on the south wall was the original front entrance. When the current owners purchased the house, the first floor of the original structure contained only one large room. The original staircase leads from the original front door to the loft. Behind this is the staircase to the basement. Cornerposts and girts are evident in the interior of the first and second storeys.

The first addition lengthened the facade to include two additional bays and raised the roof to its present height. The second storey of the original was renovated to two bedrooms and the addition provided two additional bedrooms. The second addition built at right angles to the original building reveals academic influences. The north-east room was built over a cellar which is joined to the original cellar by a narrow tunnel. On the first storey there is a central hallway with a simple staircase leading to the second storey. The room on the south-east corner has its own small chimney but the mantle has been removed. In both rooms the corner posts and girts are evident. There is no indication of a summer beam. The decorative features for the entire structure are located on the first storey of the second addition. The mantle in the north-east parlour has fine classical mouldings. The vestibule with its sidelights and transom decorate the front entrance. The pretense of front corner posts and the bubbles and ripples in the old glass indicate that this vestibule, though not original to the second addition, was constructed within a few years of it. The second storey contains two bedrooms, one on either side of the central hallway. The third addition was made to the north-west corner of the second addition and along the eastern section of the north-east wall of the original building. In order to cover this new area without rebuilding the entire roof, the builder used a saltbox roof.

The map of the town plot confirms that William Welch, an original grantee, sold three town lots, including this parcel of land, in 1770 to James Harris (from New London, Connecticut, in 1768).[12] Harris arrived with his wife Anne and two children. By 1779 they had seven children.[13] While still living in Connecticut, Harris purchased one and a half shares of land in 1766 from Cornelius Rich, an original grantee living in Middleton, Connecticut.[14] Harris acquired twenty parcels of land between 1766 and 1817.

Prosperity and a large family prompted Harris to make additions to his house. The division of the rooms and the decorative mantle indicate an appreciation for privacy and design. This increasing popularity of design is also exemplified in the symmetry of the second addition, its cornices and the lintels above the windows. Here the second addition varies from the other two houses not only in style but in motivation. The original structure and the first addition faced south to King Street, the major east-west road

12 Wright, *Planters and Pioneers*, 150.
13 Eaton, *History of Kings County*, 691.
14 Registry of Deeds, 1/158.

Figure 4: DeWolf House, Wolfville

in the town plot. The house was located very close to the road. The second addition was constructed at right angles to the existing structure and moved the main entrance from the south to the east wall. For reasons currently unknown, King Street was diverted south of this property. External factors therefore were significant in an alteration to the house.

The fourth house, the DeWolf house (Figure 4), reflects entirely academic influences. A number of factors must be considered in studying this house. Extensive renovations were made in the 1890s and 1960s. A massive oak staircase built in the 1890s altered significantly the interior of the house. In the 1960s the exterior was covered with vinyl siding and the floors and ceilings were lined with insulation. In spite of these changes, the academic style is visible. The house is located about five miles west of the Horton town plot in the east end of Wolfville. The structure is constructed of wood and has two storeys. The facade with its three bays and central entrance and the inset chimneys are symmetrical. The original floor plan has been generally maintained. A wide central hallway with a high ceiling leads from the front entrance to the rear of the house. To the right of the entrance are a parlour and a dining room which share a common chimney. To the left of the entrance is one room, the best parlour, with its decorative mantle. South of this room is the oak staircase. The bedrooms on the second storey correspond to the rooms below. On the second storey, the wide central hallway extends from the front to the rear of the house. The attic which was once a loft with windows under the gable has also been renovated. With the academic style, an addition to the facade would disrupt the balance and proportion of the design. Therefore, the addition to this house which includes a large kitchen and several bedrooms was made to the rear.

This parcel of land, on which the house was built, was purchased through a series of transactions between 1809 and 1817 by Stephen DeWolf, a member of a local wealthy family.[15] DeWolf was born in 1779 when his father owned the Atwell house. In 1802 he married Harriet Ruggles, a descendant of the Loyalists and a resident of Annapolis County.[16] He built his house between 1809 and 1817. DeWolf was described in deeds as a farmer and a merchant. Ten children were born between 1802 and 1824.[17]

This house illustrates another roof style. The truncated or flat roof, usually built on Georgian houses, were frequently enclosed with a railing and were described as "the widow's walk." It has been suggested that barrels were located on these roofs to collect rain water. Colonial houses in New England did not utilize truncated gable roofs. The DeWolf house is the earliest recorded example of this architectural style in Wolfville. Perhaps it was incorporated into the design of this house in recognition of the Loyalist sympathies of Mrs. DeWolf's family and of the British influences in Halifax as reflected in the Georgian buildings with their truncated gable roofs.

The style of the house projects balance, symmetry and proportion which were characteristic of the academic style. This indicates a dissatisfaction with the locally conceived style and a sense that any foreign style was superior to the native or local one. Form, sophistication and privacy were now valued above function, utility and openess. In early nineteenth-century Horton the academic style was appropriate for a member of a prosperous family and his Loyalist bride.

The houses which can be studied today either through extant buildings or photographs are only representative of the buildings which exist today and not of those which existed 200 years ago. The first buildings were merely shelters which protected the immigrants from the climate while they established their farms. After one or two years they built more permanent structures which were based on utility and tradition and which reflected the carpenter's response to the new locality. The vernacular buildings provided economical living, working, entertaining and sleeping space. The plain style using unadorned wood was acceptable practice. The settlers, living in an unknown land, were fearful and lacked self-confidence. Unable to rely on their own resources, they depended upon

---

15 Registry of Deeds, 6/132, 6/147, 6/301, 7/242.

16 Eaton, *History of Kings County*, 635.

17 Eaton, *History of Kings County*, 635-6.

family, neighbours and friends. Some work, such as the raising of a building, was done co-operatively. The large hall in the early homes reflected the importance of hospitality, fellowship, stability and security.

As fears diminished and self-confidence grew, people began to compete. The principle element in this competition — the insatiable hunger for land — was always present but had been generally dormant. The race to acquire more land developed for several reasons. First, the amount of land granted varied from person to person. According to Debra McNabb, land was granted according to the individual's "ability to cultivate."[18] This was determined by the age of the head of the family and the size of the family. Grants varied in size from 250 acres to 2000 acres.[19] Secondly, there was a limited amount of good farmland available in the township. And thirdly, there was no limit to how much an individual could own. Most of the Connecticut emigrants were attracted to Nova Scotia by free fertile farmland and each one accumulated as much as possible. By 1764, all the shares were distributed. Land trade became one of the few profit-making ventures in Horton.[20] Therefore people competed for the available land not in the interest of the community but in the interest of their families and themselves.

This is one indication of a general changing trend in the philosophy of North America at the time. According to Robert Blair St. George, through the seventeenth century, New England became less God-centered and more man-centered.[21] When the Planters arrived in Nova Scotia they felt themselves to be in an unknown and precarious situation and therefore they reverted to their traditional philosophy which was community-and God-centered. The effect of the vernacular style of architecture on the individual was to reinforce in his mind the proximity of God and Nature. The use of natural materials and the construction of the house close to the ground reflected the sense of man working on equal terms with Nature. The low ceilings and large hall emphasised the importance of community, stability and security for the occupant of the house and the visitor. People bundled together in the loft for warmth and assurance. Additions as shown in the Calkin and Atwell houses and in the first addition to the Harris house were fully incorporated into the original structure. Although asymmetrical facades were the result, the buildings maintained their integrity.

---

18 Debra Anne McNabb, "Land and Families in Horton Township, N.S., 1760-1830," M.A. thesis, University of British Columbia, 1986, 15.

19 McNabb, "Land and Families," 16.

20 McNabb, "Land and Families," 51.

21 Robert Blair St. George, "'Set thine house in order': The Domestication of the Yeomanry in Seventeenth Century New England," *Common Places — Readings in American Vernacular Architecture*, ed. Dell Upton and John Michael Valch (Athens, GA., 1986), 353.

As the individual gained confidence and achieved a measure of success, he saw the universe as increasingly man-centered. He was prompted to express his prosperity and sophistication through the style of his house. While one prosperous homeowner might have been content to enlarge his house, divide it into small rooms, and add a few decorative touches, another homeowner might decide that the traditional utilitarian style was inadequate in expressing his individuality and status. He would copy or borrow from the academic style which older members of the community remembered from Connecticut. The effect of the academic style on the visitor or the family member would be to reinforce the concept of man's supremacy over nature. This reflected in the significant elevation of the house above the ground and in efforts to disguise wood as marble. The high ceilings and the central hallway gave the individual increased freedom of movement. In times of prosperity, the individual in such a house would enjoy a sense of intimacy, speciality and contentment. In times of depression, however, the house would cause him to feel alone, fearful and isolated.

The homeowner was also able to show his control of his world by influencing the activities of his family and guests through the manipulation of the interior space of his house. This produced a paradox. While man thought he was expressing his individuality and his control through the use of academic style, he was being restrained by the formality which he had chosen. Although some individuality was permitted expression in the design of mantles, doorways and windows, the academic style demanded both symmetry in design and floor plan as well as the rigid specific utilization of interior space. According to St. George, "Houses that had been open social containers became private enclaves, individual shrines to perceived wealth, in which rooms grew increasingly function-specific."[22]

The academic style which influenced the Planters was generally the style used by the upper and well-to-do classes of New England in the 1750s and 1760s. These people had undergone a transformation from an open adaptive society to a closed formalized society. New England architecture reflected this metamorphosis. According to McNabb: "Communities that once had been eglatarian, homogeneous and open were stratified, differentiated and closed."[23] Prosperous Planters in Horton experienced a similar transformation and also reflected it in their buildings.

My research to date leads me to believe that our understanding of the way of life in Horton Township from 1760 to 1820 which changed from an open adaptive society to a private formal society can be enlarged and extended through the study of the architecture of the house of that period.

---

22 St. George, "'Set Thine House in Order,'" 361.
23 McNabb, "Land and Families," 17.

Houses are a primary source which the historian can analyze in order to understand the motives of the owner for constructing a particular style. That style also reflected a way of life and influenced the people who live in the house and those who visited it.

History is the study of humanity. In order to examine and understand this species, the study of homes — where people are born, sheltered and nursed; where they play, eat and sleep; and where they procreate, raise their young and finally rest before the grave — the study of homes is an essential pursuit for the historian who is eager to understand the human species in general and individuals in particular.

New Brunswick's 'Early Comers':
Lifestyles through Authenticated Artifacts,
a Research Project

M.A. MacDonald. With comments by R.S. Elliot
The New Brunswick Museum
Saint John

ELLIOT:

One might compare a competent material historian with a chess player who has these traits: the skill to set up a good game plan; patience; and especially daring — since the material history researcher must often venture into uncharted waters. This is certainly the case with the New Brunswick Museum's current project conducted by Mrs. MacDonald. Her project consists of finding and authenticating surviving artifacts which relate to the New England Planters and other Pre-Loyalist English-speakers who came to New Brunswick. Until now, research has been concentrated on the Acadians and the Loyalists, but the English settlers who came to this province in the 1750s, 60s and 70s have received comparatively little attention.

As we are all aware, written records for these Early Comers are relatively scarce and this is where material culture research can help fill the void. For the material historian an authenticated artifact is as valid as a written document for building historical information, and in some cases much more revealing. However, many of the so-called Planter artifacts, although cherished by their owners, are not in fact verified Early Comers material. In the New Brunswick Museum project, Mrs. MacDonald is working on the authentication of a large number of specific pieces to verify or refute the owner's claims. Here the analytical expertise of others outside the discipline of history must be used for basic tests of an artifact's authenticity. For example, the microscopic analysis of wood might be used to help verify or refute the oral tradition that a particular article was made in Westmorland County, New Brunswick, or chemical analysis of original paint fragments might be conducted to reveal whether the compound is characteristic of a given region or time period. This sort of hi-tech analysis is beyond the usual expertise of a historian.

Beyond doubt, the most difficult part of the New Brunswick Museum's project is this authentication of the individual specimen. Consider, for instance, the *Hazen Powder Horn* and *Kimberly Powder Horn* (Illustrations 1 and 2). The two powder horns are both of the correct period and both carry a date: the Kimberly Powder Horn is inscribed with the year 1757; the Hazen Powder Horn is dated 1761. In both cases the inscribed decorations are appropriate to the mid-eighteenth century; however, the 1757 specimen cannot be used in this project because its provenance is not

1. Hazen Powder Horn
(Courtesy of New Brunswick Museum)

2. Kimberley Powder Horn
(Courtesy of New Brunswick Museum)

verifiable. The other powder horn was owned by William Hazen of Simonds, Hazen and White trading company and has a continuous history in the Hazen family. Its silver mountings were added by a mid-Victorian descendant.

It is hoped that the careful authentication of artifacts like these will build a three-dimensional document base that historians can employ with confidence, thus shedding light on the lifestyles of the Planters and New Brunswick's other English-speaking Pre-Loyalist settlers.

MacDONALD:

At the outset, I should emphasize that this is work-in-progress. My most recent field trip took place only a few weeks ago in October 1987 and the slides of those artifacts were just received last week. All artifacts that have been photographed have survived the early stages of investigation, but the final studies are still in progress. In particular, the essential wood analysis has not yet been done.

It is regrettable that a study such as this one was not undertaken earlier. Most of the articles brought here by the Early Comers (as the Loyalists called them) in the quarter century between the late 1750s and 1783, have already vanished beyond recall. They were discarded by their owners as worn out or out-of-date, or else, more recently, removed from New Brunswick by dealers from the United States and Upper Canada — where they instantly became New England or Ontario antiques. Out of every ten artifacts that are said to have belonged to the Pre-Loyalist English-speaking settlers of New Brunswick, eight or nine have had to be eliminated — some because they were obviously wrong, others because there was no verifiable provenance.

Fortunately a few families have cherished the material possessions of their Pre-Loyalist ancestors. Centres particulary rich in such artifacts include the Sheffield-Maugerville area, Saint John and nearby localities, and the Chignecto Isthmus-Sackville-Fort Beausejour region. The discoveries range through maps and legal documents to chairs, tables and clocks, portraits, silver, china and personal military items. Before this project is concluded I hope that a few more will come to light.

The Hazen powder horn with its illustrated cities, wild animals, mottos and coat of arms, is a particularly fine example of map horns made for service during the Seven Years' War. It gives us insights into the geography and the life-styles of the day. Another significant artifact from the period is this *ceramic milk pan*, or platter, from the excavation site of the trading post of James Simonds, William Hazen and James White (Illustration 3). These three partners, including the owner of the powder horn, came from Newburyport, Massachusetts, to establish a trading post on Portland Point, at the mouth of the St. John River. This post played a major role, not only in supplying up-river settlers, but in the midst of crucial incidents

3. Simonds, Hazen and White Milkpan
(Courtesy of New Brunswick Museum)

— raids, Indian uprisings and the establishment of Fort Howe. The milk pan belongs in the category of redware, natural coloured reddish clay decorated with light-coloured slip which turns yellow in the burning. It very likely came from Newburyport, where a potter's dump of that era has yielded similar material.

The *oil portrait* shown in Illustration 4 is also connected with the Simonds, Hazen and White trading company. It is of *Elizabeth Hazen*, daughter of William Hazen, who married Loyalist Ward Chipman. She and her husband went to Boston to be painted by the famous Gilbert Stuart who produced, among other notable works, the definitive portrait of George Washington that appears on the American dollar. We have the original invoice for Elizabeth and her husband, dated 1817. It details, in copperplate handwriting, a total cost of $236.00, including the frames. This portrait, of course, was painted after the period of immigration, but it depicts a Pre-Loyalist person, towards the end of an eventful life. It is not an outstanding Gilbert Stuart, but the features are lively and well-observed, with effective execution of the lace cap and tie. This portrait, and the three following, are in the collection of the New Brunswick Museum.

4. Elizabeth Hazen Ward
(Courtesy of New Brunswick Museum)

Illustration 5 represents another Pre-Loyalist — *Elizabeth Peabody*, the daughter of Captain Francis Peabody, who colonized Maugerville. She married James White, one of the original partners. From the style of the dress, this portrait was done in the late 1820s or early 30s. It is a good commercial portrait, probably by a New England artist. The style of execution does not suggest any of the handful of painters who were active in the Maritimes at this time.

Illustration 6 depicts her son, *James White, Jr.* As a small child he watched the Loyalists land, and later became high sheriff of St. John

5. Elizabeth Peabody White
(Courtesy of New Brunswick Museum)

County. This portrait, too, is well executed by a painter with a high degree of skill. His sister, *Mary Elizabeth White* appears in Illustration 7. She became the wife of Nathaniel DeVeber, high sheriff of Queens County. These three portraits of a mother and her two children are probably by the same hand — certainly the mother and daughter are. All three strike the

6. James White Jr.

(Courtesy of New Brunswick Museum)

onlooker as strongly individualized characters, but the artist, whoever he was, did not sign these canvases. There are several likely candidates for the painter — or possibly painters — and the matter will soon be investigated.

Another portrait, shown in Illustration 8, depicts *Francis Peabody, Jr.*,

7. Mary Elizabeth White deVeber
(Courtesy of New Brunswick Museum)

the founder of Chatham. The artist is Albert Gallatin Hoit, an American who painted in the Maritimes in the 1830s and 40s. His style is more dramatic, more colourful, than that of the three unattributed paintings. It is in Loggie House, Chatham.

8. Francis Peabody Jr.
(Courtesy of New Brunswick Museum)

Illustration 9 is a miniature of *William Davidson*. He was a Scotsman from Inverness who established a lumbering colony of fellow Scots on the

9. William Davidson
(Courtesy of New Brunswick Museum)

Miramachi in 1766. After one too many Indian and American privateering raids, he moved his people to Maugerville, on the St. John River, returning north after the Revolutionary War. We do not know whether this miniature was painted in Scotland or North America, but it is nicely done.

10. Pickard Desk
(Courtesy of New Brunswick Museum)

Stylistically it appears to be late eighteenth century. It was a gift to the New Brunswick Museum from the Davidson family.

The *Pickard desk* (Illustration 10) of flame, or curly birch, was reputedly brought to New Brunswick by Moses Pickard. He came from Rowley, Massachusetts, to take up lands on the St. John. This desk, evidently a treasured possession, is mentioned in Pickard's will of 1789, and again in his son's will of 1848. It was acquired for the museum from the family. It is possible that the desk came up from Massachusetts in the 1760s, but the scroll-cut bracket feet, and especially the ogee curve of the base, were stylistically more popular later, 1770-85. The same curve appears on the end pigeonhole arches. The four main drawers are graduated, and their

11. Pickard Daver Chest
(Courtesy of New Brunswick Museum)

bail handles are replacements. The original pulls were probably of a Chippendale pattern, with flat brass backplates.

The *Pickard* maplewood dower, or blanket, *chest* (Illustration 11) still has its original handles and hinges, but the bottom rail seems to be a later addition — though not a recent one. The initials MP for Moses Pickard are carved on the ends. It is of a plain and practical design, with strong dovetailed corners, and rounded edges to its lid. This is also in the New Brunswick Museum.

Still in the Pickard family, though another branch, the *cane* shown in Illustrations 12 a and b is also said to have come from Massachusetts in 1763. In fact, family tradition has it that the cane arrived in America with the original John Pickard, in 1640. It is of reddish wood, with an ivory handle and silver ferrule. Although its very tall and slender shape suggests a mid to late eighteenth-century origin, it may be a seventeenth-century cane. It is certainly an authentic old cane, and has been passed down the generations in the Pickard family, traditionally going to the eldest male in the connection.

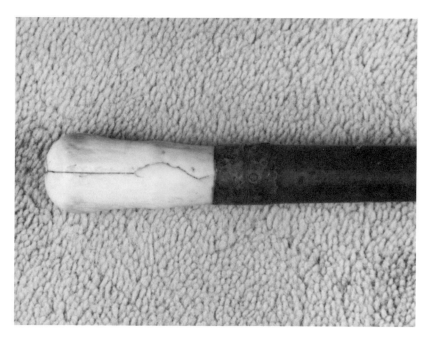

12a. Pickard Cane

(Courtesy of New Brunswick Museum)

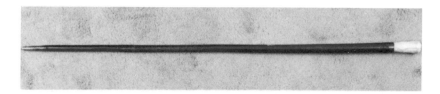

12b. Pickard Cane

(Courtesy of New Brunswick Museum)

The Otis *Pickard gateleg table* (Illustration 13) is a fine example of William Mary furniture. The square top is less frequently seen than the oval ones so often illustrated in sale catalogues and furniture reference books. The hinges appear to be original, and the mirror image turnings of the legs and stretchers are as they should be for the period. This maple table has been dated by antique appraisers to 1720-40, and it is likely that it was made closer to the end of that period. It is still in daily use, after some 250 years of well-cared-for life.

13. Pickard Gateleg Table
(Courtesy of New Brunswick Museum)

The original maps in Illustrations 14 a and b were done on the spot by *Samuel Holland* in 1758. The first is of *Fort Frederick*, at the mouth of the St. John River. It was done for Colonel Robert Monckton, who rebuilt and renamed the ruined French fort in that year. The second map is of the harbour and the course of the *St. John River* upstream as far as Grimross — present-day Gagetown. It shows a number of French place names, such as "Villeray," "le Grand Baye," and "Bay of Fundi." It was done for "Brigadier James Wolfe" and can be found in the New Brunswick Museum's collections.

The *notebook* found in Illustration 15 comes from another Pre-Loyalist family which has conserved its past. Started in 1764, at Hawnby Hall, Yorkshire, it would be continued by its owner, *William Chapman*, in Canada a decade later. The Chapman family settled in the Chignecto area of what was then Nova Scotia. William Chapman used it from 1776-77 to record the names and wages of the men of the district as they reconditioned Fort Cumberland to withstand the anticipated attacks of revolutionaries from the south. Among the names that appear are Chapman, Trueman, Anderson, Wood and Brown — "Carpenters in the King's work at fort

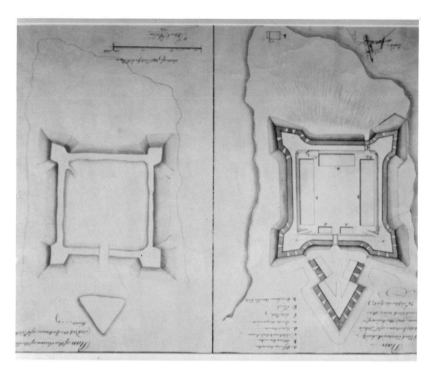

14a. Fort Frederick
(Courtesy of New Brunswick Museum)

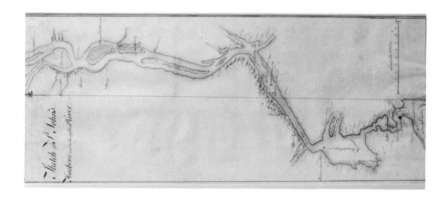

14b. St. John river
(Courtesy of New Brunswick Museum)

15. Chapman Notebook
(Courtesy of New Brunswick Museum)

comberland." They seem to have been paid about a pound a week. The notebook is at Fort Beausejour, the old French, and now the modern name of old Fort Cumberland. In addition to this record book, the Simonds, Hazen and White account books have also survived, as well as numerous deeds and grant documents.

Now we come to several artifacts from the collections in Fort Beausejour. Robert Elliot, who has published on aspects of military history, will comment on the next two items.

ELLIOT:

The *Goodwin drum* (Illustration 16) was passed down through that family from Enoch Goodwin who was a drummer boy at Fort Cumberland. The authentication or dating of such objects may be accomplished by several methods. Stylistic analysis reveals that this instrument's proportions and construction conform to like drums employed during the mid to late eighteenth century, while infrared photography may reveal an underlying crest or inscription obscured by the present crest and cipher of

16. Goodwin Drum

(Courtesy of New Brunswick Museum)

King George III, and the inscription of the 2nd Battalion of the Westmorland County militia. Chemical analysis of pigment layers may also indicate paints of different ages. However, we are also faced with difficulties due to the artifact's alteration history. For instance, drum heads would have been replaced on a regular basis. On this particular example, the rope is an obvious replacement, as are the leather ears.

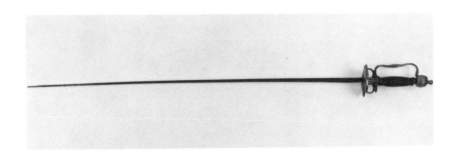

17a. Morse Sword
(Courtesy of New Brunswick Museum)

17b. Morse Sword
(Courtesy of New Brunswick Museum)

The officer's *sword* (Illustrations 17 a and b), said to have been the property of *Colonel Joseph Morse*, illustrates other problems which hamper authentication. Clearly labelled as a presentation piece, the

18. Morse Chair

(Courtesy of New Brunswick Museum)

sword's configuration conforms to officers' swords used during the Seven Years' War, despite the fact that the British Military did not adopt a set pattern until the end of that century. The inscription is most certainly of a date later than 1760, since the lettering is not characteristic of the period and the engraving cuts too deeply into the metal. The off-centre positioning of the Royal Coat-of-Arms also appears to indicate that it too was a later addition. It should also be noted that Fort Beausejour was know as Fort Cumberland by 1760, and yet the inscription provides the older name.

MacDONALD:

Another item of Morsiana is a maple, rush-seated *ladder-back chair* (Illustration 18). A plaque placed on the chairback by descendant Sir Frederick Williams-Taylor (probably the same man who had the inscription put on his ancestor's sword), says that Colonel *Morse* (1721-1770) used the chair at the fort. Morse was granted land in the area in 1764. The tale that goes with the chair is an excellent example of the pitfalls of family tradition. Colonel Morse is said to have been some seven feet tall, thus accounting for the height of the seat from the ground. But the proportions of the chair are quite wrong for the accommodation of such a big man, and furthermore there is no trace of this unusual height in records, nor of Morse having been commandant of the fort, as stated in the spurious inscription on his sword. In fact, this most probably is an accounting chair, made to fit under a high desk. Morse served as commissary officer in his previous post at Fort Oswego, and as such had much to do with accounts. The chair is a strange piece, with unusual stretcher turnings for the 1760s, and for which an Acadian influence has been suggested, and the painted leaf design on the back splats is a later addition.

Illustration 19 shows a piece of *Colonel Morse's waistcoat*. Although incomplete, it does not give the impression of a garment that would fit a seven-footer, even a frail one. But this is one of the few Pre-Loyalist textiles on hand. The silk damask fabric is of a design correct for mid eighteenth-century tastes, which favoured moderately small flower and leaf patterns.

The *Morse goblet* (Illustration 20), of silver and also located at Fort Beausejour, might have belonged to the colonel, as claimed. The classical shape and the beading are appropriate for the period, especially if this is a plated English piece. Specialized examination is in order here also.

The *Trueman glass decanter* (Illustration 21) and the *china* (Illustration 22), also demonstrates the hazards of crediting tradition. They are said to have come to this region with the original Yorkshire settlers, in the 1770s, but although they are early pieces, they were probably acquired by the second generation sometime after 1783. The handsome decanter dates to at least 1800 and more probably is early Victorian. The *teapot plate* and drum, or cylinder, *cup* are very attractive with their blue and gold decoration, but they too are later than 1783, and belong to the early part of the nineteenth century. The china has no markings.

An authentic and unusual timepiece (Illustrations 23 a and b) is one of a

19. Morse Waistcoat

(Courtesy of New Brunswick Museum)

group of tall case clocks which have survived from Pre-Loyalist times. This is the *Trueman clock*, whose brass face and works came from Yorkshire in 1774, with the William Trueman family. The case was made after their arrival in the Chignecto area. There are cherub heads in relief on the spandrels, Roman numerals for the hours, and the lower dial is inscribed with the maker's name: "R. Henderson, Scarborough." This is a listed Yorkshire clockmaker; his dates are 1678-1756. Several other Henderson clocks have been noted and described elsewhere.

This is an unusual clock because it was made with only one hand. They were not uncommon in rural districts because, in country life, the precise moment of time indicated by the second hand was seldom needed. These were less expensive pieces than two-handed, chiming clocks, and those with such added touches as moon phases and rocking ships. A similar one-hand clock is in the York Castle museum.

The case has a hood with slim turned pilasters which frame the clock face, and complex cove moldings which are echoed at the base. The door

20. Morse Goblet

(Courtesy of New Brunswick Museum)

has butt hinges of eighteenth-century pattern, one plate of which is visible. This is a plainer copy of a classic design of the period, made of local wood — perhaps by one of those carpenters who worked on the fort. Tradition

21. Trueman Decanter

(Courtesy of New Brunswick Museum)

has it that the wood is "hackmatack" — tamarack or larch — but this is yet
to be tested. The Trueman family still owns it.

Illustration 24 shows one of three black painted, seven-spindle *Windsor
chairs*, all with saddle seats in a shield shape. They are also *Trueman*

22. Trueman Teapot Plate, Cup
(Courtesy of New Brunswick Museum)

furniture, and are a puzzle as to place of origin and date. The stretcher shapes, especially, suggest a date later than the 1780s, and an American origin, possibly Rhode Island, not England. The chairs are said to be acquired from another family of Yorkshire settlers who went back to England. Wood analysis should indicate the country of origin.

A *corner armchair*, or roundabout, also reported to have arrived from Yorkshire with the family is shown in Illustration 25. The seat has been renewed, and the chair once had a high comb with crest rail, at the back, already removed when it left England. It is vernacular furniture, a simple version of transitional Chippendale, with scrolled arms and straight Marlborough-style legs and stretchers. Here, too, we need to establish the country of origin. The stocky, sturdy design does indeed suggest an English source.

Prospect Farm (the original Trueman house) is the subject of the painting found in Illustration 26. It was constructed of Tantramar Marsh mudbrick, in the late eighteenth century. The painting was done in 1917 by Dr. Elizabeth Macleod of Mount Allison University, and that same year

23a. Trueman Clock
(Courtesy of New Brunswick Museum)

23b. Trueman Clock (detail)
(Courtesy of New Brunswick Museum)

the house was demolished, because of constant shifting and cracking problems.

Illustrations 27 a and b show the Chapman house, also made of local brick, which still stands. Yorkshireman William Chapman built it on his

24. Trueman Black Windsor Chair
(Courtesy of New Brunswick Museum)

farm which now straddles the border between Nova Scotia and New Brunswick. The house dates from 1779 and is lived in today by Chapman descendants. Many design similarities mark these two houses, which probably echo the comfortable type of dwelling to which these prosperous tenant-farmers were accustomed in England. Although the execution of

25. Trueman Corner Armchair
   (Courtesy of New Brunswick Museum)

the brickwork is rough, the design of the stone and brick detail above doors and windows is skillful and well-balanced.

Another inheritance from the *Chapmans*, the works of this *clock* shown in Illustration 28 also came out with William Chapman. The softwood

26. Trueman House — Prospect Farm
(Courtesy of New Brunswick Museum)

27a. Chapman House
(Courtesy of New Brunswick Museum)

27b. Chapman House (detail)
(Courtesy of New Brunswick Museum)

case, with its fine dentil decoration on the bonnet top, is reputed to have been made on arrival here, and Peter Etter, a skilled craftsman at Fort Cumberland, who dealt in clocks and watches, is thought to have had a hand in its construction. The brass works are inscribed "Jos. Phillips, New York." This maker is listed as being active 1713-35.

28. Chapman clock
(Courtesy of New Brunswick Museum)

29a. Dixon Clock
(Courtesy of New Brunswick Museum)

29b. Dixon Clock

(Courtesy of New Brunswick Museum)

The clock in Illustrations 29 a and b is still with the family in Sackville. *Charles Dixon*, Yorkshireman, brought it out in 1772, and again the case, similar in construction to the others, was locally made. Its brass face is inscribed "John Bentley, Stockton," for Stockton-on-Tees. There are several reference listings for a John Bentley, clockmaker, in this region in the mid to late eighteenth century. The decorated spandrels on the clock face are missing, but the clock has both its hands and actually works — which is more than either of the others do.

Finally, Illustration 30 depicts the *Keillor armchair*. John Keillor and his family arrived from Yorkshire in 1772. Some of the construction details of this chair — squared Marlborough legs and stretchers, solid, sturdy shape and scrolled arms — are similar to the Trueman corner armchair, but this is a more elegant design, whose pierced back splat and crest rail are simplifications of patterns originating in Thomas Chippendale's *Gentlemen's and Cabinet-Maker's Directory*, which appeared in 1762.

30. Keillor Armchair

(Courtesy of New Brunswick Museum)

The chair has been much restored, with the seat replaced, and probably legs cut down. One family story is that the Keillor group travelled the arduous overland route from Halifax to the Sackville region, taking this one chair with them. The rest of the furniture went around by sea but was wrecked before reaching its destination. This, they say, was the only original piece they had left. The armchair is now in Keillor House, Dorchester, New Brunswick.

As can be seen from the examples shown, the authentication of such a wide variety of objects involves many fields of expertise — and there are many more artifacts under study than those shown here. For instance, a simple plank-top trestle table from New England, a Moncton-area pod auger from the Pennsylvannis-Dutch immigration, a lock from the Jemseg fort, several more clocks, two beautiful Queen Anne tables and a Paul Revere silver ladle.

Technical work on all this material is continuing and will proceed by research in libraries, by seeking the opinions of experts and by examination of comparable pieces in the northern United States. We would welcome any suggestions on solving the problems of authentication, and would also be glad to learn of any other surviving artifacts of these Pre-Loyalists English-speakers — New Brunswick's Early Comers, many of whom were New England Planters. We envisage several forms of publication, and by the time this project concludes we hope to have placed a solid segment of this exciting but neglected era in our history firmly on the record.

SELECTED BIBLIOGRAPHY

Baillie, G.H., C. Clutten and C.A. Ilbert. *Britten's Old Clocks and Their Makers*. New York, 1956.

Bailyn, Bernard. *Voyagers to the West: A Passage in the Peopling of America on the Eve of the Revolution*. New York, 1987.

Brebner, John Bartlett. *The Neutral Yankees of Nova Scotia*. Toronto, 1969.

Brown, M.L. *Firearms in Colonial America: The Impact on History and Technology, 1492-1792*. Washington, 1980.

Cunningham, Robert and John B. Prince. *Tamped Clay and Saltmarsh Hay: Artifacts of New Brunswick*. Fredericton, 1976.

Drepperd, Carl W. *American Clocks and Clockmakers*. Boston, 1958.

Fairbanks, Jonathan L. and Robert F. Trent. *New England Begins: The Seventeenth Century*. Boston, 1982.

Harper, J. Russell. *Early Painters and Engravers in Canada*. Toronto, 1970.

Jobe, Brock and Myrna Kaye. *New England Furniture: The Colonial Era*. Boston, 1984.

MacNutt, W.S. *The Atlantic Provinces: The Emergence of Colonial Society, 1712-1857.* Toronto, 1965.

Pain, Howard. *The Heritage of Upper Canadian Furniture.* Toronto, 1978.

Robinson, John and Thomas Rispin. *A Journey Through Nova Scotia....* 1774, reprint Sackville, 1981.

Roe, F. Gordon. *English Cottage Furniture.* London, 1950.

Snowdon, James D. "Footprints in the Marsh Mud: Politics and Land Settlement in the Township of Sackville, 1760-1800," M.A. thesis, University of New Brunswick, 1975.

Watkins, Lura Woodside. *Early New England Pottery.* Sturbridge, 1959.

"Remember Me As You Pass By": Material Evidence of the Planters in the Graveyards of the Maritime Provinces

Deborah Trask
Assistant Curator, Nova Scotia Museum

Actual artifacts of the Planter period in Nova Scotia are scarce. More than any other artifact type, gravestones from the eighteenth century have survived. For the most part, these are original objects, standing in much the same place and serving the same function for which they were created. A gravestone is material evidence of an individual's existence, proof that a real person lived and died. More than the inscribed information, a gravestone as an object can also provide data about the political, economic and social climate in which it was crafted. Through the careful study of material and carving details, as well as written records, it is often possible to determine where and by whom a stone was carved. This information in turn may further our understanding of the individual, community or period.

The oldest English inscribed gravestones in the Maritime Provinces were carved in New England. Those dating before 1760 can be seen in the old burial grounds of Annapolis Royal[1] and Halifax,[2] and in the collection of Parks Canada, Fortress Louisbourg.[3] In the early years of the Planter period (pre-1770) gravestones were still being imported from New England, mainly from the area around Massachusetts Bay (Figure 1). Those found outside of Halifax invariably commemorate the life of a young wife who died "in childbirth." If a male head-of-household died in this period, his grave may very well have been marked in some way, but the expense and bother of arranging with a New England stonecarver for an inscribed gravestone seems to have prohibited their importation. In some

---

1   The Bathiah Douglass stone, 1720, at Annapolis Royal, is the oldest English gravestone in the province. It has been attributed to the Boston carver Nathaniel Emmes. See Deborah E. Trask, *Life How Short, Eternity How Long: Gravestone Carving and Carvers in Nova Scotia* (Halifax, 1978), 10-11. For more on Emmes, see Harriet Merifield Forbes, *Gravestones of Early New England and the Men Who Made Them, 1653-1800* (Boston, 1927), 57-9.

2   The oldest stone remaining at St. Paul's Cemetery, Halifax (originally the common burying ground), is that of John Connors, died 1754, which is a Massachusetts Bay carved slate, with an unusual skull profile.

3   Two stones dated 1745 were found near Fortress Louisbourg, in the ruins of the hospital. Both were carved in Newport, Rhode Island. See Deborah E. Trask, "Rhode Island Stones in Canada," *Association for Gravestone Studies Newsletter*, 8, 3(Summer 1984), 10.

1. Mary Hilton stone, slate, 1774, Chebogue, Yarmouth County, N.S. Signed by the carver: "Abraham Codner Next the Draw Bridge Boston".

(Nova Scotia Museum collection: P133/84.84.10 (N-15167)
Photo: Dan & Jessie Lie Farber)

cases, as in that of Stephen Post of Cornwallis who died in 1768, a stone was carved many years later to mark the grave (Figure 2). The style and imagery of this stone dates it about 1803.[4] The vast majority of burial sites before 1770 were not marked in any permanent way.

By the early 1770s more graves were being marked with imported stones in the Planter communities along the South Shore — Yarmouth, Chebogue, Barrington, Liverpool. There survives a remarkable variety of the New England stonecarvers' works in the old burial grounds of these communities. In fact, New England stones continued to be imported to what is now Yarmouth, Shelburne and Queens counties well into the nineteenth century. A local slate carver (William Gates Archer, who also considered himself a Baptist preacher) did work in the Liverpool, and later Tusket area, from c.1808-1828.[5] We know of some sixty of his stones; they

4 Trask, *Life How Short*, 20-21. Attributed to "the Second Horton Carver," second style.

5 Deborah E. Trask, "The South Shore Carver," *The Occasional*, 9, 2(1985).

stand alongside the imported ones of the same period. Even with someone carving locally, people along the South Shore must have found it just as convenient and/or inexpensive to order or bring in a gravestone from New England. There are very few imported slates to be found in the other Planter communities of the Maritimes — one at Truro, one at Windsor and two near Granville, are all that have been found, to date.

In the Annapolis-Granville area, there is evidence that there was a skilled carver working in sandstone, probably at Saint John, where a number of his stones can also be found, from the 1790s to about 1820. In Nova Scotia, almost all of these mark the graves of Loyalists (Figure 3).

At Chipman's Corner, Kings County, in one of the old burial grounds of Cornwallis, is a rare imported Connecticut sandstone from 1785, signed by its maker, Chester Kimball of New London.[6] This marks the grave of a young man whose Planter parents' graves nearby are marked with locally carved stones. Although it is apparent, as evidenced in the South Shore communities, that stones for women and children (or young men) were more likely to be imported than were grave markers for heads of households, there are no other imported stones in the area. All other eighteenth-century gravestones in Horton and Cornwallis were carved in Horton. Nor are there any imported stones in Falmouth or Newport townships. When Shubael Dimock, grantee at Newport, died in 1781, his grave was marked by a piece of soft sandstone roughly incised (Figure 4), very different from the elaborate sandstone carvings found in Mansfield, Connecticut, whence he came.[7]

In the mid-1770s a Scottish stonecarver in Halifax, James Hay,[8] advertised that he would make gravestones; soon after, stones with simplified depictions of the same symbols were appearing in the burial grounds of Horton, Cornwallis, Truro, Onslow and Londonderry (Figure 5). This carver has been called the "Horton Carver," as his work was first identified in the Wolfville area.[9] These simple, stylized, crowned angel-heads in sandstone date from the 1780s to the mid-90s when a different carver (the Second Horton Carver) who possibly moved from the Truro area to Horton about 1795, began to interpret the image his own way (Figures 2 and 6).

---

6   For more on Chester Kimball, see Ernest Caulfield, "Connecticut Gravestones VIII," continued by Peter Benes, in *The Connecticut Historical Society Bulletin*, 40, 2(April 1975). Chester himself was a Planter baby, having been born during his parents' brief period of residency on the Saint John River, in 1763. Chester Kimball's work is also noted in James A. Slater, *The Colonial Burying Grounds of Eastern Connecticut, and the Men Who Made Them, Memoirs of the Connecticut Academy of Arts and Sciences*, Vol. XXI (Hamden CT, 1987), 35-37.

7   Slater, *The Colonial Burial Grounds of Eastern Connecticut*, 212-217.

8   For more on the prolific Hay, see Trask, *Life How Short*, 58-68.

9   Trask, *Life How Short*, 18-19.

2. Stephen Post stone, sandstone, 1768, Chipman's Corner, Kings County, N.S. Attributed carver: the Second Horton Carver, second style (c. 1801-1805).

(Nova Scotia Museum collection: P133,68.19
Photo: Deborah Trask)

3. (Nova Scotia Museum collection: P133.87.4
Photo: Deborah Trask)

3. Francis LeCain stone, sandstone, 1806, Annapolis Royal, Annapolis County, N.S.

(Nova Scotia Museum collection: P133.87.5
Photo: Deborah Trask)

4. Shubael Dimock stone, fieldstone, 1781, Scotch Village, Hants County, N.S.

(Nova Scotia Museum collection: P133.96.7
Photo: Deborah Trask)

5. Capt. Judah Wells stone, sandstone, 1791, Upper Canard, Kings County, N.S. Attributed carver: the Horton Carver.

(Nova Scotia Museum collection: P133.29.25
Photo: Deborah Trask)

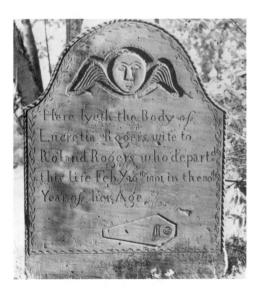

6. Lucretia Rogers stone, sandstone, 1801, Wolfville, Kings County, N.S. Attributed carver: the Second Horton Carver, first style (1798-1801).

(Nova Scotia Museum collection: P133/84.84. (N-13305)
Photo: Dan & Jessie Lie Farber)

The same craftsman may have continued to improve his skill, or perhaps a more competent competitor appeared in Horton. We know that from about 1800 to 1821, when he removed for good to Pugwash, the carver Abraham Seaman made most of the gravestones which still stand in Cornwallis and Horton (Figure 7). He was a Loyalist who owned land in Cumberland County, but resided at Horton where he carved gravestones for his Planter neighbours and in-laws, probably of Cumberland County sandstone. Some of his stones from this period can also be found at Truro, Londonderry, Parrsboro, Granville and Amherst.[10]

Another interesting Planter region of the Maritimes is Chignecto. The oldest markers are, as expected, rather crude and functional. Around Sackville and particularly Hillsborough, where good building sandstone was readily available, a different carving style evolved. Stones in this style can be seen around Shepody Bay, the Cumberland Basin, and up the Petitcodiac and Tantramar Rivers. These stones have an articulated tympanum, and are often incised with a simplified urn/lamp, sometimes surrounding the initials of the deceased (Figure 8). The stone for John Wallace, a grantee at Horton, who later moved to Hillsborough where he died "an old man, full of years," is an example of this style. The image of the urn/lamp, with a sprig of neo-classical willow, became very popular later with Saint John carvers, and their work can be found in all the coastal communities of the Bay of Fundy.

From this brief overview of the surviving gravestones of Planters in the Maritimes, it becomes clear that some insight can be gained through a study of material culture. By grouping gravestones loosely by the carving styles of individual craftsmen, distinct regions of similarity can be identified. It would seem that the place of origin of the decedent has no relevance to the source of his/her gravestone. That variable was determined by the region where his/her death occurred. The South Shore communities could readily obtain carved gravestones from New England, and there was little incentive for local craftsmen to enter the market. In the lower valley communities, similar conditions applied initially, until the closer market of Saint John developed, followed by local competition. In the upper valley and the upper reaches of the Bay of Fundy, including the Chignecto region, the local market developed early, with a ready source of materials and a more agrarian population. These are generalizations based on informal observation of surviving evidence, and not on a quantitative analysis of all existing material. In gravestone terms, the Planter period ranges from about 1760 to the mid-1830s. Only about one-tenth of all

---

10 For a preliminary study on the gravestone production of Abraham Seaman, see Deborah E. Trask and Debra A. McNabb, "Carved in Stone, Material Evidence in the Graveyards of Kings County, Nova Scotia," *Material History Bulletin*, 23(Spring 1986), 35-42.

7. William Alline stone, sandstone, 1799, Wolfville, Kings County, N.S. Attributed carver: Abraham Seaman.

(Nova Scotia Museum collection: P133/84.84.62 (N-15168) Photo: Dan & Jessie Lie Farber)

8. Stephen Millidge stone, sandstone, 1803, Westcock, Westmorland County, N.B. Attributed carver: D. Shaw.

(Nova Scotia Museum collection: P133.146.1 Photo: Deborah Trask)

eighteenth-century graves are marked, and current scholarship still has a long way to go in the identification of individual craftsmen's work.

The Planters may be considered as a group, but they were a diverse collection of individuals, dying off over a seventy year period. Therefore, in the pursuit of Planters, it is worth while to recognize this diversity and to heed the warning of the number one favorite epitaph of the eighteenth century (as seen, for example, crumbling away at the bottom of the hill below Acadia University on the grave of Sylvenus Miner, a grantee of Horton — Figure 9): "Remember me as you pass by/As you are now so once was I."

9. Sylvenus Miner stone, sandstone, 1786, Wolfville, Kings County, N.S.

(Nova Scotia Museum collection: P133.133.11
Photo: Deborah Trask)

Future Directions in Planters Studies

Phillip A. Buckner
Professor of History, University of New Brunswick

When I was asked to give a few concluding remarks about future directions for Planter Studies I thought I would begin with a brief introduction assessing why the Planters have been so conspicuously ignored in the writing of Canadian history. Unfortunately, Professor Rawlyk beat me to the punch and dealt with that topic in a far more complete and articulate way than I could have. I share with Professor Rawlyk the belief that the history of this region has been systematically marginalized and that the current generation of so-called national historians has shown little interest in an emerging and increasingly sophisticated regional historiography which ought to have reshaped traditional assumptions about the historical insignificance of Atlantic Canada.[1] (Actually I would judge from Esther Clark Wright's comments that, when it comes to the Canadian historical profession, "plus ça change.") I also agree with Professor Rawlyk that the very quality of the early scholarship, during what he once described as the first "golden age" of Atlantic regional scholarship, in particular the work of J.B. Brebner and Andrew Hill Clark, served to encourage the always mistaken belief that there was nothing pressing to be done in the field of Planter Studies.

But I also believe that there are two other factors which help to explain the relative obscurity into which the Planters have been cast. The first is the arrival of the Loyalists. It was the Loyalists who have been seen by generations of historians as the founding fathers of Canada. Partly this simply reflects the Upper Canadian bias of historians and it is hard to believe that if the first anglophone settlers in that colony had been Planters this neglect would have taken place. (But then what can you do with a province that does not even know when its own Bicentennial took place!) As Barry Cahill declared, the term Pre-Loyalist does indeed represent "a biased scholarly coinage" which has distorted the way in which we approach the studies of the Planters. To my horror I suddenly realized when he made that remark that I had used the term myself in a paper just sent to the *Journal of Canadian Studies*. In fact it is a difficult term to avoid if one wishes to describe all of the Pre-Revolutionary settlers. Yet it is, of course, a term that is essentially ahistorical since it assigns to the Planters an identity which they themselves never made — indeed which they could not make. There is a delicious irony here, of course. After all,

---

1 On this point see my "'Limited Identities' and Canadian Historical Scholarship: An Atlantic Provinces Perspective," *Journal of Canadian Studies*, 23 (Spring/Summer 1988), 177-98.

the Loyalists themselves looked down on the Planters and dismissed them (as David Bell indicated this morning) as at worst disloyal and at best lukewarm subjects of the King. Loyalist establishments at Halifax and Fredericton set out to impose their ideological standards on the Planters and the other groups in the region whose arrival pre-dated their own. As J.M. Bumsted has pointed out, they failed and the official culture of the elite was only weakly superimposed on the vernacular cultures that existed in various parts of the region. Yet in Canadian historiography the Loyalists have had their victory posthumously for it has usually been assumed that the Loyalists did succeed in imposing their values upon the earlier inhabitants of the region, now systematically marginalized as the Pre-Loyalists.

There is also a second factor which explains the Loyalist victory. Both the Planters and the majority of the Loyalists had one thing in common. They were Americans. In fact, there was to be during the decades following the American Revolution a merging of the Pre- and Post-Revolutionary migrants from the Thirteen Colonies at both the elite and popular levels, partly promoted, I suspect, through intermarriage and partly by the fact that the two groups did share so many cultural attitudes and patterns. Yet this American-based culture was itself challenged in the nineteenth century by the arrival of a much larger migration of non-Americans from the British Isles. Years ago, in an unfortunately much-neglected article on "A Study in the Historical Demography of a Loyalist County," T.W. Acheson explored the impact of this migration on Charlotte County and demolished the myth that Charlotte County can be described as a Loyalist county.[2] I certainly do not want to be accused of some kind of demographic determinism but it seems to me clear that in the nineteenth century the older American culture in the Maritimes and Upper Canada was overwhelmed by a process of Anglicization as British immigrants, British capital, British technology and British cultural values poured into the region. But when the British North Americans (as they should now be called) were forced to create their own national institutions in the latter part of the nineteenth century it was, in part, to the Loyalist myth that they turned to justify their incipient nationalism, thus simultaneously reinforcing the significance of the Loyalists and the comparative insignificance of the Planters.

I have indulged in this lengthy (and I suspect controversial) preamble because I want to make some unorthodox suggestions about future directions for Planter Studies. The strength of this conference has been its focus on the original generation of Planters: who they were, where they

---

2   T.W. Acheson, "A Study in the Historical Demography of a Loyalist County," *Histoire Sociale/Social History*, 1 (April 1968), 53-65.

came from, where they went and what kind of social institutions they established during the period of resettlement. As a number of papers have indicated there are still many questions to be answered about that period and a great deal of research to be completed. I suspect that my fellow panelists will have even more questions to add to that list. And I look forward with great enthusiasm to the book of essays that the organizers intend to produce based upon the Conference proceedings. But I disagree fundamentally with the member of the audience who queried why we should move beyond the period of Planter settlement. As a Canadian historian rather than an American colonial historian I am more interested in the post-Revolutionary history of the Planter communities than I am in their pre-Revolutionary origins. After all, the Planters established some of the most stable, resilient and homogeneous communities in Canada and if you doubt the validity of that statement look around you. I have never attended an academic conference in which there were so many interested participants from the local community. (Believe me, it did not happen when we held a series of lectures in Fredericton on the history of the Loyalists during the Bicentennial even though Fredericton is called the Loyalist city.) The reason for the popularity of this conference has little to do, I suspect, with the ability of the academics on the programme to reach out to a wider audience. What it does reflect is the persistence of so many descendants of the Planters in this region and the fact that so many of them are aware that they are the descendants of Planters. It is in this fact that the real significance of the Planters seems to me to lie: They Planted Well.

Therefore, while not abandoning further investigation into the initial period of settlement, I would like to see us move beyond that — to look at the evolution of the Planter communities over time. Can one talk even in the 1760s of a distinctly "Planter" culture or way of life? Did that culture survive the arrival of the later immigrants? Was there a substantial influx of Loyalists into these communities? Was there much intermarriage between the two groups? How do the fertility rates, the methods of soil cultivation, the commercial practices, the family organization of the Planter communities compare with other communities in the region? Many of these questions involve a systematic examination of the social history of the Planter communities but I would like to call for a much greater emphasis on the intellectual history of these communities. It may be a fact that the Planter communities were better able than other communities in the region to withstand the onslaught of Anglicization during the mid-nineteenth century. Certainly the work of George Rawlyk and David Bell suggest that. But, until detailed community studies are done of these communities in the nineteenth century, that can only remain an hypothesis.

I realize, of course, that I am outlining a programme of research that will take decades to complete but if there is to be ongoing programme of

Planter Studies at Acadia University, it is these questions that will have to be addressed. J.M. Bumsted suggested yesterday that we are here to authenticate the birth of a new ethnic group. If the Planters are to be interpreted in these terms (and I think they can be) we can and must not restrict our explorations to the first generation of settlers. For it is only by dealing with the longer term issue of the persistence and distinctiveness of the culture of the Planter communities that one can hope to assess the true place of the Planters in the Canadian mosaic and rescue them from their unmerited obscurity. This conference has begun that work but there is still a great deal to do.

Brian Cuthbertson
Head, Heritage Nova Scotia
Department of Tourism and Culture

My aim today is to urge a more systematic and less impressionistic approach to Planter Studies. It is my contention that the Planters must be viewed as forming a distinct society which evolved as part of a historical continuum from the first settlement into the present and that this society must be analysed with this in mind.

Before pursuing this thesis, I wish to reflect on the writing of Nova Scotia histories in which the Planters have figured prominently. What I find striking about our provincial historiography is how, in two significant aspects, it is different from that of other provinces and the writing of national history.

The first important departure is the predominant role played by the Public Archives in Nova Scotia, from the 1930s when D.C. Harvey became provincial archivist to the present. The PANS contribution embraces not only a succession of staff, who saw no dividing line between their archival activities and the writing of history, but equally as notable, two or more generations of graduate students who studied under Harvey. To most of you, the work of Harvey, Margaret Ells, Marion Gilroy, James Martell, C.B. Fergusson and Phyllis Blakeley needs no further comment. With that great triumph of responsible government always held firmly in their sights, their mastery of sources and forceful presentations set a very high standard. I would refer you to the recently rediscovered thesis for the university of London of Margaret Ells (herself of Planter descendant) entitled: "The Development of Nova Scotia, 1782-1812." Begun in the 1930s and completed a decade later, it was regrettably never submitted for a PhD. As a work of scholarship, it ranks equal to that of J.B. Brebner and its comprehensiveness, in my opinion, perhaps surpasses that of Brebner. Also impressive is the work of C.B. Fergusson and Phyllis Blakeley.

Between the two of them they published 43 books and phamplets, 134 articles and 59 entries in the *Dictionary of Canadian Biography*. What the Harvey school did not produce in published form was a history of Nova Scotia for any particular period. There was no equivalent of W.S. MacNutt's *New Brunswick: A History, 1784-1867*. In fact, the search for modern, published interpretations of our history over a period of time has to begin and end with what is in MacNutt's, *The Atlantic Provinces 1712-1857*. This lamentable situation is paradoxical because of the volume of output in published articles, monographs and theses was not rectified by the university historians who entered the field beginning in the 1960s. The sole exception has to be J. Murray Beck's *Government of Nova Scotia*, and more recently, his *Politics of Nova Scotia*. But these are concerned strictly with political history and constitutional development.

Contemporary historians have chosen to examine particular aspects of Nova Scotian history, often more as a theoretical exercise than as a concern for the writing of what I choose to call basic history. There has been an over-concern with methodology and an avoidance of the comprehensiveness which tells a coherent story of Nova Scotian society over a defined period of time. It is this approach, one of comprehensiveness over time, that I wish to advocate for Planter Studies. Other than what has become an obsession with their eighteenth-century religiosity, little has been published on the Planters since Brebner.

A welcome new start, however, has been made, I hope, with Debra McNabb's thesis on land holding patterns in early Horton Township. If another geographer, Andrew Hill Clark, had published his post-1755 research, we would view the Planters much differently than we do. To start with, we would see them forming a reasonably distinct society, and be able to mark out those aspects of continuity and change over time that can give history meaning for contemporary society with its increasing rootlessness. When I speak of comprehensiveness, I mean all aspects: economic, social, political, religions, cultural, architectural and so forth. Furthermore, there is a need to get away from the all too great a reliance on what I call impressionist evidence. Instead, we should be immersing ourselves in the mountains of statistical and similar evidence that is very much available. We must systematically analyze and correlate census data on individuals and families. Poll-books, numerous petitions for sundry concerns, deeds, court and probate records will also yield valuable evidence. Let us turn to these sources using, where applicable, computer technology to provide an all-inclusive profile of Planter society over time.

In my remaining time, I wish to use examples of the approach I am advocating. To begin with land holding and occupation. The common portrayal of Planter townships in western Nova Scotia is that of a rural population, almost all of whom were engaged in farming their own lands. The image is that of Joseph Howe's yeoman of Hants County, never faltering in support for reform. Well, a break-down of the 1838s census of Windsor Township shows that 41% of the heads of families were classed as labourers, only 22% as farmers. In the heated Brandy Election of 1830, for which the Windsor poll book survives, no more than 30% of the heads of households, in fact, voted. Our image holds up reasonably well in the case of Granville Township, where, in the same period, farmers accounted for about 53% of all the heads of households, and labourers only for 12%. Here also the poll book for the 1840 election survived, and a breakdown of votes by occupation is possible. In Granville we get a high percentage of turn-out for that election (70% or over). It is interesting to note that it was the farmer vote which gave a Tory victory in that election over the Reformers.

Much has been written on the various education acts passed leading up to the Free School Act of 1864. Yet there has been no attempt to determine systematically the levels of literacy. I mentioned earlier numerous signed petitions. I suggest these can form the basis for giving good indications of literacy, by using the style of signatures as a criterion. Where an "X" or a mark is used, obviously the individual was illiterate. If, however, the signature appears good, it is a fair assumption that he was able to read and write. I have used this technique, I think, with interesting results when attempting to determine the educational level of all 300 M.L.A.'s who were elected between 1785-1847. So few had attended university or could be classed as such professionals as doctors or lawyers which we assume are literate, that I had to find some way to describe the education of the vast majority. In examining the signatures of all 300, I found the vast majority signed their names with firm, fluid hands. Only a small number signed their names with a shaky scrawl, and none with an "X." I suspect that if we systematically analyze the signatures of Planters and their descendants, using many of these signed petitions, we could well be surprised by the literacy levels. We could then start investigating how these were reached in a society where schooling was supposedly so haphazard an affair. You can use the census material, the poll books, the signatures on petitions, and so on to derive an integrated political, economic, social and cultural profile of a fair segment of Planter Society at different time periods. Furthermore it is possible to compare these profiles with other societies as the Scots of Pictou County, the Germans in Lunenburg County, and the Loyalist descendants at Shelburne.

In summary, I believe that it is time we left the eighteenth century and the Newlights behind. We need now to exploit to the full the ample sources for systematically analyzing nineteenth-century Planter Society while comparing these results with those of other distinct Nova Scotian societies.

Marie Elwood
Chief Curator, History Section
Nova Scotia Museum

I was asked, as a museum curator, to give an outside view of some future directions for Planter Studies.

1. I would suggest that one future direction in which to look would be across the Atlantic Ocean. My voice has already told you that I am not a native Nova Scotian. Yet I can assure you that I am of Planter stock — but my Plantation is located where England tried out its early experiments in colonization — Ireland — and the plantation to which I refer is the Plantation of Ulster.

Within the wide context of English plantation policies in the early part of the seventeenth century consider this — that the Plantation of Ulster occurred after the sudden departure of the two leading native princes, the Earl of Tyrone and the Earl of Tyroconnell — on 3 September 1607; the event known as the "Flight of the Earls." With them departed the Gaelic civilization of Ulster. The estates of these fugitive Earls were of vast extent. These abandoned lands were declared to be forfeited to the Crown and the colonization of the territory by English and Scottish settlers — the Plantation of Ulster — began.[1]

There are parallels in this plantation and the circumstances of the Planters of Nova Scotia. Documentation of the Ulster plantation exists in the form of period maps, population census and schemes of plantation.[2] As well as written records, these English and Scottish Planters left an architectural legacy of town-plans, "Planter's Gothic" churches and farm houses, as evidence of their material history. These, and the units of settlement called townlands, the primary unit of land division, merit a comparative study with the Planters of Nova Scotia.

2. A second future direction for Planter Studies would be to look downward, below the ground. I would suggest that an archaeological excavation of a Planter site should be considered. In 1983 the Nova Scotia Museum sponsored an excavation of two Acadian pre-Expulsion houses at Belleisle, Annapolis County; the excavated specimens of building materials and artifacts from this site have considerably extended our study and interpretation of Acadian culture.

An archaeological field survey of Planter sites could lead to the excavation of domestic sites. The artifacts obtained, compared with other

---

1 See Sir Arthur Chichester, original version of his "Notes of Remembrances Concerning the Plantation of Ulster," MSS.N2.2. in the Library of Trinity College, Dublin. In *Analecta Hibernica*, No.8, Paper presented by T.W. Moody.

2 Gilbert Camblin, *The Town of Ulster* (Belfast, 1951), 117-119.

sites and combined with the documentary history, could provide a more complete history of the Planters.

3. A third direction for future study would be to look for surviving artifacts, above ground, of the Planter period. We have heard much in this conference of the written sources of information about the settlement and their agricultural methods. But there is further evidence, in the study of the vernacular architecture and artifacts associated with Planter families.

One of the earliest collections of historic artifacts formed in Canada was made in the 1860s by a Planter descendant. She was the eldest daughter of Thomas Chandler Haliburton and her interest was to find what she described as "Specimens of China Brought to the Colonies by Early Settlers." As the daughter and the wife of a Judge, Mrs. Weldon was socially well-placed to approach descendants of early settlers, like herself, to ask them for "specimens" for her collection. She visited over 200 such families and formed a collection of over 400 items which she later gave to King's College, Windsor. This collection, and her manuscript notes listing the families, have survived for over 100 years in the King's College Library.

In New England, I searched to see if a similar collection of specimens of New England settlers' effects had ever been collected from old established families — and indeed it had. Like Mrs. Weldon's this collection had been presented in the 1880s to Princeton University, where it was used for teaching purposes in the 1890s. From a vault were brought for my inspection, the notes of provenance, written by William Cowper Prime, in the period 1858-1880 when he formed this collection.

A study of such surviving artifacts with histories of ownership, along with material yielded from archaeological sites, would combine to increase our knowledge of the material culture and conditions of life of the Planters.

Finally, a word about the word "Planters." Literally, a plantation refers to the placing of plants, particularly young trees. Figuratively, the term was used in the early seventeenth century to refer to the settlement and colonization of North America and forfeited lands of Ulster. When was the term Planters used in Nova Scotia?[3]

---

3 Debra McNabb, personal correspondence, courtesy of Elizabeth Mancke indicates that the term "Planters" occurs in the Minutes of the Executive Council, 18 April 1759. Public Archives of Nova Scotia, RG 1, Vol. 188.

James H. Morrison
Dean of Arts
Saint Mary's University

As I am interested in social history I would like to look at three aspects of future Planter Studies. My major focus will be on ethnicity but I will also touch briefly on family studies and mythology. In all three themes I wish to stress a broadening of Planter research in order that an inclusive rather than an exclusive approach be encouraged in our studies of eighteenth-century Nova Scotia. All three aspects suggest a chronological broadening as well, with pre-1760 research playing an important role and oral research taking Planter Studies up to the present.

Nova Scotia is not nor ever has been an ethno-cultural monolith. Perhaps before the European invasion of the province this was true but even then there were inter-ethnic trade and marriage relations between the Micmac and other native groups. The cultural diversity of the province can be addressed at a number of levels but I will take only two. The first is the recognition of a diversity within the group that has been labelled the "Planters" who came on their own volition to re-settle a new colony. The second is the inter-relationships between the Planters and other ethnic groups of different language or colour. I am urging a consideration of the intra- and the inter-ethnocultural relations of this emerging migrant group in future research.

George Rawlyk, in his *Nova Scotia's-Massachusetts*, wrote of a "new New England," a coastal strip of peninsular Nova Scotia from Liverpool to Yarmouth and along the south coast of the Bay of Fundy to Truro and on to the St. John River. He calls these the "Yankee outsettlements."[1] E.C. Wright analyses the origins of the migrants to some of these localities in her *Planters and Pioneers*.[2] The settlers in Barrington came from Cape Cod; those in Cornwallis and Horton were mostly Connecticut in origin; Falmouth and Newport settlers emigrated from Rhode Island; Truro, Onslow and Londonderry were settled by New Hampshire migrants; and Pictou by settlers from Philadelphia. Wright does not see the group as ethno-culturally monolithic in any sense.

In some cases generational settlement patterns themselves take on a kind of cultural identity. There were, for instance, Planters who departed from Scotland to become planters in Londonderry, Northern Ireland, in the 1670s, were subsequently replanted to Londonderry, New Hampshire, in

---

1 George Rawlyk, *Nova Scotia's Massachusetts: A Study of Massachusetts-Nova Scotia Relations, 1630-1784* (Montreal, 1973), 222.

2 Esther Clark Wright, *Planters and Pioneers: Nova Scotia, 1749-1775* (Hantsport, 1982), 12.

1720, and again replanted in Londonderry, Nova Scotia, in 1760. An examination of such a group may go some way towards a new analysis of the questions of cultural integrity and cultural baggage raised by J.M. Bumsted in his presentation to this conference. What cultural continuity remains for such migrants? More bluntly, what "baggage" is brought and what "baggage" is left in each migration? What are the cultural connections and geographical connections between the old settlement and the new? How do the environmental and cultural influences shape that complex of values, morals and beliefs that become one's cultural persona and that differentiate one, perhaps radically, from others in one's group. Some presenters at this conference have identified the settlers of the Londonderry, Nova Scotia, area as Scotch-Irish and therefore not a part of the "New England" migration. Yet as Elizabeth Mancke pointed out in her fine presentation of the 1760s expansion of New England, the London-derry settlers together with those in Liverpool, Nova Scotia, pooled their efforts to maintain an important aspect of the political culture of New England. Obviously, there is intra-cultural diversity but there are also several items in the cultural baggage that are the same.

The papers presented at this conference have returned frequently to the question of Loyalist-Planter relations. The vital interaction between these two important migrant groups to Nova Scotia begins in the last half of the eighteenth century and continues into the nineteenth century and, perhaps for those with long memories and particular grudges to settle, into the twentieth century as well. There are, however, other inter-ethnic dimensions here that have not been mentioned. The Blacks, the Micmacs and the Acadians were certainly here before either the Planters or the Loyalists. Scholarly attention to Planter relations with all pre-Loyalist ethnic groups promises to yield valuable insights into colonial Maritime history.

It is clear that not all Acadians were expelled in 1755-62 and many returned to the province within less than a decade of the Planter arrivals. Some Acadians assisted the Planters in re-constructing the demolished Acadian dykes. Yet we know little about the way Acadians reacted to these Planter invaders of their one-time homeland or how the Planters interacted with the Acadians.

When the lands of Nova Scotia were opened to the New Englanders in 1759, free Blacks were offered the same opportunities as Whites to settle. However, most Blacks came as slaves. Slaves were present in Liverpool in 1760, in New Glasgow in 1767 and in Bridgetown, Amherst, Onslow and Cornwallis by 1770. In 1770, Colonel Henry Denny Denson of Falmouth, Nova Scotia, held five and possibly as many as sixteen slaves at his Mount Denson home.[3] Although the Black Loyalists have been made the subjects

---

3   Robin W. Winks, *The Blacks in Canada: A History* (Montreal, 1971), 27.

of several excellent studies, Black-White relations among the Planter migrants has yet to be investigated.

The Micmac of Nova Scotia shared the defeat of the French by the English but they were not expelled from the province. The influx of the new settlers who replaced the Acadians marked a new phase in White-Native relations. Contact between the Planters and the Micmac were in the areas of commerce and land. In the former instance the Planters operated the "truck houses" which maintained commercial contact with the native people.[4] The latter issue, that of land, was even more vital. The new colonists paid little attention to the proclamation of Lieutenant Governor Jonathan Belcher which provided guidelines as to safeguarding Micmac land;[5] consequently, Micmac land was alienated. The arrival of the Loyalists further exacerbated an already difficult situation. The Micmac method of land use was substantially altered and provisions and relief became a major point of contact between the white and the native population.

As noted above, the inter-ethnic relations between the Planters and their Black, Micmac and Acadian neighbours is an area that requires further attention if Planter "neighbours" are to escape the obscurity they hitherto shared with the Planters. The Planters, it must be remembered, brought with them their attitudes towards Blacks, Native people and Acadians that had developed in New England over the first half of the eighteenth century. A comparative look at what these attitudes entailed would be of value.

Two other aspects of future Planter Studies, family studies and mythology, also offer great promise. T. Punch has eloquently raised the possibilities of genealogy and family history. The last decade has seen a tremendous growth of interest in this old, yet new, area of social history. Without question, recent social history which now includes the study of women, labour, ethnicity and children has benefitted from the use of genealogical research. As all of these new areas are part and parcel of Planters Studies, the benefits of family research are obvious. A number of new approaches utilizing census results, oral tradition and computers can provide valuable insights into the study of the Planters and their descendants.

My third and final aspect of Planters Studies is related to those descendants noted above and the broader theme of mythology. Why in 1987 are we discussing the Planters? What traditional beliefs or long held

---

4   Elizabeth Ann Hutton, "Indian Affairs in Nova Scotia, 1760-1834," H.F. McGee, ed., *The Native Peoples of Atlantic Canada: A History of Indian European Relations* (Ottawa, 1983),
   68.

5   G.P. Gould and A.J. Semple, *Our Land: The Maritimes* (Fredericton, 1980), 24-27.

views of the Planters are prevalent and how do these coincide with the reality of what is known? What mythology, be it Acadian, Scots or Planters, has been and/or continues to be created? Do Planter descendants perceive themselves to have particular and special attributes? How much oral tradition is carried through to the present and carefully guarded by these Planter descendants?

In the article that appeared in *Historical New Hampshire* in 1985, R. Stuart Wallace examined the development of identity among the "Scotch-Irish" in New Hampshire, a group which came to Nova Scotia in the 1760s as part of the Planter migration. Wallace noted that in 1720 the "Irish" arrived in various parts of New Hampshire.[6] A century later with the emergence of such Scottish literary giants as Walter Scott, Robert Burns and David Hume a new ethnic group the "Scotch-Irish" began to emerge from those who had identified themselves as Irish. By the time Edward Parker published his *History of Londonderry, New Hampshire* in 1851, the settlers of 1720 had become Scots who spent a few years in Ireland before coming to America.[7] It was obviously better to lay a claim to a Scottish heritage in the nineteenth century than an Irish one. What of the "heritage" claims of the Nova Scotia Planters in the nineteenth century and even in the twentieth century? Again what are the mythological claims of the present descendants of the Planters? Where do the myth and the reality superimpose? The use of oral tradition by researchers may raise some interesting insights not about what "Planters" were but what they thought they were and what many descendants may still think they are.

At this conference and in our future research on the Planters we must be aware of the danger of erecting a new mythology and a new exclusiveness about an admittedly understudied group. In our efforts to right the balance in Planters Studies, let us not in our enthusiasm tip the scales.

William Naftel
Senior Historian
Canadian Parks Service, Atlantic Region

As the last speaker, on the last program, on the last day of a 2-day conference, I feel like the caboose on a train. I am not sure whether you are here because you are waiting for the crossing gate to rise or because you want to see what the last car is like. Parks involvement with the Planters is

---

6   R. Stuart Wallace, "The Development of the Scotch-Irish Myth in New Hampshire," *Historical New Hampshire*, 40, 3 & 4 (Fall/Winter 1985), 110.

7   Rev. Edward L. Parker, *History of Londonderry* (Boston, 1851), 32-33.

kind of an inherited and accidental thing. In fact, speaking of railways, it goes back to the Dominion Atlantic Railway which included in their tourist park at Grand Pré not only exhibits on the Acadians but also on the successors to the Acadians, the New England Planters. And when we took over the park from a now disinterested railway, we inherited that part of the exhibit which included the Planters.

Our current interest in the Planters arises from the decision to overhaul the Grand Pré National Park exhibits in 1978. We went through a series of public hearings in the community and elsewhere that led eventually to a decision to separate the Planters from the Acadian commemoration. As a result of that decision, we went into a further series of separate hearings to decide what to do with the Planter commemoration. Out of those hearings came a decision to develop a Planter commemoration which would involve a contribution by Parks of both artifacts and some funding to the Kings County Museum, and an out door exhibit dealing with the history of the Planters and their settlement, preferably at a landing spot such as the Starr's Point Landing on the banks of the Cornwallis River. We hope that over the next five years our plans will come to fruition.

The reason I am here today is to suggest future directions for Planter research. If, as a director of research in Parks, I had an unlimited budget, here is what I would do to fill the gaps which we have identified. I should first emphasize that despite such massive examples of military history as the Citadel, we are becoming more and more interested in the social side of history. Our experience with Acadian studies has indicated that with hard digging and persistance, we can find results where people think no results can be found. What is required is pains-taking searching through documentation, much of it available only on microfilm. The information is there and it can be found. So, as a research director with unlimited staff and funds, I would have historians go through the public records office materials relating to eighteenth-century Nova Scotia page by page. I would assign people to go through every registry office in the relevant counties of Nova Scotia and also through New England archives — not only state archives but museums and/or repositories in every town from which Planters are known to have come.

What should we do with all this material? Well, I have a list of seven or eight projects that would benefit from such an extensive documentary search.

First, I would look at the recruitment of Planters. The Nova Scotia government mounted an effective public relations campaign in New England; it appointed agents there. The message seems to have somehow penetrated every village and hamlet in the New England countryside. How was it done? We need to know more about that.

Secondly, I would like to know more about the migration process. The Planters came with furniture, cattle, household goods, etc. They were given some government assistance. How were the public and private aspects of the migration experience carried out?

Thirdly, I would like to know more about the social origins of the Planters. What kind of people were they? We have some ideas but I imagine we could find out a great deal more.

Fourthly, I would like to know the economic status of the Planters. Governor Lawrence wanted people not only with some knowledge of what they were doing but with some capital and resources. The Planters were not penniless immigrants. What did they bring with them?

Marie Elwood has touched and expounded on another interest of mine, the whole township and proprietorial system. The system as introduced in Nova Scotia by the Planters was not at that time unique. In fact, it was an old and well recognized means of planting colonies on both sides of the Atlantic. I would like to know more about its use and evolution up to the time that it gave way to land grants to individuals.

Moreover, I would like to know about trade with New England and the maintenance of family links. We know that ships went back and forth between New England and New Scotland but how long did people continue to think about families back in Connecticut as "family" and when did that link finally break so that they became strangers.

Further, I would like to know more about the evolution of Planter and Acadian relationships in the 1760s. We know that Acadians stared through gimlet eyes from the edge of the woods at these people invading their lands. Yet, by the end of the decade they seemed to be working side by side. How did these people view each other?

And finally, I would like to know about the religious beliefs of the Planters. Although many people at this conference talked about religion, there are more questions to be answered. How, for example, did the Planters pursue their religious impulses without any apparent clergy?

That is a list of eight projects and I should say that it does not look at the moment as if Parks is going to sponsor them. I am going to turn these eight projects over to you in the hope that you will find the answers for me.

Esther Clark Wright
Wolfville, Nova Scotia*

I wish to thank you very much for the privilege of being guest of honour at the banquet of the Planter Conference, and for the presentation of the certificate as Planter Scholar.

Many years ago, when I was a member of the Council of the Canadian Historical Association, Professor Creighton, *the* Professor Creighton who

---

* Banquet Address to the New England Planters in the Maritime Provinces of Canada Conference, 24 October 1987.

was the head of the Department of History at the University of Toronto, informed us that their summer seminar on Canadian History had received a grant that would enable them to carry on the Seminar away from the heat of Toronto. I suggested that it would then be possible to carry on the Seminar at centres in the West and in the Maritimes so that scholars could become acquainted with sources available in those regions. I was very quickly put in my place. It would not be necessary to go any further than Kingston where Queen's University had a very complete collection of Ontario newspapers.

So, Canadian history needed no other source than Ontario newspapers. I could discuss that proposition at length, but will content myself with one observation, that a recent book on the Loyalists shows the futility of relying on newspapers. The author draws his conclusions about the Loyalists from what the newspapers had to say about the three or four percent of the Loyalists whose names appeared in the newspapers, and completely ignores the 96 or 97 percent about whom the newspapers said nothing.

I would like to suggest to the Committee on the New England Planters that further Conferences might consider the contemporaries of the New England Planters, for instance, the German families in Lunenburg and on the Petitcodiac River (from whom Margaret Conrad and I are descended), and the English, Irish and Scottish groups of the period.

There is one warning I would like to pass on to all who study the Planters and other contemporary groups: hang on to your spelling.

Date Due

NOV 17 2001			
OCT 11 2002			
NOV 19 2008			

BRODART, CO.   Cat. No. 23-233-003   Printed in U.S.A.